Women, Religion and Education in Early Modern England

The education of women and girls in the Tudor and Stuart periods was inextricably linked to their perceived place in the religious order. *Women, Religion and Education in Early Modern England* is a study of the nature and extent of the education of women at this time in the context of both Protestant and Catholic ideological debates.

Taking a comprehensive definition of education, the author relates oral and written instruction to the spiritual, social and economic status of women. Through an examination of the role of women as recipients and as agents in religious instruction, this book offers wider insights both into the controls placed on women and the freedoms available to them.

Women, Religion and Education in Early Modern England

Kenneth Charlton

London and New York

First published 1999
by Routledge
11 New Fetter Lane, London EC4P 4EE

Simultaneously published in the USA and Canada
by Routledge
29 West 35th Street, New York, NY 10001

Routledge is an imprint of the Taylor & Francis Group

© 1999 Kenneth Charlton

Typeset in Baskerville by RefineCatch Limited, Bungay, Suffolk
Printed and bound in Great Britain by
St Edmundsbury Press, Bury St Edmunds, Suffolk

British Library Cataloguing in Publication Data
A catalogue record for this book is available from the British Library

Library of Congress Cataloging in Publication Data
Charlton, Kenneth.
  Women, religion, and education in early modern England/Kenneth
Charlton.
  Includes bibliographical references and index.
  ISBN 0–415–18148–8 (hb)
    1. Christian education of girls – England – History. 2. Women –
Education – England – History. 3. England – Church history – 1485–
I. Title.
BV1577.C48   1999
268′.4 – dc21   98–33130
                                                            CIP

ISBN 0–415–18148–8

Contents

Introduction

In the summer of 1988 Pope John Paul II issued as an Apostolic Letter *Mulieris Dignitatem (The Dignity of Women)*. Though he deals with the matter in general terms, the immediate issue he was addressing was whether women should become priests and, in saying they should not, he indicated what they *should* be – adored and cherished in the church as wives, mothers, sisters and nuns; they are 'different by nature' from men and should not, therefore, 'try to appropriate masculine characteristics'. In expressing this view he was, of course, reiterating an opinion commonly held in early modern England about the nature of women and their role in society, and a scrutiny of these earlier views will provide the ground for the purpose of this book which is to see whether, and if so, in what ways, they affected attitudes to and the provision of education for women and girls, and of their religious education in particular.

Most often, when 'education' (of whomsoever) is discussed, first thoughts centre on what is to be taught, on the content of education, and on the methods of teaching deemed appropriate to that content. The discussion may then move on to who should be the teachers, who the taught; when this education should take place and where. It is only when these, at first sight, eminently practical questions have been adumbrated and discussion is in train that we become aware that certain assumptions have been made as to whether this education should take place at all, and if so, for purposes that appear so self-evidently agreed by all as not to require expression.

In considering these two sets of issues – the practically pedagogical and the logically prior – it would be tempting to label them the 'practice' and the 'theory' of education, save that the former set require their own further distinctions to be made: between prescription and actuality, between what ought to be done and what was actually undertaken and achieved. In early modern England there was (and indeed there still is) considerable debate about each of these variables. Moreover, what actually happened, what the people of the past actually did (and even why they did it) is far from providing a complete picture of the past, since this is to ignore another 'actuality', what the people of the past actually thought and said *should* be done, their hopes and aspirations being as much a part of their 'actual' lives as their subsequent actions.

It becomes crucial, therefore, to include in any description and discussion of the part religious education played in the lives of women and girls in early modern England (or any other group at any other time) – that is, the what? the how? the by whom? the where? and the when? – an 'ought' variable, so that we weave into the cloth of education a weft of prescription through the warp of what actually transpired. Prescriptive literature, after all, concerned itself not only with 'what ought to be the case' in the future, but also with what was seen to be the *best* of current practice, just as the flood of complaining, 'now-a-daies' polemic so plainly referred to the *worst* of current practice. Moreover, to be effective, prescription had to be seen as being not so far removed from possible achievement as to be pejoratively dismissed as 'ideal', incapable of realisation. Authors themselves had to feel that their prescriptions were in some sense reasonable, and it would be taking a proper degree of scepticism too far to assert that it was otherwise. No prescriptive writer wrote as if no one else shared his views, as if those views had been plucked out of the air, out of a cloud-cuckoo land. Too often such prescriptive contributions to the debate about the religious education of women and girls have been summarily dismissed as having little to do with what actually happened, too often contrasted unfavourably with actual examples. The distinction between 'theory' and 'practice', therefore, should never be drawn too sharply, and certainly not with an implied (negative) value-judgement built into its use.

Since the study is not confined to a particular point in time, a chronological variable has also to be incorporated. Just as every moment in time has its own past, present and future, so then must 'change' figure in any complete picture. Early modern England saw great changes, at some points (such as the Protestant Reformation, the Cromwellian Commonwealth) dramatic, even revolutionary, at other times less so. But even dramatic change, though unhesitatingly embraced by some, may be grudgingly accepted by others and emphatically rejected by others. In our modern search for originality and innovation it is all too easy to forget that this period was also one in which tradition – custom – was powerfully influential, its presence celebrated by some as a matter of considered judgement (after appropriate scrutiny) but by others as a matter of unthinking acceptance, justified, if at all, in terms of 'what was good enough for my forebears is good enough for me'.[1] Moreover, tradition often took on or was accorded a sacral quality, with inherited forms of thought, feeling and action considered so self-evidently to be valued as to be immune from scrutiny.[2]

Certainly this is what was relied on by some of those in authority who sought justification for their injunctions to others, disguising vested interest as 'past experience' in order to rationalise inertia. In considering education in past times, then, the historian would do well to heed T. S. Eliot's comment about poetry:

> The work of any poet exists by reason of its connections with past work, both in continuation and divergence; what we call his originality is simply his special relationship to tradition, and each poet's relation to that tradition changes the tradition itself.[3]

The complexity of the issues as well as the contradictory nature of the debates will clearly preclude a simple developmental sense of 'change' – whether for better or for worse – in the chronology of religious education in early modern England. Change, if it does take place, is rarely neat; it is certainly not linear, nor uniform on all fronts. It is messy, untidy, even chaotic in its production of unintended consequences.

It will be seen then, that a study of religious education such as this will require an inclusive rather than an exclusive use of the term 'education' and, more particularly, an avoidance of the equating of 'education' with 'schooling', if by that is meant what is transacted in the formal institution called 'school'. That other educative agency, the church, long pre-dated the school, and Osbert Sitwell's observation that he was 'educated during the vacations from Eton' reminds us that the family, pre-dating both school and church, continues to have a role as an educative agency. Moreover, outside these three relatively enclosed environments, the big wide world has also to be considered, if only because those in authority constantly used it through processions, progresses and pageants, as well as public forms of punishment (of which the Marian burnings were only the most extreme) to press home particular messages to the populace. The relative influence of any one of these forms of education has been a matter of perennial debate in the past, and remains so to this day. The heterogeneity of educational experience is not, however, in doubt. The history of education is no longer concerned simply with schooling in schools, but it is most certainly about teaching and learning, about a cultural negotiation – what Bouwsma has called 'the preservation, cultivation and transmission of meaning'.[4]

The distinction implied above between 'formal' and 'informal' education is useful though hardly watertight, and certainly this applies to any consideration of the religious education of women and girls in early modern England, whether they were recipients or agents in that education. The formulation 'women, religion and education' has therefore been preferred since, though for the most part they were recipients of religious education, they were also on important occasions prime movers in the matter, and in the case of mothers crucially so. Plenty has been written about the 'learned ladies' of the past, but remarkably little about how far and in what ways they acquired their learning and, more importantly, passed on their learning to their own children. That some women in the past were 'learned', 'cultivated', 'educated' in the achievement sense, is not difficult to demonstrate. Precisely how they came to achieve that learning, by what means, at whose hands, is rather more difficult. And it is even more so when we seek to find out whether and how they transmitted this to their children, *a fortiori* when it is the many women to be considered rather than the few. The aim here, then, is to consider women and girls not only as the target of educational provision, but also as agents of both prescription and provision. The reproductive function of the older generation *vis-à-vis* the younger worked essentially to maintain differential roles for their male and female members and, whilst gender identity could be the product of self-education, there was no doubt in the minds of most that gender differentiation was to be the accepted aim of the education of the younger generation by the older.

No historian writing in the late twentieth century about women and girls – least of all a male historian – can proceed without some reference to the literature of feminism, both in general and with reference to his own chosen topic and period. If he chooses to write about women, he would be extremely insensitive if he did not feel some fellow sympathy for Daniel entering a den which some feminists have insisted should be reserved to themselves. What this particular male historian has learned, not *de novo*, but with an increasingly immediate awareness, is the continuing influence of a male-orientated cultural biography. One's education as a historian has, of course, insisted on the need to be aware of one's own involuntary biases – but not with the stridency of the reminders provided by some representatives of the feminist movement, as for example when Renata Duelli Klein asserts, 'In my view there is no room for men in Women's Studies, *none whatsoever*.'[5] This may no longer be a view shared by all or even a majority of Klein's feminist colleagues working in the field of history, and in any case this is not the place to enter into a full-scale critique of 'feminist history'. Suffice it to say that this particular study is not intended to be a feminist history, if that involves a form of presentism which co-opts early modern female writers to the cause of twentieth-century feminism, which seeks to find harbingers of late-twentieth-century liberated women, or which deplores the failure of certain writers of the early modern period to share late-twentieth-century views as to what the status and role of women should be. There remains the far from completed task of recovering the lived experience of women, of retrieving and making visible that particular part acting both in public and in the relative privacy of the family. But the dramatist provides only *clues* about their characters, clues which he knows full well will be interpreted in quite different ways by different members of his audience; indeed, it is part of his art to so arrange his clues that such reactions are produced. It is for others to insist that dramatic literature should be approached as 'words on the page' or as 'performance on the stage' – and even (as they commonly do) to insist that theirs is the only legitimate way of proceeding. The historian, however, is interested in how far the people of the past, of his chosen part of the past, may be found in the text, and – though this is more problematic – how far these people reacted, by report, to the attitudes and behaviours of the writer's characters.

Conscious of the complexities of the task, the problem of presentation has to be faced. The topic is a taxonomist's nightmare. The neatest break-down would be to make a class-based distinction and to divide the book into the education of the few and the education of the many but since neither of these, in the matter of religious education, is specific to itself such a presen-tation would result in a good deal of repetition. The points which will be addressed are, therefore:

1 whether girls and women should be educated and, if so, on what grounds and for what purposes (whether and why);
2 who should be educated (who);
3 at what stage in a female's life should her religious education take place and where should it be located (when and where);
4 what should be the content of that education (what);
5 what methods of teaching were deemed to be desirable and efficient (how);
6 who would be the teachers (by whom).

In each case – whether and why? when and where? what? how? for whom? by whom? – multiplicity and heterogeneity rather than simplicity and homogeneity will predominate and, with the provisos mentioned earl-ier, each will require a consideration of its own prescription and its own practice, with the variables of gender, age and class constantly needing to be borne in mind.

None of the materials (or indeed the concerns) of the book is susceptible of quantification in any statistical sense of the term.[12] Where household and family size, age of menarche, age of marriage, etc. are referred to in general terms, I have relied on current historiographical literature (which has its own methodological problems). My interest lies in actual rather than aggre-gated people, in individuals struggling to shape their lives to suit their own particular situations and purposes, though plainly I wish to know whether and in what degree particular attitudes and practices were shared or not. But such knowledge can be quantified only in the roughest sort of way by the collection and comparison of particular instances, by the cumulative weight of fragmentary evidence, which is the historian's traditional (though far from perfect) way of proceeding. All kinds of factors, some quite contingent, others inherent in the topic and period under discussion, combine to limit the number of instances which can be presented. In a sense all the women referred to are extraordinary, in that they have left a mark on the historical record, but the haphazard nature of their survival precludes any use of the term 'sample', especially since the evidence is heavily weighted towards the upper and middle classes. The difficulty of detecting the voices of ordinary people is, moreover, compounded when the voices sought are female.

This is not a book simply about women and girls, but about males and females and their inextricably bound relationships, and how these affected and were affected by conceptions such virtue, obedience, citizenship, power.[13] However, since it was a preoccupation of the period, it is also about sex differences, and how far and in what terms these were to be identified, and then maintained or minimised by the social mechanics of education in our extended sense of the term. Without doubt, it was believed in the early modern period that sex differences were 'natural'. From the moment of conception the sex of a child was endlessly discussed – strength of kick, position in the womb and so on – and, theological exhortation notwithstanding, a boy-child was preferred, giving rise to expectations and aspirations which not surprisingly led to disappointment and differential treatment of siblings, not least in their education. As with sex differences themselves, it was but a short step from contemporary anatomy and physiology to value-judgement and the ideology of the 'eternal feminine' – in a Christian and male-dominated culture. Even so, 'identification' on the part of the child and 'labelling' on the part of others did not necessarily work in the same direction of the current male hegemony, as we shall see when we come to consider women as the target of educational prescription, as the agent in educational practice, as the consumer of educational provision – a consideration which will lead us into the affective as well as the cognitive life of women. Whether it is possible, as Lucien Fèbvre hoped, to reinstate the emotional life of the past and to enter the shadowy regions of motive, of expectation, of aspiration, of the workings of individual conscience and choice,[14] a consideration of our topic can hardly avoid the attempt, as long as we remember that the tensions between freedom of choice and submission to authority were not the monopoly of one sex.

Myra Reynolds and Dorothy Gardiner have pioneered the field of women's education, to be followed, with their varying emphases, by Carol

Camden, Ruth Kelso and Dorothy Stenton.[15] Yet it was not too long ago that Joyce Irwin, commenting on the comparative lengths of the chapters in which she gathered her extracts of *Womanhood in Radical Protestantism 1525–1675* (1979), noted that 'the chapter on women's education is relatively brief'. Rosemary Masek, a year later, concluded that 'The story of women's education is an important part of the whole history of Tudor–Stuart education which has yet to be written.'[16] Back in 1965, my own book *Education in Renaissance England* grossly under-represented women, and even in 1982, when Women's Studies were much more visible, Rosemary O'Day allocated not much more space to the topic in her *Education and Society 1500–1800*. More recently, Roland Bainton, Retha Warnicke, Diane Willen, Joan Douglass, Patricia Crawford and Margaret Spufford have made important contributions to a history of the religious life of women in the early modern period. This particular contribution, surprisingly, is the first to attempt a systematic consideration of a major aspect of women and education in that period. One devoutly hopes it will not be the last. Indeed, the present healthy state of Women's Studies will almost certainly ensure it will not, as the recent perceptive and questioning article by Penny Corfield makes clear.[17]

1   Attitudes to women

NATURE AND NURTURE

A society concerned (to an almost obsessive degree) with religion and, most immediately, with the scriptural basis of that religion not surprisingly turned first and foremost to the scriptures for statements about the nature of women, from which it would be possible to justify claims about women's status in society and an education deemed appropriate to that status (albeit in a society with a male Godhead, a male Saviour and a male priesthood, and in a society largely governed by men). Again, not surprisingly, the scriptures served to provide proof-texts for just about every kind and level of claim in the matter. Shakespeare was merely reflecting a common awareness when he had Antonio warn Bassanio that 'the Devil can cite scripture for his purpose'.[1]

Human nature, and the efficacy of education in controlling or modifying it, had for long been a matter of discussion by classical authors, by the early Christian Fathers and by medieval theologians. Much of the 'pagan' thought on the matter was assimilated into Christian theology, but always in the context of notions about 'childhood' and its modification by 'original sin'. Even so, theological doctrine was rarely homogeneous, and Reformation theology hardly improved matters, especially when it attempted to simplify the presentation of doctrine to suit the perceived needs and capabilities of the newly enfranchised 'priesthood of all believers'. Moreover, despite their insistence on man's post-Lapsarian 'depravity', few Reformers wished to abandon their humanist predecessors' emphasis on the dignity of man, and on man's 'natural' faculty of reason, which above all things enabled him to distance himself from the world of 'brutish beasts'.

The problem was further complicated by differences of opinion not only about the spiritual state of a new-born infant but also about the nature and length of childhood itself. For most writers, 'infancy' took the new-born nature and nurture, has to be set. Without doubt, women in the early modern period 'enjoyed' (as we say nowadays) 'a bad press'. In much of the literature they not only shared with men the stigma of being 'born in sin', but they were additionally and crucially the direct descendants of Eve, the initiator, as it was claimed, of the events which led to the banishment from Paradise. A commonplace feature of most discussions about the nature of women, therefore, would be its starting point, Eve-woman the seducer, and its proof-text, the story of the Fall as told in Genesis, Chapter 3, repeated in 1 Timothy 2.13–14 and usually glossed as the fall of Adam at the hands of Eve. At the same time, however, woman was described as 'the weaker vessel', the comparative adjective of which should remind us that for the most part the debate about the nature of women was determined by reference to the nature of men, a procedure as common at the end of our period as at its beginning. The words of the Elizabethan Homily 'Of the State of Matrimony', 'for the woman is a weak creature, not endued with like strength and constancy of mind', are echoed a hundred years later, for example, in Richard Baxter's *Christian Directory*:

> It is no small patience which the natural imbecility of the female sex requireth you to prepare. Except it be very few that are patient and man-like, women are commonly of potent fantasies, and tender, passionate, impatient spirits easily cast into anger or jealousy or discontent, and of weak understandings and therefore unable to reform themselves. They are betwixt man and child. Some few have more of the man, and many more of the child.[15]

Commonly, too, the ambiguity of the adjective 'weaker' was conveniently ignored by those who wished to present a misogynist point of view, though the literature of misogyny was far from homogeneous in its treatment of the matter. On the one hand, women were regarded as objects of ridicule, derision or contempt. They were by nature idle, garrulous chatterers, brainless, indiscreet gossips, unable to keep a secret; they were querulous, wayward, prodigal, capricious, obstinate, contrary and contentious. In one sense, then, their 'weakness' could be dismissed as of no great importance, as a mere inconvenience. As Zanthia complains in Marston's *The Wonder of Women* (1606):

> We things cal'd women [are] only made for show
> And pleasure, created to bear children
> And play at shuttlecock[16]

In another, more reflective sense, however, their 'weakness' was a matter of concern, something to be warned against. Idleness, for example, meant the neglect of that traditional charge to 'keep' the goods that it had been the responsibility of the husband to 'gather', a neglect of the role of the 'good-wife', the 'huswyf', etc. Proverbs 31 provided the appropriate proof-text for treatise and sermon, with Aristotelian dictum thrown in for good measure.[17] Moreover, idleness and garrulity in a woman inevitably led to gossip, which would endanger the secrets of her husband's trade or office, his 'misterie'. 'Trust a woman? Never! Never!' exclaimed Flamineo in John Webster's *White Devil* (1612), and Portia's agonised asides in Shakespeare's *Julius Caesar* would have struck a chord in many members of the Shakespearean audience:

> Constancy, be strong upon my side!
> Set a huge mountain 'tween my heart and tongue!
> How hard it is for woman to keep counsel!

and later

> . . . . . Ay me! how weak a thing
> The heart of woman is!

Sir John Harrington, on the other hand, congratulated his wife Mary on

> thy good silence . . . for thanks to the sweet god of silence thy lips do not wanton out of discretion's path, like the many gossiping dames we could name who lose their husband's fast hold on good friends rather than hold fast on their own tongues.[18]

In the same way, 'inconstancy' as an aspect of the condition 'weaker' was treated not only at a relatively frivolous level – forever changing her mind as to the best colour for her dress – but also as an exemplification of the inconstant love, leading to cuckoldry, which was treated as a subject for bawdy humour, and adultery, which was certainly not regarded in the same lighthearted way.

Another aspect of a woman's nature, her propensity for 'contention' – treated as a matter for humour in John Heywood's collections of epigrams (1566) or in Anthony Copley's patently chauvinist *Wits, Fits and Fancies* (1595) – was for others of much greater significance, potent of danger not derision, and certainly nothing to be scoffed at, for it symbolised that disturbance of harmony and concord which was considered essential not only to the well-being of personal relationships but also to the stability of family and commonwealth. Richard Hooker, for example, characterised it as a general social and political ill.[19] Shrewish wives abound in the literature – Noah's wife, Socrates' Zantippe, Aristotle's Phyllis, Chaucer's Wife of Bath are all recalled in the early modern period as exemplars, from *A C Mery Talys* (1526), Erasmus' pert Maria in his Colloquy 'Courtship' and the story in *Pasquil's Jests* (1604), taken from Poggio, of the husband who went upstream in search of his drowned wife because in life she had been so contrary, to their many counterparts in Elizabethan and Jacobean drama, as for example in Leonato's warning to Beatrice, 'By my troth, niece, thou wilt never get thee a husband if thou be so shrewd [shrewish] of tongue', and Matteo's comment in Thomas Dekker's *II The Honest Whore* (1630), 'There's no music when a woman is in the consort.'[20]

In all these characterisations of a woman's nature it was her patent lack of the male's ability to reason which made her in some sense sub-human when contrasted with her male counterpart. When Julia, discussing her choice of various suitors with Lucetta, her waiting woman, in Shakespeare's *Two Gentleman of Verona*, is asked 'Your reason?', she replies 'I have no other but a woman's reason. I think him so because I think him so.' The same response is made by Middleton's Violetta in *Blurt Master Constable*: 'I have a woman's response. I will not dance because I will not dance.'[21] When women presented a petition to the House of Commons in April 1649 they were told by the Sergeant-at-Arms that

> the matter you petition about is of a higher concernment than you understand; that the House gave an answer to your husbands; and that therefore you are desired to go home and look after your own business and meddle with your housewifery.[22]

More threateningly, however, there appeared to be an easy transition from chattering scold to shrewish virago – and thence to fearsomely dangerous witch. When men came to portray women as scold, shrew, virago and witch they were coming close to expressing, if not overtly acknowledging, their basic apprehension of the powers of women. Edmund Tilney warned his readers to beware of the 'masterful shrew'. William Whately claimed that 'if a husband hath made himself an underling to his wife' he would at the same time have contributed to the production of a 'misshapen house'. Discussing the duties of wives in his *Of Domesticall Duties*, William Gouge stressed that 'if the fear of God possess not their hearts, though they be the weaker vessel, [they] do oft make their husbands plain vassals to them'.[23]

In each of these cases, and there were many more, 'weaker' seems not to be the appropriate adjective. When Hamlet exclaimed 'Frailty, thy name is woman' he was referring not to that 'tenderness, soft and mild with a kind of womanly sweetness' that Castiglione had considered so desirable, nor even to 'this fair defect of nature' which Milton referred to in *Paradise Lost*, but to the other end of the continuum, to woman as sexual predator.[24] Woman's 'fervency' was a commonplace of misogynist literature and dramatic personification. Lear's embittered tirade against Regan was a typical characterisation, to be seen also in Isabella in Marston's *The Insatiate Countess* and in Roxena in Middleton's *Hengist King of Kent*.[25] In this portrayal of woman as lustful, lascivious seducer, what was at the same time being exemplified was her capacity for deceit for ends other than sexual satisfaction, using her seductive powers to gain ascendancy over an individual male or over a state which he alone should rule. She was thus wilfully ignoring the allegedly 'natural' passivity of woman, and in so doing usurping the 'active' role of man.

Alternatively, if a woman presumed to become more man-like by acquiring a learned education she might still be derided as what the eighteenth century came to call a 'blue-stocking'. Jonson, for example, constantly ridiculed such women in his plays as 'collegiate ladies' and Herrick was not unusual in praying for an 'unlearned' wife.[26] The 'merry' riposte in Heywood's *Gunaikeion* (1624):

> I desire me to have a woman to be my wife that shall have no more tongue to answer me to a question than yea or nay; or to have more wit than to distinguish her husband's bed from another man's[27]

was merely a commonplace which 'Jane Anger' had already identified in her *Jane Angers Protection Against Women* (1589). Moreover, if she were seen to be acting in an independent fashion, a woman's behaviour could easily be deplored as (literally) 'monstrous' or 'Amazonian'. Lady Macbeth's 'unsex me here' and Goneril's 'I must change arms at home, and give the distaff into my husband's hands' are echoed throughout the literature, dramatic or otherwise, with polemicists citing Medea, Delilah, Jezebel and Joan of Arc (amongst other exemplars) to buttress their case.[28] When Middleton's Follywit insisted ' 'Tis an Amazonian time' he was at the same time commenting on what was regarded as a currently dangerous social phenomenon – the number of itinerant and therefore uncontrolled women, such as the Southampton women who, in 1580, were seen to 'keep themselves out of service and work for themselves in divers men's houses [and] take chambers and so live by themselves masterless'.[29] The literature had a long line of these dangerously independent women – Long Meg of Westminster, Mary Ambree, Mary Frith (alias Moll Cutpurse in Middleton's *Roaring Girl*), and Margarita in Beaumont and Fletcher's *Rule a Wife and Have a Wife* who warned Leon:

They both have the name of human being whose nature
reason differentiates from that of the beasts; both,
I say, are equally suited for the knowledge of
learning by which reason is cultivated.[39]

Sir Thomas Elyot's Candidus, arguing in Socratic fashion on behalf of women, soundly trounces his misogynist opponent, Caninus, who is forced to conclude: 'I see well enough that women being well and virtuously brought up, do not only with men participate in reason but some also in fidelity and constancy be equal unto them.' Montaigne echoed the humanist position when he asserted 'I say that both male and female are cast in the same mould; except for education and custom the difference is not great between them.'[40] The puritan Roger Carr continued the theme: 'Most true it is that women are as men, reasonable creatures, and have flexible wits both to good and evil, the which with use, direction and good counsel may be altered and turned.' Nor was the view particular to Protestants. The Jesuit, Henry Garnett, told his female followers 'your husbands over your soul have no authority, and over your bodies but limited power'. William Austin put it most comprehensively:

> In the sex is all the difference, which is but only in the body. For she hath the same reasonable soul, and in that there are neither hees nor shees; neither excellency nor superiority; she hath the same soul, the same mind, the same understanding, and tends the same end of eternal salvation that he doth, in which there is no exception.[41]

Occasionally it was claimed that in some respects women were to be regarded as superior to men. 'Jane Anger', for example, argued the case for women on two fronts, pointing out that 'Adam was moulded out of the dusty clay of the earth; she was framed out of the purified body of man.' William Austin went further, by noting that women were the *last* on earth to be created: 'from minerals, vegetables, birds, beasts, man. Every work being still more perfect of all, he rested.' Anthony Gibson argued from current humoral theory that

> as women are much more moist than men . . . they are therefore not like men in the public theatre the subject of very tragical faults . . . The nature of a woman being inclined to sadness discovers wisdom, makes her prudent and apprehensive; whereas men are commonly rash and unruly, because divers appetites transport them to many frivolous and fleeting considerations, which might fault you shall find few women, or none at all infected with.

Richard Braithwait made the same point in more general terms:

> And if that ancient philosophical maxim hold good: 'That the tem-
> perature of the soul follows the temperature of the body' we must
> necessarily conclude that as their outward temperature and composure
> is more delicate, so their inward affections must be more purely refined.
> No violent passion so predominant which their mild temper cannot
> moderate.[42]

The superiority of women was also urged by reference to classical and
biblical stories. The patient and long-suffering Griselda, for example, was
constantly cited, from Chaucer, Petrarch and Boccaccio onwards, when it
came to a search for models of Christian behaviour.[43] Lucretia, Penelope
and others were similarly evidenced. From the Bible Susannah figured
largely as an exemplar,[44] alongside Mary Magdalen, Esther, Sarah, Ruth,
Abigail, and of course, even in Protestant circles, Mary, the mother of Jesus,
cited for example by Thomas Becon, in his *New Catechisme*. The dramatic
literature, too, provided examples of women whose actions showed them to
be eminently more rational in their behaviour than their menfolk – Her-
mione, Paulina and Perdita in Shakespeare's *Winter's Tale* and Rosalind, Viola
and Portia in other plays, as also Fletcher's eponymous heroine in *Bonducca*
and Evadne in Beaumont and Fletcher's *The Maid's Tragedy*.

By the mid-seventeenth century claims on behalf of women, based on a
rejection of traditional views about the 'weakness' of their nature, were
becoming increasingly evident. Texts from France such as Jacques de Bosc's
L'Honneste Femme (1632) and Pierre le Moyne's *La Gallérie des Femmes Fortes*
(1647) were translated into English, as later were Poulain de la Barr's *De
L'Egalite des Deux Sexes* (1673), Madeleine de Scudéry's *Conversations Nouvelles
sur Divers Sujets* (1686) and Fénelon's *De L'Education des Filles* (1687).[45] In the
second half of the century, too, English women writers produced their own
texts, with the prolific Margaret Cavendish, Duchess of Newcastle, leading
the way with her *Philosophical and Physical Opinions* (1655) and *The World's Olio*
(1655), to be followed by Bathsua Makin's *An Essay to Revive the Ancient
Education of Gentlewomen in Religion, Manners, Arts and Tongues* (1673), Hannah
Woolley's *The Gentlewomans Companion* (1675), Mary Astell's *A Serious Proposal
for the Ladies* (1694), Lady Mary Chudleigh's *The Ladies' Defence* (1701), and
other lesser writers. Moreover, such women continued to be supported
by their male counterparts, from Abraham Darcie, *The Honour of Ladies*
(1622), and Edward Fleetwood, *The Glory of Women* (1652), to George Savile,
William Walsh and Daniel Defoe. Even the periodical press joined in,
with the *Athenian Mercury*, for example, discussing in 1691 'Whether or not it
is proper for a woman to be learned' and concluding:

On the whole since they have as noble souls as we, a finer genius and generally quicker apprehensions, we see no reason why women should not be learned now as well as Madam Philips, van Schurmann and others have formerly been.[46]

For the most part, the word 'nature' was taken to imply something innate, inherent, unchanging – but in one degree or another, since few argued that it was unchangeable. As many recognised, the difficulty lay in maintaining any change in a woman's (or a man's) nature that might have been wrought by 'nurture'. Whatever position was taken on the Mary–Eve continuum, there nevertheless remained the possibility of regeneration, which in turn raised the issues of when, how, by whom, etc., that is the educational or more strictly the pedagogical problem of 'nurture' as a means of either reinforcing or changing 'nature'.

'Nurture', of course, meant different things to different people. For some it was merely a teaching and learning process whose purpose was to learn how to be a Christian in all aspects of life, in accordance with the current orthodoxy, statutorily ordained. Others went further than this, and whilst acknowledging that the post-Lapsarian Christian could be saved only by God's grace, nevertheless insisted that the aim of the process was to learn *why* a Christian should live her life in that way. Nurture could thus help a Christian to recognise this and so to order her life and her relations with other Christians in family, parish and state that, with a repentant heart, she could be embraced by God's forgiveness, and at the end achieve that salvation which every Christian sought. The very existence of catechisms of all kinds for all sorts and all denominations, together with the constant and repeated exhortations to catechise and be catechised in order to 'seek to enter the pathway to salvation',[47] provides ample evidence of this. Even so, the place of reason in nurture had a considerably limited scope. It rarely meant following the argument, in strictly logical fashion, wherever it led and for the most part, as we have seen, women were considered to be especially limited in the matter, since what was regarded as their 'natural' inferiority meant they could have their argument dismissed, not because it was illogical or misinformed, but because it had been put forward by a woman. As Milton has Delilah acknowledge in *Samson Agonistes*:

> In argument with men, a woman ever
> Goes by the worse, whatever be her course.[48]

Even so, the literature of the period is full of biological, and more particularly horticultural, metaphors which stressed not only the need for but also the possibilities of nurture. The child becomes the soil to be tilled or the green twig to be bent, the teacher is the wise gardener, clearing stony ground, tilling the soil, sowing the seed, grafting and pruning the tree, striking roots, each of the metaphors emphasising the possibilities of nurture in the growth and development of the child – of course, always in preferred ways and directions. Even more potent was the *tabula rasa* metaphor, through which the likening of a child at birth to a piece of wax or clay signalled the possibility of nurture for virtuous behaviour and the avoidance of 'misshapen' members of the commonwealth.[49] By emphasising not only the blankness but also the malleability of the material, writers were able to prescribe a much more positive approach to nurture, in contradistinction to the curbing tendency of their opponents, with whom the bridle metaphor predominated. As William Gouge put it, 'There is necessity that children be taught piety, because they are not born but made Christians.' At the same time, the metaphor was used to emphasise the need for the earliest possible starting of a child's education, long before entry in to some kind of formal 'schooling', which, since the vast majority of children would not enter school, reinforced the message of parental responsibility for nurture.[50]

Alongside such metaphors and continuing to be quoted throughout the period was the story, culled from the much-translated and plagiarised Plutarch (though originally told by Lycurgus, the fourth-century BC Attic Orator), of the two young dogs, one pure-bred and trained in the kitchen, the other a mongrel and trained in the field. When food was presented the pure-bred dog went straight to it, whilst the mongrel went off after game in the field – not the 'controlled experiment' of the twentieth-century psychologists but a story whose lively simplicity was made the more persuasively effective by its constant repetition in all kinds of text over a long period of time. It was used by Erasmus who drew the moral from it that 'while nature is strong, education is more powerful still',[51] a conclusion which is repeated when the story is retold in the several translations of Plutarch produced during the early modern period, or whenever an author needed to make the point as, for example, in Peter de la Primaudaye's *The French Academie* (1586), Richard Braithwait's *English Gentleman* (1630), and Matthew Griffith's *Bethel or a Forme for Families* (1633).[52]

In following through the weaker vessel metaphor, no one argued that nurture would be a complete waste of time; even the most pessimistic view of human nature believed it to be a duty to attempt the curbing process. Some indeed argued that a woman was in need of *more* not less education precisely because of her 'weakness'. Others, however, went beyond this essentially prophylactic view of education to insist on the need to *foster* a girl's Mary-like potentialities. This humanist insistence on the influence of nurture on nature was early applied to the education of girls by Leonardo Bruni in his short piece *De Studiis et Literis* (*c*.1405),[53] which he wrote for the benefit of Baptista, the younger daughter of Antonio, Count of Urbino, a view which was repeated in the writings of Vives and More at the beginning of our period. But it was Richard Mulcaster, the successful Master of two leading London boys' schools, who systematically applied the argument, in the long chapter on girls' education which he included in his text *Positions* (1581). In it he likened parents who would not educate their daughters to those who forbade their children to use their left hands:

> nature has given them abilities to prove excellent in their kind [he claimed] . . . that naturally they are so richly endowed, all philosophy is full, no divinity denies . . . young maidens deserve the train, because they that have treasure bestowed them by nature to be bettered in them by nurture . . . That young maidens can learn, nature doth give them, and that they have learned, our experience doth teach us.

He went on to give a list of classical exemplars followed by 'our most worthy princess . . . for whose excellent knowledge and learning we have most cause to rejoice'.[54]

Yet, even if the possibility of nurture was acknowledged by some, there still remained the question of whether it was desirable. Some, of course, doubted its efficacy, as Mulcaster noted: 'But some Timon will say, what should women do with learning? Such a churlish caper will never pick out the best, but be always ready to blame the worst.'[55] When Francis Bacon, for example, wrote in his essay 'Of Nature in Men' that 'Nature is often hidden, sometimes overcome, seldom extinguished' he was clearly referring in his title to males (in the plural) and not to generic 'man', though this is implied in the rest of the essay. Yet when he comes to exemplify his argument he takes Aesop's fable of the cat who, having been turned into a woman, 'sat very demurely, at the board's end, till a mouse ran before her'.[56] The initial aphorism would have been commonplace in Bacon's day, but Aesop's tale and its application to women would also have been readily accepted. The downfall of Lady Anne Frankford in Thomas Heywood's *A Woman Killed with Kindness* (1607) would have been taken by some at least of Heywood's audience as providing an example of a well-born, well-educated and well-beloved wife reverting to the alleged type. The behaviour of Tamyra in Chapman's *Bussy D'Ambois* (1607) would have produced a similar response. Sir Miles Sandys made the same point directly in his *Prima Pars Parvi Opuscula* (1634) when he asserted 'To make them scholars were frivolous . . . learning in a woman is like a sundial in a grave'. James I, on being told of a young woman's learning, acidly asked 'But can she spin?' Even that affectionate husband Sir John Harrington expressed the same sentiment in his epigrammatic poem 'Of Women Learned in the Tongues':

> You wish me to a wife, fair, rich and young,
> That had the Latin, French and Spanish tongue.
> I thanked, and told you I desired none such,
> And said, One language may be tongue too much.
> Then love I not the learned? Yes, as my life;
> A learned mistress, not a learned wife.[57]

Alexander Niccoles, offering 'certain precepts' in his *Discourse of Marriage and Wiving* (1615), advised a young man that he should 'make thy choice rather of a virtuous than a learned wife'.[58] Nor were such comments the preserve of the treatise writers. As the contemporary proverb put it, 'A learned wife seldom proves good.' Even the balladeers had something to say on the matter:

> Their soaring thoughts to books advance,
> 'Tis odds that may undo 'um,
> For ever since Dame Eve's mischance
> That villainous itch sticks to 'um.[59]

Elizabeth Jocelin, a caring mother anxious to do her best for her offspring, nevertheless warned her daughter to hide what knowledge she had rather than 'boast it', though a century later Lord Chesterfield offered the same advice to his son: 'Wear your learning like your watch in a private pocket; and do not merely pull it out and strike it merely to show you have one.'[60]

Those, then, who acknowledged the possibility, even desirability, of nurture nevertheless recommend only a limited and in the end limiting curriculum, one aimed at curbing the 'natural' tendencies of women as with a bridle, confining them to the limited sphere of the home, where once again they would carry out their 'natural' function in society. Vives had recognised the tendency early on: 'I perceive that learned women be suspected of many; as who sayth, the subtlety of learning should be a nourishment for the maliciousness of their nature',[61] before going on to deny the validity of the suspicion. But with some the attitude persisted. When Sir Ralph Verney heard in 1652 that his god-daughter 'Nancy' (Ann Denton) wished to learn Latin, Greek and Hebrew he gently tried to dissuade her: 'Good sweetheart be not so covetous; believe me, a Bible . . . and a good plain catechism in your mother tongue, being well read and practised, is well worth all the rest, and much more suitable to your sex.' At the same time he advised the girl's father, 'Let not your girl learn Latin nor shorthand. The difficulty of the first may keep her from vice, but the easiness of the other may be a prejudice to her, for the pride of taking sermon notes hath made multitudes of women most unfortunate.' Of his own 8-year-old daughter Peg he wrote: 'She grows a great girl and will be spoiled for want of breeding . . . being a girl she shall not learn Latin, so she will have more time to learn breeding hereafter; and [needle]work too'.[62] In emphasising the need for religious education Sir Ralph would have found no objectors, but neither would his stress on housekeeping skills. Comenius himself, advocating universal elementary education, was, nevertheless, quite clearly of the same mind:

> And let none cast in my teeth that saying of the apostle: I permit not a woman to teach (I Tim. 2.12), or that of Juvenal in the sixth satire: See that thy lawful wife be not a chatterbox that she express not the simplest matter in involved language nor be deeply versed in history; or the remark of Hippolytes in Euripides: I detest a bluestocking. May there never be in my house who knows more than is fitting for a woman to know . . . These opinions, I opine, stand in no true opposition to our demand. For we are not advising that women be educated in such a way that their tendency to curiosity shall be developed, but that their sincerity and contentedness may be increased, and this chiefly in those things which it becomes a woman to know and to do; that is to say, all that enables her to look after her household and, to promote the welfare of her husband and her family.[63]

Even during the mid- and late seventeenth century then, the debate offered nothing that was new in content about either the nature or the possibilities of the nurture of girls and women. What those who contributed to the 'defence' literature did was to confirm, in more explicit and comprehensively argued terms, claims that the position of women in society was the result not of a 'weaker' or 'inferior' or even 'dangerous' nature, but of custom which denied them educational opportunities appropriate to their natural abilities. Dramatic literature, sermon, moral tract and treatise continued to be used as a vehicle to depict women in their various roles and guises – as, indeed, did the broadside ballad:

> The weakness of a woman's wit
> Is not through Nature's fault.
> But lack of education fit
> Makes Nature oft to halt.[64]

Despite an increasing number of women contributing to these kinds of literature, the vast bulk of it was written by men. But in the end the males had to come back to an acknowledgement of the positive stance which implied that 'nurture', whether of girls and women as educands or by mothers as educators, was not only possible but desirable. No one denied the proposition that parents should be responsible for the nurture of their children, or that mothers should have the prime responsibility for the education of their young offspring. The question, therefore, was no longer whether but how these tasks should be carried out.

None of this, however, is to say that by the end of the seventeenth century women had achieved 'equality' with men (however we define that elusive term), merely that the misogynist answer to the question 'whether' a woman's nature was susceptible of nurture did not go unanswered. Traditional assumptions and ascriptions about women and prescriptions about their education, though questioned, even challenged and denied, nevertheless remained predominant precisely because they were accepted as such by many educated (or even uneducated) women, who were ready, albeit resignedly, to follow the advice of such as George Savile, Marquis of Halifax, to his daughter: 'You are therefore to make the best of what is settled by law and not vainly imagine that it will be changed for your sake'[65] – even though that law was man-made and firmly buttressed by custom.

Yet to argue that the 'defences' and the claims to be found in them were singularly unsuccessful is to ignore the detail of individual lives – male and female – where women *shared* the decision-making of family (though not national) life and, on occasion, where women assumed the dominant position. The 'shrew' literature for example, was not a complete figment of the male imagination; it was a literary way of reflecting an actual life situation, deplored by some women as well, apparently, as by most men. Though 'Teach her to live under obedience'[66] was a universal prescription for the education of girls, so also was it for boys. The disobedient child, male or female, was seen to be in direct contravention not only of parental authority, but also of an authority based on and upheld by the divine sanction of the Fifth Commandment.[67] The difference lay in the next stage of nurture. Whilst a young woman was enjoined to be obedient to her husband, a young man was enjoined to ensure that his wife was obedient to him, though glosses on the nature of that relationship varied enormously in their attempt to resolve the underlying problem of power and consent. At the same time, the man himself continued to live under obedience to the crown and its officers at all levels, as the Elizabethan Homily 'Against Disobedience and Wilful Rebellion' and innumerable texts with titles such as *Of Government and Obedience* and *How Superior Powers Ought to be Obeyed* made abundantly clear.[68]

In the early modern period very few explicitly encouraged parents to educate their children to 'do better' than themselves. The whole drift and justification of prescription was encapsulated in the Primer of 1549, where the task of education was seen as a preparing of children for adult life that would be appropriate to their 'station'.[69] In the end, debate was couched in terms which remain with us to this day, as 'realistic' parents and teachers insist that their task is to prepare the child for 'the real world', the world as it is – 'Here it is, in you jump' – not even 'Here it is, take it or leave it.' In this view the task is certainly not to teach children to 'think for themselves', a process which openly, if on occasion apprehensively, acknowledges that it might possibly result in their contemplating the possibility or desirability of *changing* that world into something different, possibly even 'better'. In the early modern period neither the achievement of spiritual maturity at the *rite de passage* of confirmation, nor its later concomitant, participation in the Eucharist, were ever intended to indicate at the same time the achievement of a parallel political maturity, least of all for women. In its use of 'evidence' provided by 'authorities', whether classical or biblical, theological or philosophical, the nature–nurture debate in early modern England shared with its modern counterpart a willingness of some to seek ways and means of justifying a previously determined stance and to ignore in the meantime 'evidence' which did not fit that stance.

STATUS

A crucial corollary to any view of the nature of women and their education was the status ascribed to or claimed by them as a consequence of that view. The word itself was not used in the early modern period. Instead, terms such as 'state', 'estate', 'condition', 'degree', 'sort' were used[70] – and always in the sense, explicit or implicit, of the Prayer Book's catechetical gloss on the Tenth Commandment, 'that state of life unto which it shall please God to call me'.[71] In liturgy, sermon, catechism and treatise, status assymetry, to use the sociologist's term, was regarded as very much a part of one's God-given vocation.[72]

In practice, the bench-mark was the status of the male, in comparison with whom the female, of whatever class, was customarily accorded a position of inferiority and subordination. Moreover, such ascription meant that it was much more difficult for a woman (assuming she so wished) to *achieve* a higher status. Indeed, if and when she did achieve what men had achieved, for example, learning or power, whether in the family or in the state as queen, regnant or regent, or even by behaving courageously, her acquisition of power or her assumption of behaviour considered to be the monopoly of the male would often lead to calumny or blame.

Despite Calvin's assigning of Paul's restrictions on women – the covering of the head, the keeping of silence in church and their various extrapolations – to 'things indifferent', particular to Paul's historical situation and therefore subject not to divine law but to human decision, he nevertheless shared the cultural commonplace of his time, the Great Chain of Being, the failure to maintain which would lead to chaos and the breakdown of social stability. Shakespeare's much-quoted Ulysses speech on degree, 'Take but degree away, untune that string. And hark what discord follows',[73] was expressing, albeit in remarkably memorable language, a commonplace of the period, indicated, for example, in the differential 'Prayers for all conditions and sorts of men'[74] (and women) and in the contemporary distinction between 'gentlemen of continuance' and those 'newly come up'.

Of course, such views prevented neither an actual rising in the social scale, nor criticism of such change. In the same way, the politics of gender – the ways in which position, and therefore power to apply influence or control, affect the ways men and women treat each other – was not as simple as polemicists (of whatever view) would have had their readers believe. The generalisation that girls were subject to their fathers and wives subject to their husbands is far too simplistic to provide an adequate picture of what was considered to be the appropriate social status even of 'maids' who, as the mass of contemporary, 'now-a-daies', whingeing complaint constantly reiterated, seemed to challenge or ignore the wishes of their parents with impunity. It remains unhelpful, therefore, to think in terms of, say, 'the status of Tudor women', when there are numerous, often contradictory, indicators of the differential statuses which particular women claimed, were accorded or achieved in the different aspects of their lives.

The legal rights of women, severely limited as they were, at least in theory, nevertheless provide one sort of clue to their status in practice. Though not the legal equivalent of men – or, as Pearl Hogrefe has more precisely put it, having 'a more precarious legal personality than men'[75] – women were nevertheless not simply legal nonentities, not simply chattels, the property of their fathers or their husbands. As a spinster or a widow – *femme sole* – a woman enjoyed the same proprietorial rights as a man. If her husband died intestate and with issue, a widow was entitled to one third of the estate (one half, if without issue), plus the right to her dower, that is, half the property he held during his life. She could make a will and bequeath her goods as she wished; she could and very often did act as an executrix of her late husband's will; she could sue and be sued. As a married woman – *femme couverte* – she did indeed lose these rights, surrendering them on marriage to her husband, 'as when a tributary joins the main river'.[76] As always, however, much depended on the actual relationship between two particular people, a situation well recognised by the author of *The Lawes Resolutions of Womens Rights or The Lawes Provision for Women* (1632): 'I know no remedy, though some women can shift it well enough. The common law here shaketh the hand with divinity',[77] the more so if, as increasingly she did, a woman resorted to the Court of Chancery, which increasingly took on testamentary cases (traditionally the monopoly of the ecclesiastical courts) and which mitigated much of the intractability of the common law by its relatively informal and quick process and its consequent cheapness.[78]

Of greater importance than legal restrictions and rights, however, were those social and moral codes which were much more susceptible to interpretation and therefore productive of variety in attitude and behaviour. Perceptions of and attitudes to marriage are a case in point. In the Protestant churches it was universally insisted that the married state was not only honourable, instituted by God, but a divinely enjoined duty on the part of the Christian faithful. Moreover, the emphasis was now on its superiority to the state of celibacy, with the biblical injunction 'Go forth and multiply' echoed in sermons, treatises and dramatic literature alike. Barnaby Rich used the techniques of rhetoric to make the point: 'Marriage is not only commended, but it is also commanded by the Almighty Himself.' William Vaughan could not resist making an additional point: 'He that shunneth marriage . . . is to be esteemed a wicked wretch (as the Pope is).' John Donne directed his shaft towards young women, insisting that 'foolish maids . . . accuse their parents in condemning marriage'. Shakespeare's Parolles adds a reference to the Fifth Commandment in his assertion to Helena that 'To speak on the part of virginity is to accuse your mothers, which is most infallible disobedience.' The disguised Viola takes a different line with her remonstrance to Olivia in *Twelfth Night*:

> Lady you are the cruellest she alive
> If you will lead these graces to the grave
> And leave the world no copy.[79]

Such comments lead on to a further indicator of the status of women, that provided by the debates about the absolute need to defer to parental wishes in the choice of marriage partner. Medieval canon law[80] had recognised that agreement between the two persons concerned, *per verba de presenti*, was sufficient to make a marriage valid, without intervention from priests, parents or friends, though young people were advised for the sake of familial harmony to consult with and persuade their parents. With the Reformation and Counter-Reformation, all churches sought means to control their flocks by emphasising the need for parental consent and priestly oversight. The prescriptive literature argued the case on two fronts: whilst children should heed the Fifth Commandment, parents should not unduly impose their will. The agreement of all parties was the ideal to be sought after. Bishop Gervase Babington was not unusual in choosing his words: 'As children owe a duty to parents to ask their consents, so every parent also oweth this to their children not violently to force them against their likes, for whoso marrieth marrieth for himself and not his parents.'[81] Henry Parker alluded to the matter in his discussion of the relative rights of subjects and princes:

> In matrimony there is something divine . . . but is this any ground to infer that there is no human consent or concurrence in it? Does this divine institution of marriage take away freedom of choice before, or conclude either party under an absolute formalization?[82]

What was generally condemned was the making of financial gain the sole consideration in the choice of marriage partner, 'the buying and selling among parents' as Samuel Hieron put it,[83] a practice which Thomas Fuller saw as having wider consequences when he warned ' 'Tis to be feared that they who marry where they do not love will love where they do not marry and they jeopardise not only their own marriage but the whole commonwealth.'[84]

Some women made plain their willingness to defer to parental wishes, or at least to seek their consent. In 1644 Anne Murray, for example, declined to accept Thomas Howard's offer to marry her secretly against her parents' wishes, whilst at the same time reserving to herself the right to refuse marriage without her own consent.[85] Dorothy Osborne had a similar message for William Temple, though they later overcame the opposition of both families and married with their blessing.[86] Anne Clifford must have been mature beyond her years when, in August 1605 when she was aged 15, she discussed her own marriage with her father, though in the event neither of her two marriages was a great success.[87] At a more popular level, the balladeer put similar sentiments into the mouth of one of his young maids:

> Kind sir, I have a mother, beside a father still,
> Those friends above all others, you must ask their goodwill.[88]

Each of these was taking up the position assigned to Katherine, daughter of the King of France in Shakespeare's *Henry V*, to Robert Greene's Melissa in his *Perimedes the Blacksmith* and to Thomas Deloney's 'Mistress Page' in his ballad 'The Lamentation of Mr Page's Wife'.[89]

Others, on the contrary, insisted on staking a claim on their own assessment of their status by refusing to accept their parents' wishes in the choice of marriage partner, a piece of behaviour much disapproved of by commentators. Roger Ascham, for example, deplored the fact that 'even girls dare, without all fear though not without open shame, where they list, and how they must marry themselves in spite of father, mother, God, good order and all.'[90] Richard Allestree was equally forthright in his condemnation: 'But of all acts of disobedience, that of marrying against the consent of the parents is one of the highest.'[91]

The audiences of Shakespeare and his contemporaries would have been very familiar with the behaviour of those of his women characters who had either defied or were in the process of defying parental wishes in the matter – Desdemona in *Othello*, Hermia in *A Midsummer Night's Dream*, Imogen in *Cymbeline*, for example. Similar examples in real life are not far to seek. Back in 1469 Margery Paston had shocked her family by insisting on marrying, against all advice, her mother's bailiff, Richard Calle.[92] Anne More, daughter of Sir George More of Mosely, and Elizabeth Evelyn, daughter of the diarist, both resorted to secrecy in their respective marriages to John Donne in 1601 and a nephew of Sir John Tippett in 1685.[93] Elizabeth Freke followed a similar path in 1671 when she married her cousin, Percy Freke. Lady Katherine Manners agreed to convert to the Anglican faith against the wishes of her father, the sixth Earl of Rutland, in order to marry her love, George Villiers, in 1620. Mary Boyle refused to marry her father's choice, before marrying Charles Rich, her own choice. Much the same kind of opposition faced Katherine, the daughter of Sir Richard Chomley when she indicated her decision to marry 'one Dutton, a gentleman but a younger brother' who was at the time a servant to Sir Richard. She eventually married the man of her choice 'which Sir Richard in some sort connived at which was too late to prevent'.[94]

Some parents were, however, only too ready to apply the sanctions they knew they had to hand. Daughters of relatively wealthy parents knew that their marriage portion, their dowry, could be withheld and their jointure, the annuity promised to the bride by her prospective father-in-law, could similarly be put in jeopardy, if they refused to accept parental wishes. With very little property or money involved those lower down the social scale enjoyed greater freedom, though doubtless the practice of young newlyweds starting their life together in one of the parental homes, or even a conscientious willingness to heed the Fifth Commandment, might well have influenced decision-making in the matter. Even so, Edward Chamberlayne was not alone in noting that a father's testamentary powers 'kept their children in great awe'.[95] Sir Roger Townshend of Raynham in Norfolk, for example, left £200 each for the marriages of his daughters, Anne and Elizabeth, so long as they married with the advice and agreement of their mother, Eleanor.[96] Sir Ralph Verney insisted in his will of 1525 that 'if any of my aforesaid daughters will not be advised nor ruled in the preferment of their marriage by my executors . . . it shall be at their liberty to diminish part of the sum bequeathed until she be reformed'.[97] Peter Slingsby of Marton, Boroughbridge, even extended such sanctions to his two 'base begotten' daughters, Alice and Joan. In his will of 1570 he bequeathed them 20s per annum until their marriage. On marrying each was to receive £11, a sum which would be withdrawn and re-allocated to the other if in choosing a husband either was not 'ordered and obedient' to his three male executors.[98] The elder daughter of Richard More of Grantham, having contracted to marry a London silk vendor without her father's consent, was allowed only 40s towards her marriage.[99] A more dutiful younger daughter was allowed £200. The 1624 will of Richard Latimere, vicar of Polesworth, allowed his daughter Alice 20 marks 'provided that she be ruled by her mother, her brother and her uncle Francis'. Anne Hallam's portion of £120 would be reduced to £20 if she married against her mother's wishes.[100]

Gilbert Burnet (1643–1715), later Bishop of Salisbury, faced a different sort of problem in each of his two marriages. In the autobiographical section of his posthumously published *History of My Own Times*, he reported that Margaret Kennedy, his first wife, agreed to marry him only after many years of friendship, 'for as she had no mind to lose my company she had as little mind to marry me . . . [since] she saw marriage as such an inequality would much lessen her'. In the same way Mary Scott, his second wife, 'continued unmarried until she was 27 years old, resolving not to marry till she saw a person she could like'.[101] Mary Rich, Margaret Cavendish, Alice Thornton and Dorothy Temple each reflected in later life on their earlier reluctance to forgo the relative independence of the unmarried state,[102] despite its obvious drawbacks in the cultural ambience of their day. Young men and women alike faced the dilemma in wishing to recognise filial duty whilst preferring a partner of their own choosing. Few would enjoy the benefit of the advice that Philip Henry gave his children: 'Please God, and please yourselves, and you shall never displease me.'[103]

It was in circumstances as varied as these that many arranged marriages resulted in a variety of outcomes. Writing to his son Henry Hastings, in 1613, Henry, fifth Earl of Huntingdon, recalled that 'I was myself married when a child and could not have chosen as well myself and not been so happy in any woman I know', though he judiciously went on to say 'but because one proves well it must not beget a conclusion'.[104] Rachel Wriothesley's short-lived first marriage to Francis Vaughan was arranged, though her second to William Russell was a decided love-match of their own choosing.[105] Mary Bracknell's marriage in 1629 when she was 13 to Ralph Verney then 15, was plainly not the result of independent decisions on their part, yet their partnership survived long periods of separation during the Civil War.[106] Francis, Lord North, on the other hand, reflecting on his own relatively unhappy arranged marriage, concluded that parents 'ought to leave their children full freedom, with their consent, in so important a case'.[107] At the other end of the spectrum, however, were the unfortunate cases where a father resorted to extreme measures to enforce his wishes. Sir Edward Coke, for example, forcibly abducted his daughter from her mother's care, tied her to a bedpost and had her severely whipped until she agreed to marry the mentally unstable brother of the Duke of Buckingham.[108] The daughter of Sir Thomas Holte of Aston Hall near Birmingham died in the upper room where her father had imprisoned her for refusing to marry in accordance with his wishes.[109] Even so, most parents would have agreed with the line taken by Thomas Hilder who, whilst complaining 'how much then are those parents to blame who train their powers over their children beyond due limits in laying out engagements and commands of them', nevertheless went on to advise young people that they should seek parental consent on both sides in order to fulfil the Fifth Commandment, whilst condemning those that did not 'as the greatest of thieves in the world' by thus breaking the Eighth Commandment.[110] As was so often the case in such texts, he did not go on to delineate the 'due limits'.

At the root of the matter of a woman's status in the choice of marriage partner, and indeed her status as a married woman, was the continued ambivalence of attitudes to what we now call romantic love, which many of the older generation regarded as merely an aberrant adolescent fantasy with no firmer base than what John Stockwood called 'unbridled and unsettled lust'.[111] Philip Stubbes likewise warned against young men who were without sufficient resources for marriage, yet 'cared nothing so long as they lived with their pretty pussy to huggle withal'.[112] When William Painter included 'The goodly history of the true and constant love between Rhomeo and Julietta' in his *Second Tome of the Palace of Pleasure* (1567) he did so to 'disclose the hearty affections of two incomparable lovers ... [and] what dangers either sort incur which marry without the advice of parents'.[113] In this he was merely echoing the purpose of Arthur Brooke who five years earlier had produced *The Tragicall Historye of Romeus and Juliet written first in Italian by Bandell and nowe in Englishe by Ar. Br.*

> and to this end (good reader) is this tragical matter written to describe unto thee a couple of unfortunate lovers, thralling themselves to unhonest desire, neglecting the authority and advice of parents and friends, conferring their principal counsels with drunken gossips and superstitious friars (the naturally fit instruments of unchastity), attempting ill adventures of peril that attaining of their wicked lust, using

auricular confession (the key to whoredom and treason) for the furtherance of their purpose, abusing the honourable name of lawful marriage to cloak the shame of stolen contracts, finally by all means of unhonesty hastying to a most unhappy death . . . Hereunto if you apply it you shall deliver my doing from offence and profit yourselves.

Richard Baxter made much the same point: 'Take special care that fancy and passion overrule not pleasure and friends' advice in the choice.'[114]

By the end of the period, however, an increasing number of texts advising 'How a lady ought to approve and reject a suitor' gave some indication of how far a young woman might act independently in her choice of marriage partner. Whilst some few flew in the face of all advice, others showed their willingness to at least attempt to reconcile the multiplicity of often conflicting pressures – religious, economic and social as well as emotional – which could be brought to bear 'in so important a case'. Having married, a woman could claim and was indeed accorded a status higher than that of her unmarried sister. Showing every sign of rejecting the proposed marriage to Demetrius, her father's choice, Hermia in *A Midsummer Night's Dream* (I.i.72–3) was reminded in no uncertain terms by Theseus, Duke of Athens that, if she did not follow his wish, she would die or at the very least be reduced to entering a nunnery, there to be restricted to 'Chanting faint hymns to the cold fruitless moon'. At a lower social level the waiting woman, Charlotte, in Chapman's *Bussy D'Ambois* used a more down-to-earth metaphor: 'Ye must gather us with the ladder of matrimony or we'll hang until we be rotten.'[115]

But it is in the numerous qualified glosses on 1 Peter 3.1ff., 'Likewise, ye wives, be subject to your husbands', a favourite text of the patriarchalists, that we get perhaps the best indicator of woman's perceived status in marriage. Alternatively, Ephesians 5.22, 'Wives submit yourselves unto your husbands', would be used and this would be reinforced with a justificatory reference to the Fifth Commandment, glossed as usual in the widest terms, as in Robert Cleaver's *Plaine and Familiar Exposition of the Ten Commandments*, 'so the apostle speaketh to wives: "wives obey your own husbands" in obedience to the commandment'. Francis Seager had already put it in more familiar terms in his *School of Vertue* (*c.*1550 and many times reprinted):

Ye wives love your husbands
And obedient be;
For they are your heads
And above in degree.[116]

ually, husbands were warned that it was their responsibility to maintain the position of authority over their wives which had been divinely granted to them. James I's advice to Prince Henry could not have been more succinct or commonplace: 'Rule her as your pupil . . . it is your office to command and hers to obey.'[117] In his verse commentary on the various virtues and vices of the day, Anthony Sherley described obedience in the household, as in the state, as 'a religious glue':

> The only true physician
> Rebellious sores to heal.[118]

William Whateley was more direct in making his point:

> that house is a misshapen house and . . . a crump-shouldered or hunchbacked house where the husband has made himself an underling to his wife, and given away his power and regiment to his inferior . . . let her set down this conclusion in her soul: my husband is my superior, my better; he hath authority and rule over me; nature hath given it to him . . . God hath given it to him (Gen. 3.16).[119]

Or, as the anonymous *Mothers Counsell* put it, 'If a man's folly make a woman his equal, her pride will soon make herself his superior.'[120]

Yet this does not tell the whole story by any means. Throughout the period we are faced with the ambiguities of familial metaphors and analogies, and innumerable glosses frequently hedged the injunction round with conditional clauses, giving a clear indication that the 'subjection' was not intended to be as absolute as that laid down in the prayer designed for wives in the Edwardian Primer of 1553:

> God give me grace, I most entirely beseech thee, to walk worthy of my vocation, to acknowledge my husband to be my head, to learn thy blessed word of him, to reverence him, to obey him, to please him, to be ruled by him, peaceably and quietly to live with him.[121]

The problem of how to reconcile patriarchy and affectionate mutuality remained perennially difficult to answer. When Eulalia, in Erasmus' colloquy 'Marriage', asserted that 'A woman's highest praise is to be obedient to my husband', she was expressing the conservative view which her neighbour Xantippe plainly did not share.[122] The Protestant reformers who followed Erasmus continued to elaborate the gloss in their own way, but with the same qualifications. Glosses on the second Edwardian Prayer Book's three-fold purposes of marriage – procreation of children, a remedy for sin and mutual society and comfort – all recognised that none of these was a sufficient reason in itself. But by the end of the sixteenth century writers and preachers increasingly placed the greatest emphasis on the third. The degree of emphasis would, of course, depend or vary with the commentator's position on the conservative–radical continuum, though we should never discount the possibility of a degree of self-interest in the praise of marriage to be found in the writings and sermons of Protestant clerics. Most, however, would go only so far as William Gouge: 'for all degrees wherein there is any difference betwixt person and person there is least disparity betwixt man and wife'. The wife's position (he went on) is 'the nearest to equality that may be, a place of common equity in many respects wherein a man and wife are, after a sort, even fellows and partners'.[123] This is no clerical prevarication, but a recognition of the complexities of marital relationships, nowhere more evident than in the final speech of Katherine in Shakespeare's *Taming of the Shrew*.

The difficulty of making a connection between mutual love and wifely obedience was ever present in the marriage literature of the period, especially when glosses on the Fifth Commandment extended the injunction to man and wife, as John Whitgift did, for example, in his sermon at St Paul's Cross in 1583. John Donne was commenting on many of the attitudes of his time when he reminded his congregation, on the subject of wives, 'To make them gods is ungodly and to make them devils is devilish; to make them mistresses is unmanly and to make them servants unnoble; to make them as God made them, wives, is godly and manly too.'[124]

Jeremy Taylor was not unusual in arguing 'A husband's power over his wife is paternal and friendly, not magisterial and despotic', going on, as many others did, to spell out the dilemma implicit in customary attitudes to marriage, which he described as 'the queen of friendships'.[125] Partnership metaphors abound in an effort to clarify a complex relationship, as in the rib metaphor to which we have already referred.[126] That marriage was seen as an alliance of economic resources, at all levels of society, should not, however, inhibit us from examining the terms of the alliance and the evidence for other motivations. The desirability of a mental compatibility was emphasised by humanists such as Vives and More. David Clapham, translating Agrippa, reminded the prospective husband to 'Choose a wife not a garment; let thy wife be married unto thee not her dower.' Edmund Tilney made much the same point by insisting that 'equality is principally to be considered in this matrimonial amity, as well of years as the gifts of nature and fortune. For equality herein maketh friendliness.'[127] Henry Smith advised that 'to begin this concord well' young couples should 'learn one another's nature and one another's affections and one another's infirmities, use you must be helpers and you cannot help unless you know the e'. In other words, 'the man and the wife are partners, like two oars in a boat'.[128] William Whatley used the more usual terminology when he likened husband and wife to 'two oxen that draw in one yoke'. Some, such as William Gouge, pitched the argument at a more material level: 'there should be some equality betwixt partners that are married, in age, estate, condition and piety',[129] a view which is to be found in Thomas Heywood's description of Frankford and his wife Anne in *A Woman Killed with Kindness* (1607):

> You both adorn each other, and your hands,
> Methinks are matches; there's [e]quality
> In this fair combination; you are both scholars,
> Both young, both descended nobly;
> There's music in this sympathy; it carries
> Comfort and expectation of much joy.

The musical metaphor was also used by Peter de la Primaudaye in his *French Academie* (1618), when he wished his married couple to be 'in perfect harmony like as in music'.[130] John Donne, on the other hand, put the emphasis elsewhere when he insisted that the young couple need 'not always [be] like in complexion, nor like in years, nor like in fortune, nor like in birth, but like in mind, like in disposition, like in love of God and of one another'. But, in the end, and all the conditional clauses notwithstanding, prescription began and ended with the position of the husband.[131] Dod and Cleaver's *Godly Forme of Household Gouvernement*, one of the most popular of marital manuals, could stand for most of the genre:

> all in the family are not to be governed alike . . . There is one rule to govern the wife by, another for children, another for servants . . . those husbands who use their wives but as servants are but very fools, that judge and think matrimony to be a dominion . . . [a wife] may in modest sort shew her mind, and a wise husband will not disdain to hear her advice and follow it if it be good.

implying, of course, that it would be the husband who would decide what was deemed to be 'good'.[132]

Some wives were plainly willing to accept an inferior status as part of Christian duty. For example, in 1632, Lady Mary Peyton advised her daughter Anne, newly married to Henry Oxinden of Barham, 'withal be careful that whatsoever you do, to love, honour and obey your husband in all things that is fitting for a reasonable creature' and in so doing to 'show yourself a virtuous wife whose price is not to be valued'. Lady Cotton similarly wrote to her daughter, 'You have subjected yourself to him and made him your head'. Elizabeth Walker's advice to her daughters, Margaret and Elizabeth, could not have been more customary, citing Proverbs 12.4 and 31.7 as well as 1 Peter 3, 1–6. Lucy Hutchinson was her own witness:

> Never man had a greater passion for a woman, nor a more honourable esteem of a wife; yet he was not uxorious, nor remitted he that just rule which it was her honour to obey, but managed the reins of government with such prudence and affection that she who would not delight in such an honourable and advantageable subjection must have wanted an unreasonable soul.[133]

Yet manual and sermon prescription notwithstanding, some wives refused and some husbands were either not inclined nor indeed able to follow the norm. Despite the evidence of successful and happy marriages, some failed to live up to all that was expected of them, and thus attitudes to and teaching about divorce and separation further contribute to our understanding of the status of women, whether ascribed or achieved. A reiteration of the basic proof-text, Matthew 19.6, 'What therefore God hath joined together let no man put asunder', constantly reminded the faithful of their marriage vows and of the need to live 'for better or for worse', in companionate harmony and mutual toleration of each other's faults, apart from those occasions when it was subsequently alleged and proved that secular, financial and property contracts had not been honoured – cases which could be settled in Chancery not by divorce but by restitution. A marriage could be annulled only by resort to the ecclesiastical courts, and then only for non-consummation or the infringement of forbidden degrees.[134]

John Whitgift, drawing the attention of the Lower House of Convocation to a number of evils within the church, included the too easy granting of divorce as one of them, and attempted to put matters right in his Constitutions of 1597. Yet the fact that he had to refer to the matter several times in subsequent years points to a failure to implement the policy efficiently or consistently. Brawling, scolding, beating continued to be denied as grounds for divorce – for men as well as women – though doubtless among all classes there were cases of separation by simple desertion. In other words, as Thomas Gataker put it, divorce should not become available to either party simply because it was felt a mistake had been made.[135] It was put in more homely terms by the anonymous author of *The Mothers Counsell* (1630): 'she that forsakes her husband because she dislikes his manners is like her that forsakes the honey lest the bee might sting her'.[136] Some, as we might expect, insisted on the absolute veto implied in the injunction that marriage was for life, and referred the parties concerned to the advice of John 8.11 and the Christian virtue of forgiveness.

Nevertheless, adultery produced a perennial problem. John Calvin's commentary on the text concluded that if adultery were condoned no crime would be punishable, and Edmund Bunney, who produced an abridged version of the *Institutes* in translation, repeated the view in his *Of Divorce for Adulterie and Marrying Againe: That Thing Is No Sufficient Warrant So To Do* (1610), noting in his Preface 'how few of all sorts there are that are able to see how strict and insoluble the bond of wedlock is, after that it be rightly joined together . . . not only the common sort . . . but even the better also'.[137] Yet others, seeing that the emphasis on John 8.11 focused all attention on the sinning wife, wished also to bring an adulterous husband to account. Henry Smith, for example, was willing to concede that 'As God hath ordained remedies for every disease, so hath He ordained a remedy for the disease of marriage. The disease of marriage is adultery, and the medicine thereof is divorcement.' No one condoned adultery but increasingly the prescriptive literature, recognising the standing of the wife in marriage, was unwilling to condone 'the double standard'. Indeed, some such as William Gouge and Jeremy Taylor argued that since the wife was the 'weaker vessel' the sinning husband was more culpable than the sinning wife.[138]

The matter was further complicated by the possibility of religious difference between the husband and wife. Andrew Kingsmill, for instance, made it plain that 'the believing woman already married to an unbelieving man should not use his infidelity as an occasion to part him . . . I Cor. 7', and went on, 'I counsell you to continue for the hope of sanctification'. But plainly this did not satisfy some women.[139] Anne Askew, whose marriage to her 'unchristian' husband was arranged by the respective fathers 'for lucre', was a case in point. As John Bale tells her story:

> Notwithstanding, the marriage once past, she demeaned herself like a Christian wife, and had by him (as I am informed) two children. In process of time by oft reading the sacred Bible, she fell clearly from the old superstitions of papistry to a perfect belief in Jesus Christ, whereby she so offended the priest that he at their suggestion violently drove her out of his house, whereupon she thought herself free from that uncomely kind of cloaked marriage by this doctrine of St Paul, I Cor. 6.[140]

Foxe celebrates the lives of other women, contemporary with Askew, who held fast to their reformed religion in the face of aggressively unbelieving husbands. Later, the Quaker, Alice Hayes (1659–1720), left her first husband, Daniel Smith, who took away her clothes as she prepared to go to meetings, though they were eventually reconciled and (as she reported) he 'continued to his life's end a loving and tender husband and an indulgent father to our children'.[141] Unusually, both William Whately and William Gouge acknowledged the possibility of divorce by mutual consent, though Whateley was obliged by the Court of High Commission to repudiate his allowance for divorce by separation or desertion which he made in his *Bride Bush* (1608) when he came to publish his *Care-cloth . . . the Cumbers of Marriage* (1624). Milton, following his prime source, Martin Bucer's *De Regno Christi*, accepted that marriages break down for a variety of reasons, and that these should therefore be accepted as grounds for divorce, with the wife having as natural a right to divorce her husband as her husband had to divorce her.[142]

A woman's status was also a matter of crucial concern in the constant debates about wife-beating. In one particular, women were accorded equality with men in that the judicial form of corporal punishment, public whipping, was applied, especially in cases of petty larceny, to men and women alike. In the 1592 Quarter Sessions, Margery Moor was ordered to be 'whipped openly in and upon two several market days throughout the full market of Axbridge in Somerset, being naked from the waist upwards', for producing a bastard child. For the same offence in 1608, Margery Chalcrofte was ordered 'when fit and able to travel [out of the parish] to be whipped through the next market town'. At the Sessions of 1613 it was ordered that Elizabeth Stuckey of Mochelness 'shall be on Saturday next about twelve of the clock whipped at Langport up and down the market until her back be bloody'. In 1659 Sir Richard Brownlow noted in his day-book that he had ordered 'to be whipped 20 stripes apiece Tealby of Hockenby for stealing two sheep and Dorothy Dawkins for stealing red cloth for a petticoat'.[143] Whipping was also considered to be an appropriate punishment for Barbara Blaugdone who had the temerity to speak out in church at Exeter, and for Elizabeth Williams for addressing a crowd of undergraduates outside Sidney Sussex College in Cambridge.[144] The Assize records are full of such cases, and in the cases of grand larceny the full rigours of capital punishment were enforced, with women being sentenced to be hanged along with men.

Within the marital home wife-beating (or indeed husband-beating) was not a common-law offence – though cases could be brought before the consistory courts or be dealt with informally by the parishioners themselves by 'rough ridings'. Household and marriage manuals, however, were almost universal in their disapproval of such behaviour in the relative privacy of the home. Thomas Becon, for example, fiercely criticised husbands who 'like stable curs urgently entreat them, beat them, buffet them, and put out of doors, handling them rather like dish clouts than like honest wives, unto the great slander and ignoring of wedlock'.[145] Richard Whitforde had earlier urged husbands to take a pragmatic view since, as he argued, 'a shrew will sooner be corrected by smiling and laughing than by a staff of strokes'. A later balladeer, appealing to a wider audience, used the same argument:

> Some men will beat their wives, but that's the way
> To make them obstinate and go astray.
> But if thou seest her strive to wear the breeches
> Then strive to overcome her with kind speeches.[146]

William Vaughan took a different tack when he insisted that 'the husband must not injure his wife ... for a woman is a feeble creature and not endowed with such a noble courage as the man'.[147]

Such injunctions plainly acknowledged that wife-beating was not unknown. Indeed, the common law recognised the right to do so, and proverbs such as 'A spaniel, a woman and a walnut tree / The more they are beaten the better will they be'[148] encouraged husbands still further. Yet there is plenty of evidence that some wives were only too ready to reply in kind to such treatment. Many would have recognised Erasmus' Xantippe, who responded to her husband's threatening her with a stick by snatching up a three-legged stool and reminding him that he was dealing with a spirited woman. Once again the balladeer echoed the same sentiment when his 'fair and virtuous wife', having recounted how she had responded to her husband's beating by using her own ladler on him, concluded:

> Young married women pray attend
> To these few lines which I have penned.
> So you will clearly understand
> How I obtained the upper hand.[149]

But the prescriptive literature, manual and sermon alike, consistently argued from a matter of principle. The Second Book of Homilies, read in churches throughout the land, put it in uncompromising terms: 'But yet I mean not that a man should beat his wife. God forbid that, for that is the greatest shame that can be.' Henry Smith spoke in gentler but no less compelling vein when in a marriage sermon he reminded his young couple (and presumably his congregation) that 'her cheeks are made for thy lips and not thy fists'. The author of *The Glasse Of Godly Love* (1569) urged the husband to 'take heed that he turn not his authority to tyranny'. William Ames' considered form of words was nevertheless entirely characteristic of the genre:

He may and ought to restrain her by such means as not repugnant to conjugal society, as by admonitions, reprehensions and the denial of some privileges which are due to a good and obedient wife. But it is by no means part of any husband to correct his wife with blows.[150]

Jeremy Taylor was as uncompromising as the Homily when he referred to 'the barbarous inhumanity of striking the wife'. The pseudonymous author of *The Husbands Authority Unvail'd* (1650), indicating to his readers that 'The style is nothing lofty, but low and professedly humble to all men', made it plain that 'The scripture yields neither precept nor example for beating a man's wife.'[151]

Rarely accorded status in the prescriptive literature, which often attempted to dissuade her from remarrying and made her a figure of fun and even derision in the dramatic literature, a widow is an actual fact found to be operating at a remarkably independent level.[152] A further indicator, then, of a woman's status is to be found in the number of occasions on which a wife and a widow rather than a male relation or friend, is nominated in the husband's will as his sole executrix. A wife could perfectly legally be nominated to such an office. Patrick Hannay, in delineating *A Happy Husband* (1618), acknowledged this, though he did not recommend it, whilst Sir William Wentworth, advising his son Thomas in 1604, was adamant: 'Make sure you make your son, not your wife, your executor.'[153] Even so, there are numerous examples of husbands nominating their wives, and this not solely as a token of loyal affection, Deryk Leke, for example, nominating his wife 'for the cause she hath helped me with great pains to get that I have, therefore it is right that I should remember her'.[154] Nor was the practice a new one. The Celys regularly made their wives their nominees. Roger Townshend did the same for his wife Eleanor in 1493. Christopher, Lord Conyers, nominated his wife as his sole executrix in 1538, as did Henry de Clifford his wife Margaret. Henry's son Ingram followed his father's example when he nominated his second wife Ursula. Nor was the recognition of status implied in such a practice confined to the aristocracy. In 1526, the Bristol merchant, Matthew Smyth, willed his wife Alice to that office.[155] In his will of 1542, Thomas Barnardiston made his wife, Anne, his sole executrix. John Donne's mother, Elizabeth, was similarly named in the 1576 will of her husband John senior. James West, yeoman of Banbury, made a complicated will in 1625 but nevertheless nominated his wife as executrix, 'for I am well assured she may take the executorship upon . . . she having always carried herself as a very loving and dutiful wife to me'. Lettice, wife of Lucius, second Viscount Falkland, and Mary, wife of Charles, fourth Earl of Warwick, were both charged to execute the wills of their husbands, in 1642 and 1673 respectively. In 1683 Jane, wife of

Ralph Josselin, was executrix of her husband's will, and Ralph's son, John, followed his father's example in nominating his wife Martha. In 1691 Sir Dudley North did the same.[156]

Occasionally, both wife and daughter were called upon to act. In 1582 Giles Entwistle of Entwistle in Lancashire nominated his wife Alice and his daughter Anne. John Cleye, husbandman of (Temple) Normanton nominated his wife Joan and daughter Ezabell in his will of 1561, whilst Alen Lyngard, husbandman of Walton, named his wife Emote and daughter Margaret in his will of 1559. At the end of the early modern period, in 1679, Elizabeth Scarrow of Carlisle nominated her four daughters to the office.[157] Moreover, women showed their ability to engage in disputes with male executors of their husbands' wills, as did Alice Spring, widow of Thomas Spring who died in 1523, when she challenged her husband's executor, Thomas Jermyn, about control of the family's fortune. Anne, widow of John de Vere, fourteenth Earl of Oxford, faced the same difficulties. After the death of her father in 1581, Lady Mary Willoughby battled for nearly 40 years with his half-brother who laid claim to the estate. More famously, Anne Clifford, with the support of her mother Margaret, the Dowager Countess, fought with her uncle, the executor of the will of her father George, third Earl of Cumberland. It was probably with this experience in mind that she made her daughter, Margaret, Countess of Thanet, her own executrix.[158]

Officially inoperative whilst her husband was alive, a widow often continued his business as a member of his guild. Virile as young apprentices doubtless were, it is unlikely that an active and experienced widow would be too easily seduced into marriage by a younger man without some awareness of what she was engaging in. Widows frequently appear in the records of the Stationers' Company, for example, as independent printers, as well as on the title pages of books printed by them. Other guild and municipal records show them operating as vintners, inn-keepers, glove- and shoe-makers (dressmaking did not become women's work until the latter part of the seventeenth century), though women were never accorded the status of office-holder in these guilds. Lower down the social scale, women – unmarried, married and widows – are to be found as wage-earners, as servants, laundresses, dairymaids and of course as wet-nurses and midwives. Button-making, lace-making, silk- and stocking-knitting also provided women with earning opportunities, which would in turn afford them a degree of autonomy, in what was, nevertheless, a male-orientated world.[159]

Occasionally we find women acting as business partners, formal or informal, or notice them negotiating an entrance into freehold or leasehold land. The merchant's wife in Marinus van Rymerswaele's painting 'Money-changer and his wife' (dated 1536, now in the Prado) depicts a wife intimately and knowingly involved in the business of counting the cash handled by her husband, against an account book in her own hands. The painting is so realistically and minutely detailed that it would hardly have been intended as representing anything other than a relatively common occurrence at that level of society, the sort of contribution which, for example, Sabine Johnson and Grace Wallington made to their husbands' business affairs, as also the Nuremberg wife, Magdalena Paumgartner, did to those of her husband, Balthasar.[160]

Notwithstanding the urgings of misogynist literature to beware of garrulous wives who would fail to keep a husband's secrets, the mutuality prescribed in sermon and treatise and the sort of transactions objectified in van Rymerswaele's painting are nowhere more clearly to be seen than in the numerous cases where wives were entrusted in their husbands' absence with what was normally considered to be a man's work, the management of family estates. The evidence ranges over the whole period and applies to a remarkably wide social spectrum. Lady Agnes Paston's participation in the ordering of the Paston estates during the 1430s whilst her lawyer husband, William, was away, is paralleled in the case of Thomasin Hopton, second wife of John Hopton, of Blythburgh in Suffolk in the 1460s.[161] Whilst Arthur Plantagenet, Viscount Lisle, was serving the king as Lord Deputy in Calais in the late 1530s, Lady Honor, his wife, was at work in London acting on his behalf in the protracted lawsuits regarding the ownership of tin mines in Cornwall, about the collection of rents, the payment of bills, and a host of other matters, to say nothing of maintaining his precious political standing and contacts at court. Lady Elizabeth Kytson's 1596 account book shows her purchases, amongst other things, of grain and livestock.[162] The letters of Jane Smyth, wife of lawyer Matthew Smyth, absent in London going about his legal business, show her keeping him up to date in a highly informed way of the work in progress on their estate at Ashton Court near Bristol, of the purchase of cattle at fairs in Wales for fattening on the home farm, as well as the negotiations for extending their land holdings. Her husband died in 1583, leaving her with her eldest son, Hugh, aged only 8, whereupon she continued to manage the estate and to further increase it until her death in 1594. Her daughter-in-law, Elizabeth, similarly acted in the 1620s.[163] Both Joan, wife of John Thynne, and her sister-in-law Maria, wife of Thomas Thynne, were actively engaged in the estate affairs of their husbands in the late sixteenth and early seventeenth centuries. The young Benedicta Hoskyns, wife of lawyer John Hoskyns, was involved in a similar way back in Herefordshire during the 1610s whilst her husband was practising in the Middle Temple.[164] At much the same time Sir John Coke wrote to his wife Marie, 'If corn bear so good a price I hope you send good store to make and thresh out apace to deceive the rats, for the killing whereof take what course you think fit.' Henry Oxinden wrote in similar vein to his wife Katherine in 1655:

> Pray let the best care be taken that the conies [rabbits] do not bark the trees in the cony place or orchard, and if need be that they be fothered with hay; but I say the less of things because I leave all to thy care as if I were not in being at all.

Throughout their married life his letters constantly say 'I leave all my businesses at home to your menagerie' and 'but I leave this to your discretion knowing thee to be careful and knowing how to advise'. Dame Margaret Verney, wife of Sir Edmund Verney (the Standard Bearer to Charles I), had oversight of the family estate whilst her husband was at court, as did her daughter-in-law, Mary, whilst her husband Ralph was in exile in France during the Civil War. Mary had, in fact, received most of her education as a child bride in the 1630s in the household of Dame Margaret.[165]

Nor were the wives of the highest in the land exempt from such duties. Sir Robert Sidney, writing to his wife, Barbara, in 1594, acknowledged 'I need not send to know how my buildings go forward, for I am sure you are so good a housewife you may be trusted with them.' Margaret Clifford managed the family estates during the many absences at sea of her husband, George, third Earl of Cumberland. In a letter of 20 February 1621 to Lady Jane Cornwallis, Lucy Russell, Countess of Bedford indicated that 'I intend to turn Combe [Combe Abbey, in Warwickshire] wholly into money, both to make myself a free woman from debt and with the rest of it to raise as good an estate for life as I can, having now no one but myself to provide for'. Margaret Cavendish reported that her widowed mother was 'Very skilful in leases and setting of lands and court-keeping, ordering stewards and other like affairs.'[166] Dorothy Sidney, wife of Robert, second Earl of Leicester, was plainly *au fait* with estate business whilst her husband was away on embassy in France in the late 1630s, and was in constant correspondence not only with her husband but also with the family lawyer, William Hawkins. Mary Rich, Countess of Warwick was intimately involved in the ordering of her estate in Essex, as was Lady Brilliana Harley at Brampton Bryan in Herefordshire. Lady Judith Barrington, who married Sir Thomas Barrington in 1624, not only attended to the family estates at Hatfield Broad Oak in Essex during her husband's absences in parliament in the 1630s, but also managed to pay off the debts of her first husband, Sir John Hobart, and similarly undertook the management of h:~ ~states, including the auditing of his accounts, in an effort to reduce the his many debts.[167] Nor were some husbands slow to acknowl wives' contributions. Sir Roger Twysden called his wife 'the s estate'. Thomas Knyvett wrote to his wife Katherine in 1642, 'I know I cannot have a better steward than thyself to manage our affairs'. William Blundell, the recusant Royalist, said that his wife, Anne, had been 'the ark who hath saved out little cockboat at Crosby from many a storm'.[168]

Such participatory activity on the part of wives was not of course confined to the landed and business classes. In an age when the clergy of rural parishes often engaged in agriculture, farming the demesne lands themselves, their wives also took their share of the duties involved. Elizabeth Walker, wife of the Reverend Anthony Walker, rector of Fyfield in Essex, supervised the farm labourers and household servants, and shared the work of the dairy and brewhouse – as well as bearing and educating her ten children. Anne, wife of Robert Bolton, rector of Broughton in Northamptonshire, 'to whose care he committed the ordering of his outward estate, he only minding the studies and weighty affairs of his heavenly calling', which included, alongside his pastoral duties, the writing of numerous godly books, was similarly involved.[169] Not surprisingly, much of the evidence of women taking on such responsibilities refers to the occasions when husbands were away from home or abroad on business, diplomacy or in exile, or on their death. Yet a wife's skills and expertise in these matters were obviously not new-born on the husband's departure. They could only have been built up over the years by active participation during his presence, and with his approval.[170]

But of all the status-accorded roles for women, those of housewife and mother were pre-eminent. Subject to the over-riding authority of a husband – in theory at least, for practice would be determined by the characters of the partners concerned – the status of a woman as mistress of her own domain was not in doubt. That in the marital home there should be a division of labour was never questioned, justified as it was by Aristotelian dictum, biblical proof-text and commentaries thereon. What was debated, however, was whether the traditional role assigned to wives carried with it a status appropriate to the responsibilities undertaken. The writers who used the metaphor of 'the cock flyeth to and fro to bring all things to the nest . . . [and] . . . the dam keepeth the nest, hatcheth and bringeth forth her young'[171] did so with a wealth of customary authority for such a division of labour, which nevertheless also used the 'weaker vessel' metaphor. Conversely, an inept 'huswyf' was regarded as a contradiction in terms, a case of title without entitlement since 'prudence', that pre-eminently female virtue in the domestic sphere, required a careful weighing of balances, a calculation of consequence, an acceptance of deferred gratification.

It was, of course, taken for granted that women of 'the lower orders' had no option but to engage in housewifely duties, but the diary of Lady Margaret Hoby, of Hackness in Yorkshire, written during the years 1599 to

1605, gives the most detailed account of a woman of some substance similarly engaged. The diary is full of entries recording that she was 'busy in the kitchen . . . busy about the reckonings . . . busy preserving . . . busy in my garden all the day almost . . . all the day setting corn' and so on.[172] Elsewhere we have to rely on reportage at second hand, such as that of Sir John Oglander who was full of praise for the contribution his wife had made to their overcoming a period of acute shortage of money:

> But with God's blessing and our care we rubbed it out and lived most contentedly. I could never have done it without a most careful striving wife . . . [who] . . . was up every day before me and oversaw all the outhouses; she would not trust her maids with directions, but would wet her shoes to see it done herself.[173]

Sir Hugh Cholmley reported in similar vein about his wife Elizabeth, as she went round her whole domain 'from hop-garth to hen-yard, from linen closet to larder'. Richard Baxter praised his wife Margaret for her excellence in matters 'prudential and practical' on which he 'never knew the equal'.[174] Doubtless not all wives were able or willing to match these standards of housewifely virtue, as John Smyth, steward to the Berkeley family, reported of the Lady Anne and her daughter-in-law Katherine:

> country housewifery seemed to be an essential part of this lady's constitution . . . [she] would betimes in winter and summer mornings make her walks to visit her stables, barns, dairy house, poultry, swine-troughs and the like, which housewifery her daughter-in-law the Lady Katherine Howard, wife to the Lord Henry her son, seeming to decline and betake herself to the delights of youth and greatness; she would sometimes to those about her swear 'By God's blessed sacrament, this girl will beggar my son Henry'.[175]

Plainly the old adage 'When Adam delved and Eve span' was too simple a notion to fit the blurring of class and gender boundaries. Plenty of evidence points to a modification in practice of the principle so frequently quoted from the Pauline texts. Equally plainly this was not simply a pragmatic arrangement to meet exceptional circumstance, but a more reflective enactment of that principle of mutuality for which other biblical texts provided a justification, and which was ultimately based on a theological exegesis of the notion of 'vocation' in its multiple meanings. A deep residual attachment to gender relations based on patriarchal power was not as all-dominant and all-pervasive as we might believe. The traditionally assigned roles for men and women and the gendered distinction between public and private were practised only in the broadest of senses, with many women willing and able to undertake responsibilities outside the home as well as within at the request and approval of their husbands.

We have seen something of the debate about the nature of women's spirituality, a debate which generally resulted in a high degree of agreement in their favour. Yet women still found it necessary to assert their ecclesiastical status when faced with the practice of the established church, in which there was a uniformly efficient veto on their holding clerical office and on their preaching from the pulpit of the parish church. On the other hand, their ability to disrupt the service with fervent comments is amply recorded in the records of the ecclesiastical courts. Similar, less formal means of expressing their religious conviction when this did not coincide with established doctrine and practice were seized upon by many women, urged on, as they were, by reminders of the example of active women in biblical times – Priscilla and Aquila arguing with Apollos in their home after hearing him in the synagogue (Acts 18.26); the apostles' wives sharing in their husbands' witness in the upper room (Acts 1.14); Phoebe bearing St Paul's letter to the Romans (Romans 16.1); the women remaining at the Cross and later witnessing the resurrection. These and more were frequently cited by authors, male and female, seeking a more active role for women in the established church and outside it.

The prime status claim, frequently made by women denied a preaching role in the church, was the claim that there was no authority in scripture which denied women the right to bear witness in public by preaching the Word of God. If Anglican orthodoxy was likely to cite 1 Corinthians 14.34–5, 'Let your women keep silence in the church, for it is not permitted unto them to speak', or 1 Timothy 2.11–12, 'But suffer not a woman to teach, nor to usurp authority over man, but to be in silence', opponents would seek justification by reference to Joel 2.28, Galatians 3.28 or Acts 2.17–18. Such claims were made not only by women such as Margaret Fell, Elizabeth Hooton and a host of other Quaker women, as well as the likes of Mary Cary, Eleanor Davies, Anna Trapnel and others, but also by male supporters such as George Keith, George Fox and Richard Farnworth.[176]

But preaching did not exhaust the means whereby women sought to assert their equality of status in matters of religion. When *c.*1555 a Willingham man walked to Colchester in search of spiritual enlightenment, he stopped at an inn where he found two men and two 'women gospellers' discussing the divinity of Christ. John Bunyan later recalled that it was the sound of three or four women sitting at a door in the sun in Bedford and talking about the things of God which set him on the path to piety.[177] Many other women were from the early days of the Reformation active in support of their husbands in familial conventicles. In 1521 for example, Alice, wife of Richard Colyngs of Ginge near Burford in Oxfordshire, was reported as being

> a famous woman among them, and had a good memory and could recite much of the scriptures and other good books; and therefore when any conventicle of these men did meet in Burford, commonly she was sent for to recite unto them the declarations of the Ten Commandments and the Epistles of Peter and James.

John Foxe recorded many like her.[178] In the seventeenth century some few women took it upon themselves to act as prime movers in the setting up of separatist churches. Katherine Chidley for example, was instrumental in the setting up of such a church in Bury St Edmunds, and, more famously perhaps because more fully recorded, Dorothy Hazzard, wife of the incumbent of St Ewins in Bristol, set up a church in Broadmeads in the city in 1640, which she continued to influence until her death in 1675. Where church lists exist, most of them show a preponderance of female membership. A 1645 Norwich congregation showed a membership of thirty-one men and eighty-three women. Of the twelve founder members of the Baptist church in Bedford in 1650, later to be joined by John Bunyan, eight were women. In 1671, three-quarters of the membership of the Broadmead church were women.[179]

The consistory court records are full of individual women being presented for asserting their claim to be independent-thinking members of God's church.[180] In 1557, four women of Essex, for example, were hauled before Bishop Bonner in London for refusing to express their belief in the doctrine 'that there are in the catholic church seven sacraments, instituted by God, and by the consent of the holy church allowed, approved, received, kept and retained'.[181] In the diocese of Norwich in 1570, a woman expressed her disagreement by asking why she should 'go gupping up to the priest for a piece of bread and a sup of wine' when both of these were available to her in her mistress's house.[182]

Though these were, of course, matters of high theology which would usually not arise more than once a year in most parishes, the doctrine was frequently challenged. Attendance at church was quite another matter, and women regularly appeared alongside men in the lists of those presented for non-attendance. Nor was such behaviour simply a matter of local concern for individual parsons. In 1580, for example, Walsingham himself wrote to John Watson, Bishop of Winchester, noting that notwithstanding the latter's success in persuading parishioners in his diocese to come to church, many of their wives 'do not only continue obstate by refusing . . . but also do use in their ordinary meetings among themselves unrevered speeches of the religion now established, defacing the same as much as in them lieth'.[183] For those who did attend the parish church, the customary refusal of the church to allow them to sit alongside their husbands and fathers offered some women yet another opportunity to indicate their disapproval of the traditional allocation of pews to men and women separately. Very occasionally we come across evidence of husbands supporting their wives in the matter. In 1620, for example, Mr Loveday was presented by the churchwardens of his parish church of St Alphege, Cripplegate, within London, for sitting in the same pew as his wife. The problem was not of course a new one. Sir Thomas More had earlier expressed his fear of the difficulties that would arise if such practices were persisted in.[184] Moreover, successive bishops' visitation articles and churchwardens' presentments are witness to continuing claims and practices by women in disagreement with the church's position on the status of women to be 'churched' as an act of 'cleansing' after childbirth.

Though some women could rely on the support of their husbands, others were not so fortunate in their familial relations, and found it necessary to resist their husbands' attempts to make them conform to his preferred religious affiliations. In such cases, women were plainly refusing to accept the customary injunctions of those who insisted on a wife's Christian duty to obey her husband in all matters. Anne Askew, Elizabeth Bowes, Anne Locke and Anne Wentworth are only the more famous of those who left their husbands rather than succumb to a hated form of religion. Others acted in different ways. When the wife of Roger Wigston, for example, was hauled before the Court of Star Chamber for allowing the Marprelate printers to use the marital home at Wolston in Warwickshire, she was fined £1000 and sent to prison. Her husband, on the other hand, claiming that his wife was the prime instigator, was fined only 500 marks (£333 6s 8d) and escaped imprisonment.[185] Despite her husband's opposition Elizabeth Cary, Viscountess Falkland, persisted in her adherence to the Roman Catholic faith and persuaded six of her children to embrace her beliefs. Margaret Clitherow similarly defied her husband in pursuing her faith, and ultimately suffered death by pressing at the hands of the authorities. Less dramatically, Alathea, wife of Sir John Holland, was refused permission by him to catechise her children in her own faith, though her persistence resulted in her daughter, Catherine, becoming a nun. These were but a few of the women whose influence was well recognised by Richard Hooker when he drew attention to them as 'diligent in drawing their husbands, children, servants, friends and allies the same away . . . [being] . . . bountiful towards their preachers who suffer want, apter to procure encouragements for their brethren'.[186] Nor should it be concluded that such influence and affirmation were the monopoly of recusant or radical women, either in their actions or in their writings. The relatively high profile of such women tends too easily to obscure more sober women, Protestant and Catholic alike. Mildred Cecil, wife of Queen Elizabeth's chief minister, apparently wrote nothing that was printed and was certainly never presented before a church court, yet she was described by the Spanish ambassador in one of his dispatches with the words 'She hath great influence with her husband . . . [and] . . . appears a much more furious heretic than him.'[187]

Needless to say, there was no shortage of writers (usually male) willing to condemn women who made claims on their own or others' behalf for that 'insolency' which James I, as part of his campaign against 'mechanick' preachers, called on his bishops to stamp out. Thomas Hobbes was echoing a common complaint when he asserted that 'every boy and wench that could read English thought they spoke with God Almighty and understood what he said'. In his *County Contentments or The English Housewife* (1615), Gervase Markham was perfectly willing for a wife to act 'as an example, an incitement and spur to all her family', but not if this led to their 'usurping to themselves a power of preaching and interpreting the Holy Word, to which they ought to be but hearers and believers, or at the most but modest persuaders'.[188] John Taylor concluded his tract *Lucifer's Lackey* (1640) with the couplet, 'When women preach and cobblers pray / The friends in hell make holiday.' John Vicars was more adamant in tone, considering it was intolerable 'to see bold impudent housewives without all womanly modesty to take upon themselves . . . to prate . . . after a discoursing and narrative manner, an hour or more, and that most directly contrary to the apostle's inhibition'.[189] If such critics were not outraged or fearful, they were often simply derisive or dismissive. When Elizabeth Young, for example, a mother of three and aged 'forty years and upwards', was arraigned before Bishop Bonner and his officials for distributing Lutheran books in 1558, one of her accusers exclaimed:

> Thou hast read a little in the Bible or Testament and thou thinkest that thou art able to reason with a doctor that hath gone to school thirty years. Why, thou art a woman of fair years; what shouldst thou meddle with the scriptures? It is necessary for you to believe and that is enough. It is more fit for you to meddle with thy distaff than to meddle with the scriptures.

Her responses showed that she was well able to defend herself and her views.[190] When Anne Stubbe argued with her brother-in-law, the puritan cleric Thomas Cartwright, about the advisability of separating from the Elizabethan church, he responded to her arguments with the dismissive 'remember your frailty as a woman'. Queen Elizabeth herself found such independence of thought as outrageous as the officers of her predecessors, complaining that 'some maids have not sticked to control learned preachers and say "such a man taught otherwise in house"'. At the end of our period, John Locke concluded 'reason must be our last judge and guide . . . [but] . . . the greatest part cannot know and therefore must believe' – what they were told, presumably.[191]

Whether these examples of independent thought and action on the part of women rendered the ideology of spiritual autonomy 'a powerful solvent of the established order and unity'[192] is highly doubtful, certainly in anything other than the short term, but their very existence should remind us that some women at least were unwilling to be passive accepters of the status assigned to them by traditional Pauline doctrine and contemporary church custom. Whilst the majority of godly women were likely to wear their piety discreetly, even submissively, others saw an egalitarian stance as the essential consequence of their claimed spiritual equality with men, including the right, even duty, to interpret the Word of God as they, and not their menfolk, understood it. George Abbot, speaking to the Court of High Commission, was voicing a view with which most Anglican – and some puritan – clergy would have concurred when he insisted that 'when you have reading, preaching, singing, teaching, you are your own ministers; the blind lead the blind'. Many women would have accepted the first but denied the second of these assertions, claiming that such activities would, on the contrary, lead to *clarity* of vision, a clarity they were manifestly capable of achieving. At the end of the period, Amey Hayward was not alone when she prefaced her *Female Legacy* (1699) with 'A Word of Advice to the Female Sex':

> Come female sex, and labour more apace
> And do not spend away your day of grace;
> Our souls let's value at a higher rate
> And look about us ere it is too late.[193]

Earlier, whether in published text or private letter, women were more likely to defer – or appear to defer, since the substance of what some of them wrote suggests a degree of dissembling which recognised the politics of gender whilst attempting to maintain their own integrity. Catherine Parr, for example, defending herself and her ladies before the king, her husband, against the plotting of Wriothesley and Gardiner, laced her remarks with 'I a poor silly woman . . . womanly weaknesses . . . natural imperfection' and an acknowledgement of Henry's 'natural superiority' – at the same time confounding her critics. Anne Locke in her *Markes of the Children of God* (1590), a translation from the 1586 original French of Jean Taffin, was careful to acknowledge

Because great things by reason of my sex I may not do, and that which I may, I ought to do, I have according to my duty, brought my poor basket of stones to the strengthening of the walls of Jerusalem, whereof (by grace) we are all both citizens and members.[194]

In 1592 Catherine, Countess of Northumberland wrote a letter to her husband, Henry the eighth Earl, full of national and family financial affairs, but concluded with

For mine own part being but a woman, I can no more but pray for your good success and speed, seeing the matter is too weighty for me to give advice upon and too chargeable to intermeddle withal, being not able to travail therein myself.

When she translated *The Mirrour of Knighthood* in 1578, Margaret Tyler felt it politic to defend her translating a book of chivalry since it was regarded as 'a matter more man-like than becometh my sex'. Anne Finch, Countess of Winchelsea, was rather more forthcoming in her poem:

Alas! A woman that attempts the pen,
Such an intruder on the thoughts of men,
Such a presumptuous creature is esteemed,
The fault can by no virtue be redeemed.[195]

Mary Throckmorton must have had an unusually good rapport with her father, Thomas Throckmorton, when she wrote to him in 1607 about a dispute with a neighbour: 'I have answered his letter as a woman, very submissively, if that will serve, for I perceive they cannot endure to be told of their faults.' On the other hand, having played a very active part in the founding of Wadham College, Oxford, Dorothy Wadham nevertheless wrote to the Fellows in 1616, 'My experience in such matters is small.'[196] Despite an apparent willingness to acknowledge her status as a woman, especially in matters of religious doctrine, Lady Jane Englefield of the Catholic family of Montague, was nevertheless perfectly willing and able, in a 1617 exchange of letters with her cousin Sir Henry Slingsby the elder, to stand her ground:

And for my part being a woman it little beseemeth me to meddle with controversies of so high a nature, which makes me wonder much that so wise a man as your self would present unto me such a kind of letter – ('how to reduce me into unity of belief with yourself') – whereunto lest you might tax me with pride or incivility I have in some sort like a woman made answer to show that I am not altogether so ignorant in points of religion as you esteemed me to be.

Henry Oxinden was not merely playing the gallant when, replying to a letter from Unton, Lady Dering in 1647, he wrote:

> I conceive that expression of yours, viz that as a woman you are altogether unable and unfit to undergo the care of the estate left to your sister's children, is only inserted but of the modesty of your nature, for, pardon me, if I can possibly understand it otherwise. For believe me, as a woman, I say as a woman, you are able not only to manage a private estate, but also to govern a kingdom if called thereunto.

Elizabeth Cary, Viscountess Falkland, was even more unyielding when in her translation *The Reply of the Most Illustrious Cardinall Perron to the Answeare of the Most Excellent King of Greate Britaine, the First Tome* (1630) she wrote:

> I will not make use of that worn-out form of saying, I printed it against my will, moved by the importunity of friends; I was moved to it by my belief that it might make those English that understand not the French, whereof there are many, even in our universities, read Perron.[197]

There were in addition women who, by nature or circumstance, felt it necessary to ignore the customary passive role assigned to them. The period of the Civil War threw up many examples on both sides of the political spectrum of women who, alongside or in the absence of their husband or even alongside their parents, showed a bravery in the face of the enemy which in some of the earlier prescriptive literature would have been described and criticised as unwomanly and 'Amazonian'.[198] Lady Brilliana Harley for example, offered defiance to the royalist governor of Hereford, Sir William Vavasour, when he besieged her home at Brampton Bryan in 1643. The siege was raised on 9 September, but Lady Brilliana died on the 31 October following, soon after the siege was raised.[199] Despite being in an advanced stage of pregnancy, Lady Anne Savile, wife of Sir William Savile, was a stout defender of Sheffield Castle in 1644. Her husband died during the siege and her child was born on the day after she was forced to surrender.[200] Nor was such behaviour confined to upper-class women. The daughter of the royalist divine Matthew Griffith was caught up in the siege of Basing House in Hampshire. Her taunts of the Roundhead soldiers so provoked them that they shot and killed her. Mrs Yaxley, wife of the parish priest of Kibworth in Leicestershire, was faced with the prospect of being dispossessed of her home by royalist soldiers. Her husband was willing to go peaceably but she resisted, throwing stones after the oppressors and threatening to burn down the house, whereupon the soldiers fired on her, blinding her and disfiguring her face.[201]

Less dramatic, but equally indicative of women's readiness to act on their husbands' behalf are the cases of wives intervening when their husbands had been imprisoned for one reason or another. Margaret Douglas, Countess of Lennox, for example, engaged in a long-drawn-out correspondence with William Cecil, on behalf of her husband imprisoned in the Tower in 1562. Even when the Earl was released and restored to favour, Lady Margaret continued to pester Cecil over the financial straits of her family. Lucy Hutchinson even went to the length of forging her husband's signature in an effort to obtain his release, and Anne Fanshawe, also faced with her husband's imprisonment, stood in the rain outside his prison until 'the water ran in at the neck and out again at her heels'.[202] On other occasions, wives had to fight challenges to the terms of their husbands' wills. After the death of her second husband, Sir William Wentworth, Elizabeth, Lady Scrope, had to defend her marriage settlement which was disputed by her son Richard. Lady Elizabeth Russell was another who wrote to Cecil, her brother-in-law, this time on behalf of her daughters Elizabeth and Anne, whose inheritance was being put in jeopardy by Lady Warwick. Later she joined Lord Hunsdon and 29 other inhabitants of Blackfriars in a petition to the Privy Council against 'one Burbage who hath lately bought room near Lord Hunsdon's and is converting it into a common playhouse which will be a great annoyance to the neighbourhood'.[203] More famous, perhaps, was the long struggle that Lady Margaret Clifford and her daughter Anne persisted in over the will of Margaret's husband which her uncle attempted to subvert. Lady Mary Fitzhoward was merely one of many who, after the death of her husband in 1626, sought the assistance of the Court of Chancery in the matter of her jointure against Thomas Howard, Earl of Suffolk and his son Theophilus.[204]

A claim to independent status by women was also apparent when 'diverse women of the cities of London and Westminster' petitioned parliament in May 1649, arguing that

> since we are assured of our creation in the image of God and our interest in Christ equal unto me, as also of a proportionable share in the freedom of the Commonwealth, we cannot but wonder and grieve that we should appear so despicable in your eyes as to be thought unworthy to petition and represent our grievances to this Honourable House.

John Pym obviously considered such a woman to be 'unworthy' in this sense when, in response to a petition for peace delivered by Mrs Ann Stagg in 1642, he wrote 'we intreat you to repair to your houses and turn your petition to prayer at home for us'. Whether Mrs Stagg and her companions did as they were bid we know not, but certainly Elizabeth Lilburne continued to print and organise petitions after the imprisonment of her husband John in 1641.[205] Even braver and more dramatic exemplars of women who refused to accept their prescribed role in society were those who in the time of Mary Tudor were willing to suffer the extreme sacrifice of burning at the stake in order to safeguard their religious convictions. Less dramatic but equally indicative were those such as Elizabeth Humphries who during the Civil War was fined 40 nobles for uttering 'The devil take the Parliament', and Alice Jackson who was imprisoned for her remark that when she saw two sheep's heads on a pole she wished they were the king's and Prince Rupert's.[206] In these many ways, and to a greater or lesser degree, then, we see women playing a role and claiming a status which was far removed from those which most male writers of the period were willing to accord them.

Women thus claimed a status and acted out roles both in public and in private, which did not conform to the over-simple formula of domination–submission which a selective reading of the Bible and the plethora of misogynist literature would have indicated. The insistent volume of calls for wives to obey their husbands and daughters to obey their fathers and to acknowledge them as their superiors suggests that some women behaved as they wished, refusing to fit into the feminine mould designed for them by men. Equally, there were those who accepted their designated role and status, whether through ignorance or fearful resignation, or as a matter of their perceived Christian duty. Others, too, paid lip-service to social convention, a pattern of dissembling recognised even by their menfolk. Whether women were as 'chaste, silent and obedient' as many texts and sermons prescribed turns therefore on which women and what circumstances are being considered, and *a fortiori* when the religious education of those women in those circumstances is being considered. Even then the appeal was almost always to a man's sense of duty, only rarely to a woman's sense of injustice. It was not until the nineteenth century that a kind of political arithmetic – Dicey's notion of women being 'half the nation' – and discussion was brought into the arena of equality between the sexes.

2   The media

Any discussion of the education of girls and women in the early modern period must recognise the centrality of their religious education, an aspect which in its aim – 'that the child by carnal generation may become the child of God by spiritual regeneration' as Richard Greenham put it, or in Milton's words 'the end then of learning is to repair the ruins of our first parents by regaining to know God aright, and out of that knowledge to love Him, to imitate Him, and to be like Him'[1] – embraced all social classes, seeking to remind them of their Christian calling through a variety of means which 'caught' high and low, rich and poor, literate and illiterate alike. The enjoinders to 'Wait on God' and to 'Rest in the Lord; wait patiently for Him' were rarely intended to imply a total passivity in a Christian's life. On the contrary, salvation had to be actively prepared for and sought, as much by self-education as by education at the hands of others, even though the sinner was in the end dependent on God's grace.[2] In a variety of ways, the flock – male and female – had not only to be instructed in doctrine and its behavioural expression in everyday life, but also to prepare itself for such a life (and death). Moreover, what was claimed to be a woman's 'natural' propensity for piety was almost a commonplace in the period.[3] Christopher Hatton's 1563 comment about Lady Mary Egerton of Ridley in Cheshire, that her unwillingness to 'confirm herself to Her Majesty's proceedings' was to be explained by reference to a 'certain preciseness of conscience incident to divers of her sex, without reason or measure oftentimes',[4] was later echoed by Thomas Pomfret, the memorialist of Lady Christina Cavendish, Duchess of Devonshire, when he reported that

> prayers and pious readings were her first business, virtues almost natural to her sex, the devout sex the Fathers called it, as if the very inclinations of women were to religion ... The softest natures [he

continued] are usually the most pliant, and the softest natures usually are women, and devotion takes first and surest roots in their tender breasts.[5]

William Alexander, Earl of Stirling, put the thought into verse in his *Recreations with Muses* (1637) with his aphorism 'The weaker sex, to piety more prone.'[6] Richard Hooker complained of the 'eagerness' of women which made them 'diligent in drawing their husbands, children, servants, friends and allies the same way . . . [noting] how all near about them stand affected as concerning the same cause'.[7]

The ritual of divine service, though for some an empty formality, was for others a meeting place for both public and private devotion, in which and through which its members would be enabled to praise God, to seek His love and forgiveness through prayer, and to hear His Word, initially through the Lessons, and then through its exposition and clarification in the sermon. The Protestant Reformation, it has been said, was 'the religion of the Word', with the Bible as the main curricular component of the religious education of its adherents. But the primary principle of the self-authenticating authority of the Bible, whether in theological debate or in the ordering of everyday life, was far from being unambiguous, either to the clergy or to the laity, and more rather than less so to the 'godly' with whom we will of necessity be primarily concerned. Behind the certainty of the Sixth of the 39 Articles – 'Holy scripture containeth all things necessary to salvation', echoing Cranmer's Preface to the Great Bible of 1540 – lay the possibilities of doubt and heterodoxy arising from the need to expound it in church and to study it at home. It was one thing to assert – and it was repeatedly asserted – that Holy Writ had a single unified meaning that could be read and understood by all, that 'There is but one true, proper and genuine sense of scripture arising from the words rightly understood which we call the literal.'[8] Such assertions not only got over the pedagogical difficulty of intelligibility but they also conveniently denied the Church's traditional insistence that the Bible often implied more than it literally stated, that it could be understood, therefore, only through the identification of several (traditionally four) levels of meaning,[9] which required careful exegesis by the clergy, who themselves needed the support of the hermeneutical tradition of biblical scholarship (however cleansed by the philological and historical skills of the Erasmians). But the theologians' failure to agree about such crucial biblical concepts as revelation, redemption, salvation, the meaning of the words 'The body and blood of Christ',[10] and not least the Christian conception of God Himself, with its fluctuating characterisations – who is 'Our Father'?; what is He like, this personal, loving, merciful, understanding being, who was at the same time impersonal, omniscient, omnipotent and occasionally terrible and full of wrath? – presented enormous difficulties to clergy and laity alike. Henry VIII himself was fully aware of the problem when, addressing his parliament in 1545, he complained 'Alas, how can the poor souls live in concord when you preachers sow amongst them in your sermons division and debate?'[11] Leonard Wright, writing in 1591, reckoned that not much had changed in his own time:

> when the church is grown like a jarring instrument out of tune . . . and the honourable profession of divinity is much like the tailor's craft . . . the one through daily inventing of new fashions is ever in learning . . . and the other by continual devising strange articles is never learned . . . as though religion consisted only in speculation, without action, learning without doing or knowledge without execution, to the great discouraging and amazing of many a simple soul . . . for whose comfort I have penned this little volume.[12]

No one was surprised that in such a situation many of the laity felt free to place their own interpretation on the Word of God. In this, as in all matters relating to the education of a hitherto uneducated group, the state and the church faced a real dilemma. In achieving freedom – freedom from the Pope, as from a necessarily mediating priest – Protestants in authority had to maintain their newly won position against new forms of heterodoxy.[13] Prescription and conformity – 'for the right understanding of God's true religion now truly set forth by public authority' as one of Elizabeth's proclamations put it[14] – thus became necessary to maintain the flock in the new orthodoxy and especially to induct the younger generation. Milton's 'licence they mean when they cry liberty' had been clearly recognised a century earlier, as for example by Nicholas Ridley: 'for the Christian, liberty is not licence to do what thou list'.[15]

The claim that all should have access to scripture inevitably implied the provision of a vernacular Bible for the benefit of those for whom the existing Latin Bible was a closed book. As the versions of Tyndale and Coverdale became available, reports came in that, for example, 'divers poor men of Chelmsford . . . bought the New Testament of Jesus Christ and on Sundays did sit reading in the lower end of the church, and many would flock about to hear their reading'.[16] Moreover, with Cromwell's Injunctions of 1538, it became state policy that such a Bible should be authorised and made available:

> Ye shall provide one book of the whole Bible in English and set up the same in some convenient place within the said church that you have

> care of, where your parishioners may most commodiously resort unto
> the same and read it . . .

though subsequent proclamations made it clear that the text was to be read
'humbly, meekly, reverently and obediently . . . without murmurs or grudg-
ings' so that the flock might 'learn thereby to observe God's commandments and to obey their sovereign lord and high powers'.[17] Even so, such
was the formal authority of the clergy that the folio Bible on the lectern –
whether the Great Bible of 1539, or the Bishops' Bible of 1569 or eventually the Authorised Version of 1611 – became their preserve, though as
early as 1541 Becon was asking

> but how many read it? Verily a man may come into some churches and
> see the Bible so enclosed and wrapped around with dust . . . that with
> his finger he may write upon the Bible this epitaph: *ecce nunc in pulvere
> dormio*, that is to say 'behold I sleep now in the dust'.[18]

However, if the purpose was to acquaint the flock with the contents of the
Bible, this would be to ignore the fact that each Sunday the form of service
in the Book of Common Prayer would include a reading from the Psalms
and of the Lessons, passages from the Bible which were planned to cover
the complete text in the course of the year, the Old Testament 'and so once
every year', and the New Testament 'and so twice every year'. In addition,
the choosing of a biblical text and its expounding was a function of the
sermon, to be preached by a cleric licensed by the bishop. In the absence of
such it was ordered that a set of printed sermons, the Homilies, should be
read to the congregation, thus overcoming not only the problem of a shortage of fully trained clergy but also of possibly heterodox interpretations of
particular passages of the Bible.[19]

In these ways, then, the flock, literate and illiterate, could be made
acquainted with God's Word. Reading the Bible for oneself, however, was
quite another matter. When the Act for the Advancement of True Religion
and the Abolishment of the Contrary was passed in 1543 it restricted the
private reading of the Bible to noblemen, gentleman and merchant householders, and expressly excluded artificers, apprentices, husbandmen and
women. Gardiner feared that the vernacular Bible would 'beguile the
people into refusal of obedience'.[20] Indeed, some would have insisted
that only the clergy should have the privilege.[21] Cranmer spotted another
problem when he criticised

> such persons as in time of divine service do read the Bible. They do
> much abuse the King's Grace's intent and meaning in his Grace's

injunctions and proclamations, which permitteth the Bible to be read not to allure great multitudes of people together, nor thereby to interrupt the time of prayers, meditations and thanks to be given to Almighty God, which especially in divine service is and of consequence ought to be used, but that the same be done and read in time convenient privately, for the condition and amendment of the lives of the readers and such hearers as cannot themselves read, and not in contempt or hindrance of any divine service or laudable ceremony used in church.[22]

Carrying the Bible into church to follow the readings, or more dangerously, to check on the preacher's exposition of the text of his sermon, continued to produce problems for those in authority who wished to maintain some form of control over the religious education which took place in church.[23] Moreover, the problem went wider than that, as the king well recognised, when, in 1545, he complained to parliament that he was 'very sorry to know and hear how unreverently that most precious jewel, the Word of God, is disputed, rhymed, sung and jangled in every ale-house and tavern, contrary to the true meaning and doctrine of the same'.[24]

All the (admittedly imperfect) data we have about levels of literacy indicate that, though among the upper and middle classes illiteracy was almost unheard of after the middle of the sixteenth century, for the rest, the vast majority, illiteracy rates were very high indeed, and even more so for women and girls.[25] Despite the invention of movable type and the spread of the printed book, pamphlet and broadsheet, early modern England remained for a large majority an essentially oral culture.

In the matter of religious education then, alongside the ritual of the Book of Common Prayer, the sermon remained one of the most important methods of spreading the Word 'for such hearers as cannot read'. 'Preach the Word, be urgent in season and out of season; convince, reprove, exhort with all long suffering and doctrine'.[26] Paul's words to Timothy were a commonplace of Protestant ideology, used by all shades of opinion about the role of the reformed clergy. Nor were the laity exempt from such exhortation. Latimer reminded his congregation of Paul's words to the Romans: 'We cannot be saved without faith and faith cometh from hearing the Word.'[27] The point was echoed with his usual imagery by John Donne: 'The ears are the acqueducts of the waters of life.'[28] Yet, as with every radical or revolutionary movement, once the aims of the Protestant reformers had been achieved, the maintenance of orthodoxy, uniformity and conformity became the over-riding concern. Though Grindal reminded Queen Elizabeth 'where preaching wanteth, obedience faileth',[29] it was quickly realised that sermons could easily become a vehicle for heterodoxy as for orthodoxy. It was not for nothing that Elizabeth insisted during the first year of her reign that all preaching should cease 'until consultation may be had by parliament, by Her Majesty and by her three estates of this realm', and that subsequently she continued the attempt to control the clergy by the issue of licences to preach and by republishing the Edwardian Homilies, with important additions, to be read by those not licensed.[30] No Homilies were more popular with the hierarchy than those 'On Obedience' and 'Against Disobedience and Wilful Rebellion', the latter being added after the 1569 Revolt of the Northern Earls. Glosses on the Fifth Commandment, which poured from the presses in increasing numbers, insisted that the injunction contained therein applied not simply to parents but to schoolmasters, clerics, magistrates and kings as well. The Queen's Stuart successors faced the same problem. James I complained of 'itching tongues', and insisted that the increasingly popular afternoon sermon be confined to catechising or to a gloss on the Lord's Prayer, the Creed or the Ten Commandments. Charles I was merely acknowledging what was usual when he remarked that 'people are governed by pulpits more than the sword in times of peace'.[31]

But, as we have seen, it was the possibility of heterodox interpretations of the scriptures which caused the sovereign and the bishops most cause for concern. The matter was further complicated by the fact that whatever form of control was used – statute, proclamation, injunction, licensing, Homilies, a Book of Common Prayer and an authorised translation of the Bible – the early modern state was relatively powerless to enforce attendance at church, to control what was said in the pulpit or indeed to ensure that the sermon was preached or the Homily read, a situation well recognised by Thomas Tymme who reported in his *A Silver Watchbell*:

> But now either through negligence or laziness we sit at home, or if we come to church it is either to hear news or eloquent phrases from the preacher, or to undermine or entrap him, or peradventure to fetch a nap or two, or to meet a friend.[32]

This echoed in part Latimer's earlier story of the gentlewoman who regularly attended 'St James of Acres', since (she averred) 'I never fail of a good nap there'. Even so, Latimer told his congregation 'I had rather ye should go a-napping to the sermons than not go at all.'[33] But it was the power of the reformist elements in the church, with their emphasis on the exposition of scripture in the pulpit, that led Laud and his bishops to play down the relative influence of the sermon, to emphasise the liturgy and the sacraments, and in 1633 to suppress the Feoffees for Lay Impropriations, which had been set up to endow and support lectureships, expressly charged to preach the Word.[34] Those who followed the preacher of their choice and who attended more than one sermon per week were constantly, though ineffectually, criticised by those on the conservative wing of the church, who saw such behaviour as a challenge to the status of both the clergy and heads of households. Control in matters religious required not only a set of orthodoxies – of doctrine and of practice – but also an institutional machinery for the monitoring of such practice and the inhibiting of heterodoxy, tasks which became increasingly difficult to maintain in the face of sincerely held and deeply felt beliefs, even among those who were willing to conform to the rituals of the established church.

OUT OF CHURCH

But for those who could not read, the sermon was not the only means whereby they could be provided with the necessary instruction. Conforming members of the established church and radicals alike enjoined their literate members to assist in the religious education of their less fortunate brethren. As early as 1530 Richard Whitford was urging the readers of his *Werke for Householders*:

> You that can read gather your neighbours about you on the holy day, especially the young, and read them this poor lesson. For therein be such things as they be bound to know or can say: that is the Pater Noster, the Ave Maria, the Credo, with such other things as do follow.[35]

Whitgift reported in his time 'of the many examples in England of those which being not able to read themselves, by means of their children reading to them at home, receive instruction and edifying'.[36] Richard Rogers, puritan lecturer and schoolmaster at Wetherfield in Essex, asked the rhetorical question 'Who shall read?' and offered a remedy for those who could not: 'Let them use the more diligence in praying, hearing the Word preached and godly books read by others.'[37] Nicholas Bownde went further: 'Therefore so many as can read let them do it on the Lord's Day, and they that cannot, let them see the want of it be so great in themselves that they bring up their children to it.'[38]

Urgings such as these did not go wholly unobserved. John Foxe, for example, reported the case of one Agnes Priest, a Marian martyr of Exeter, who

> albeit she was of such simplicity and without learning, yet you could declare no place of scripture but she could tell you the chapter, yea she would recite you the names of all the books of the Bible.

When questioned by the bishop she acknowledged that her knowledge of the scriptures had been acquired partly from 'godly books that I have heard read'.[39] A century later the memorialist of John Bruen of Stapleford in Cheshire reported that though Robert Passfield, one of Bruen's servants, was

> a man utterly unlearned, being unable to read a sentence or write a syllable, yet he was so well taught of God that, by his own conducting and God's blessing upon his mind and memory, he grew in grace as he did in years, and ripe in understanding and mighty in the scriptures, so much that he became a very profitable index to the family to call to mind what they had learned, and recover what they had lost by slip of memory; and not only so, but a godly instructor and teacher of young professors, to acquaint them with the Word and to exercise their hearts unto godliness.

As an aid to his memory, and obviously ignorant of the current methods, he made for himself a girdle of leather, 'this instrument of his own invention he framed and used (as others do their pen and writing) for the better help of his understanding'. At the end of the period, *The Whole Duty of Man* continued to recommend 'if they cannot read they should be taught without book some form of prayer'.[40]

Notwithstanding the reservations and attempts to control the reading of the Bible and other godly books by the laity, the printing presses continued to produce a variety of aids which aimed at providing a comprehensive means of religious education to supplement that provided in church. A folio Bible was, of course, far too expensive for purchase by most householders for familial use, and so a constant stream of Bibles (and parts of Bibles), printed in quarto, octavo, and the later even duodecimo, appeared in the bookshops and in the packs of the itinerant pedlars,[41] supplemented from 1560 to 1644 by the immensely popular Geneva Bible.[42] Churchwardens' Accounts which record the purchase of 'a Bible in great volume' show a remarkable variation in price, though rarely under 10s, depending on whether it was bound or not at the point of purchase.[43] Even then the cost of transporting it to the parish and the chains required to secure it had to be added. In 1578 an 'English Geneva Bible' was purchased for the church of St Mary's in Cambridge for 17s. In 1620 the churchwardens of Great Wigston in Leicestershire paid £2 for 'a new Bible', presumably the Authorised Version, prudently selling the 'old Bible' for 10s.[44] In the 1616 inventory of the goods of John Foster, stationer of York, his 'Bibles in folio of the larger sort' were valued at £2 8s, with 'five Bibles of sorts' showing valuations ranging from £1 8s to 6s 8d. No value was attached to his 8 quarto and 4 octavo Bibles, but the 'small bybell' left by the widow Jane Ward of Ipswich in 1606 was valued at 2s, and the 'littell Bible' which Brilliana Harley asked her husband to send to their undergraduate son, 'Ned', in 1629 probably cost much the same.[45] It was an 'English Bible of the smallest volume' that Princess Elizabeth had requested to be purchased for her when she was confined at Woodstock in 1554.[46]

After the Bible the most important 'godly' book was John Foxe's *Actes and Monumentes of These Latter and Perilous Days*, commonly called The Book of Martyrs. Originally published in Latin in Strasburg in 1554 and again in Basle in 1559, it appeared in English in 1563 in a folio volume not far short of 2,000 pages. Thereafter it was printed, much enlarged in two double-column folio volumes and later in a three-volume edition.[47] It achieved a degree of official status when Convocation required that it should be purchased for use in all cathedral churches, but parish churches too began to buy the set, as was the case in 1573 when the churchwardens of St Michael's, Cornhill, in London, bought a copy with a chain and lock, for £2 2s 6d, and in 1635 when the churchwardens of St Mary's church in Devizes, Gloucester, bought a set and had them set up with chains in the church. A three-volume set was bought for the parish church of Cheltenham with a gift of £5 provided by a London merchant who had once lived there. They were mounted on a revolving stand 'to the end that the same may be free in common for all to read at convenient times'. As late as 1693 'three Books of Martyrs', presumably a three-volume edition, were still being handed on to the new churchwardens of St James' church in Chipping Campden.[48]

Such editions, like the 'Great Bibles', were obviously too expensive for all but the most prosperous, but with others in mind Timothy Bright produced an abridged version in 1589, reducing the 1563 version to a smaller two-volume edition, the first volume of 508 octavo pages and the second of 288 pages, this latter covering the events of the sixteenth century. Later, a quarto edition of 792 pages was printed. Various other 'martyr books' were produced including Thomas Brice's *A Compendious Register in Meter Conteining the Names and Pacient Sufferyngs of the Membres of Jesus Christ* (1559), Myles Coverdale's *Certain Most Godly and Fruitful and Comfortable Letters of Such True Saintes and Holy Martyrs of God* (1564), John Taylor's *Book of Martyrs* (1639) and Clement Cotton's *The Mirror of Martyrs* (1613), which latter was dedicated to Lucy, Countess of Bedford and her mother Lady Anne Harrington, Cotton describing himself as 'sometime their ladyships' unworthy servant'. In his 'Preface to the Reader' he explained that he had written his 432-page duodecimo volume for those who either lacked the time to read or the money to purchase Foxe's two-volume original. His effort must have found a readership for it was reprinted in expanded form and appeared in a sixth edition in 1685. In 1693 Nathaniel Crouch, writing under his pseudonym,

Robert Burton, printed his duodecimo *Martyrs in Flames or the History of Popery*, in which alongside the martyrs of Henry VIII and Mary Tudor he memorialised Continental martyrs and celebrated England's safe deliverance from the Armada, the Gunpowder Plot, the Fire of London and the Popish Plot of 1678. Like Cotton he urged in his 'Preface to the Protestant Reader': 'Let this be a looking glass to my honest countrymen who have neither money nor time for perusing greater histories.'

But none was as popular or influential as Foxe's own compilation. It was recommended reading in Thomas Salter's *A Mirrhor Mete for all Mothers, Matrones and Maidens Intituled the Mirrhor of Modestie* (1579), by Philip Stubbes in his *Anatomie of Abuses* (1583), as well as in Thomas White's *Little Book for Little Children* (1674) and in Benjamin Keach's *Instructions for Children* (1693). Benjamin Harris produced his own version and included it in his *Protestant Tutor Instructing Children to Learn to Spell and Read English* (1679). Richard Baxter recommended it in his *Compassionate Counsel to All Young Men* (1681). Moreover, in its various versions Foxe's book was widely read. The two-volume edition was listed as being in the possession of Lady Mary Grey. The diary of Lady Margaret Hoby records its being read in her household, along with the works of Greenham, Cartwright and Perkins. It was read too by Lady Mary Rich, by Katherine Brettergh and by Elizabeth Wallington. It figured in the Sunday evening reading to the extended family of Nicholas Farrar at Little Gidding, and was obviously well known to Brilliana Harley, who in 1639 sent her son 'Ned' a translation of those parts of Calvin's *Life of Luther* 'that was not in the *Book of Martyrs*'. Elizabeth Walker later included it in the 'prudent choice of books of instruction and devotion' which she drew up for the benefit of her two daughters.[49] It is reported that Francis Drake took a copy to sea in 1577, and the work was included in the collection of books sent out to their factors by the East India Company. Simonds D'Ewes had a copy of the abridged version in his library. The yeoman Adam Eyre noted his reading of the book in 1647 and 1648, as did the merchant Roger Lowe in 1666. John Bunyan took a copy with him to jail and, attesting to its continuing popularity, John Wesley produced yet another abridged version in 1750.[50]

Foxe's book was plainly a work of Protestant propaganda, a celebration and exhortation as well as a record, and as such has been subjected to historiographical scrutiny. Yet it has emerged as being a work of 'reasonable accuracy', bearing in mind the conditions in which Foxe worked and the purpose of his endeavour.[51] But alongside it, hundreds of other 'godly books' streamed from the printing presses in the form of epitomes, collections of prayers for every part of the Christian's day, summaries and expositions of doctrine, as well as 'commonplaces' from the scriptures. What these different types of books had in common was an aim to continue the religious education of the flock outside of church and within the confines of the family. The Geneva Bible – much more widely used than the official Bishop's Bible or even the later Authorised Version – though itself innovative, not simply in its doctrinal orientation but also in its presentation, had a marginal gloss of Genesis 17.23 which insisted that 'Masters in their families ought to be preachers in their families, that from the highest to the lowest they may obey the will of God.' The responsibility thus placed on householders was recognised to be heavy and not without its difficulties, since

> parents will do them more harm at home than both pastor and schoolmaster can do abroad . . . It is not enough to bring thy child to be catechised at church, but thou must labour with them at home after a more plain and easy manner of instruction so that they may the better profit by the public teaching.[52]

Godly books for the use of the lay reader were, of course, available in the late medieval period. The *Speculum Vitae*, a late-fourteenth-century poem, was based on the seven penitential petitions of the Lord's Prayer, the seven vices, the seven sins, the seven virtues and the seven beatitudes. *The Prick of Conscience*, the *Lay Folk's Catechism* and the early-fifteenth-century *Dives et Pauper*, centring on the Ten Commandments, as well as a number of Lollard texts, provided a limited amount of material for a limited number of people.[53] Caxton's translation and printing in 1483 of *The Golden Legend* provided a more readily accessible form of the Latin *Legenda Aurea*, a retelling of stories from the Bible and of lives of the saints, though as a 444-page folio it was too expensive for most.[54] But by the late 1530s, texts such as these were being replaced by a variety of texts written by reforming Protestants, the only exception being Thomas à Kempis' *Imitatio Christi*, which in the sixteenth and seventeenth centuries was translated and paraphrased no fewer than sixteen times, seven of these being appropriately modified for the Protestant reader, the most popular of these being Thomas Rogers' *The Imitation of Christ* (1580) and John Worthington's *The Christian's Pattern* (1654) which had a printing history continuing into the eighteenth century.[55]

But popular as these were they were overwhelmed in number by the flood of Protestant helps for the laity,[56] in the first instance helps to get to know their Bible. Richard Taverner's *Commonplaces of the Bible* (1538) was frequently reprinted. Thomas Paynell's *The Piththy* [sic] *and Most Notable Sayings of all Scripture gathered by Thomas Paynell after the manner of commonplaces very necessary for all those that delite in the consolations of the Scripture* (1550) was his own 150-page paraphrase of the whole Bible. *A Postill or Exposition of the Gospels that are usually read in the churches of God upon Sundays and Feast Days, written by*

Nicholas Hemming a Dane . . . and translated by Arthur Golding (1569) was a short
set of commentaries on passages of the Bible, citing first a text (with chapter
and verse) and then – *post illa* – a gloss or explanation of its meaning. The
clergy were not slow to make their own contribution, as for example John
Bradford's *Godly Meditations Upon the Ten Commandments* (1567) and Thomas
Cooper's *Brief Exposition of Such Chapters of the Old Testament as are usually read
in the church at Common Prayer on Sondayes set forth for the better helpe and instruction
of the Unlearned* (1573). Others concentrated on a particular part of the
Bible, as did John Newstub in his *Lectures . . . upon the Twentieth Chapter of
Exodus* (1577), which he dedicated to Anne, Countess of Warwick, and
Gervase Babington in his *Certaine Plaine Brief and Comfortable Notes upon Every
Chapter of Genesis* (1596). John Lawson directed his schoolmaster's discerning
perception of the problem by producing his *Gleanings and Expositions of Some
of the More Difficult Places of Scripture* (1646), as did Simon Wastell, master of
the Free School of Northampton, with his *The True Christians Daily Delight
being the Summe of Every Chapter of the Old and New Testaments* (1623), a duodecimo volume of 198 pages with each chapter done in verse which he
hoped would be 'a comfortable companion whether thou walkest abroad or
stayest at home'.[57] Anne Wheathill followed the medieval tradition of *florel-
egia* by putting together *A Handfull of Holesome (though Homelie) Hearbs Gathered
out of the Garden of Gods Most Holie Word* (1584). John Northbrook's *The Poor
Mans Garden Wherein are Flowers of the Scriptures and Doctours Very Necessary for the
Simple and Ignorant to Read* (1573) was nevertheless a more substantial affair,
in which the 'flowers' (extracts) were grouped together under headings such
as 'All sorts of people ought to know and read the scriptures', 'That the
scriptures are easy to be understood of the simple people', 'Ignorance of
the scriptures is very dangerous', 'The scriptures are sufficient to debate and
decide all doubts and controversies', 'The Pope is Anti-Christ'. Despite his
title, *Medulla Bibliorum. The Marrow of the Bible. A Logico-theological Analysis of
Every Severall Book of the Holy Scripture* (1652), William Ainsworth, its author,
considered it 'useful for all Christian families', providing a two- or three-
page analytical summary of each chapter, followed by a poem written by
himself appropriate to the text. One of the most popular of such texts was
the anonymous *Doctrine of the Bible or Rules of Discipline Briefly Gathered Through
the Whole Course of the Scriptures*. First appearing in octavo in 1606, it was
rapidly reprinted in duodecimo size, reaching a 31st printing in 1699.
Thomas Adams' enjoinder may stand as exemplar for this type of help:

> Beloved, let the Word of God dwell in you plentiously. Do not give it a
> cold entertainment as you would to a stranger and so take your leave of
> it, but esteem it as your best familiar and domestical friend, making it
> your chamber-fellow, study-fellow, bed-fellow, the resting place in your

heart . . . search the scriptures, read, observe . . . it must be digested by meditation and prayer.[58]

Though a reading of the Bible and an application of its messages to the business of everyday life were the most immediate aims of many writers, there were plenty of more general books available for the godly reader, books such as *The Institution of Christian Man* (1537) and its revised version *A Necessary Doctrine and Erudition for Any Christian Man* (1543), which provided expositions of the Creed, the Seven Sacraments, the Ten Commandments, the Pater Noster, the Ave and the Articles of Religion. Robert Hill's *The Pathway to Prayer and Pietie* (1613) included with its exposition of the Lord's Prayer, 'an apology for public and private prayer', 'a preparation for the Lord's Supper', 'a direction to a Christian life', 'an instruction to die well', together with 'divers prayers and thanksgivings'. The section on the Lord's Supper was separately printed as *A Communicant Instructed* (1613). Such a *vade mecum* was repeated many times over, as in John Downame's *A Guide to Godlynesse* (1622), Abraham Fleming's *The Diamond of Devotion* (1602), John Ball's *A Short Treatise Containing all the Principal Grounds of Christian Religion* (1629), Jeremy Taylor's *The Rules and Exercises of Holy Living* (1650) and *The Rules and Exercises of Holy Dying* (1651), and Samuel Craddock's *Knowledge and Practice* (1659).

Each of these examples of the different kinds of godly book could have been multiplied many times over. But they did not exhaust the resources available to those who sought guidance to support their own and their children's and servants' lives. As Margaret Spufford and Tessa Watt have shown, there was also a continuous supply of much cheaper material sharing the same aim, produced by the printers of chapbooks and broadside sheets.[59] The likes of John Bruen, who had two Bibles on display in hall and parlour, and doubtless a supply of other works in the closet, and Margaret Hoby, whose Bible- and book-reading are well documented in her diary, have to be noticed alongside a larger but individually unidentifiable group of people who could read but did not have the wherewithal to purchase the books already mentioned. It was for these that the chapbooks and broadside sheets were produced.[60] The Records of the Stationers' Company show them being produced from the 1570s onwards. The single-sheet broadside *A Right Godly and Christian ABC Shewing the Duty of Every Degree* did not excel in its versifying but its religious intent was plain:

> Arise and wake from wickedness;
> Repent and thou shalt live;
> Or else with sword and pestilence
> The Lord God will thee grieve.
> . . .

Young folks be sober, chaste of mind
Let God's Word be your guide.
Make clean your hearts before the Lord
And never from him slide.[61]

A Looking Glass for the Soule Worthy to be hung up in Every Household in the Kingdom and to be Looked at Daily gives an indication of how these sheets were intended to be used, sheets such as *The Duty of Children to Parents*, *A Plain Exposition of the Lord's Prayer*, *A Scripture Table: Some Plain Directions for the More Profitable Hearing of the Word Preached*, *A Hundred Godly Lessons that a Mother on her Death-bed Gave to her Children*, as well as more overtly partisan exhortations such as *A Christian Belief Concerning Bishops* or *A Table Pointing Out Such Places of Scripture . . . Condemning the Principal Points of Popery*.

Arthur Dent's classic 430-page *Plaine Mans Pathway to Heaven* was abridged in a 24-page chapbook form by John Hart in 1659 with the same title, whilst Allestree's *Whole Duty of Man* appeared as a broadside abridgement in 1674. In the post-Restoration period many of the octavo and duodecimo books, priced at 2d or 3d, were advertised by their printers in other godly books, as for example at the beginning of Andrew Jones' *Dooms-day or The Great Day of the Lord Drawing Nigh* (12th ed., 1660) and T.P.'s *God's Call to the Unconverted Sinner* (5th ed., 1663).

The religious content of broadsheet and chapbook is mixed, though in general traditional, rarely venturing into the niceties of Protestant doctrine which characterised some of the larger godly books offered by the book-sellers. Margaret Spufford found in her examination of the Pepsyian collection of 'small godly books' that 'religion . . . in chapbooks is a gloomy one. There is little proclamation of the love of God shown in Christ compared with emphasis on fear of death, judgement and wrath of God.' Whether the evidence justifies her conclusion that the chapbooks presented a 'perverted gospel' remains in doubt, as Eamon Duffy has attempted to show.[62] Certainly the broadsheets show a more complex picture.

The broadside single sheet was thus put into service in the religious education of the laity. The format was also used, but with the addition of a recommended tune and a conscious capitalising of the format of the popular ballad, when metrical versions of the psalms were produced with the explicit aim of countering the (alleged) profanity of many of the broadside ballads then current. Myles Coverdale, for example, produced his *Goostly Psalms* (before 1539) to replace, as he said, the 'ballads of filthiness', hoping as a result that 'carters and ploughmen . . . and women sitting at their rocks or spinning at their wheels' would 'not pass their time in naughty songs of fleshly love and wantonness . . . and the common sort of ballad'.[63] Thomas

Becon made a similar juxtaposition in the expectation that 'both old and young would once leave their lascivious and unclean ballads, and sing such godly and virtuous songs as David teacheth them'.[64]

As always there were dangers in such use, recognised equally by the puritan Richard Rogers who urged his congregation to 'sing David's psalms with David's spirit; sing with spirit and sing with understanding; regard that more than the tune', and the Anglican Lewis Bayley who warned, in his 'Rules to be observed in the singing of psalms':

> Beware of singing divine psalms for an ordinary recreation, as do men of impure spirits, who sing holy psalms intermingled with profane ballads. Remember to sing David's psalms with David's spirit . . . Be sure that the matter makes more melody in your hearts than the music in your ears.

George Wither had similar misgivings:

> For though many sing them, very few remember to think of what they sing. Certain I am that no scripture is half so frequently read or sung as they are; and as sure it is that no book is so little understood . . . Many of them had rather sing some good ballet of Robert Wisdom's than the best of these prophetical odes.[65]

By the mid-seventeenth century the original translations were beginning to appear out-of-date, as William Barton, minister of St Martin's, Leicester noted, introducing his new versions, *A Century of Select Hymns and Spiritual Songs* (1659), which he followed with *Four Centuries* . . . (1660) and *Six Centuries* . . . (1680) 'finding withal that the ancient usage and speech in Sternhold and Hopkins' translation was become obsoletely contemptuous to many people of this age'.[66] By then the singing of psalms as part of the religious education of the flock had long been a permanent feature in both church and household.

But popular as psalm-singing became it was overshadowed in importance by the contemporary belief in the efficacy of petitionary prayer, which meant that the laity had also to be instructed in its proper use. The Lord's Prayer was, of course, one of the earliest formularies to which the young Christian was introduced, though such a supplication was but one of many which were made available. Moreover, the Homily 'The Place and Time of Prayer' was at pains to emphasise that the church was not the only place where prayer could be efficaciously engaged in, nor the Book of Common Prayer the only source. Prayer, both communal and private, played an essential part in domestic piety, with texts constantly reminding readers that preparation, manner and place were matters requiring careful consideration. 'To pray without understanding is not praying but mumming'; 'prayer is a familiar conference with God'; 'a respiration of the soul'; 'prayer is the greatest duty and the greatest privilege of a Christian'. 'It is his intercourse with God, his remedy from sin, his cure of griefs ... by which we ascend to God in spirit whilst we remain on earth; call upon God in time of trouble and He will deliver you'; 'Prayers ... repeated without understanding and so out of their right ordinance and use, are they any better than a charm? Is it not rather a service unto the Devil than unto God?'[67]

Suitably warned on all sides of such dangers, the godly were provided with a plentiful supply of texts which gathered together prayers for every aspect and point within the Christian day – on rising in the morning and retiring at night, before and after meals, before and after the sacraments, before and after childbirth, thanksgivings for God's mercies and petitions for His forgiveness for transgressions. Many of the texts were small enough to go into the pocket. Thomas Becon's *Pomander of Prayer*, originally 306 pages in its 1558 edition, measured 2¼ by 3¼ inches in a 1565 edition, whilst Thomas Tymme's 252-page *The Poor Mans Paternoster* was 1½ by 2½ inches in a 1598 edition. The anonymous *Tablet for a Gentlewoman* (1574), even smaller at 1 by 1½ inches, nevertheless included in its 198 pages a series of 29 prayers for all occasions, followed by 'The Litany with certain other godly prayers'. Each of these prayers betrayed a thoroughly traditional view of a woman's place in society, including 'A prayer for maids' which insisted that 'There is nothing that becometh a maid better than silence, shamefastness and chastity both in body and mind, for these things being once lost there is no more a maid but a strumpet in the sight of God.' James Canceller's *The Alphabet of Prayers* (1565), Edward Chapman's *A Form of Prayer for all Christian Families* (1583), Samuel Hieron's *A Help unto Devotion* (1618), John Cosin's *A Collection of Private Devotions* (1627), Michael Sparke's *Crums of Comfort* (1628), Daniel Featley's *Ancilla Pietatis or The Handmaid of Private Devotion* (1626) and a host of similar texts from all sides of the religious spectrum, most running to several editions, provided both a justification for and an exhortation to engage in private and family prayer as well as the means for carrying it out.

As with advice on how to read the scriptures, so too manuals were produced to guide the practice of prayer with meaning. Expositions of the Lord's Prayer were readily available, for example Francis Bunny's *Exposition of the Lord's Prayer* (1602), and William Burton's of the same title (1602), together with Robert Hill's *Christ's Prayer Expounded. A Christian Directed and Communicant Prepared* (1606), Arthur Dent's *A Learned and Fruitfull Exposition upon the Lord's Prayer* (1624), Henry Scudder's *A Key to Heaven or The Lord's Prayer Opened and so Applied* (1620), William Gouge's *A Guide to Goe to God or An Explanation of the Perfect Pattern of Prayer, the Lord's Prayer* (1626). Others offered more general direction, as did Elnathan Parr in his *Abba Father or A Plaine . . . Direction Concerning the Framing of Private Prayer* (1615) which he dedicated to Lady Jane Cornwallis. 'Breath is the instrument of the life of the body; prayer is the breath of the soul' he urged, and it was crucially important for the 'weaker Christians who are as yet babes newly beginning to cry Abba Father'. Moreover, 'as a musician first tunes his instrument before he plays on it, so both the mind should be put in frame and the matter forethought when we pray to God'. He then went on to give guidance on how to construct a prayer, with examples, before concluding with an exposition of the Lord's Prayer.[68] George Downame produced his *Godly and Learned Treatise of Prayer* in 1640 and Samuel Slater his *Discourse of Closet (or Secret) Prayer from Matt. 6.60* in 1691 and at the end of the period Matthew Henry's *Method of Prayer* (1710) and Isaac Watts' *Guide to Prayer* (1715) enjoyed enormous popularity in their many editions. A common feature of all such texts was their emphasis on the importance of private 'closet' or 'secret' prayer as a supplement to the communal prayer of godly households and that of the church service.[69] Oliver Heywood, for example, in his *Closet Prayer a Christian Duty* (1671) complained:

> The power of godliness is much spoken of, but (I am afraid) very rarely to be found amongst (even) famous professors. Most content themselves with external, visible duties, which formalists may carry on with as much seeming zeal and applause as sincere worshippers. A formal spirit is the disease of the present day . . . There are thousands in the world will run miles to hear a sermon yet will not set themselves solemnly to the duties of meditation, self-examination or secret prayer.

He was at pains to insist that 'I write not to please learned scholars, but to profit plain Christians' and compared his own 127-page 'small piece . . . more portable as a pocket book or vade mecum' with the 477-page 'otherwise excellent piece', *The Prime Key to Heaven or Twenty Arguments for Closet Prayer* (1655) of Thomas Brooks, 'preacher at St Margaret's New Fish Street' in London. Like other authors of such texts, Heywood reminded his readers that 'If you have not a convenient room indoors, yet a good heart will not disdain to go to meet its beloved in any cote or barn or wood. Isaac walked into the fields to pray and meditate.'[70] When John Featley compiled his collection of prayers *A Fountaine of Teares . . .* (Amsterdam, 1646) he explained that he had done so because

I was first invited to this task by the means of a gracious and virtuous gentlewoman who much complained that her sex was so much neglected by divines that they had not penned devotions for all of their several sufferances that are common to many . . . For her dear sake these soliloquies and prayers were fitted for females and taught to speak in the persons of the weaker vessels.[71]

The gentlewoman in question was Mrs Elizabeth Keate, wife of the London grocer Gilbert Keate, though her complaint was not well based since the majority of collections[72] included prayers designed for the use of women during pregnancy and childbirth. These were often copied, sometimes in modified form, into the 'diaries' and commonplace books of women such as Elizabeth Egerton, wife of John Egerton, second Earl of Bridgewater, who wrote out 'A prayer in time of labour', 'A prayer after I was brought to bed', 'A prayer when I continued with child after I thought I should have fallen in labour', 'A prayer before communion at Easter, being at the same time with child' and so on.[73]

As always the difficulty lay in providing texts for a very wide range of reading skills, texts which, seeking a practical and affective spirituality, incorporated a 'more plain and easy manner of instruction'. Arthur Dent's *Plaine Mans Pathway to Heaven* (1601) and Lewis Bayly's *Practise of Pietie* (*c*.1612) were nevertheless over 400 and 500 pages in length respectively, the third edition of the latter being expanded to 1031 duodecimo pages. Towards the end of the century it began to appear in large Roman print for the use and benefit of older readers,[74] and continued to be printed on into the early nineteenth century. Joseph Alleine's *An Alarm to the Unconverted* (1672) sold 20,000 copies when it first appeared and a further 50,000 when it was reprinted as *A Small Guide to Heaven* in 1685. Yet its turgid 214 pages, with six or more biblical texts per page, were not much better than Arthur Dent's *Pastime for Parents* (1606), intended as he said to be 'a recreation to pass away the time with children', and in no way unusual in including among its 430 pages passages such as:

Father: How then do you conceive of the Essence and being of the Godhead?

Child: That the Substance or Essence of the Deity is of all things most simple and single, and is neither divided, multiplied nor compact of any elementary quality.

Father: Express your mind more fully.

Child: This I mean, that the divine nature is of one simple, uniform, immaterial, immutable, illocal, eternal, omnipotent, omniscient, infinite, void of all mixture.[75]

It is not surprising, then, that William Vaughan could complain:

> Do we not see pamphlets, ballads and playbooks sooner sold than
> elegant sermons and books of piety? Unless a book contain light mat-
> ters as well as serious it cannot flourish nor live jovially, but like Saturn
> standeth still on the stall.[76]

Even so, 'books of piety' were not in short supply nor of course were they
all like Dent's or Alleine's. There were plenty like Francis Inman's *A Light
unto the Unlearned or The Principles of the Doctrine of Christ* . . . (1622), 'set down
briefly for the use of young and ignorant persons . . .' as a result of which
'they may receive great profit by the scriptures they read and the sermons
they hear . . . and so come better prepared to the Lord's Table'. Indeed,
John Rhodes produced his *Countrie Mans Comfort* (1637) precisely for those
who asked 'What shall we do in the long winter nights? How shall we pass
the time on Sundays? What would you have us do in the Christmas holi-
days?'[77] John Norden's *Pensive Mans Practice* (1584) ran into 40 editions in as
many years, Arthur Dent's *Plain Mans Practice* (1601) to 25 editions by 1640,
whilst John Dod's *Exposition of the Ten Commandments* (1603) had 19 editions
by 1635. By the end of the century the most popular of all such books was
The Whole Duty of Man, first published anonymously in 1658, which 'laid
down in a plain way for the use of the meanest reader . . . divided into XVII
chapters, one which being read every Lord's Day the whole may be read
over thrice in that year'. At first attributed to the pen of Lady Dorothy
Pakington, it was finally established to be the work of Richard Allestree, and
covered every aspect of a Christian's daily life from the suckling of infants,
the education of children, the duties of children to their parents and of
wives to their husbands, as well as the absolute need of parents' consent
before marriage. In considering these it was in fact a thoroughly traditional
manual, which probably accounts for its popularity.[78]

In 'Popular and Unpopular Religion', Chapter 5 of his *The Religion of
Protestants*, Patrick Collinson considers the difficulties entailed in using the
term 'popular', and concludes that 'the "religion of Protestants" in its more
intense and fully internalised form was never popular in the plain and
ordinary sense'. But by insisting on such criteria he effectively debars from
consideration those 'comformable' Protestant attenders at the parish church
whose religious belief and allegiance was rarely 'more intense' and only
with great difficulty 'fully internalised'.[79] Indeed, attendance itself is a
doubtful index of piety or godliness, whether at church or at the Marian
burnings. In its degree of admonition or encouragement, in its attempts to
reduce anxieties or revive flagging spirits, the literature we have just considered was varied indeed. The attempt has now to be made to identify the

'godly' and their religious education, with a due recognition of the sources available and an expectation that even the godly, as opposed to the apathetic and uncaring, will turn out to be as varied in their belief, their understanding and their allegiance as their place on the social spectrum. Above all, the attempt will bear in mind John Downame's reminder to his readers that

> as in civil affairs that knowledge which is gotten by reading and mental discourse is of little use or worth until it be perfected by practice and experience, so is it much more true in the knowledge of Christianity.

Or, as Elizabeth Warren put it:

> The pratick part of religion and holiness is the acting of precepts in a pure conversation, not contenting ourselves with a naked theory, but clothing it comely with pious practice, that our doing and suffering in the cause of God may outstrip all hypocrites and carnal professors.[80]

3   The methods

The wide variety of provision meant that an equally wide range of methods
were used to enjoin, encourage and enable the flock in its religious education. After centuries of learning by means of oral repetition, the appearance of the printed book could hardly be expected to produce an overnight
change to silent reading.[1] Even for the literate minority, listening remained a
major means of acquiring religious knowledge, whether through the sermon or the Lessons in church, or through listening to the reading of the
Bible or of passages from other godly books at home.[2] Moreover, despite
the transformation of the parish church as a result of Protestant icono-
clasm, some stained glass remained to tell the biblical story or to remind
parishioners of the biblical saints. In addition, the tables of the Ten Commandments remained for the edification of the faithful when in 1561 it
was ordered that the Decalogue should be painted on the walls or displayed
on boards in every parish church.[3]

Listening and seeing were thus as much a part of the religious education
of the literate as of the illiterate. The same was true of the reliance on
memorising prayers and passages of the Bible by the age-old means of
constant repetition, acknowledged for example in the Royal Injunctions of
1536 and 1547,[4] or by the more consciously focused use of versification
and, in the case of the psalms, by the additional use of simple tune struc-
tures. Preachers were also called upon to assist the memories of their
hearers. Manuals on the preparation of sermons abounded, urging
preachers to structure their sermons into more readily remembered sections
and to make use of recapitulation before moving from one section to the
next. Moreover, 'silver-tongued' Henry Smith was not alone in preparing
sermons especially designed to educate his listeners in 'The Art of Hearing'.[5] The printers themselves also made a major contribution as facilitators
by providing title pages, tables of contents, even occasionally what we now
call alphabetical indexes, as well as marginalia giving textual and biblical
references. Towards the end of the period some printers provided texts in

large print for the benefit of the elderly reader.[6] But their major contribution was to provide godly books of all kinds in the vernacular tongue, in all sizes and at all prices. In so doing they not only contributed to the religious education of the literate godly but must also have encouraged the spread of literacy itself.

LEARNING TO READ

The almost universal insistence that the religious education of children should be started early raised all kinds of ways and means problems – problems of basic pedagogy. More particularly, an insistence on the importance of learning to read required in addition a consideration of the methods which might be used to achieve what was, after all, a skill characteristic only of a minority of the population. At the same time, a recognition of the religious needs of an illiterate population meant that a whole range of aids to memorisation had to be produced. Even those who were provided with the means to learn to read were put through a systematic process of oral teaching in which memorisation by speech as well as by visual recognition was made an essential part.

The 'how?' of a literate religious education started with the horn book, a single sheet of paper pasted to a wooden board with a handle, sometimes covered with a skin or horn for protection during use.[7] At its top the alphabet in upper and lower case was set out, and below the Lord's Prayer and perhaps the Ten Commandments. To follow, the parent or teacher would have the assistance of a variety of learning-to-read texts, which commonly started with a listing of the individual letters of the alphabet in a variety of type faces, black letter, Roman, upper and lower cases, which in turn would be followed by an indication of the vowels and consonants, together with lists of syllables, starting with two-letter words, then those with three, four, and up to as many as seven syllables. As Chaytor has put it, for the child learning to read 'the task is to construct from visual printed symbols an acoustic image which he can recognise'.[8] Learning to say, to pronounce, was thus the first exercise in learning to read aloud. Learning to read silently came later in the process, and then only by those who had become habitual readers.

Few writers of such texts would have disagreed with Richard Mulcaster's enjoinder concerning these elementary stages of learning to read that, in considering his pupil, the teacher should have regard to 'his memory, his delight, his capacity and his forwarding', and that above all the whole process should be 'short in precept and much in practice'.[9] William Kempe, for example, was insistent:

let him not learn by rote, spelling one syllable and shuffling up the rest without distinct spelling. As if he would learn this word mercifulness, suffer him not, as some would, to go on thus: m-e-r, mer, c-i-f-u-l-n-e-s-s, mercifulness. But according to the letters and syllables, which are as precepts in this behalf, let him learn it by reason thus: m-e-r, mer, c-i, ci, merci, f-u-l, ful, merciful, n-e-s-s, ness, mercifulness. For if he repeat the former syllables with every other added unto them, he shall have all in perfect memory when he cometh to the end, where otherwise he may err or forget.

Kempe was, however, well aware that 'the scholar shall find one hindrance and stumbling block, in that the practice doth not always agree with the precepts', in which case:

> these and such like difficulties are as rough ground in the way of a learner, which he cannot stride over unless the master do lead him as it were by the hand, supporting him again and again lest he fall, which must needs be tedious to them both for a while.[10]

Edmund Coote, too, recognised the need for reinforcement in his teaching, as when he followed each section on syllables with sentences for reading, consisting of words from the previous section: 'Boy, go thy way up to the top of the hill, and get me home the bay nag; fill him well and see he be fat'. Francis Clement, on the other hand, though following the usual practice in the matter of introducing letters and syllables, chooses as his examples words such as 'neighbours', 'manifold', 'communication' etc., and his examples of the syllable ph- are Philip, physician, physic, philosophy, phantasy, physiognomy.[11]

For the most part, however, the examples and the recommended reading matter have a distinctly religious content. Following Becon and others, Mulcaster was explicit in indicating the purpose of the exercise:

> Reading, if for nothing else it were, as for many things else, it is, is very needful for religion, to read that which they must know and ought to perform . . . If they hear first and after read of the self-same argument, reading confirms the memory . . . by reading of some comfortable and wise discourse, penned either in the form of histories or for direction to live by.[12]

Coote's *English Scolemaister* thus included a short catechism, followed by prayers, metrical psalms and excerpts from Proverbs. Brinsley recommended that the Primer and the psalms be used before moving on to the

New Testament, whilst Charles Hoole similarly insisted that before a child is led to the Bible he should be weaned on the Lord's Prayer, the Creed and the Ten Commandments, together with psalms and prayers.[13] In his *The English Primrose . . . the easiest and speediest way both for the true spelling and reading of English as also for the true writing thereof that was ever publickly known to this day* (1644), Richard Hodges, schoolmaster in Southwark, appended a reader which included all these elements. Benjamin Harris, in his *The Protestant Tutor Instructing Children to Spell and Read English Grounding them in the True Protestant Religion* (1679), was much more overtly partisan in his aim, complaining of 'the vast number of Popish primers, catechisms, manuals and a multitude of such Romish tracts which they intended to have dispersed like a general infection among the youth of this nation'. He therefore addressed his book, whose 146 16° pages measured 2 by 3 inches, 'to all Protestant parents, schoolmasters and schoolmistresses of children . . . to teach them to spell and read English, and to create in them an abhorrence of Romish idolatry at the same time'. To this end his text therefore included as reading matter 'An Account of the Burning of the Pope at Temple Bar in London Nov. 17, 1697' (Queen Elizabeth's Accession Day), and reports of 'The Spanish Invasion 1588', 'Gunpowder Treason 1605', 'The Massacre of Ireland 1642', 'The Massacre of Paris 1655', 'The Burning of London by the Papists 2 Sept., 1666'. His 18-page catechism reflected the same bias:

Q. What religion do you profess?
A. The religion commonly called the Protestant in opposition to Popery.
Q. Are we bound to own the Pope's interpretation of scripture?
A. No. 2 Peter 1 20–21.
Q. May the Pope absolve us from the oath of allegiance?
A. No. Eccles. 8.2.

Then follows 'A Little Book of Martyrs or The History of the Kings of England, with an Account of the Cruelties Exercised by the Pope and his Clergy for Several Hundred Years', starting with William the Conqueror's 'Norman Yokeland' and concluding with 'Queen Mary imitating Jezebel / Advanced against the monster of Hell', with a list of martyrs appended below.

Benjamin Keach's *The Child's Delight or Instructions for Children and Youth*, aiming to teach 'an easy way to spell and read English, directing parents in a right and spiritual manner to educate their children', included a set of versified Commandments and a detailed catechism, besides recommending that the child should read the *Book of Martyrs*, presumably in one of the abbreviated versions then available.[14] Tobias Ellis' 'Epistle to the Reader' in his *The English School Containing a Catalogue of all the Words in the Bible . . . being the readiest way for teaching children to read* (5th ed. 1680) was equally explicit in setting down his aim:

> an expeditious, plain and pleasant way to bring very young ones of competent capacities in a very reasonable time to read the whole Bible over distinctly, and to the knowledge of the principles of godliness, sufficient through the blessing of God to their salvation.

For 'the most ancient and ignorant people' his hope was that 'at least they may be able to read the Creed, the Lord's Prayer and the Ten Commandments, and to have them exactly in their memories to make way for their explication, so that they perish not for want of knowledge'.[15] John Locke's advice on teaching children to read was based wholly on the notion that it should be made a pleasurable activity, to which end he suggested that ivory dice should be provided with the letters of the alphabet pasted on their sides, in the expectation that they would be learned as if a game. The letters, he argued, 'were best to be the size of those of the folio Bible to begin with, and none of them capital letters. When once he can read what is printed in such letters he will not be long ignorant of the great ones'. In the matter of learning to read, 'let him never be driven to nor chid for; cheat him into it if you can, but not make a business of it'. As for reading the Bible, 'I think the promiscuous reading of it through by chapters as they lie in order is far from being of any advantage to children, either for the perfecting of their reading or principling their religion, that perhaps worse could not be found.' Much better, he argued, is for the parent to choose Bible stories 'such as the story of Joseph and the brethren, of David and Goliath, of David and Jonathan'. The Lord's Prayer, the Creed and Commandments should be learned by heart by having someone repeat them to the child and the same method should be used to master the catechism, 'a question every day or every week as his understanding is able to receive and his memory to retain them'.[16]

But the illiterate still had to be catered for, and in this the Christian church had always been prepared to use the visual medium, from the fish symbol of the early Christians and holy relics and statues of saints to the elaborate stories in the stained glass of the medieval cathedrals and churches.[17] The illiterate adherents to the various forms of Protestantism, faced with whitewashed walls, plain glass, and the Homily 'On the Perils of Idolatry', had recourse only to the oral medium, though those who had access to Foxe's *Book of Martyrs* could share with their illiterate friends and family the experience of his detailed woodcuts. For those embarking on the road to literacy the simplest visual aid was to be found in the form of pictorial alphabets which Hans Holbein had pioneered in the 1530s.[18] John Hart was one who used the technique in his *Methode to Read English* of 1570, as later did Benjamin Harris in his *New English Tutor . . . to which is added Milk for Babes*. He elaborated his pictorial alphabet by adding a couplet to each woodcut, and included illustrated poems 'On Death', 'On Judgement', 'On Heaven', 'On Hell', together with an illustration of the Pope (naked save for his triple crown) with various parts of his body identified with the human vices. Though Comenius' *Orbis Sensualium Pictus* (1658) was originally designed for the teaching of Latin with the aid of a pictorial alphabet and other woodcuts, its Englishing by Charles Hoole in the year following its publication, again to help his own grammar school boys, would have made it available for those learning the elements of their own tongue. Apart from its inclusion of a pictorial alphabet, Thomas Lye's *The Child's Delight* (1671), addressed to 'the able and industrious instructors of youth in England, especially such as are concerned in teaching the English tongue', was entirely orthodox in its content and method. Stephen Batemen's earlier *A Christall Glasse of Christian Reformation Wherein the Godly May Behold the Coloured Abuse Used in This our Present Time* (1569) had a woodcut to illustrate his list of virtues and vices – with sloth being illustrated by a dozing schoolmaster in his classroom. This apart, a more misogynist text could not be imagined. The illustrated title page of Daniel Featley's *Ancilla Pietatis* (1623) was a more positive identification of the piety of women. Benjamin Harris elaborated the pictorial alphabet in his *Protestant Tutor* (1679) by adding a couplet to each woodcut:

A	In Adam's Fall We sinned all.
J	Sweet Jesus He Died in a tree.
O	The royal oak It was the tree That saved his Royal Majesty[19]

Works such as these poured from the presses throughout the period. But for many of the reformers and their adherents, reading the Bible for oneself continued to be regarded as an essential part of religious education. Erasmus had led the way with his *Paraclesis*, the introduction to his 1516 translation of the New Testament, which had been quickly Englished by William Roye as *An Exhortation to the Diligent Studye of Scripture* (1529). It was one thing, of course, to exhort, as Immanuel Bourne amongst many others did in his sermon preached at Paul's Cross in 1617: 'Get ye to the Bible that most wholesome remedy for the soul', or to claim with William Gouge that 'there is a secret virtue lurking in the holy scriptures (which is God's own Word) more than in any books of men. No books are more easy than many parts of scripture and no histories more admirable and delightful.' The Edwardian Homily 'A Fruitful Exhortation to the Reading and Knowledge of Holy Scripture' was nevertheless careful to insist that the flock should 'Read it humbly with a meek and lowly heart to the intent you may glorify God not yourself with the knowledge of it'. Jeremy Taylor was instructing his hearers as well as reminding them of the virtues of the subject of his funeral sermon, when he reported, of Lady Frances Carbery's constant reading of the Bible, that she read

> not to the purposes of vanity and impertinent curiosities, not to seem knowing, or to become talking, not to expound and rule, but to teach her all her duty, to instruct her in the knowledge and love of God and of her neighbours, to make her more humble, and to teach her to despise the world and all its gilded vanities, and that she might entertain passions wholly in design and order to heaven.[20]

A different kind of help had therefore to be provided which would guide the flock in its private reading of the Bible. Edward Vaughan's *A Methode or Brief Instruction Very Profitable for the Reading and Understanding of the Old and the New Testaments* (1590) was an early example in which he divided the books of the Bible under four main headings – legal, historical, sapiential and prophetical – with the encouraging reminder that 'by observing this ordering you shall be able to judge nearly where every matter that cometh in your hearing doth lie in the Bible, or what scripture soever you shall read elsewhere'.[21] Nicholas Byfield's *Directions for the Private Reading of the Scriptures* (entered Stationers' Register, 21 February 1617; 2nd ed., 1618; 3rd ed., 1626) provided detailed and explicit guidance for his parishioners at Isleworth, Middlesex, as well as for his wider readership, aiming especially at 'the godly that are unlearned'. His text provided, first, headings and summaries of each of the books of the Bible, with analytical tables appended. Next came a daily calendar of reading 'so that the whole Bible might be read over in a year'. The work was rounded off with guidance as to 'Rules or titles of things to be observed in reading', such as 'Places that showeth the affection I should bear God', 'Places that show me how to carry myself in church', 'Promises that may comfort me against outward crosses', 'Comforts against death', and so on, all this within the space of 95 duodecimo pages. Similar, though less precisely detailed, instruction was to be found in more general texts such as the enormously popular *The Practise of Pietie*

Directing the Christian How to Walke that he may Please God by Lewis Bayly, Bishop of Bangor. First published about 1612 and running into more than 40 editions by 1640, it included a chapter on 'How to read the Bible with profit and ease once over every year', with the injunction 'and read not these chapters as matters of historical discourse but as if they were so many letters of epistles sent down from God out of heaven unto thee; for whatsoever is written is written for our learning'.[22] In his small *Search the Scriptures. A Treatise Showing that all Christians Ought to Read the Holy Books, with directions to them therein* (1685), Simon Patrick was not unusual in urging his readers 'these books ought to be much in our hands, in our eyes, in our ears, in our mouths, but most of all in our hearts'. In his *Several Methods of Reading the Holy Scriptures in Private* (1718), Samuel Blackwell, Rector of Brampton-by-Dingley in Northamptonshire, offered five different ways, in decreasing detail, of reading the Bible. William Lowth, prebendary of Winchester, in his *Directions for the Profitable Reading of the Holy Scriptures* (1708), indicated his hope that 'the careful reading of the Holy Scripture would enable Christians to recover the spirit of piety which is visibly decayed and almost extinguished amongst us'.[23]

LISTENING AND MEMORY AIDS

Memorising passages from the Bible was a practice regularly enjoined upon the godly, and here again there was no shortage of texts designed especially for their use. An early example is to be found in Richard Whitford's *Worke for Householders* (1530) in which he provides

> a short table that doth in sum contain the whole life of Our Saviour Jesus Christ, that such persons as wish to learn it by heart and have it ready in mind may lightly [easily] order and lay it up, as it were in a chest or coffer.[24]

Ezekiel Culverwell's posthumously published *A Ready Way To Remember the Scriptures* (1637) was a typical example of the genre, in which each chapter of the Bible is summarised thus:

> Genesis: Chap. 1: Creation, 1; God's image, 26; Man's sovereignty, 26; All very good, 31.
> Chap. 2: Sabbath, 3; Eden, 8; Tree of knowledge, 17; Woman, 22; Naked and not ashamed, 23.
> Chap. 3: Fall, 6; Punishment, 16; Cursed, 17; Thrust out of Paradise, 23.

Some of these the reader was recommended

> to say over every day . . . and the better to keep the contents in memory to
> say over daily that which is past . . . (which I conceive may be a good
> exercise for the training up of children of ten years old and upwards),
> for by reading over these contents a man well exercised in the scriptures
> may in one hour see the principal matters in the whole New Testament.

An even more abbreviated form was used by Edward Beecher in his *The
Christian School or Scriptures Anatomy . . .* (1676) which he set out in a highly
simplified fashion:

Chap	Genesis
1	Adam made 27
2	Eden planted 8
3	Man ensnared 6
4	Abel's death 8
5	Enoch's walk 24[25]

Whilst some authors relied on abbreviation as an aid to memory others used
alphabetisation, as in Robert Allen's *An Alphabet of the Holy Proverbs of King
Solomon* (1596), produced as he said 'for a help to our weak and frail memories'.[26] E. C., who described himself as 'a country minister' of some twenty
years' standing, used the same method in his *An ABC or Holy Alphabet conteyn-
ing some plaine lessons gathered out of the Word to the number of letters in the English
Alphabet to enter young beginners in the school of Christ* (1626), as did John Clarke in
his *Holy Oyle for the Lampes of the Sanctuarie or Scripture Phrases . . . Alphabetically
Disposed* (1630).

The oldest aid to memory was, of course, versification where rhythm and
rhyme could be called on. Poetry as 'a functional instrument of storage' was
used in pre-alphabet days, when the repetition of the Homeric story helped
to preserve a set of cultural values in a non-literate society, as was the case
later with the sagas of the northern world. In England, it was not until the
sixteenth century that any significant attempt was made to versify parts of
the Bible. William Samuel's *Abridgemente of Goddes Statutes in Myter* (1551) was
an early example, with an aim similar to that of Richard Robinson who
produced his *Certain Selected Histories for Christian Recreations with their Several
Moralizations Brought into English Verse* (1576), with each 'moralization thereof
aptly applied' and followed by a summarising 'argument'. William Hunnis
used the same technique on a smaller canvas with his *A Hyve Full of Hunnye
Contayning the Fyrst Booke of Moses Called Genesis Turned into English Meetre*
(1578), in which he dealt with each chapter in turn and provided a verse

summary as a preface to each, the whole being supplemented with marginal glosses.[27] John Shaw's summarising of the Bible in Latin verse, *Biblii Summula* (1621), was translated into English verse in 1629 by Simon Wastell, master of the grammar school at Northampton, under the title *Microbiblion or The Bibles Epitome*, with indications of the verse numbers as his text proceeded:

> At first Jehovah with his word
> Did make heaven[2] earth and light
> The firmament, the moon and stars[14]
> Thy glittering sun so bright.
> By Him the earth[11] was fruitful made
> And every creation[31] good
> He maketh[26] man like Himself
> And doth[29] appoint his food.

Wastell anticipated criticism of his versifying abilities by insisting 'I have purposely laboured to speak plainly to the capacity and understanding of the simple and ignorant, rather than by poetical strains to please the ear and eye of the serious learned readers'.[28] A printing of the work was forthcoming as late as 1683, under the title *The Divine Art of Memory Wherein is Contained the Sum of the Holy Scriptures in Acrostic Verses*. John Rhodes' *Countrie Mans Comfort or Religious Recreations Fitte for All Well Disposed Persons* (1637) versified the Creed, the Ten Commandments and a selection of graces before meals and other prayers, at the same time bidding his readers

> First learn to honour God aright;
> Let love and fears thereto provoke.
> Obey the king with all thy might;
> Submit thyself to parents' yoke.

Rhodes' allegiances were further made plain by the addition of a 'A Song reproving Papists for the Gunpowder Treason' and 'A Prayer for the King's State', all of which, he urged, were not for 'the wise and learned' but for 'the scholars of petty schools, the poor country man and his family, who will ask these vain questions, sometimes saying 'What shall we do in the long winter nights?'[29] John Bunyan's *A Book for Boys and Girls or Country Rimes for Children* (1686) followed a versification of the Ten Commandments with 74 verse 'meditations': 'Upon an egg', 'Upon the peep of day', 'Upon a flint in the water', 'Upon a mole in the ground', 'Upon the cuckoo', etc., each of which was supplemented by 'comparisons' which pointed the moral. The meditation 'Upon an instrument of music in an unskilful hand', for example, is followed by the 'comparison':

> The unlearned novices in things divine,
> With this unskilled musician I compare.
> For such, instead of making truth to shine,
> Abuse the Bible and unsavoury are.[30]

Reading and memorising the Bible, in whatever form, was one thing. Much more contentious, however, was the exposition of its message, fraught as this was with the danger of heterodox interpretation. Based on the notion of 'sola scriptura', the reformed standpoint insisted that all a Christian needed for guidance was to be found in the scriptures. The accumulated tradition of the church universal, the commentaries of the Christian Fathers and their medieval successors, it was argued, no longer had any force. But a further gloss, that the words of the Bible were literally true, obvious in their clarity to all believers, plainly presented problems to those in authority, for it quickly became clear that not all the godly were reading the scriptures 'aright'. Nor could the laity be expected to bear in mind the traditional (though hotly debated) niceties of the theologians' four-fold differentiation of meaning. The earlier attempts to solve the problem by restricting the reading of the Bible to certain sections of the populace had obviously failed and been abandoned, but once the earlier restrictions had been eased (and under Elizabeth more and more of the clergy leaned towards one form of puritanism or another), reading the Bible at home was increasingly enjoined upon the flock. The concomitant danger of such reading being supplemented by discussion and interpretation was quickly spotted. When Elizabeth Young had defended her interpretation of the nature of the sacraments, the Bishop of London's Chancellor expostulated:

> Why, thou art a woman of fair years [she was over 40]. What, should thou meddle with the scriptures? It is necessary for you to believe and that is enough. It is more fit for thee to meddle with your distaff than to meddle with the scriptures. Thou has read a little in the Bible or Testament and thou thinkest that thou art able to reason with a doctor that hath gone to school thirty years.

Later, Queen Elizabeth herself complained that

> every merchant must have his schoolmaster and nightly conventicles, expounding scripture and catechizing their servants and maids, in so much that I have heard how some maids have not sticked to control learned readers and say 'Such a man taught otherwise in our house'.

Thomas Adams continued the chorus of dispraise when he declared 'There is scarce a man that can read English, scarce a woman that can make herself ready to church, but will presume to teach the minister.'[31] As we shall see, women themselves were becoming increasingly critical of the limitations put on the exercise of their piety by a culture which enabled men to monopolise the content and the method of their religious education, though at the end of the period Mary Astell still had to insist that, since women were still not taught to read the Bible for themselves in the original languages, when they made use of translations and commentaries written by men, they had no way of knowing what distortions had crept into the texts recommended to them.

The complexities involved in considering a historical shift from an illiterate society and culture to a literate one, and of a continued majority of illiterates in the latter, have been authoritatively treated by Eric Havelock, Walter Ong and many others.[32] We have throughout tried to remind ourselves that even in a post-Gutenberg culture, with the printing presses pouring forth a wide range of instructional literature, those in authority, as well as the educators who endeavoured to put into practice their injunctions, had always to remember the needs of as well as the requirements which were heaped upon the population as a whole. It was necessary, therefore, to base induction, indoctrination and the retention of doctrine on traditional means of communication, on word of mouth, as the primary means of education, in which memorisation, whether by repetition or by other means, had to be assisted. Literacy had provided what might be called an artificial memory. What was spoken had to catch the attention if it were to stand a chance of being retained. But more importantly, if memorisation was to be made an efficient method of learning and retaining, it had in some way to be made a pleasurable activity. It was not for nothing that the proof-text Isaiah 28.9–10, was constantly cited, and that the metaphor 'milk for babes' became a favoured indication of the elements of religious education throughout the period, applied to adults as well as children.

'Search the scriptures' (John 5.34) was, then, a crucial though problematic enjoinder in the religious education of the laity. But the Bible was far from being the only medium through which that education was transmitted. More important, both as text and method, was the very old medium of the catechism. Once again, variety became the enemy of uniformity, and when Thomas Sparke explained in his *Catechisme or Short Kinde of Instruction* (1588):

> I would have thee (Christian Reader) . . . to understand that by a catechism is here meant a form of instruction, briefly, soundly and plainly containing the first and necessary principles of Christian religion,

examples whereof (God be thanked) there are abroad in print amongst us here in England good store . . .

he was running directly counter to the efforts of those in authority to confine such instruction to an officially approved version. Royal and diocesan Injunctions and subsequent Visitation Articles, repeated in the 1604 Canons, constantly required the clergy to

teach the children and young folks the catechism, examine and oppose them in the same, and that yearly at every Synod and General Chapter they shall give the names of all parents, masters and dames that shall refuse or defer to send their children, servants and apprentices to learn the catechism, and all such, as being sent, stubbornly refuse to learn or be taught the same.[33]

The catechisms in the 1549 and 1552 Prayer Books, together with the shortened version of Nowell's catechism of 1570, were the officially approved versions of the Anglican Church, but catechising rapidly became one of the most flexible instruments of religious education, flexible that is in size and contents, through retaining the essentially authoritarian question and answer format that made it so much preferred by all denominations. During the Commonwealth period, the Anglican catechisms were replaced by the longer and shorter catechisms of the Westminster Assembly, but in the meantime a very large number of versions had been produced.[34] These varied in size from the 13-question form of the Edwardian Prayer Book, the five pages of D. W., *Certain godlie instructions verie necessarie to be learned by the younger sorte before they be admitted to be partakers of the holie communion* (1580), the seven pages of Christopher Watson's *Brief Principles of Religion for the Exercise of Youth* (1581), the 12 pages of Ezekiel Rogers' *The Chief Grounds of Christian Religion Set Down by Way of Catechizing Gathered long since for the use of an Honourable Family* (1648), the 19 pages of John Stalham's *A Catechism for Children in Yeeres and Children in Understanding Chiefly Intended for their Instruction in Families* (1644), the 26 pages of John Craig's *The Mother and Child. A Short Catechism . . . gathered out of Mr Cragge's Catechisme. . .* (1611), all of which of necessity used the starkly simple form:

Q.   Who made you?
A.   God
Q.   Why did God make you?
A.   To serve Him.

Francis Inman gave a clear indication of his intended users as well as of the scale of the problem when he directed his 10-page catechetical *Light unto the Unlearned or The Principles of the Doctrine of Christ Set down most briefly for the Use of Young and Ignorant Persons* (1622) to the

> many poor servants and labourers, many that are of trades and manual sciences, many aged persons of weak and decayed memories . . . of these, some never learned so much as to read, some very little, and most of them have or will have small leisure to learn long discourses . . . yet all have immortal souls . . . of these care must be had.

In his *Plain Method of Catechizing with a Prefatory Catechism* (1698) Thomas Doolittle recommended to his 'Reverend Brethren' that they distribute the book to their parishioners at 12d, with free copies to the poor, emphasising that it had not been printed in 'smaller print' since this would 'be made useless to the weak eyes of ancient people (whose instruction in catechising I much aim at)'.[35]

The 'long discourses' to which Inman referred usually took the form of an 'exposition' of the catechism's various sections, of which John Mayer's 593-page *English Catechism or A Commentarie on the Short Catechisme Set forth in the Book of Common Prayer . . . Profitable for Ministers in their Churches, for Schoolmasters in their Schools and for Householders in their Families* (1621), and William Slatyer's 743-page *The Complete Christian . . . Delivered in a Plain and Familiar Explication of the Common Catechism for the Benefit of the Younger Sort* (1643) were typical examples. Plainly, however, these assumed a much more sophisticated knowledge of the Bible as well as of doctrine, were obviously intended only for the very literate (and most assiduous) members of the godly community, and were a far cry from the shorter texts which assumed they would be learned by heart as the basic requirement for those wishing to be admitted to the communion table. When the Puritan divine John Ball produced his *Short Catechisme . . . Contayning All the Principal Grounds of Christian Religion* in 1615 he explained that

> our desire herein is to teach the simple Christian how he may grow from grace to grace and from faith to faith, and to further such godly householders as desire to instruct and train up their children and servants in the information and fear of the Lord but want leisure or ability to furnish themselves out of longer and more learned treatises.[36]

Its 246 duodecimo pages nevertheless reached a 54th edition by 1688, despite the appearance of a 20-page abridgement as *A Catechisme Shorter than the Short Catechism Compiled Principally by Mr Ball. . .* in 1649. Richard Greenham was not far short of the mark when he insisted that

> Catechising is the ford wherein a lamb may wade; more exact know-
> ledge is the gulf wherein an elephant may swim . . . children must be
> taught precept by precept, line by line, sometimes in the catechism to
> inform them, sometime in histories to refresh them

and he was perceptive enough to acknowledge the more efficient use of the
Tridentine Catechism by his Catholic opponents: 'if ever they get ground of
us again it will be by their more diligent exacting of their catechising'.[37]
Robert Cawdrey recognised that even the shorter forms of catechism
might still present difficulties, 'especially for the eldest folks and also the
younger sort', and suggested therefore that 'some brief catechism of the
quantity of half a sheet of paper' would provide a better way of starting
instruction, in the hope that the pupil would then progress to one of 'two or
three sheets'. This he indicated would be the province of the householder.
As to the minister in church, he suggested that he should 'ask his people, one
after another, one and the same question, that by so often hearing of it they
may the more easily conceive it by heart'. In addition, reinforcement could
be achieved 'by asking them suddenly out of order which is the sixth, the
tenth, the fourth commandment . . . and also backwards and forwards in
the questions'. At all times, moreover, ministers should avoid speaking 'like
parrots and poppinjays in words without understanding'.[38] Stephen Egerton
shared Cawdrey's misgivings, and in his *Briefe Methode of Catechising*, a
52-page duodecimo volume, he provided, alongside a 19-page catechism,
a 7-page abbreviation and a 1-page 'brief summary wherein the former
40 questions and answers are brought to four'. Setting out his catechism
in a particular way:

Q	How did God make man?	Man:
A	He made man, both male and female, in a most happy estate, according to his own image, in perfect knowledge and righteousness.	Col. 3.10 Eph. 4.24
Q	Did man thus made continue in this blessed estate?	Man's fall:
A	No: they fell from it and became most cursed and miserable creatures.	Gen 3.12 Eccles. 7.31

he nevertheless added:

> I would advise thee, Christian Reader, to reform the common fault,
> and with all care and diligence to turn to the places which are noted,
> that thy faith and conscience may be grounded not upon the speeches
> of men, but upon the words of the Holy Ghost.

Egerton supplemented his catechisms with an 11-page 'Form of examining such as are to receive the Lord's Supper', and a 6-page 'Another familiar means of instruction, the most plain and easy of all the rest, which parents and masters may with great fruit propound to their families, especially before the communion' which had a running heading 'A familiar instruction for children'. First entered in the Stationers' Register in 1593, Egerton's *vade mecum* became one of the most popular of catechetical helps, reaching a 44th edition by 1644, combining as it did a reasonably orthodox content with a precise awareness that a wide variety of ages and intelligences needed their own particular provision. Towards the end of the century the anonymous author of *The Art of Catechising or The Compleat Catechist* (1691) divided his text into four parts: I The Church Catechism resolved into easy questions; II An Exposition of it in a continued, full and plain discourse; III The Church Catechism resolved into scripture proofs; and IV The Whole Duty of Man reduced to questions to be answered by a single Yes or No, 'fitted for the meanest capacities, the weakest memories, the plainest teachers and the most uninstructed learners'.[39]

As a method of religious education 'catechising' has to be considered with extreme care, in view of the wide range of those in need of such education – 'children in years and children in understanding' – and the wide variety and level of texts made available for use outside of church. As a method, rote memory (with all its acknowledged disadvantages) was plainly relied on for oral instruction through the shorter texts. The larger texts, designed to be read and inwardly digested, required more than basic literacy plus a reasonable degree of religious understanding on the part of the reader. As we shall see however, catechising, at whatever level, continued to be a favoured method of instruction, whether 'by heart' or 'by head'.

EXAMPLE AND EXEMPLARS

In the family setting, direct attention was paid to the fact that 'religious education' consisted not simply of 'religious knowledge' – of the Ten Commandments, the Lord's Prayer, the Creed and the sacraments – but also of everyday 'religious behaviour', the Christian virtues which were expressed in the multitude of conduct books and 'Advices', and which were to be the immediate end-product of all public and private worship and prayer, reading and exhortation. At the same time it was clearly recognised that Christian action was in the end public action, and that this entailed a political dimension. Prayers for the sovereign and others in authority, and sermons on obedience and against 'wilful rebellion' were supplemented and reinforced in the familial catechisms by the glosses on the Fifth Commandment ('Honour thy father and thy mother') which were precise and explicit in emphasising that 'honour' was due to all those 'set in authority above us', including the Crown, the magistracy, the clergy, schoolmasters and 'our elders'.

It was for this reason that a major aspect of the kind of religious education which made use of a non-literary method was the common emphasis on example on the part of parents and teachers. In their sections on the duties of parents in the religious education of their children, marriage and householder manuals frequently urged parents to ensure that in their own behaviour they gave their children no improper signals. Children's powers of imitation and identification, it was argued, could be applied to that which was considered to be proper as well as to that which was considered improper. In his *The Education or Bringing up of Children translated out of Plutarche* (1533), which he wrote (as he said) for the benefit of his sister Margery Puttenham, Sir Thomas Elyot insisted that

> Above all things it is most expedient that the fathers be a true example to their children, not only in doing none evil but doing many good acts and faites, that beholding their father's lives as it were in a mirror, the children may eschew all foul or unseemly act or word.[40]

Among the clerics Bullinger was certainly not alone in reminding parents that their 'godly and honest conversation in the presence of their children [will] teach them more virtues and good ways than their words. For words although they may do much, yet shall good examples of living do more.'

For Robert Cleaver, 'verbal instruction without example of good deeds is dead doctrine'. William Gouge likewise insisted that 'Example is a real instruction and addeth a sharp edge to admonition.' Reflecting on current belief, George Herbert was sure that children were 'moulded more by example of parents than by stars at their nativity'.[41] The schoolmaster William Kempe, likening a child to an empty vessel which was 'most apt to receive that which is first taught, and that stickest deepest in memory whether it be good or bad', went on to point out:

> The parent's first care is, so soon as his child beginneth to speak, to provide that he use none other company than such as are both honest and civil, as well in behaviour as in language. He shall therefore seclude his child from barbarous nurses, clownish playmates and all rustical persons; neither shall he himself speak in the hearing of the child either wantonly or otherwise any rude or barbarous speech, much less shall he teach him any lewd or unhonest talk, as many do.[42]

Robert Bolton similarly noted that 'children are ordinarily apt, out of kindly instinct and natural lovingness, from many and strong motives to imitate and follow their parents either in baseness or better carriage to Heaven or Hell'. Thomas Hilder contrasted the relative efficacy of precept and example with the warning that

> if this be done only by precept and not by example, there is small hope of doing them any good, for a man may teach his child or servant the way to Heaven by precept and the way to Hell by example.[43]

As always, parents came in for a good deal of criticism in this matter. 'Where,' asked Laurence Chaderton, 'be those parents and masters which do teach in their families unto their children and servants the love and fear of God, walking in the midst of their houses in uprightness of heart?' Edward Hake was more peremptory: 'Children by their nature are evil, and being evil they are by the example of their parents made worse'.[44] Hezekiah Woodward was more considered, but equally critical:

> Now must parents be doing, if they will evidence their care; and now they must consider well what they do. The child imitates strangely; it is taken like an ape wholly by example. The parent's practice (I mean the parent at large, him or her that have oversight of it) is the child's book, it learns by it, so it speaks, so it hears, it is fashioned after it, it is catechized by it. It is its school and church. The parent's house must promote the child in point of information, more than can a school or church ... Yet parents be too ready to refer all thither, and so put off from themselves ... The parent commonly doth just nothing, the master must do all, look to the child's book and manners both.

John Donne on the other hand tended to be more optimistic: 'as your sons write by copies and your daughters by samplers, be every father a copy to his son and every mother a sampler to her daughter, and every house will be a university'.[45]

Some parents were, however, well aware of the complex processes of identification. In 1570 Walter Mildmay wrote to his son, Anthony, 'Beware what thou sayest and doest in thine own house, for thy example is a guide to thy wife, children and family.' In a letter of advice to his son, Sir Henry Slingsby reminded him that 'though precepts induce, examples draw, and more danger there is in a personal example than any doctrinal motive'. He went on:

> Return my blessing to your sister, my dear Bab, and tell her from a

dying father that she needs no other example than from her virtuous mother for all her directory, in whose steps I am confident she will walk religiously. Her modest, blameless demeanour can promise nothing less.

In a letter to his friend Robert Busby in 1649 concerning the education of their sons, Sir Ralph Verney averred in much the same way that 'a father's good example will doubtless prevail much with him and all other good children'.[46]

It was for this reason, too, that manuals constantly warned parents of the possible deleterious effect that the behavioural example of servants could have on their young children. Thomas Salter, for example, in his *Mirrhour Mete for all Mothers and Matrones* ... (1579) urged his readers to ensure that they 'shall in no wise permit them to have acquaintance with kitchen servants or such idle housewives as commonly of custom do thrust themselves into the familiarity of those of "good calling". The 1598 English translation of Bruto's *La Instituione di una Fanciulla Nata Nobilemente* (1565) made much the same point:

> always be wary ... that she be not acquainted with maids, servants and other prating women ... staying by the fire to hear their tales and prating speeches ... Be careful to follow the steps not only of her betters but also (which is of much more importance) of the wise and virtuous, and not of her inferiors, like fools and those that have no understanding.[47]

The lawyer John Hoskyns wrote 'A Note to Instruct the Servants' for his clerk William Taylor, in which he ordered that they should 'In no case speak any lewd word before my children'. Grace Mildmay reported that she had been warned by her parents, Sir Henry and Lady Anne Sherrington, that she should shun the serving men of the household, 'whose ribald talk and idle gestures and evil suggestions were dangerous for our chaste ears and eyes to hear and behold'. John Donne had considered it his good fortune that his parents 'would not give me over to servants' correction'.[48] Brilliana Harley, on the other hand, expressed her concern for the influences her young son Robin was being subjected to by spending too much time with the servants of her household. Elizabeth Walker was obviously quick to see the danger, her husband recalling that she 'would strictly charge the servants not to teach her children foolish stories or teach them idle songs which might tincture their fancies with vain or hurtful imaginations', a view shared by Roger North, who noted in his autobiography that his mother had ensured that her children picked up 'no ill habits by conversing with servants'.[49]

The difficulty, as John Earle pointed out, was that 'Nature and his parents alike dandle him and 'tice him with a bait of sugar and a draught of wormwood',[50] a criticism which is to be found echoed in the innumerable texts which deplored the habit of parents of young girls in spending time and money on preparing them for the niceties of the *beau monde* at the expense of their religious and moral formation. The citing of what we would now call role models was therefore, in the early modern period, a common feature of all kinds of prescriptive literature. From the Ancient World the fortitude and wifely faithfulness of Penelope and the patience of Griselda were constantly reported; from the Bible itself the helping Lydia, the chaste Susannah, the judicial Deborah, the housewifely Martha, the pious Mary, sister of Martha, the steadfast Mary Magdalene and, above all, the Blessed Virgin Mary, were all called to bear witness to the Christian virtues which were considered to be especially appropriate for women and girls to copy. *The Golden Legend* was replaced by the Book of Martyrs and later by Samuel Clarke's biographical volumes. As Foxe himself put it in his preface:

> so by reading this we are better made in our own livings, and besides are better prepared unto like conflicts . . . more wisely by their doctrine and more steadfast by their example. To be short, they declare to the world what true Christian fortitude is and what is the right way to conquer.[51]

The poets too recognised the power of example as part of religious and moral education. George Puttenham, for instance, was of the opinion that 'No kind of argument in all the oratory craft doth better persuade and more universally satisfy than example.' Edmund Spenser made a similar point in his letter to Sir Walter Raleigh, prefacing *The Faerie Queen* (1590, 1596):

> The general end therefore of all the book is to fashion a gentleman or noble person in virtuous and gentle discipline . . . In which I have followed all the antique poets historical, first Homer who in the persons of Agamemnon and Ulysses hath ensampled a good governour and a virtuous man . . . then Virgil whose like intention was to do in the person of Aeneas; after him Ariosto comprised them both in his Orlando, and lately Tasso discovered them again . . . To some I know this method will seem displeasant, which had rather have good discipline delivered plainly in way of precepts, or sermoned at large, as they use, than thus cloudily enwrapped in allegorical devices. [However] . . . So much more profitable and gracious is doctrine by example, than by rule. So I have laboured to do in the person of Arthur.

Thomas Heywood aimed at a wider audience but used the same method in his *Gunaikeion* (1624), which comprised 'a collection of histories [as he described them] which touch the generality of women . . . their virtues and noble actions . . . their vices and baser conditions . . . of all degrees'.[52]

But the ancient past was not the only source of such exemplars. The seventeenth-century practice of preaching funeral sermons continued to make use of the method. Some preachers put forward arguments for refusing to make mention of the lives of the deceased person as an appendix to their exposition of a text considered appropriate to the occasion. Most however did and, in offering a potted biography at the conclusion of the sermon, drew the attention of the congregation to the exemplary passages in the life of the deceased, urging them to follow a similar path. Samuel Clarke reinforced the message by including the funeral sermon details of a dozen women, including that of his own wife, in his *Lives of Sundry Eminent Persons . . .* (1683).

Thomas Gataker was one such preacher, reminding his hearers at the funeral of Mrs Rebecca Crisp that:

> Good examples (as the heathen man observeth) are of great force and are therefore (not without cause) so frequently expounded in God's Word. They prevail oft more than precepts. Precepts show us what we should do. Examples go further and show us how we may do it.[53]

Arthur Ducke explained in a prefatory letter to William Gouge, who had preached the funeral sermon for Ducke's wife Margaret, that he wished the sermon to be printed 'whereby I may more easily transmit it to our two children to remain with them . . . which will, I hope, raise in them by God's grace a desire of imitation of the piety and virtues of their mother'.[54]

AMBIENCE: PUNISHMENT AND REWARD

Repetition, practice and example were, then, crucial aspects of the oral education of girls and women, whether literate or not. Equally important for the efficiency with which these techniques were implemented was the ambience in which the learning took place, and this in turn depended, as we have seen, on particular views of the nature of childhood. Plainly, a teacher or parent who believed that some degree of pleasure on the part of the child would maximise the efficiency of his or her teaching and of the child's learning, would have different attitudes to matters such as repetition, discipline, rewards and punishment, from those who did not.

As always, those in authority found themselves confronted with justification for procedure in the matter selected from biblical texts. Most frequently cited were those from the Book of Proverbs itself: 'He that spareth the rod, hateth his son; but he that loveth him chastiseth him betimes' (13.24); 'Chastise thy son while there is hope, and let not thy soul spare for his crying' (19.18); 'Withhold not correction from the child for if thou beatest him with the rod he shall not die. Thou shalt beat him with the rod, and shalt deliver his soul from Hell' (23.13–14); 'Foolishness is bound in the heart of the child; but the rod of correction shall drive it far from him' (22.15); 'The rod and reproof give wisdom, but a child left to himself bringeth his mother to shame' (29.15).

With biblical exculpation such as this it is not surprising that 'correction' featured largely in the prescriptive texts, and that clergy took one or other as texts for their sermons. Thomas Cogan, in his *Well of Wisdome* (1577), used the terminology of Proverbs 23.13–14. Williame Kempe included 22.15 and 29.15 on the title page of his *Education of Children in Learning* (1588). Writing to his wife from prison in 1593, John Penry urged her to have great care for the religious upbringing of their young children with the injunction

> Break their affections while they are yet green, by instructions out of the Word, and corrections meet for them. Yet you know that parents must not be bitter unto their children, especially Snib, not the eldest [Deliverance] because you know the least word will restrain her.

The memorialist of John Bruen similarly reported that Bruen, master of a very large and godly household in Cheshire, 'did not spare to use the rod of correction as God's healing medicine to cure the corruptions of children and to heal their souls of their sins by the same'.[55] When she was pregnant and fearing for her life, Elizabeth Jocelin wrote her *Mothers Legacie* (1624). Her prefatory letter to her husband urged him 'and dear love, as thou must be the overseer, for God's sake, when it [the forthcoming child] shall fail in duty to God or the world, let not thy indulgence wink at such folly, but severely correct it'. Samuel Clarke reported that his wife Katherine was 'not sparing of the rod when there was just occasion'.[56]

Though such actions and their biblical justifications could be cited many times over, this was not the whole story by any means. Sir Thomas Elyot argued for the use of a light touch in the matter of correction:

> I will not that parents should be sharp or hard to their children, but sometimes to remit or forgive the offences past, and to remember their own fragility and youth, like as a physician do mix better medicines

with delectable liquors, finding the means to join pleasure with profit . . . By such means the wildness of youth, like a colt wisely wayed and broken, is made gentle and sober.[57]

Thomas Becon's *Catechism* warned parents that in correcting their children they ought to be 'gentle and favourable', and always willing to couch explanations of their actions in terms of a transgression of God's Commandments and an assurance of their affection: 'Punish according to the fault and also according to the nature of the child . . . for some are brought as soon to amendment by words as by stripes'.[58] In 'A compendious form of education' appended to his *A Touchestone for This Time Present* (1574) Edward Hake resorted to verse to make his point:

Nay, let our rods that we shall use
Be admonitions mild;
And if we chide, as chide we must,
See bitterness exiled.[59]

Despite his title page, in his text William Kempe enjoined the master to make sure that he 'punish according to the fault', using admonition and rebuke before resorting to the rod, and using a range of punishments such as 'restraining that liberty of recreation which otherwise would have been granted' or 'sometimes by service of drudgery as maybe the sweeping of the school'. He concluded that 'Generally of all these corrections none may be differed when it is fit time, none executed before due time', the aim always being to 'allure scholars to virtue and to drive them from vice, sometime the one, sometime the other . . . [like] the cunning physician that tempereth his bitter medicine with sweet and pleasant drink'.[60] The author of *The Education of Young Gentlewomen* (1598), translating Bruto, offered much the same advice, insisting that if correction were felt to be in order then 'let it be done with mildness than with vigour', with beating regarded as 'a beastly and inconvenient kind of correction'.[61] Addressing her *Mothers Blessing* (1636) to her sons George, John and William, their father being dead, Dorothy Leigh entreated them to bring up their children with 'much gentleness and patience. What disposition soever they be of, gentleness will soonest bring them to virtue; for forwardness and curtness doth harden the heart of a child, and maketh him weary of virtue'.[62] William Perkins was careful to remind his reader-parents that

the first instruction of children in learning and religion must be so ordered that they may take it with delight, for which purpose they may be somehow allowed in moderate manner to play and solace themselves in recreation fitting to their years.

Robert Codrington was addressing both governesses and mothers when he insisted 'taunts are for fools and blows for beasts that understand not reason'. Henry Newcome recounted in his autobiography that he had once dreamed of striking one of his children in anger: 'I was much ashamed at it, but glad it was but a dream. But I desire to take warning hereinby.' Even the conservative Richard Allestree moderated his prescriptions:

> To this great duty of education of children there is required as means, first encouragement, secondly correction . . . When all fair means, persuasions and encouragements prevail not . . . first tried in words . . . but that prevail not, then proceed to blows . . . Proverbs 13.24 . . . but correction must be moderate . . . not given in rage.[63]

On the other hand, the commonplace Old Testament attitudes to children, especially those of the poor, remained a force in the writings of the end of the century, as for example in Bishop White Kennett's reminder to his Charity School sermon congregation: 'Children are made tractable and submissive by being early accustomed to awe and punishment and dutiful subjection. From such timely discipline the public may expect honest and industrious servants.' Though Susannah Wesley had obviously no expectation of such a life course for her large brood, the educational regime she initiated and presided over in the Anglican parsonage at Epworth was not much different in its ambience.[64]

WHEN?

With all these various forms of instruction available to those godly persons who wished to benefit from them, the question remains, when was this religious education to start in a child's life? When, for example, might it be expected that a child should be taught to read the Bible and other godly books? When should catechising start? When should a child begin to prepare or be prepared for the partaking of the sacraments? In the early modern period, as now, there were no agreed answers to these questions, but debated they were, as constituting a crucial stage in the life-long religious education of the flock.

Though primarily concerned to argue for the liberal education of the young nobleman, Erasmus made plain in his *De Pueris Instituendis* (1529) the absolute necessity of beginning religious and moral education as soon after birth as possible. Using metaphors, commonplace in classical authors, that continued to be used throughout the early modern period, he urged:

Press wax while it is softest; model clay while it is still moist; pour precious liquids only into a jar that has never been used before; and only dye wool that has just arrived spotless from the fullers.

Moreover, he continued, parental example was crucial in the early years of infancy:

Nature has given small children as a special gift the ability to imitate; but the urge to imitate evil is considerably stronger that the urge to imitate the good ... After all, nothing clings more tenaciously than something that is poured into empty minds.

It was for these reasons, then, that

Children are taught these first beginnings of good behaviour and proper devotion before they can even speak; these principles remain with them into adulthood and contribute in no small way to the growth of true spirituality ... Goodness, then, is best instilled at an early age, for once a certain pattern of behaviour has been imprinted on a young and receptive mind that pattern will remain ... As soon as a child is born he is ready for instruction in right conduct, and as soon as he is able to speak he is ready for learning his letters.[65]

The early reformers continued to insist that a child should be introduced as early as possible to the prayers of the primer and to biblical passages. Bullinger, for example, recommended parents to 'teach them first certain godly sentences though they yet cannot understand them, yet let them commend them to memory and practise them in speech', and went on to provide a long list of appropriate examples, such as 'Without God there is nothing good' and 'God loveth virtue and hateth vice'.[66] Richard Greenham reminded his readers that Hannah delivered her son Samuel to Heli, the father of Joseph, Mary's husband, for instruction as soon as he was weaned (I Samuel). Thomas Burroughs urged parents to 'do it betimes ... [for] we know not how soon God may be pleased to work upon the hearts of our children, even the youngest of them'.[67]

Food metaphors also played an important part in persuading parents of the importance of early religious upbringing. The *virgo lactans* motif of Renaissance painting was carried over into the prescriptive literature of education, typified by works such as Robert Abbot's *Milk for Babes Drawn out of the Breasts of Both Testaments* (1646). But the metaphor was used throughout the sermon literature of the period, as for example by Henry Smith, using I Peter 2.2 as the text for his 1592 sermon 'Food for new-born babes':

First, because it is the only food of the faithful, as milk is the only proper food for babes. Secondly, because it is not hard and intricate, but plain and easy to be conceived as milk is easy to be digested. Thirdly, because it is sweet and comfortable to the soul, as milk is sweet and pleasant in taste.[68]

William Perkins, *The Art of Prophesying* (1607), John Syme, *The Sweet Milk of Christian Doctrine* (1617), William Crashaw, *Milk for Babes or A North Country Catechism* (1618), John Phillips, *The Way to Heaven* (1625) and James Naylor, *Milk for Babes and Strong Men* (1661) all utilised the same metaphor, as did Peter Sterry in his exhortation to his son Peter at Emmanuel College, Cambridge:

Lay the mouth of your soul by faith to the breasts of the Godhead laid forth in Christ, swelling with all fullness, longing, delighting to be drawn, yea, of their own accord sprouting forth their milky stores unto your face and bosom.

In a more reticent way, Lady Anne Clifford recalled that 'By the bringing up of my said dear mother, I did, as it were, even suck the dear milk of goodness which made my mind strong against the storms of fortune.'[69]

Texts for the guidance of 'all Christian householders', marriage treatises with their comprehensive coverage of the duties of both husbands and wives, even the later marriage sermons, all stress the importance of starting the religious education of children in the early stages of infancy, though of course differing in their emphases. Richard Whitford's *Werke for Householders* (1530) insisted on the need for early attention to the matter by recommending that 'as soon as they can speak, let them first learn to serve God and say the Pater Noster, Ave and Creed', though an earlier work, *The Ordynary of Chrysten Men* (1506), was careful to point out that 'some would learn more at the age of four or five than others would at seven and eight'. William Perkins used a different criterion by urging parents 'to sow the seeds of godliness and religion in the heart of the child so soon as it comes to the use of reason and understanding', with the reminder (on another occasion) that:

It is not sufficient to say all these [The Ten Commandments] without book unless you can understand the meaning of the words, and be able to make a right use of the Commandments, of the Creed, of the Lord's Prayer by applying them inwardly to your hearts and consciences, and outwardly to your lives and conversations.[70]

Thomas Gataker, however, felt bound to insist that:

It is an idle conceit of many that godliness and religion is not for children, that some things concern them not. There is no age freed from it . . . It is a general and fatal mistake that we believe children incapable of understanding till they have some proportion of reason as to understand what is good and what is ill.

Yet Thomas Hooker was equally sure of the opposite view:

for a child to consider the mysteries of life and salvation is almost impossible; he is not yet come to that ripeness of judgement of his years from 20 years until he come to be 40 or thereabouts when the works of reason put forth themselves. Then his apprehension is quick to conceive a thing and his memory is strong and pregnant to retain a thing apprehended.[71]

Many parents nevertheless reported with pride, or at least satisfaction, on the ability of their young children to read or to recite passages of the Bible or their catechism by heart. Dorothy Leigh advised mothers 'that all your children may be taught to read beginning at four years old or before, and let them learn until ten'. Oliver Heywood reported that his wife was 'able at six years of age to write down passages of the sermon in the chapel', whilst the memorialist of William Gouge's wife Elizabeth reported that she taught her children

so soon as they were capable, the principles of religion wherein some of them so profited as before they were three years old they were able distinctly to answer all the questions of a catechism which her husband published.

Elizabeth Walker taught her children to read 'as soon as they could pronounce their letters, yea before they could speak plain', and her daughter Mary was able to read the psalms and learn passages from the Bible before she died aged 6. Anne, daughter of Quaker Thomas Gwin of Falmouth, was a good reader by the time she was 3½, wrote tolerably well before she was 5 and in her 'teens wrote her own prayers. She died in 1715 aged 23.[72]

But, as always, the problems of learning by heart or by head were well recognised. John Donne for example, in a sermon preached at Paul's Cross in 1622, told the story of a young girl, 'not above nine years of age', who was brought to him:

we could scarce propose any verse of any book or chapter of the Bible but that the child could go forward without book. I began to catechise the child and truly she understood nothing of the Trinity, nothing of any of those fundamental points which must save us, and the wonder was doubled how she knew so much, how so little.

Whether or not many adults would have 'understood' the Trinity, learning by heart must have caused many situations such as the one described by Donne, perhaps not surprisingly when such as William Charcke could insist 'so needful a thing it is in religion often to beat in the first grounds', a practice which could produce many who could 'say the catechism . . . without piercing into the sense of it', as George Herbert had reason to complain.[73]

Much the same point was made by the puritan divine John Rogers when he spurred on his congregation with the words 'But do you believe and cannot prove it?', that is, identify and justify one's belief by reference to an appropriate biblical proof-text, insisting that 'scripture knowledge' was merely a means to an end and not an end in itself. George Abbot, speaking in the Court of High Commission, voiced a view which many clergy, puritan as well as Anglican, would have echoed, when he insisted, using Matthew 15.14, 'when you have reading, preaching, singing, teaching, you are your own ministers; the blind lead the blind'.[74] Yet, though puritans would have accepted the first of these assertions they would mostly have denied the second, claiming that on the contrary the whole educative aim of such activities would lead to *clarity* of vision.

Any consideration of the 'how?' and 'when?' of education inevitably leads to an awareness of the complexities of language use and the difficulties involved in measuring levels of understanding, *a fortiori* when the education of a largely illiterate community is attempted. 'Knowing' the catechism, for example, often meant nothing more than 'saying' it, repeating the answers provided, and going no further than 'the elements' – the Lord's Prayer, the Ten Commandments and the Creed. Donne's young girl 'knew' her scriptures, but would not be alone in her inability to interpret the text, least of all to offer doctrinal justification. The distinction between indoctrination and education has remained to plague educators,[75] despite their insistence that understanding remained their chief aim. Stanley Fish's exploration of the meaning of the notice 'Private Members Only' at the Johns Hopkins University Club produced no problem of interpretation for the members of that community, but a wide variety of meanings, legitimate but mostly ribald, from his undergraduate class.[76] When the language of religion caused so many problems for early modern divines it is not surprising that the laity shared their difficulties. Archbishop Abbot would certainly have categorised Erasmus as too 'bold' when the latter asserted in the preface to his 1516 edition of the New Testament that 'only a few can be learned, but all can be Christians, and all can be devout, and – I shall boldly add – all can be theologians'.[77]

4 Women as recipients

THE FAMILY AND RELIGIOUS EDUCATION

Controlling the clergy by licensing and visitation was difficult enough, but controlling what went on in private, albeit godly, houses, even when restricted to immediate members of the family, was seen by the establishment as a matter of grave concern, especially when it became clear that some of the godly were allowing others, not members of the household, to join in the praying and reading and, more dangerously, in discussion of the scriptures' meaning in a quite heterodox way. The enjoinder of Matthew 18.20 notwithstanding, for some of the more conservative godly the family and its religious life was seen not as an essential part of the education of the flock, but as a conventicle, potentially subversive of that Christian faith 'now truly set forth by public authority', to say nothing of a challenge to the status of the ordained and licensed clergy. In 1520 'seven godly martyrs' were burned in Coventry for teaching their children and family the Lord's Prayer and Ten Commandments in English, and John Foxe made much of such attacks on familial religious education in his Book of Martyrs.[1] Tyndale's denial that a vernacular Bible would inevitably cause insurrection was repeated by Thomas Lever in 1550.[2] Even so, Whitgift's Articles of 1584 insisted that 'all preaching, reading, catechising and other suchlike exercises in private places and families whereunto others do resort being not of the same family be utterly inhibited', and considered such practices to be a 'manifest sign of schism and a cause of contention in the church'. Queen Elizabeth herself noted with irritation that

> every merchant must have his schoolmaster and nightly conventicles, expounding scriptures and catechizing their servants and maids, in so much that I have heard how some maids have not sticked to control learned readers and say 'such a man taught otherwise in our house'.

George Abbot had in mind Jesus' criticism of the scribes and pharisees, as reported in Matthew 15.4, when, in the Court of High Commission, he expostulated 'when you have reading, preaching, singing, teaching, you are your own ministers; the blind lead the blind'.[3] As in any ideology-ruled group, the problem of heterodoxy was perennial. Indeed, as Eamon Duffy has reminded us, heresy has been as traditional in the Christian church as orthodoxy.

But the dilemma took a particularly acute form in the Protestant churches with the problem of how to control the newly won freedom of a 'priesthood of all believers', whose individual members faced their own personal conflict between an instinctive, aggressive wish for autonomy, with its consequent threat to personal stability, and a wish for authority figures to carry out their nurturant and protective function through a process of passive gratification rather than rational acceptance after due consideration of all the possibilities. Milton's 'licence they mean when they cry liberty' had clearly been recognised a century earlier, for example by Nicholas Ridley: 'for the Christian, liberty is not licence to do what thou list'.[4] What started as a freedom movement – freedom from the Pope and from the priest as a necessary intermediary in the spiritual life of the flock – soon became one of strict control at all levels of society. 'Conferring' within the family was accepted, indeed enjoined from the 1536 Injunctions onwards. But when others were invited to join in the 'exercises', the meeting became a 'conventicle' not conducive to church unity and requiring the intervention of the 'apparitor' and possible appearances before an ecclesiastical court.[5] For example, in 1587 John Leeche, the puritan schoolmaster of Hornchurch in Essex, was hauled before the archdeacon's court, and not for the first time, on the grounds that 'He useth to catechise or preach in his own house every Sabbath day, whereunto others resorteth, not being of his family.' John Etherington was similarly charged before the Court of High Commission. He denied the charge but admitted that he was 'always ready to speak to my neighbour and friend and children whatsoever I have known and understood of the Word and ways of God'. The Reverend Oliver Heywood recalled how his father

> associated himself with God's people, promoted days of fasting and of prayer, conference and other Christian exercise. In my childhood I can remember many days of that nature, and the apparitor searching them out, and one appointed in the entry to deafen the noise of such as were praying in the parlour.[6]

Thomas Knyvett reported to his wife with disapproval the occurrence of 'conventicles every night in Norwich, as publicly known as sermons in the daytime, and they say much more frequently'. Samuel Clarke remembered that, when he was a minister at Shotwick in Cheshire, every three weeks 'all the professors both men and women' would assemble in a circuit of 'all the rich men's houses' for a day of 'prayer, discussion of some particular question, and especially the instruction and testing of the younger sort'.[7]

Even so, it was generally recognised that religious education could and should take place in the familial situation, though always as a supplement to the primary place of instruction, the parish church. From Tyndale's *Obedience of the Christian Man* (1528) onwards, royal and diocesan injunctions were reinforced by prescriptive treatises dealing with the duties of the various members of a household, which included the religious education of children and servants as part of 'the office and duty' of the father and mother. Occasionally, the more explicit 'fathers and mothers both' was used. William Caxton's *Boke of Good Manners* (1487) had a section 'How the father and the mother ought to teach their children'. In the preface to his *New Catechisme* (1560) Thomas Becon referred to both parents, though the ensuing dialogue is between father and son. Bullinger went into detail:

> Let both the father and the mother at home privately do their endeavours to teach their children the Ten Commandments, the Apostles' Creed and the Lord's Prayer, and let them teach a brief and ready rule out of the scriptures for the understanding of the sacraments. Let them many times and often cause them to repeat the catechism, and beat into their heads such sentences as are most necessary to put them in memory of their faith and duty of life.

The subsequent sections, however, started with 'Let the father . . .', though in his *Childes Patrimony* (1640) Hezekiah Woodward was careful to point out that 'I mean the parent at large, him or her who have oversight of it'.[8] Though more often than not, the term 'parents' is replaced after a page or two by 'fathers', 'householders' or 'masters of the household', William Perkins was not alone in reminding his readers that the family was 'the seminary of all other societies . . . the school wherein are taught and learned the principles of authority and subjection'[9] and there is no shortage of prescriptive evidence about 'parents' (in the plural) and their roles and responsibilities in the education of their children, whether in liturgies, canons, injunctions, sermons, prayers or didactic treatises about and for the family. Robert Cleaver was repeating a commonplace when he insisted:

> For although there never be so good laws in cities, never so pure order in churches, yet if masters of families do not practise at home, catechising and disciplining in their houses and joining helping hands to

magistrates and ministers, they may in truth (but unjustly as many have done) complain that their children and servants are disordered and corrupted abroad, when in truth, they were disordered and corrupted and marred at home.

Josias Nichols, again, was recommending a thoroughly traditional menu when he urged his readers, the heads of households, to spend two hours per week 'to instruct your children and servants' by starting with 'some short stories or sentences of holy scripture', which would then be followed with a stint of catechising and of 'interpretations' of biblical passages.[10] George Webbe was similarly explicit:

> In the evening . . . cause thine households to come together, then either read thyself or cause some of thy family to read something out of the Bible or out of some godly book, expounding the same. Examine thy family in that which they hear read, catechize them in the principles of religion, sing psalms together with them to God's glory. So shalt thou find the evening thus spent in this kind of exercises will bring them much more joy and comfort to thine heart than spending the evening in cards, dice and other kinds of gaming wherein worldlings do take their felicity.

In 1655 Richard Baxter was still making the same point about the efficacy of household instruction when he advised ministers to

> get masters of families to their duties and they will spare you a great deal of labour with the rest and further the success of your labour . . . you are like to see no general reformation until you procure family reformation.[11]

Baxter's comment implied a certain neglect on the part of householders, and of course he was not alone in his criticism, though not surprisingly the families of ministers provide examples of positive instruction. John Carter kept a household which his son described as 'a little seminary' where thrice daily he gathered around him his wife, children and servants to read to them from the scriptures. Oliver Heywood reported in his diary that 'my sons have very towardly plied their books, read chapters, learned catechisms, got some chapters and psalms without book. John repeated the 12th, Eliezer the 10th of Revelation last night in bed, blessed be God'. It would be reasonable to suppose that he would have been similarly assiduous had he had daughters. Heywood also left a detailed account of how his father-in-law, John Angier, led his family and his 'tablers' in daily religious exercises.[12]

The godly households of Herbert Palmer, Thomas Gataker and Thomas Cawton similarly saw a good deal of pious instruction. Of the women of the Henry family we shall be hearing something later, but plainly Philip Henry played a large part in the religious upbringing of his two sons and four daughters.[13]

But clerical households held no monopoly of such activities. Though Erasmus likened Sir Thomas More's household to Plato's Academy he nevertheless continued, 'But I do the house injury in likening it to Plato's Academy. I should rather call it a school or university of Christian religion ... Their special care is piety and virtue' – and it was here that More's daughters Margaret, Elizabeth and Cecily, his niece Frances Staverton, as well as his ward and subsequent daughter-in-law Anne Cresacre and his adopted daughter Margaret Giggs, were educated.[14] The house of Sir Nathaniel Barnardiston, Kedlington Hall in Suffolk, was described by the family chaplain, Samuel Fairclough, as 'a spiritual church and temple wherein were daily offered up the spiritual sacrifices of reading the Word, of prayer morning and evening, or singing psalms constantly after the evening meal'. Robert Rich, second Earl of Warwick, whose appetite for sermon-going was well known in his day, ensured that his own household 'heard the most useful and powerful sermons upon the most useful and practical points of divinity, and had Sunday sermons repeated in his presence to the whole family'.[15] John Bruen's memorialist reported that he made his house at Bruen Stapleford in Cheshire into 'a little Bethel, a house of God', where he and his wife catechised their children, and where 'family exercises in religious duties [were] like putting on and bucklering unto us the whole armour of God', with morning and evening prayers, psalm-singing and Bible-reading regularly engaged in. At the same time he

> set upon a desk both in his hall and in his parlour two goodly fair Bibles of the best editions and largest volume (as they were printed, some in larger and some in lesser folios) and these he placed to be continual residentiaries, the bigger in the parlour and the lesser in the hall.[16]

Sir Robert Brooke brought his wife, family and servants to the parish church of Yoxford in Suffolk for the Sunday service, held a 'repetition' of the sermon at home that evening, insisted on daily prayers morning and evening with readings from the scriptures, and engaged a catechist to come to the house fortnightly. Sir John Holland kept a similarly pious regime, though in his case his main motivation seems to have been a wish to maintain a strict control over the influence of his Catholic wife Alethea on their daughter Catherine. Sir John Hartopp took shorthand notes of the sermon each Sunday so that he could repeat its message to his family thereafter.[17]

In the more affluent households, a domestic chaplain would be charged not only with leading family worship but also with the religious education of the children and servants. Richard Whitford was an early example as chaplain in the household of William Blount, fourth Lord Mountjoy, the patron of Erasmus, as were William Tyndale, tutor to the children of Sir John and Lady Anne Walsh of Old Sodbury in Gloucestershire, Alexander Seton and John Parkhurst in the late 1530s and early 1540s in the family of Charles Brandon, Duke of Suffolk, and on the latter's death in the household of Catherine Parr.[18] John Aylmer was responsible, as chaplain in the household at Bradgate in Essex of his patron Henry Grey, Marquis of Dorset and later Duke of Suffolk, for the tutoring of Jane Grey who reported to Roger Ascham that her tutor 'teacheth me so gently, so pleasantly, with such allurements to learning', in direct contrast to the rather harsh treatment she received from her mother and father.[19] John Foxe started his career after university as tutor to Thomas, the son of Sir William and Lady Anne Lucy, and subsequently to Thomas, Jane and Charles Howard, the children of Frances, widow of Henry Howard, Earl of Surrey, after the latter's execution for treason in 1547, when they were put in the care of Mary Fitzroy, Duchess of Richmond, Surrey's sister. It was to Thomas that Foxe dedicated the 1559 Latin edition of the *Book of Martyrs*.[20] At another social level Samuel Fairclough, domestic chaplain to the Barnardiston family of Kedlington Hall in Suffolk, recalled the piety of Sir Nathaniel Barnardiston, who had

> at any one time ten or more servants of the eminency for piety and sincerity that I never saw the like at one time . . . truly they made his house a spiritual church and temple wherein were offered up the spiritual sacrifices of reading the Word, and prayer every morning and evening, or singing psalms constantly after evening meal, before any did rise from the table.

Such was the ambience in which Sir Nathaniel's children, eight boys and an only girl, Jane, were raised.[21]

In the recusant household of Sir Thomas and Lady Muriel Tresham during the 1560s, Thomas Bramston was tutor to their six daughters and two sons. Elizabeth, the widow of Sir William Petre, retained John Woodward as family chaplain after the death of her husband in 1572. In 1582 his successor John Payne was hung, drawn and quartered in Chelmsford for treason, only to be replaced by William Hudson.[22] Humphrey Wildblud was engaged by Lady Anne Bacon at Gorhambury to catechise her household, which also had the benefit of domestic sermons from the young Hugh Latimer. Thomas Hooker was similarly employed as chaplain and tutor in the household of Francis Drake and his wife Joan at Esher in Surrey. Though Margaret Hoby had no children of her own, her chaplain, Richard Rhodes, followed a similar pattern of religious practice in her household at Hackness in Yorkshire.[23] Jeremy Taylor was successively chaplain to the families of Francis, Earl of Carbery and of Thomas Wriothesley, fourth Earl of Southampton. Before joining Sidney Sussex College as a founding fellow, Thomas Gataker, the later puritan divine, was chaplain to the family of William Ayloffe of Braxted in Essex, later moving to London to tutor the family of Sir William Cooke.[24]

Not all such appointments worked out as well as the employer had hoped, as was the case of William Chillingworth, engaged as chaplain-tutor to the family of Elizabeth Cary, the devout Catholic convert, who suspected him of trying to convert her children to the Protestant faith.[25] John Duncon, chaplain to Elizabeth's staunchly Anglican eldest son, Lucius, and his wife Lettice, seems, on the other hand, to have been entirely satisfactory in his office, though Lucy Hutchinson took a poor view of her tutor, 'my father's chaplain, a pitiful dull fellow'. Thomas Pierson was chaplain in the household of Oliver St John, third Baron Bletloe in Bedfordshire, where he preached to the family every Tuesday and Friday after supper, catechised and prayed with the servants and heard sermon repetition and singing of psalms with the whole family present.[26]

Thomas Cawton was a young Cambridge graduate when in 1633 he was appointed as chaplain-tutor to the family of Sir William Armine. Here for four years, in addition to leading the family in prayers, offering 'a plain exposition of the scriptures' and catechising, he also instructed the servants, thereby, his memorialist tells us, showing his 'readiness to instruct the meanest and lowest capacities, suiting himself to them and all things to all that he might win some'.[27] Anthony Walker followed a quite usual career path in becoming, immediately after proceeding MA, tutor to Mary Lewkenor, the step-daughter of Dr John Gauden (later Bishop of Worcester). He held this post for three years before becoming chaplain in the household of Charles Rich, the fourth Earl of Warwick, where he forged a close spiritual relationship with Lady Mary Rich in the education of her children, before taking up the living of Fyfield in 1662. Gauden himself had been chaplain in the household of Lady Anne Rich, daughter-in-law of Robert, second Earl of Warwick, and it was to her that he dedicated his *Whole Duty of a Communicant*, which became a popular text after his death in 1662.[28] Obadiah Sedgwick held a similar position with Sir Horatio Vere and his wife Lady Mary. Robert Abbot, 'preacher of the Word' at Southwick, Hampshire, was engaged as tutor to the four daughters of Lady Honoria Norton of Southwick. He dedicated his *Milk for Babes* (1646) to Lady Honoria, and the appended four sermons to his four charges. Edmund Barker was chaplain for eight years to Lady Elizabeth Capel, wife of Arthur, Lord Capel, and their nine children, preaching her funeral sermon in 1661.[29]

Unfortunately very few such tutors-chaplains have left more than the scantest of records of their activities. An exception is offered by the career of John Thornton, who graduated BA from Trinity College, Cambridge, in 1646, and almost immediately afterwards was appointed family chaplain in the Woburn household of William Russell, fifth Earl of Bedford and his wife Anne, at the then handsome salary of £30 per annum. His charges as tutor included the boys William, Francis, Edward, Robert, James and George, and the girls Anne, Diana and Margaret. The accounts he kept reveal that when each child reached the age of four he or she was given two Bibles, one in Latin and the other in English, plus a catechism and a Book of Common Prayer. Later, when they were seven, they were each bought a copy of Baxter's *Sincere Convert*. Diana, apparently her tutor's favourite, later received another Bible 'of the fair minion print' costing 12s 6d, as well as copies of Byfield's *Principles* and James Fisher's *The Wise Virgin*. Plainly their religious education was not being neglected.[30]

Some women continued their search for religious enlightenment by corresponding with clerics who had, in some instances, previously been their chaplains. Luther, Calvin and Loyola each carried on such correspondence with women of their acquaintance.[31] Lady Jane Grey corresponded with Heinrich Bullinger, and in a letter to him referred to her correspondence with Martin Bucer, who had likened her to Saint Paula and her daughters Blessilla and Eustochium who had corresponded with St Jerome, though Jane herself asked Bullinger to 'excuse the more than feminine boldness of me who, girlish and unlearned as I am, presume to write to a man who is the father of learning'.[32] John Knox carried on a long correspondence with his mother-in-law, Elizabeth Bowes. Far from dismissing Elizabeth's rather importunate, almost obsessive, seeking of advice on matters spiritual, Knox persisted over a number of years in his efforts to help her find answers to her spiritual doubts and questionings, even going so far as to acknowledge that he himself suffered in much the same way, especially over the problem of faith and works.[33] In the mid-1570s Edward Dering, Rector of Pluckley in Kent, discussed spiritual matters in letters to a variety of women, including Katherine Killigrew, 'Mistress Barrett', Mary Honeywood, Lady Golding and Lady Mildmay. John Bradford, an indefatigable correspondent with 'believers' and 'professors', shared with John Philpott a correspondence with Lady Elizabeth Fane, 'that liberal benefactor of God's saints', as Foxe described her, from their prison cells prior to their martyrdom.[34] Coverdale collected and printed a host of such letters in his *Letters of the Martyrs* (1554), as did Foxe in his own *magnum opus*.

After he had left the Barrington household Lady Joan Barrington continued to correspond with Ezekiel Rogers, her former chaplain. Lady Mary Vere kept up a voluminous correspondence with a variety of clerics, including William Ames and Obadiah Sedgwick (both of whom had been chaplains in the Vere household in The Hague), Laurence Chaderton, John Burgess, John Dod, Richard Sibbes, and especially John Davenport, with whom she exchanged letters over a period of 20 years, continuing even when he had gone to New England.[35] Lady Dorothy Pakington, too, corresponded with a wide circle of clerics, including George Morley, Bishop of Winchester, and John Fell, Bishop of Oxford. She also provided a home for the deprived former chaplain to Charles I, Dr Henry Hammond, whose *Practical Catechism* (1644), written expressly to counter that of the Westminster Assembly, became extremely popular after the Restoration and reached a 13th edition in 1691. Lady Anne Finch, later Viscountess Conway, corresponded with the Cambridge Platonist Henry More, and Margaret Godolphin, wife of Sidney Godolphin, wrote habitually to George Benson, Dean of Hereford, seeking his guidance on matters of the spirit.[36] Both Mary Astell and Lady Damaris Masham corresponded with the scholarly John Norris, Rector of Bemerton near Salisbury, about religious issues arising from his writings. Norris published his *Reflections upon the Conduct of Human Life . . . in a Letter to an Excellent Lady* in 1690, and in a reprinted edition in the following year named Lady Masham as the recipient. Mary Astell's correspondence was published in 1695 as *Letters Concerning the Love of God Between the Author of the Proposal to the Ladies and Rev. John Norris.*[37]

In this way, then, women of 'the better sort' contributed to their chosen religious network, by initiating as well as responding in a sequence of letter-writing which served to supplement the more usual forms of spiritual edification.

When there was no chaplain in the household, the task of educating the children was occasionally undertaken by a male tutor or a female governess, though evidence for the latter is much more infrequently found. Moveover, the evidence for either is usually extremely vague and lacking in detail, especially in relation to the religious education of the children, indicating more often than not the mere existence of such a person. An autobiographical report such as that of Lucy Apsley is typical: 'When I was about seven years of age I remember I had at one time eight tutors in several qualities – language, music, dancing, writing, needlework – but my genius was quite averse from all but my book.' Anne Halkett offered some detail:

> My mother . . . paid masters for teaching my sister and me to write, speak French, play on the lute and virginals, and dancing, and kept a gentlewoman to teach us all kinds of needlework . . . But my mother's

greatest care ... [was to ensure that we were] instructed never to neglect to begin and end the day with prayer and orderly each morning to read the Bible, and ever keep the church as often as there was occasion to meet there, either for prayer or preaching.[38]

But by whom Anne and her sister 'were instructed' is not revealed.

The practice of utilising the services of a female governess was not new, of course. Women had been so charged throughout the medieval period, and Chaucer had taken it as normal practice when in 'The Physician's Tale' he warned

And all you ladies that in middle life,
Are put in charge of younger gentlefolk
. . . . . Teach them then for Jesu's sake
And never slacken; virtue is at stake.[39]

Nor was the practice confined to 'gentlefolk'. Royal children had long been put under the supervision of 'Mistresses', 'governesses' or 'tutors', though the paucity of detailed evidence generally makes it difficult to discern precisely what was required of them other than a general supervision of the 'household' of the royal prince or princess. Prince Henry, for example, who was born in 1421 and succeeded to the throne in 1422 as Henry VI, had Alice Butler as his 'Mistress'.[40] We know that the daughters of Henry VIII were tutored in the classical languages, Mary by Richard Fetherstone, John Cheke and Richard Cox, and Elizabeth by William Grindal and Roger Ascham. But in what sense Lady Margaret Bryan was a 'governess otherwise Lady Mistress' to the infant Mary and then to the infant Elizabeth, other than as a supervisor of their households and the servants therein, we do not know, though it would not be unreasonable to suppose that she would have had some direct and indirect influence over the children's moral and religious formation. Mary was 11 years old when her mother Catherine of Aragon was banished by Henry VIII, and thus in infancy and early childhood had the undoubted benefit of a caring and well-educated mother, who for a time had engaged Ludovicus Vives as Mary's tutor. Elizabeth, on the other hand, was not yet 3 when her mother Anne Boleyn was executed and she was put in the charge of Lady Margaret at Hunsdon. In the absence of, say, a chaplain to sit by Elizabeth as she learned to read and say her catechism, it would be entirely reasonable to suppose it was Lady Margaret who undertook these responsibilities herself, though in the much-quoted letter to Thomas Cromwell it was the ordering of the household and Elizabeth's lack of suitable clothes and her troublesome teeth that primarily concerned her on that occasion. By the time

Katherine Ashley took over as Elizabeth's governess the princess was a self-assured young teenager, who nevertheless found in her 'Kate' a staunch ally through troublesome times. From the age of 4 Mary herself had had the benefit of the supervision of the devout Margaret Pole, Countess of Salisbury, a relationship which lasted for 13 years, before the Countess's discharge in 1533 for refusing to give up the princess's jewels. The king's 'Instructions' to the Countess in 1525 are frustratingly lacking in detail, ordering only that she should 'give most tender regard to all such things as concern the said princess, her honourable education and training in all virtuous demeanour'.[41]

In 1605 James I wrote to Sir Robert Carey, 'we have made choice of your wife Lady Carey, one of the ladies of the Privy Chamber of the Queen, to have charge of our second son, Duke of York, in respect of his tender years'. Prince Charles was then 5 years old, but once again we have little evidence as to how Lady Carey carried out her duties or what assistance, if any, she had in tutoring the young prince, though she did write to the king in October 1607 complaining of the poor quality of the food provided for him. Plainly, however, if the king had not believed that she would be a good influence on the boy's upbringing she would not have been chosen as his 'governess'.[42] James's daughter Elizabeth, the future 'Winter Queen' of Bohemia, was also allocated a tutor, on this occasion in the person of Sir John Harrington at his home at Combe Abbey near Coventry. After the execution of Charles I, his daughter Elizabeth was tutored by Richard Lovell at Penshurst and later by Bathusa Makin, the author of *An Essay to Revive the Antient Education of Women* (1673), who had previously held a similar position with Lucy, the daughter of Lady Eleanor Davies, and with the latter's granddaughter Elizabeth.[43]

The practice is also to be found amongst the aristocracy and gentry. In 1517, for example, the Wardrobe Accounts of Edward Stafford, the third Duke of Buckingham, record payments to a 'nursery governor' (presumably a woman) for the Duke's daughters.[44] In the same way, the account books of Sir Henry Sidney for the 1570s show that his younger children, Robert, Mary, Thomas and Ambrosia, were placed in the care of Robert Mantell (Mantle) and his wife Jane, and in 1576 Philip Sidney made it his responsibility to have £20 paid 'to my sister's old governess Mrs Jane Mantell . . . which is due unto her for her wages which my father owed her'.[45] During the 1530s, in the household of Sir Anthony and Lady Anne Cooke at Gidea Hall near Romford in Essex, their five daughters received an education comparable to that of the daughters of Sir Thomas More. One of the girls' tutors was Giles Lawrence, who in 1550 became Professor of Greek at Oxford. Whilst on a visit to the Cookes, Walter Haddon paid a visit to 'the little academy' and reported that 'whilst staying there I seemed to be living among the Tuscalans, except that the studies of women flourished in this Tuscany'.[46] After tutoring Barbara Lucy and her brothers at Charlecote, the martyrologist John Foxe moved to London to act in that capacity to the orphaned children of Henry Howard, Earl of Surrey, in the house of Mary Fitzroy, the Duchess of Richmond.[47] Grace Sherrington, one of the three daughters of Sir Henry and Lady Anne Sherrington of Lacock Abbey in Wiltshire, reported in her diary that she had 'the experience of a gentlewoman, niece unto my father, and brought up by my mother from childhood, whom afterwards she trusted to be governess of her own children'. All we know of her is her name, 'Mistress Hamblyn', though in such a devoutly puritan family it may safely be assumed that she made a contribution to the religious formation of Grace and her sisters.[48]

In the 1630s John Harrison, chaplain to Sir Thomas and Lady Frances Barrington, received a stipend of £30 per annum, with duties to include the tutoring of their daughter Lucy and her younger brothers. Frances Egerton (1602–64), who later married Sir John Hobart, was, as her memorialist tells us:

> early betrusted to the tuition of a French gentlewoman, learning French before she could distinctly speak English, which she retained to her dying day. [In addition she learned] how to handle the lute, sing and dance and to read and cast accounts nimbly and exactly, and to use her needle and order the affairs of the household ... Partly by the diligence of her governess, partly by the care of one Mr Moor [her father's chaplain] partly by the superintendent care of my lord her father, she was fully instructed in the principles of religion ... and private devotions (as to which her governess was her most faithful mentor).[49]

Richard Kidder, born in 1633 and later to become Bishop of Bath and Wells, is as uninformative as most in reporting his early upbringing, telling us only that he had been educated at home by a 'gentlewoman', who nevertheless 'taught me so effectually that I was nearly fit for the grammar school'.[50] In the same vein Elizabeth Livingstone, who later married Ralph Delaval, reported that her parents 'appointed a French Protestant gentlewoman since I was seven years old that I should perfect that language'. Later, when she was 10, she was put under the supervision of a 'Mistress Carter, who began more perniciously to insinuate presbyterian principles into me'.[51] Samuel Daniel, the poet, is reported as having been the tutor of Lady Anne Clifford, but in what way he carried out his duties we have no evidence to show, and much the same is true of Mrs Anne Taylor, who is referred to as Anne's 'governess'.[52] The same has to be said of Andrew

Marvell, tutor from 1651 to 1653 to Lady Mary Fairfax, only child of Lord Thomas Fairfax, the parliamentary commander.

With such a frustrating paucity of detail about tutors and governesses and their role in the religious education of children in the familial situation, it is not surprising that their contribution rarely figures in the records, which all too often show attention being paid to that aspect of their education referred to as 'accomplishments' – singing, dancing, lute and virginal playing and, much more occasionally, modern languages.

ADVICES

Girls and women received advice about their religious education in a wide variety of forms, as well as from a wide variety of people, with the range of religious texts available to them, for example, rapidly increasing in quantity after the early years of the Reformation. In addition, they were increasingly confronted with 'Advices', which, not surprisingly, had a high religious content, and which for the most part were quite different from those addressed to their brothers. The majority were, of course, written by men. One of the earliest, Leonardo Bruni's formal 'letter' to Baptista Malatesta, written *c.*1405, started by emphasising, in typical humanist fashion, that 'the foundation of all true learning must be laid in the sound and thorough knowledge of Latin', and 'though she had before her, as a subject peculiarly her own, the whole field of religion and morals', he goes on to insist that

> the cultivated Christian lady has no need in the study of this weighty subject to confine herself to ecclesiastical writers. Morals, indeed, [he continued] have been treated of by the noblest intellects of Greece and Rome. What they have left us upon Continence, Temperance, Modesty, Justice, Courage, Greatness of Soul, demands your sincerest respect.

It is in terms such as these that he concludes the section with the admonition 'Let religion and morals, therefore hold the first place in the education of a Christian lady.' Yet nothing is proposed about her daily religious practice or reading, and thereafter the bulk of his advice relates to a typical humanist study of language and literature.[53]

When this is compared with similarly addressed advices towards the end of the period the difference in approach and attitude is clearly shown, as for example in Hugh Peter's *A Dying Father's Last Legacy to an Only Child . . . Advice to his Daughter Written by his Own Hand During his Late Imprisonment in the Towere of London and Given her a Little Before his Death*. It was published in 1660, a year after his death, and in it he encouraged Elizabeth to undertake the most rigorous daily religious observance – Bible-reading, prayer, meditation, self-catechising – offering also Christian advice about relations with others, about calling, about marriage and death, and in each case recommending appropriate authors and texts for her edification. In addition he suggested that she keep a spiritual diary:

> Keep a book by you (I mean it literally) in which every night before you sleep you set down on the one side the Lord's gracious providence and dealings with you, and your dealings with Him on the other side.

Above all, he urged, 'the Fourth Commandment is the key to all the rest, for how shall the rest be practised if not taught, and how taught if not time allowed'.[54] Thomas Hilder prefaced his *Conjugall Counsell . . .* (1653) with 'the author's paternal advice to his children', Samuel, Mehetabel and Anne. 'Though your bodies are very dear to me [he wrote] I desire your souls may be more precious.' To that end he appended a long list of moral aphorisms, with a biblical proof-text alongside:

Be very strict in the observance of the Sabbath.	Exodus 28.10–1 [sic]
Keep within the limits of your calling.	I Cor. 7.24
Keep your hearts always waking.	Cant. 5.2
Endeavour to keep a good conscience in your whole life, which will be your continual feast, Proverbs 15.15 (for so the Geneva translation renders it).	Acts 23.1

At the same time he recommended a wide range of authors: Perkins, Hall Usher, Preston, Sibbes, Byfield, Bolton, Jeremiah and Daniel Dyke, Symonds and Smith, with a warning to avoid 'all heretical and schismatical treatises and authors', and above all to 'prefer the good and safety of church and state before your own'.[55]

Sir Henry Slingsby's *A Fathers Legacy to his Sonnes* (1658) was primarily addressed to Tom and Harry, but he managed to slip in a note to their sister 'Bab', reminding her that she had 'no other example than her virtuous mother, in whose steps I am confident she will walk religiously'.[56] Despite his title, *The Young Mans Guide in his Way to Heaven . . .*, Thomas Robins offered his guidance 'for the instructions of young men and women in the ways of piety and true holiness', with the entirely conventional advice

> Hear the Word preached, read the scriptures diligently and other godly books; be sure to pray to God morning and evening . . . if thou canst not pray, buy a book of godly prayers till God enables you to pray without book.

At the same time he recommended that his readers should refer to Mr Baxter's *Directions for Family Duties* for guidance on how they should 'reverence, respect and honour thy parents, as a child of God ought to do'.[57] George Savile had much general advice to offer in his *The Lady's New-Years Gift or Advice to a Daughter* . . . (1688), but proved a severe critic in respect of women's piety:

> religion doth little consist in loud answers and devout conversions in church, or praying in an extraordinary manner. Some ladies are so extreme at stirring at church one would swear the worms in their consciences made them so unquiet . . . Let your earnestness therefore be reserved for your closet, when you may have God Almighty to yourself. In public be still and calm, neither undecently careless or affected in the other extreme . . . Religion is exalted reason . . . it dwelleth in the upper region of the mind . . . [yet] there are many who have an anguished devotion, hot and cold fits, long intermissions and violent raptures; this uneveness is by all means to be avoided.[58]

The Advice to an Only Child . . . *Containing the Summe and Substance of Experimental and Practical Divinity* (1693), addressed by O. H. to 'Daughter', was originally written 'for the private use of an only child, now made public for the benefit of all . . . by an ejected minister'. A comprehensive manual, it covered every aspect of Christian life from rising in the morning to retiring in the evening, together with advice about specific situations, with chapters on 'Of Obedience', 'How to manage your converse in company', 'How to manage solitariness', 'How to spend the Lord's Day', 'Of Prayer', 'Of reading the Word', 'Of hearing the Word profitably'. In this case no mention is made of sermon note-taking or note-making, only an admonition to listen to the sermon attentively and to follow this up with a careful rehearsal at home in the privacy of the closet. Similar detail about Christian behaviour was provided in George Hickes' *Instructions for the Education of a Daughter* (1770), which *inter alia* had long sections on 'How the first principles of religion may be instilled' and 'Instructions for the practical part of religion'.[59]

In a quite different mode, and accessible to a much wider audience by virtue of its relative cheapness, was the anonymous *The Maidens Best Adorning or A Directory for the Female Sex Being a Fathers Advice to his Daughter* (1687), published as a single broadsheet and using verse as its medium:

> Take scripture for your guide,
> Make room for Christ
> Bad company (as poison) shun.
> . . .

Be much in prayer, it is the begging trade,
By which true Christians are the richest made.
Of meditation get the blessed art
And often search thy own deceitful heart.

Frequently decried as the medium for bawdy verse tales, the broadside sheet was nevertheless constantly used to present religious and moral advice, as in *A Divine Poem Written by Mary Wells*, who recommends it as 'a fit token' for 'all young men and maids', in the hope that it would replace profane songs and ballads. Each verse started with a letter of the alphabet in turn, as did *A New Years Gift Being a Help to Heart Converse by Way of Change and Challenge in Morning Exercitation and Evening Examination, Alphabetically Digested for the Help of Memory*. Others of the genre included *The Old Gentlewomans Last Legacy to her Sons and Daughters on her Deathbed*, *A Hundred Godly Lessons that a Mother Gave to her Children*, and its variant *An Hundred Devout Admonitions Left by a Dying Mother to her Children*, the substance of which is to be found also in the pedlar-distributed 'penny godlinesses', the chapbooks which Margaret Spufford has examined in detail, with titles such as *The Dying Christians Pious Exhortation* and *Godly Counsel to his Wife and Friends*. It was books such as these which Frances Wolfreston collected and which, in the printer's advertisements at the end, incidentally provide evidence that Dent's *Plaine Mans Pathway to Heaven* was available in suitably abbreviated form, price 2d.[60]

Alongside the texts written with specific religious advice in mind were the family memoirs written, as their dedications make clear, for the express edification of the children of the family whose history is being retold. Mostly written by fathers, who nevertheless directed their remarks to their daughters as well as their sons, these were conscious pieces of historical writing which deliberately set out to report on ancestors as moral exemplars for future younger generations. Sir John Bramston, for example, made it clear at the beginning of his autobiography that he wrote

> That posterity, therefore (I mean my own descendants), may know something of myself and my father, besides our names with pedigree or line of descent. I have set down some things (though few) done by myself not unworthy, many things by my father worthy both of their knowledge and imitation.[61]

More often, of course, such advice is to be found given *en passant* in family correspondence, or occasionally in more urgent circumstances. Faced with impending martyrdom, John Bradford wrote to his mother Elizabeth a letter in which he added:

> I require you, Elizabeth and Margaret my sisters, that you will fear
> God, use prayer, love your husbands, be obedient unto them, as God
> willeth you. Bring up your children in God's fear, and be good house-
> wives. God bless you both.

John Penry was in a similar situation in 1593 when he wrote to his daughters, Deliverance and Comfort, with the enjoinder 'Keep yourselves in this
poor church when I leave you, or in some other holy society of the saints . . .
Learn to read the Word of God . . . your mother will teach you', and a
reminder to be kind to strangers as the Scots had been to them, and to pray
for the Queen. Imprisoned in the Tower and nearing his execution on a
charge of treason in 1569, Thomas Howard, Duke of Norfolk wrote a
similar letter of advice to his son Philip and his daughter 'Nan', in which he
especially urged them to maintain a daily reading of the Bible.[62] In more
normal circumstances Catherine Hastings, Countess of Huntingdon, wrote
in 1573 to John Manners, Earl of Rutland, on his marriage, 'I trust you have
chosen well, and I am sure of it if the report be true that she fears God,
loves the Gospel and hates Popery.' The Earl's son and heir, Roger, wrote to
his younger sister Bridget in 1589 as she was about to leave home to take her
place at court in the Queen's Privy Chamber:

> Serve the Queen . . . with all meekness, love, and obedience . . . give
> reverent behaviour to all elders and superiors . . . use much silence, for
> that becometh maids, especially in your calling. [But] first and above all
> forget not to use daily prayers to the Almighty God to endue you with
> His Grace.[63]

Roger Hill's letter to his married daughter, Mrs Abigail Lockey, urged her
to

> despise not the day of grace which is able to build you up and give you
> all inheritance among them that are sanctified . . . A prize is now put in
> your hands; improve it to the utmost; put it not off. This is the best day
> to work in before the troubles and cares of this world come upon you;
> give all diligence now to make sure of the Lord Jesus Christ . . . seek the
> Lord daily as in private and public.

William Blundell offered similar religious advice to his 17-year-old daughter
Jane, on her leaving home in 1658, with her younger sister Margaret, aged
14, to join the Poor Clares in Rouen.[64] In 1670 Sir Edward Harley (the
'Ned' to whom in his youth his mother Lady Brilliana had written so
frequently) wrote to his newly married daughter 'Brill'(iana):

You must be careful to keep the family in good order and that all come to prayers constantly night and morning, and that prayers be in seasonable time. Be very watchful over yourself that not anything divert you from the morning and evening worship of God in secret and constant reading of the scripture and some other good book, and warn your sisters from me to do the like. Tell your brothers that I hope they will be careful in reading their book, praying and saying their catechism every day.

His later letter (1696) to his grand-daughters 'Betty' and 'Alys' thanked them for their letters and referred to Betty's 'indisposition':

I doubt you are not careful to avoid eating what is unwholesome. You must remember that your life is given you to glorify God. Therefore it is a sin to misemploy the moments of life and also to do anything that may unfit you for the service of God. The scripture teacheth that whether we eat or drink, we should do all for the glory of God. I hope you and your sister and your brother are careful every day in reading and praying, not only as a task but as the special excellency of life in act of worship, drawing near to God with reverence and godly fear, remembering that God is a consuming fire to all profane hypocrites, that so, as Psalm 43 verse 4, you may approach to God as your exceeding joy. Put you and your sister and your brother Ned in mind not to lose precious time which cannot be recalled, but if lost must be accounted for in eternity.[65]

Letters such as these were by no means untypical. John Evelyn's to Margaret Godolphin was of a more formal nature, offering detailed advice for each day of the week. Some days were to be devoted to reading secular works of history, natural history and mathematics, all of which would, nevertheless, 'give you a scheme and prospect how God has governed the world through various successions, and how piety and virtue have always triumphed at last', as well as contributing to 'your understanding of many important passages of scriptures, and furnish you with matter for contemplation'. On other days a programme of religious readings was prescribed, including 'some of the most choice pieces of practical and contemplative devotion, church history and the lives of holy persons', though 'very little controversy, for it is fruitless and tends more to passion than conviction'. Margaret was also urged to

transcribe verses, passages, fragments and sentences, which I advise you to note with your blacklead in your daily course of reading scriptures . . . write them down on loose sheets (to be afterwards stitched together) under the several titles and commonplaces properly assigned.[66]

In much the same vein, during his exile in the Netherlands in the mid-1660s, Sir James Harrington, writing in 1665, addressed a long letter to 'My true yoke-fellow' (Katherine) and his 'dearly beloved' 12 children as a preface to the 'Scripture Catechism' he had composed for their edification. In the letter he reflected on the domestic regime he had painstakingly followed when he was with them, which included

weekly catechising, morning and evening expounding the Holy Scriptures, and praying with you, besides my constant repetition of sermons, preparation and particular examination of you on the Lord's Day, and monthly sacraments; and often remembrance of you as to your daily exercise of private prayers, reading of the scripture and the works of God's faithful ministers.

With these reminders he entreated his children, 'O, let not my above twenty years of labour be in vain.' In addition he composed a 'Directory Letter', a copy of which he sent to each of the 12 children, in which he made a long list of 'exhortations' and 'dehortations' to act as guides to their future religious life.[67] William Penn's *The Fruits of a Father's Love, Being the Advice of William Penn to his Children Relating to Their Civil and Religious Conduct, Written Occasionally Many Years Ago and Now Made Public for the General Good by a Lover of his Memory* (1726) was a much more ambitious piece of work, though in content not much different from others of the genre:

Read daily the Old Testament for history, chiefly the psalms for meditation and devotion, the prophets for comfort and hope, but especially the New Testament for doctrine, faith and worship . . . Have few books, but let them be well-chosen and well read, whether of religious or civil subjects; reading many books is but taking off the mind too much from meditation.

Throughout he emphasises the virtues of humility, meekness, thrift, charity and above all obedience, with each of the points he makes liberally provided with biblical proof-texts.[68]

These examples of men offering advice – injunction would perhaps be a more accurate description – were addressed to daughters as well as sons. Women, too, acted as agents in the matter, whether informally in family letters or more formally in treatise or 'epistle'. The role of mothers in all of this will be noted later, but Diane Willen has recently drawn attention to such 'spiritual reciprocity' in the letters which passed in the 1640s between the Fairfax sisters, Mary Arthington, Dorothy Hutton, Elinor Selby and Frances Widdrington, in which the married daughters of General Lord Fairfax constantly exhorted or consoled each other in matters of the spirit. Anthony Fletcher has done the same in reference to the correspondence between members of the Busbridge and Temple families and the Pierson and Jeakes families in Sussex.[69] Networks of religious counselling such as these admirably supplement the correspondence between domestic chaplains and their patronesses, and the earlier mid-Tudor traffic between imprisoned divines and their female supporters which we have already noticed. In their various forms 'advices' defined gender roles in religious as well as secular terms, besides indicating preferred religious adherence and observance. That these were all too often stereotypical does not reduce their importance in the religious education of women and girls.

5　Away to school

IN THE HOUSEHOLD OF ANOTHER

At home or in church were not, of course, the only places where girls were 'schooled' in the early modern period. Following on the medieval tradition of sending girls as well as boys to spend their childhood in another, preferably socially superior, household, many parents of high social standing continued to send their daughters to join another family, where they would be expected to receive the kind of education considered appropriate to their class and inevitably share, in whatever degree, in the religious life of the household. It is important to recognise that this was but one method of socialisation amongst several for such girls, a plurality which was itself expressed in the public–private debate in education, a debate which recognised the reductionism of the common idea that the sending of children away to this kind of schooling was simply an expression of a lack of affection on the part of parents. As always in individual cases, motivation would not only be different but also mixed, and in the records rarely indicated, though inevitably an affirmation of social hierarchy and gender subordination would figure largely in the expectations of parents who negotiated the details of such education for their daughters. None of the evidence, however, would seem to confirm that such a mode of education 'betrayed a want of affection in the English', or was followed merely in order that their children would 'have better manners',[1] or 'to reduce the possibility of incest and Oedipal tensions'.[2] As always in the period, 'custom' and status were the prime movers in the matter, with religious allegiance a built-in factor.

Nicholas Orme has used the domestic correspondence of the mid- and late fifteenth century to show the practice at work in the families of the Pastons, Stonors and Plumptons.[3] The letters which passed between Arthur Plantagenet, Viscount Lisle, his second wife Honor Basset and their agent John Husee tell a similar story of the placing of the Plantagenet and Basset daughters, with Husee's letter of 18 June 1536 to Lady Lisle giving a good indication of the intricate planning and negotiating which were required for the placing of daughters. Having spent a year under the supervision of Dame Elizabeth Shelley, Abbess of St Mary's in Winchester, Bridget Plantagenet was sent, when she was about 7, to the household of Sir Anthony and Lady Jane Windsor, Sir Anthony reporting to her father in September 1538 'she is very spare and hath need of cherishing, and she shall lack nothing, in learning or otherwise, that my wife can do for her'.[4] Bridget's sister Elizabeth was likewise sent to the household of her half-brother Sir John Dudley, the son of Lisle's first wife Elizabeth.[5] Their step-sisters, the Basset girls, were also sent away from home for the early years of their education. At the age of 13 Catherine Basset was sent to live with Eleanor, Countess of Rutland. Between 1533 and 1538 her sisters Anne and Mary were sent overseas to northern France to be housed not far from their father, who was the King's Deputy and Governor of Calais. Anne went to join the household at Pont de Remy near Abbeville of Mme Jeanne de Riou, who assured her parents 'I will treat her like my own daughter. The young lady is one who can easily be taught.' She stayed there for three years. Mary was not far away in Abbeville with the family of Mme Anne de Bours.[6]

Lady Margaret Beaufort, mother of Henry VII, had several young ladies in her charge, alongside other young aristocratic gentlemen, some of them wards of court of her son.[7] In the equally pious household of Sir Thomas More we find Anne Cresacre, only daughter of Edward Cresacre, a Yorkshire landowner who had died in 1519, placed there by Wolsey when she was about 12 years old, and remaining to marry More's son John in 1529. In addition, there were Frances Staverton, a niece of Sir Thomas, and Margaret Giggs, adopted by More, who married a fellow of the household, John Clement, each of them educated alongside More's own daughters, Margaret, Elizabeth and Cicely and step-daughter Alice.[8] Margaret Pole, Countess of Salisbury had in her household her two granddaughters, Margaret and Catherine, two great-granddaughters, the daughters of her grandson, Sir Arthur Pole, as well as the unrelated Joan Cholmley, Elizabeth Cheney and Alice Densell.[9] In the late 1540s Lady Neville, wife of Sir Anthony Neville, had in addition to her own three daughters the daughter of Sir Thomas Fenton and three other gentlewomen, Anne and Catherine Topliffe and Ursula Clifton.[10] When she was 9 the wardship of Catherine, daughter of William, tenth Lord Willoughby, was purchased by Charles Brandon, Duke of Suffolk, and it was in his house that she was brought up under the tutelage of his first wife Mary Tudor, sister of Henry VIII and Dowager Queen of France, together with the latter's two daughters by her previous marriage, and her neice Lady Margaret Douglas, daughter of the Earl of Angus and Queen Margaret of Scotland. Catherine later married Charles Brandon as his fourth wife and, on his death, as Dowager Duchess of Suffolk was a fervent supporter of the reforming party in religion, in her turn maintaining several 'children of honour' in her household at Grimsthorpe in Lincolnshire.[11]

Four of the six daughters of Edward Seymour, the disgraced Lord Protector Somerset, were committed by the Privy Council to the guardian-ship of their aunt Elizabeth Cromwell, widow of Thomas Cromwell's son Gregory. Margaret, aged 5 and Francis, aged 3, the two younger children of Sir Henry and Lady Anne Willoughby, were sent on their father's death in 1549 to the care of their uncle, Henry Medley. When she was 6 Margaret was presented with her own copy of the Bible. She later continued her education as lady-in-waiting to the Duchess of Suffolk, and went with her to the court of Queen Mary Tudor, and ultimately to that of Queen Elizabeth.[12] In 1572 the widowed Jane Tuttoft wrote to her 'loving cosen' Nathaniel Bacon of Stiffkey:

I give you hearty thanks for bringing up my daughter in your house-hold. Let her learn to write and read and cast accounts, and to wash and brew and to bake and to dress meat and drink, and so I trust she will prove herself a great good housewife. As you requested I am sending £4 for you to give her.[13]

Elizabeth Manners lost her husband John, fourth Earl of Rutland, in March 1588. In the following June she wrote to the Countess of Bedford:

Now that my daughter [Elizabeth] has recovered I commend her to you and resign all the power which I have over her. I beg you will form her in such course both for education and maintenance you think fit, remembering the small stipend allotted to her by my lord. Her educa-tion has been barren hitherto, nor has she attained to anything except to play a little on the lute, which now, by her late discontinuance, she has almost forgotten. I have committed to my daughter her whole year's annuity the employment whereof I commit to your discretion.[14]

In 1597 Sir Robert Sidney, then in the Low Countries on government service, wrote to his wife Barbara, who had already played an active part in the early religious education of their children, urging her to join him and suggesting that the time had come for their two eldest daughters, Mary and Katherine, to be placed in the household of another for their continued education. Mary, then 'almost ten', he proposed should be placed with Catherine, Countess of Huntingdon, and Katherine, 'Kate', then 'almost eight', with Anne Rich, Countess of Warwick, each of these ladies well known for the care with which they looked after those placed with them.

Mary, apparently, was 'tearful' at the thought of not being able to join her father, though in fact she would have joined several other young ladies in the charge of Catherine Hastings, the widow of 'the Puritan Earl' Henry, third Earl of Huntingdon. They included the future diarist Margaret Dakins, Lady Margaret Hoby, whose first husband was Walter Devereux, who with his sisters Penelope and Dorothy were also resident members of the household. In a postscript to a letter to Sir Julius Caesar in 1618, Lady Catherine quite justifiably claimed 'I think there will be none make question but I know how to breed and govern young gentlewomen.' As part of the 'breeding' process, this deeply religious woman doubtless made it plain that she 'governed' in accordance with the Fifth Commandment.[15] A similar reputation was claimed for Lady Elizabeth Cholmley by her husband Sir Hugh, who noted in his *Memoirs* that 'divers (of the best of the county) desired to have their daughters in service with her'. Having been brought up by her parents 'in the nurture and admonition of the Lord', Ellen Bentley married the Reverend Asty of Stratford in Suffolk, her memorialist reporting that 'when she was first married several gentlewomen sent their daughters to be with her that they might live under her instructions, and the Lord made her very useful to them', and with the same purpose in mind the relations of Mary Mounteford, who died in 1656 aged 93, ' a woman of so great virtue, so modest, so devout and so well-grounded in religion that she never swerved from the doctrine and discipline of the Church of England in the worst of times', sent their children to be educated in her religious household.[16]

George Clifford, later Earl of Cumberland, became a ward of Francis, second Earl of Bedford, when he was 11, and was brought up in the Duke's household at Woburn, 'that very school of virtue', where he was to meet their daughter, Margaret Russell. The two were married in 1577, he aged 19 and she 16, whereupon they went to live with his mother Lady Clifford at Craven Castle in Cumberland, later to produce a daughter, Lady Anne Clifford, who under the guidance of her mother ultimately 'knew well how to discourse of all things from predestination to slea-silk'.[17] Nor were the daughters of royalty exempt from this mode of education. In 1603 Elizabeth, the eldest daughter of James I and Anne of Denmark, was placed in the household of Sir James and Lady Anne Harrington at Combe Abbey in Warwickshire, where with their daughter Lucy (later Countess of Bedford) she was joined by the daughter of Sir Robert Carey, and Theophilia, the daughter of Sir Thomas Berkeley, Lucy in turn taking Sarah, the daughter of Sir William Harington of Bagworth.[18] Mary Gunter lost both of her parents in infancy when she was committed to the care of 'an old lady, a strong papist', who died when Mary was 14, whereupon she was sent to live in the Protestant household of Sir Christopher Blount, whose wife Lettice,

Countess of Leicester by her former marriage to Robert Dudley, weaned her away from her early Catholic upbringing, taking away all her Catholic books and causing her to give an account of the sermons that were preached in the household twice on Sundays. As part of her 'conversion' she vowed that she would read over the whole Bible once every year, and did so for the next 15 years, keeping notes and learning passages by heart. She remained with the Countess for 22 years, dying in 1622.[19] Lady Joan Barrington, daughter of Sir Oliver Cromwell and sister of the future Protector, had in her household alongside her five daughters, Elizabeth, Mary, Winifred, Ruth and Joan, her god-daughter Mary Towse, daughter of William Towse, Sergeant-at-Law of Takeley in Essex, and Mary's sister Jane, together with Mary Whalley, daughter of Sir Richard Whalley, Lady Joan's brother-in-law.[20] On occasion, of course, a pious upbringing was not the only or indeed the prime reason for sending a daughter to another's household. Sir Edward Molineux, for example, sent his two daughters to the house of his cousin to be brought up, as he said, 'in virtue, good manners and learning, to play the gentlewoman and good housewife, to dress meat and oversee their households'. Henry Thorndike was more tersely direct in sending his niece to live with the Isham family in Northamptonshire 'that she might find match by having the honour of being in your house' – though in such a godly environment as the Ishams insisted upon, the young lady would also have been assured of a godly education.[21]

The greatest household to which a girl could be sent was, of course, the royal court, an old chivalric tradition by which both boys and girls were sent from home to learn the appropriate mode of service to their elders, as well as to acquire courtly manners and to participate in the religious pattern of the royal household. The practice continued virtually unchanged in the sixteenth and seventeenth centuries, and nowhere more so than in the pious ambience of the household of Henry VIII's Queen, Catherine of Aragon. It was to this place that in 1517 Catherine Parr's newly widowed mother Maud went as a 21-year-old lady-in-waiting to the Queen, accompanied by her three young children, Catherine aged 3, Anne aged 2 and the infant son William, there to be joined eventually by the young Princess Mary with whom they were brought up, alongside Katherine Willoughby and Joan Guildford, daughters of Catherine's other ladies-in-waiting. At the Queen's instigation the princess was in the mid-1520s to be tutored by Juan Luis Vives, who produced for his young charge a plan of education, *De Ratione Studii Puerilis*, and for a wider audience *De Institutione Foeminae Christianae*. These were both dedicated to Queen Catherine, whilst to the Princess he dedicated his *Satellium sive Symbola*, a collection of moral axioms and advices. When Catherine Parr was brought to the court of Catherine of Aragon to be brought up with Princess Mary she could not have known that one day she would be Queen with a similar group of young women under her supervision, including another future queen, Lady Jane Grey.[22]

The court of Queen Elizabeth was also used as a 'school' for numerous 'maids of honour', among whom were Elizabeth Vernon, who later married Henry Wriothesley, Earl of Southampton, patron of Shakespeare and John Florio. However, this was without first getting the Queen's permission, thereby incurring the latter's displeasure and a spell for both of them in the Fleet prison. Also at court at this time were the sisters Lettice and Cecilia Knollys and Catherine and Philadelphia Carey, as well as Anne Russell, daughter of Francis, second Earl of Bedford, who was later to marry Ambrose Dudley, Earl of Warwick.[23] Mary Sidney, daughter of Sir Henry and Lady Mary Sidney and sister of Philip, with whom she was later to collaborate in the translation of the Book of Psalms, was in 1575 when she was 13 sent to the court of Queen Elizabeth where she became a lady-in-waiting, as her mother had been before her. Two years later she was married to Henry Herbert, the second Earl of Pembroke, 25 years her senior.[24] The household of Queen Henrietta Maria was of course quite different in its religious orientation, but it was to there that Margaret Lucas, later Duchess of Newcastle, was sent, following her mistress on the outbreak of war first to Oxford and then to France. Elizabeth Livingstone (later Delaval) was also at court aged 18, serving in the Privy Chamber of Queen Catherine, wife of Charles II.[25] Margaret Blagge, whose father the royalist colonel died when she was 8, was placed at court in 1664, when she was 12, her mother Mary being maid-of-honour to Anne Hyde, Duchess of York. It was one of her companions there, Anne Howard, who introduced her to John Evelyn, who had such an influence on her as a young woman. Anne Finch was maid of honour to the Catholic Mary of Modena, second wife[26] of James II. The practice of obtaining a place at court for young ladies of quality was thus continued throughout the period and, in each case, during their most impressionable years they would amongst other things have absorbed the religious ambience of the place, sometimes accepting and following, at other times rejecting, the doctrine and practice which surrounded them.

ACADEMIES

In the early seventeenth century the parameters of the public–private debate as to whether boys should be educated at home by a private tutor or sent away to one of the increasing number of grammar schools which took in boarders were somewhat widened when applied to the education of a certain class of girls. Nunneries and convents were no longer available unless a girl were sent abroad, but the continuing practice of educating girls at home or in the household of another family was supplemented by the quite new opportunity of sending them away from home to a boarding school for the education of daughters of gentlemen. It was taken for granted that grammar schools were the reserve of boys, though there were exceptions – the statutes of the grammar school founded at Banbury in 1594, for example, allowing that girls could be admitted, though none 'above the age of nine, nor longer than they may learn to read English'. Those of the small grammar school founded in 1571 (though not built until 1590) in the village of Harrow-on-the-Hill by the will of John Lyon expressly forbade the admission of girls.[27] The Founder's Rules drawn up by Thomas Saunders for the school he founded in 1637 at Uffington in Oxfordshire were quite explicit:

> Whereas it is the most common and usual course for many to send their daughters to common schools to be taught together with and amongst all sorts of youths, which course is by many conceived very uncomely and not decent, therefore the said schoolmaster may not admit any of that sex to be taught in the said school.[28]

Whilst these examples tell us something about the social attitudes of the particular founders, they also give some indication that the segregation of boys and girls was not as all-embracing as might appear. Even so, it was early recognised that schools should be set up expressly for girls, Thomas Becon, for example, insisting that:

> It is expedient that by public authority schools for women children be erected and set up in every Christian commonwealth, and honest, safe, wise, discreet, sober, grave and learned matrons made rulers and mistresses of the same, and that honest and liberal stipends be appointed for the said schoolmistresses which shall travail in the bringing up of young maids.

Richard Mulcaster, himself a successful grammar-school master, made much the same point in his *Positions* of 1581.[29] The seventeenth century saw an increased recognition of the need for such provision. Comenius and his circle of followers were insistent that if the kingdom of God were to be achieved on earth then the religious education of all, high and low, girls as well as boys, should become a priority. In his plan for a *Reformed School* (1650), John Dury made it plain that though boys and girls should be strictly segregated:

> The main scope of the whole work of education, both in the boys and

girls, should be none other than this: to train them up to know God in Christ, that they walk worthy of Him in the gospel, and become profitable instruments of the Commonwealth in their generations. And in order to do this, two things are to be taught to them. First, the way of godliness, wherein every day they are to be exercised by prayers, reading of the Word, catechetical instructions and other exercises subordinate to the life of Christianity. Secondly, the way of serviceableness towards the society wherein they live, that they may be enabled each in their sex respectively, to follow lawful callings for profitable uses, and not to become a burden to their generation by living in idleness and disorderliness, as most commonly those do which come from the schools of this age.

None of this was out of the ordinary, nor indeed was Dury's criticism of females in respect of

the ordinary vanity and curiosity of their dressing of hair and putting on of apparel, the customs and principles of wantonness and bold behaviours, which in their dancings are taught them, and whatsoever else doth tend only to foment pride and satisfy curiosity and imaginary delights, shall be changed by this our course of education, into plain, decent cleanliness and healthful ways of apparelling themselves; and into such exercises of hearts, heads and hands, which may habituate them through the fear of God to become good housewives and careful housewives, loving towards their husbands and their children when God shall call them to be married.[30]

In his proposals for an education for all members of the commonwealth, Dury was of necessity talking about an elementary level of education, but his criticisms were plainly directed against the 'daughters of gentlemen' and the new boarding schools, 'academies', which were now being provided for them. It was to provide a reformed alternative to such schools that Edward Chamberlayne proposed the founding of *An Academy or College Wherein Young Ladies and Gentlewomen May at a Very Moderate Expense be Duly Instructed in the true Protestant Religion* (1671). Those girls who were kept at home for their tuition, he argued, were too easily 'corrupted or betrayed by servants'; those who were sent abroad 'returned otherwise virtuous but generally tainted with and inclined to Romish superstitions and errors'. But he reserved his chief criticism for

the maiden schools in or about London where either through the unskilfulness or negligence or covetousness of the mistresses, too much minding their private profit, the success hath oft times not answered the expectations of their parents and friends, whereof there are divers lamentable examples and grievous complainings.

Instead, he proposed the purchase of a large house near London, with a chapel, hall, lodgings and 'rooms for all sorts of necessary offices, with gardens, orchards and courts'. A divine of the same parish would be appointed chaplain, a 'grave and discreet lady' would be the 'governess', to be assisted by 'divers and other matrons'. Only in such an environment would it be acceptable to hire visiting teachers for singing, dancing, music, needlework and cooking. Prospective parents were invited to invest in the financing of the institution, with the money subscribed to be put under the trusteeship of the Mercers' Company. In the event of failure, subscriptions would be returned with 5 per cent interest. Like so many of the projects of the period we have no further evidence of the scheme, or of the fate which awaited Daniel Defoe's similar proposal for an 'academy for women' in his *Essay Upon Projects* (1697), with one to be set up in every county and 'about ten in the city of London', thus (he claimed) putting an end to 'one of the most barbarous customs in the world, considering us a civilized and Christian country, that we deny the advantages of learning to women'.[31]

Significant too, however, was the increasing part played by women themselves, not only in arguing for a greater equality of the sexes but also in following this up with proposals for the better education of girls and women as an essential means of achieving such a change. We have only the indirect report of John Duncon, memorialist of Lettice, Viscountess Falkland, the devout wife of Lucius Cary, that she had hoped to help in the foundation of houses

> for the education of young gentlewomen and the retirement of widows (as Colleges and Inns of Court and Chancery are for men) . . . hoping thereby that learning and religion might flourish more in her own sex than heretofore and have such opportunities to serve the Lord without distraction . . . but these evil times disabled her quite.

Mary Astell's *Serious Proposal to the Ladies for the Advancement of their True and Great Interest*, which she published in two parts in 1694 and 1697, was a considered discussion of the education of women and particularly the place of religion therein, complaining that girls and young women were too often

> taught the principles and duties of religion but not acquainted with the reasons and grounds of them, being told 'tis enough for her to believe, to examine the why and wherefore belongs not to her. And therefore,

though her piety may be tall and spreading, yet because it wants foundation and root, the first rude temptation overthrows and blasts it.

But, as she was not alone in claiming, 'the soil is rich, and if well cultivated would yield a noble harvest'. She therefore aimed to produce someone

> who is a Christian out of choice, not in conformity to those about her, [one who] cleaves to piety because it is her wisdom, her interest, her joy, not because she has become accustomed to it . . . [who] acquires a clear understanding as well as a regular affection, that both together may move the will to a direct choice of good and steadfast adherence to it.

A religious education based on reason and understanding would, she claimed, redirect those 'whose piety blazes higher without understanding . . . having more heat than light' and whose 'zeal outruns their knowledge'. Moreover, a good deal of blame should be attached to those parents who, in the education of their children,

> have taught them perhaps to repeat their catechism and a few good sentences, to read a chapter and say their prayers, though perhaps with as little understanding as a parrot, and fancied that this was charm enough to secure them against the temptations of the present world and waft them to a better.

Astell was plainly aiming at a more highly educated group of women than most parents and clerics would have contact with, and she acknowledged this in her proposal to

> erect a monastery . . . or if you will a religious retirement . . . a seminary to stock this kingdom with pious and prudent ladies whose good example, it is to be hoped, will so influence the rest of their sex that women may no longer pass into those little useless and impertinent beings which the ill conduct of too many has caused them to be mistaken for.

But she faced and, in the end, was unable to resolve the dilemma that faced all those women of the period who argued for greater equality for women but recognised the huge range of capacity when the detail of provision had to be decided. Like many before her she asked the rhetorical question, 'What is it but the want of an ingenious education that renders the generality of feminine conversations so insipid and foolish and their solitude so insupportable?', yet felt it politic to accept that 'women have no business with the pulpit, the Bar and St Stephen's chapel [that is, parliament]' and to reassure her male readers that 'we pretend not that women should teach in church or usurp authority where it is not allowed them; permit us only to understand our own duty . . . to form in our minds a true idea of Christianity'. To her conservative way of thinking, a woman's Christian life would be confined to

> prayer and praise . . . spiritual and corporal works of mercy as relieving the poor and healing the sick, mingling charity to the soul . . . instructing the ignorant, counselling the doubtful, comforting the afflicted and correcting those that erand do amiss . . . [together with] daily performance of the public offices after the cathedral manner.

Competent in these matters, some such women might become 'tutors to the daughters of gentlemen' and 'stock the kingdom with pious and prudent ladies . . . able to teach in schools of the better sort', a proposal which anticipated Charles Kingsley's Queen's College in London by 150 years.[32]

When John Batchiler printed his *The Virgins Pattern*, in which he memorialised 'the life and death of Mistress Susanna Perwich . . . who died July 3 1661' when she was 25 years old, he dedicated it 'To all the young ladies and gentlewomen of the several schools in and about the city of London and elsewhere'. His reason for doing so arises from the fact that Susanna was the daughter of Robert Perwich, who had a school for the daughters of gentlemen in Hackney in which she had finished her own schooling and had then become a teacher.[33] Hackney was at the time a salubrious suburban village to the north of the City of London, in which many prosperous middle- and upper-class people had taken up residence, and in which were to be found several schools of a similar kind and clientele. One of the earliest to be mentioned was that of Mrs Winch, which is known as a result of a notorious episode in 1637 when a pupil of the school, the 14-year-old Sarah Cox, an orphan with a goodly portion, was abducted whilst walking on nearby Newington Green by Roger Fulwood, brother to Katherine, one of Sarah's school friends, who had failed in an earlier attempt to persuade Sarah to marry him. Fulwood took the girl to Southwark House, the London residence of the Bishop of Winchester, and forced through a form of marriage, with the aid of spurious documentation. Sarah was finally rescued, and after the case was brought to court delivered of a declaration of nullity.[34] It was in the following year that the 8-year-old Katherine Fowler arrived in Hackney to join the school run by Mrs Salmon, later to marry and as Katherine Phillips to make her name as the poetess 'the Matchless Orinda'.[35] The two eldest daughters of Sir John Bramston were also sent to Mrs Salmon's school on the death of their mother in 1648, and in his notebook Samuel Sainthill of Bradninch, north of Exeter in Devon, recorded his outgoings for the teaching and boarding of his sister at the school during the period 1651–3.[36] Mary Aubrey, a cousin of the antiquary, also attended the school, and in 1675 Ralph Josselin's two daughters Mary and Elizabeth arrived with their mother from Earls Colne in Essex, Josselin noting in his diary, 'God bless them in their education, both in soul and body.'[37] In 1695 Sir Richard and Lady Mary Newdigate sent their daughters Anne ('Nan') aged 16 and Elizabeth ('Betty') aged 13 to a school in the village run by Mrs Beckford, to be joined in the following year by their sister Jane ('Jinny') aged 14.[38]

The Hackney schools were plainly supported over the years by the prosperous parents of young ladies but no records of the schools have survived. However, Samuel Pepys, in typical fashion, recorded in his diary his visit on Sunday 20 April 1667 to Hackney parish church, St Augustine's, chiefly in order to run his eye over the 'young ladies' of the schools, whom he deemed 'very pretty'.[39] The same is true of other schools of a similar kind which were to be found in the villages which circled London in the seventeenth century. To the north of Hackney in the village of Tottenham was to be found the school for the daughters of gentlemen which Bathusa Makin ran and advertised in a 'Postscript' to her *Essay to Revive the Antient Education of Women* (1673) at a fee of £20 per annum.[40] A few miles to the east of Hackney in Islington the Dissenter Esreal Tong (or Tongue) had an academy for girls in the 1660s, in which it was claimed that all were able to construe a Greek gospel by the time they were 14.[41] Just to the south, in Stepney, a school run by Mrs Friend was attended by Anne Heather, sent there as an orphan by the City's Court of Aldermen at an annual fee of £21, and later in 1638 Sir Edward Nicholas sent his daughter Susan there.[42] In the 1620s Sir Simonds D'Ewes' two sisters, Mary and Cecilia, attended a school in Walbrook, a little to the east of Stepney and not far from St Paul's, kept by 'a poor merchant's wife'. Cecilia died there in 1620, aged 10, and D'Ewes reported that on the Sunday before her death she repeated the greater part of the sermon she had heard that day, and inquired about some chapters and verses in the Bible which she could not find for herself.[43] Near the river just south of Greenwich in Deptford was located a school known as Ladies Hall, some of whose girls took part in Robert White's masque *Cupid's Banishment*, which was performed in Greenwich at court before James I's wife Queen Anne of Denmark, probably as the eight 'woodnymphs', listed by name in White's published text, who sang 'In joy is Cupid gone'. It was to this school that Lettice, the daughter of Sir Richard Newdigate, was sent in 1620 when she was 15, at a fee of £22 per annum.[44] Upstream to the east at Putney was the school that the eldest daughter of Mrs Margaret Ducke attended, one of several in the area, since John Evelyn recorded in his diary for 17 May 1649 that he went 'to Putney . . . to see the schools and colleges of the young gentlewomen'.[45] After the death of his wife, in 1678, aged 31, Francis North, Lord Keeper Guildford, turned his mind to the continuation of the education of his young family. His two sons, Francis and Charles, he sent to his mother, his daughter Anne to the home of his sister Lady Wiseman (later Countess of Yarmouth) in Chelsea, 'where also there was [as Roger North reported] a good school for young ladies of quality, which was an advantage'. Whether Anne actually attended the school we do not know, but the school in question was probably that run by Josias Priest and his wife, newly removed from 'Leicester-Fields'. It was for the young ladies of this establishment that Henry Purcell wrote his opera *Dido and Aeneas*, and it was to this school that Edmund Verney, eldest son of Sir Ralph, took his daughter Mary ('Molly') aged 8, where she joined Betty Denton, daughter of Dr William Denton and sister of Sir Ralph's god-daughter and niece 'Nancy' Denton. Elizabeth Palmer, who in 1680 married John Verney, had already been a pupil there.[46]

The concern of the Verney family for the education of their children is well documented in the extensive family correspondence, a concern which was complicated by Sir Ralph Verney's exile in France during the 1640s. He had his son Edmund ('Mun') and his daughter Margaret ('Peg') with him in Blois, whilst 'Jack' remained at home with his mother, Lady Mary. The family was thus quite used to children living away from home, but it was the education of Sir Ralph's youngest sister Elizabeth ('Betty'), she of the 'cross, proud and lazy disposition' who appeared to be 'in love with her own will', which proved to be the greatest worry to the family.[47] The possibility of placing her or sending her away to school was often discussed. Several attempts to place her with relatives proved to be unsuccessful, and when she was finally sent to live with her older sister Margaret, wife of Sir Thomas Elmes, she unilaterally discharged herself and returned home, prompting Sir Ralph's wife Lady Mary to conclude in a letter to Sir Ralph 'nobody will take her'. Finally, Sir Ralph suggested:

> If it be thought for Betty's advantage to be sent to a school, though it be dear, I am content to be put to that charge. It seems the mistress demands £25 a year for diet, teaching and all things . . . She is a strange, perverse girl and so averse to going thither that she doth stick to threaten her own death by her own hands, though my girls (who have been there) give all the commendation that can be of that school.

Her uncle, Dr Denton, agreed with the proposal, acknowledging that it would be 'a great change' but hoping that 'this being abroad may do her more good than if you had given her £500 and no breeding'. A few days later he reported, 'On Friday last, with many tears and much regret Betty went to school, but I droled it out and left her.' The move seems to have succeeded, for in October Dr Denton wrote, 'I never saw so great a change in countenance, fashion, humour and disposition (and all for the better) in any body; neither could I imagine it possible it could have been wrought so soon.' Betty eventually married a clergyman, the Reverend Charles Adams, her torrid adolescence apparently firmly left behind her.[48]

The metropolis and its environs were plainly well served in the provision of boarding education for the daughters of gentlemen. Provision in the provinces was by definition more scattered, though the evidence is more often than not equally lacking in detail other than the existence of such schools. For example, all that is known of the schooling of Margaret and Mary Kytson, daughters of Sir Thomas and Lady Elizabeth Kytson of Hengrave Hall in Suffolk, is derived from an account book which recorded expenditure 'For a drinking at Thetford and the children going to school at Norwich' in January 1573, Norwich lying about 30 miles away to the east of their home. A different kind of source, the Sandwich Orphans' Book, provides evidence that between 1592 and 1594 Thomasine Wolters, an orphan with property producing an income of £10 a year, was sent to a boarding school in Canterbury at a fee of £8 per annum during which time she was provided with 'a book containing all the service and the singing psalms' at a cost of 2s 6d. Later, in 1626, the same accounts report that Elizabeth, the daughter of Robert Wild who had died at sea, was boarded with the wife of William May at 10s a quarter for 'schooling, shoes and flannel waistcoat' together with 'a book to teach her to read'.[49]

The diary of John Dee was terse in the extreme, recording only that in 1590 on the 21st of May his daughter Katherine was 'put to Mistress Brayce' at 'Brayferd' when she was 9. Rosemary O'Day has noted a late-sixteenth-century unpublished letter from Anne Higginson to Lady Ferrers of Tamworth Castle reporting the details of a boarding school in Windsor whose unnamed mistress was charging £32 per annum (plus extras) for the 20 girls who were boarding with her. By comparison with the fees charged in the London boarding schools we have already noted this was an expensive establishment, though Anne reassured Lady Ferrers that she had already placed some of her own 'kindred' there.[50] Sir George Courthope reported in his *Memoirs* that when his mother died in 1620, when he was 4 years old, his two sisters Anne and Frances were sent to a school in Westerham in Kent to board with 'a gentlewoman whose name was Isley'. He was sent to a presumably local school where he learned the elements of Latin grammar, before going first to Merchant Taylors' School and then to Westminster School before entering University College Oxford when he was about 14 in 1630 – a good example of no expense being spared on the prolonged education of the boy of the family.[51] John Haynes was a relatively prosperous merchant in Exeter but he afforded only day schooling for his daughter Susannah who, when she was 6, was taught by a widow, Mrs Clark, at 2s 6d a quarter in 1642 and 1643. The boarding school which Mrs Parnell Amye ran in Manchester was in 1648 reported as charging £11 per annum for schooling and lodging with the usual extras for dancing and music.[52] Each of Henry Oxinden's three daughters were sent away to school, Margaret and Elizabeth, whose mother was Oxinden's first wife Anne Peyton, attending the school run by a Mr Beavan at Mersham, about 15 miles from the family home at Barham in east Kent. The schoolmaster was recommended to Oxinden by Unton, Lady Dering, wife of Sir Edward Dering and near neighbour at Surrenden:

> besides the qualities of music both for the virginals and singing (if they
> have voices) and writing (and to cast accounts which will be useful to
> them hereafter) he will be careful also that their behaviour be modest
> and such as becomes their quality, and that they grow in knowledge and
> understanding of God and their duty to Him which is above all . . . his
> wife is an excellent good woman and his daughter a civil well-qualified
> maid, and both work very well. I presume you will think £30 a year for
> both reasonable when you consider the hardness of the times and that
> there is more trouble with girls than boys.

The two girls were 12 and 11 when they went off to school. Their younger sister Katherine ('Kitty') who was born in 1644, daughter of Oxinden's second wife Margaret Culling, was sent in 1652 to the school run by Mrs Margaret Jackson in Canterbury who, according to Lady Dering, was 'connected in the Precincts' though Mrs Jackson's letters to Kitty's parents rarely mention what kind of religious education the girl was receiving. Oxinden had on one occasion to defend his Margaret against some comments, made by his cousin Elizabeth Dallinson, about the class of her parents. She was, he wrote,

> a yeoman's daughter . . . but such a yeoman as lived in his house, in his
> company and in his sports and pleasures like a gentleman, and followed
> the same with gentlemen . . . and he bred his daughter, according to
> herself, maintaining her four years at school amongst other gentlemen's
> daughters at the same cost and charges they were at.[53]

Ralph Josselin's daughters who went to the Hackney school in 1675 had started their schooling away from home, Mary to White Colne in 1668 when she was 10 and Elizabeth to Bury St Edmunds in 1674 when she was 13. Their elder sister Jane had gone to Mrs Piggott's school at Colchester in 1656 when she was 10, though whilst she was there she resided with her father's cousin John, Ralph noting in his diary 'The Lord bestow his blessing in mercy on her there, his prudence was very visible in her going.'[54] Another diarist, Ralph Thoresby, reported his sister's leaving to go from Yorkshire to Leicester to attend Mrs Falkland's school there, but of the school we know nothing more. Before she married Ambrose Barnes of Newcastle-upon-Tyne, Mary Butler went by sea with her widowed mother from that town to go to school in Windsor, about which we know as little as we do about the education of her own daughters, Mary, Anne, Sarah and Hannah who, we are told by their father, were kept at their needle by their mother 'after they had left boarding school', the whereabouts of which remains a mystery. As little can be said of Sarah Davy (née Roane) who reported 'It pleased the Lord my time being expired at school to return me my father's house.'[55] Linda Pollock has noted from manuscript account books that Sarah and Martha Worsley were at school incurring fees of about £10 per annum in the late 1650s and early 1660s, that the fees for the schooling of Betty Wittenwronge in 1685 came to £18 for the year, and that the quarterly bill for the two daughters of Anne Phelips was £11 12s 10d in 1699, though once again no details of their curriculum are forthcoming.[56]

The journal and account book for the Reverend Giles Moore fortunately tell us a little more about his expenditure on and placing of his niece and adopted daughter Martha ('Mat'). On 20 March 1669 he noted that 'I was with Mistress Chaloner and bargained with her at £12 per annum for the board and schooling for Mat, which at first she would not yield to, but at last by Mr Taylor's interposition she yielded.' On 19 April he 'took a journey to London carrying with me my little maid whom I placed at school. I bought her a new gown and petticoat costing £1 16s and a primer 8d'. On 20 June 1671 he sent £1 10s for 6 weeks' board at Mistress Chaloner's, and later another 25s together with a Bible and New Testament which cost him 7s. He was obviously a careful though relatively generous account keeper, recording that 'The exact amount I laid out upon her from the time of my resolving to take her to the day of her marrige [at which he officiated] besides her diet and washing in my house was £163 12s 6d.'[57] It would have been more helpful if Celia Fiennes had included rather more detail of her visit to Shrewsbury in 1698 than the bare entry to her journal: 'Here is a very good school for young gentlewomen for learning [needle]work and behaviour and music', but unfortunately hers is no more than typical.[58] It has to be said that religious formation was so expected in all levels of education that it would have been taken for granted rather than commented on.

ELEMENTARY SCHOOLS

With such an emphasis on church and household as the primary educative institutions it is not surprising that, in the matter of basic religious education, that other recognised institution, the school, should not be considered to be as important as an alternative or as a supplement to those traditional avenues. On the relatively few occasions when schooling had been associated with the setting up of a chantry, some form of elementary education became available but, after the dissolution of the chantries in the 1530s, where a school was refounded it was invariably as a grammar school for boys only. Undoubtedly, a schooling in the elements of the vernacular was provided in such schools, though only as a preliminary to the learning of Latin, as for example in Plymouth schoolmaster William Kempe's *The Education of Children in Learning* (1588) where it was recommended that such a programme should be continued only until the boy 'be about seven years old, at which time he shall proceed to the second degree of schooling, which consisteth in learning the grammar'.[59] Richard Mulcaster in his *Elementarie* (1582) had been more concerned to justify the claims of the English tongue but, though he argues at one point that by teaching reading in school he aims to 'lay the ground first of learning, in religion towards God and in religion itself to observe the law and ordinances of my country',[60] he nowhere develops this aim as the primary purpose of the education of all children, as the early Protestant reformers had done. Nor does he consider it necessary to establish schools for this purpose as Thomas Becon had done in his *New Catechisme* (1559).[61]

Such a comprehensive system of elementary schooling continued to be called for, especially during the period of the Commonwealth. William Dell, for example, called for schools to be built in all towns and villages, stipulating at the same time that 'in the villages no women be permitted to teach little children but such as are the most sober and grave', and that 'in these schools they first teach them to read in their native tongue, which they speak without teaching, and then presently as they understand, bring them to read the Holy Scriptures'.[62] Dell's stipulation with respect to women teachers was not new, of course. Francis Clement had, in 1587, complained that

> children as we see almost everywhere are first taught either in private by men and women altogether rude and utterly ignorant of the due composing and just spelling of words, or else in common schools most commonly by boys, very seldom or never by any of sufficient skill.[63]

Charles Hoole, himself a grammar-school master of long experience, writing in the late 1630s, acknowledged that

The petty school is the place where indeed the first principles of all religion and learning ought to be taught, and therefore rather deserveth that more encouragement should be given to teachers of it, than that it should be left as work for poor women or others, whose necessity compel them to undertake it as a mere shelter from beggary.[64]

William Walker, the master of the grammar school at Grantham, was similarly concerned that elementary schooling was left to 'ignorant schoolmasters and school madams, whose reformation were well worth the inspection of gravest authority'.[65]

Complaints and comments such as these provide indirect evidence that schooling at this elementary level was indeed available, though obviously not in the systematic fashion that the early reformers would have wished. However, early signs of provision are also evident in the church's attempts to control education at all levels through diocesan injunctions and visitation as well as through the licensing of teachers. The 1536 Royal Injunction required of the clergy

that ye do instruct the children of your parish such as will come to you at the least, to read English, so that thereby they may the better learn to believe, how to pray and how to live to God's pleasure.[66]

In practice, an injunction such as Bonner's of 1555: 'That schoolmasters of any sort be not admitted till they be by their ordinary or by his authority examined and allowed'[67] tended, with some few exceptions, to be applied only to male teachers of Latin grammar, even though subsequent injunctions and visitation articles, as well as the 1604 Canons, continued to be couched in 'catch-all' terms such as 'None shall teach school without licence' and visitation articles continued to enquire 'whether any do presume to keep school within your parish or teach any children before he be duly examined and licensed by the ordinary for his sufficiency, life and conversation' and to insist that 'we shall not suffer or permit any to teach schools whether publicly or privately in any private houses within the parishes unless they shall bring licences first from us under our hand'.[68] The 78th of the 1604 Canons stipulated that curates desirous to teach should be licensed before others 'for the better increase of his own living, and training up of children in the principles of true religion'.[69] The Act of Uniformity of 1662 exacted an oath of non-resistance as well as the usual licence from all schoolmasters, a requirement exemplified in Sheldon's 1665 visitation article which obliged churchwardens to enquire whether

the said schoolmasters, ushers, schoolmistresses or teachers of youth, publicly or privately, do themselves frequent public prayers of the church and cause their scholars to do the same, and whether they appear well-affected to the government of His Majesty and the doctrine and discipline of the Church of England.[70]

The 'catch-all' nature of such orders is reflected, too, in the variety of licences actually issued. In addition to the majority of licences issued to teachers in grammar schools, we find cases such as that of John Barnwick who was licensed to teach boys the abcedarium and English letters in the parish of Walpole, in Suffolk, in 1582, or of Richard Prist in the following year to teach the art of writing, abcedarium and English letters in Methwold, in Norfolk. Thomas Woodwerde of Belford, in Northumberland, was licensed 'according to his enablement and education to keep a school and to teach children to read and write the English tongue and to cast accounts'. In 1607 David Palmer was licensed to teach English and writing at Watford in the diocese of London.[71] Provision at this elementary level is also indicated in the records of presentment of those who were found to be teaching without licence. The 1565 visitation of the Archdeaconry of Essex produced the report that in the parish of 'Westtilberye' 'One John Goose teacheth certain youth of the parish the Absye [ABC] and to read, unlicensed'. In 1581 in the Archdeaconry of Canterbury, the churchwardens reported that 'There is one John Bussher our clerk that teacheth some to read and some to sing but whether he be licensed thereunto we know not.' In 1613 Roger Hartfield of Arundel in Sussex presented 'an honest and poor man [that] doth teach small children to know their letters and read English, unlicensed'. In response to the Articles of Enquiry of 1579 in the Achdeaconry of Chichester, the vicar of Stoughton, in Sussex, reported that 'We have no schoolmaster here but I do teach the youth in the English tongue.'[72]

But the problem of unlicensed teaching proved, unsurprisingly, difficult to solve. As late as 1682 it was noted that 'It is to be wished that order be taken according to law with all unlicensed schoolmasters and schoolmistresses and keepers of private academies, whereof there are great numbers in and about London.'[73] Apart from the obvious issue of religious conformity, there were economic reasons why teachers (of either sex) at the elementary level would wish to avoid paying the fee exacted for the issuing of a licence, to say nothing of the cost of travelling to the place where the archdeacon's official was waiting to record the issue of the licence. Moreover, as Rosemary O'Day has pointed out, there is a considerable methodological problem facing the historian who wishes to make use of ecclesiastical records for study of the history of elementary education in the early modern period. From the prescriptive evidence it would appear that the church, through its bishops and their officers, had an intense interest in the monitoring of the content and the teaching of such provision. But the practical implementation of such policy depended to a very large extent on the efficiency with which these men approached their responsibilities. Nor did every bishop pursue those who did not conform with the fervency of a Bancroft, a Laud or a Wren. The same would be true of the church-wardens whose responsibility it was to respond to the articles of visitation and to present those who were found, or indeed known, to be unlicensed or who failed to exhibit a licence previously issued. In the 1590 Visitation Returns for the diocese of Ely, for example, it was reported that though 20 parishes reported the presence of a schoolteacher, 45 made a return of 'nullus' and 86 remained blank.[74] Even so, records are there to be used, and if they cannot reveal precisely how many elementary teachers were operating at this elementary level nor how efficiently they operated, they do at least provide direct evidence that at particular points in time named men and women were providing such education, albeit to a very small proportion of the population.

Studies of particular dioceses and localities[75] have also revealed the existence of schools which had been endowed for the provision of an elementary form of education for a group of children who would never enter a grammar school or academy, and it is in this area of education that we begin to notice provision being made explicitly for girls to be educated outside of the home, in a formal institution where learning to read had as its primary aim an ability to read the Bible and other godly books. The bulk of the evidence for such endowed elementary education is to be found in wills (continuing, until 1858, to be under the jurisdiction of the ecclesiastical courts) wherein the rents from donated lands or the interest from a capital sum were indicated to be put to the provision of education for the children of those 'sorts' of parents usually labelled 'poor', 'humble', 'labouring', 'decayed'. Often such testaments provide only the barest detail – a sum of money and the number and 'sort' of children to be provided for – as in the case of Michael Wentworth's provision in 1587 of £5 per annum for a master to teach five poor children at Stradbrooke in Suffolk. In 1562 in the village of Wenhaston in the same county, William Pepyn left £20 to educate poor children in 'learning, godliness and virtue', provision which was supplemented in the following year by the will of Reginald Lessey, who left a piece of land in Blythburgh for the same purpose.[76] In 1635 the will of the London draper Charles Parrett left, among other bequests, the sum of £5 for the 'instructing and teaching to read in the English tongue poor children born and bred' in the parish of Boebrickhill in Buckinghamshire.[77] Two years later in the same county, John Pym left an annuity of £10 to be paid to a master for the teaching of ten poor children at Brill. By a deed of

31 December 1642 Robert Dewhurst and his sister Catherine provided land, from the rents of which a school was to be built in Cheshunt, with a house for the master whose salary would be a generous £20 per annum, to teach the poor children of the parish to read 'that they might know God the better', as well as to write and cast accounts. The school survived, and in 1908 was a public elementary school with 230 pupils.[78] At Brampton in Derbyshire the 1679 will of Peter Calton left the seemingly inadequate income of 10s per annum to provide for the teaching of two boys, yet subsequent supplementary endowments enabled the school to continue throughout the eighteenth century.[79] In the same way, the £2 per annum from the rent charges of 11 acres at Easton in Leicestershire, which Thomas Collins bequeathed in his will of 1669 for the teaching of four poor children, was supplemented in the eighteenth century, and the school continued on into the nineteenth.[80]

Other benefactors provided a little more detail. In 1586 for example, George Whately of Stratford-upon-Avon granted lands in Henley and other parts of Warwickshire, half the rents of which were to provide for a schoolmaster to teach 30 children reading, writing and arithmetic in Henley-in-Arden. The children were to be between 8 and 13 years old, were not to remain for more than three years, and were eligible for admission only if they had attended the Sunday school in the town for at least six months previously.[81] In 1638 Sir Edward Alleyne left £100 in his will to purchase within 12 months of his death land in trust for the schooling of poor children of the parish of Hatfield Peverel in Essex. Other sums were provided for the purchase of cottages, and out of the total income £5 was to be paid by the trustees to a schoolmistress for the teaching of 11 children.[82] In the same year, the London glazier Abraham Wall left £4 per annum for a schoolmaster to freely teach poor children of Heptonstall in Yorkshire, his birthplace, together with £1 per annum for the purchase and distribution of Bibles. The initiative received an enormous boost and virtual refoundation in 1643 when the Reverend Charles Greenwood of Thornhill provided a capital sum of £410 for its support, together with £100 for the building of a schoolhouse. The will of Robert Rayment of 1661 left a house and land to provide an income of £10 to be paid to the minister and churchwardens of Buckden in Huntingdonshire for a schoolmaster to teach the English tongue and the grounds and principles of true religion according to the Church of England to those of the village 'as shall be too poor to pay'.[83] The Lichfield draper and Commonwealth MP Thomas Minors left money in 1677 for a school in which were to be taught 30 poor boys to 'read in English books until they could read the Bible', a provision which one of his trustees, William Jesson, augmented in 1685 by a bequest of 20s per annum to buy Bibles for the poor scholars. Francis Willoughby made similar provision in his will of 1672, which left £4 per annum for a master or mistress to teach the poor children of Middleton in Warwickshire, together with a sum of £20 to purchase Bibles for them.[84] Anthony Walker, the rector of Fyfield in Essex by his will of 1687 (he died in 1692) left two houses in Fyfield and 56 acres in High Ongar in trust to Sir Francis Masham and others to establish a school in which a schoolmaster would be paid £8 per annum to teach the poor children of the parish of Fyfield, together with one from Ongar and one from Willingate, to read, write and cast accounts and to say their catechism. One pound was allocated for the purchase of books and paper for the poorest sort of children, plus £1 for Bibles. He also left two tenements in Fyfield for the residence of the schoolmaster or dame and the church clerk, the rent of the adjoining pastures to go to the keeping of the houses in repair.[85] In 1679 William Austin of Trumpington, Cambridge, left 14 acres of land in Bottisham to put four of the poorest children born in Trumpington to school 'until they can read a chapter in the Holy Bible perfectly, and then a Bible to be given to them and they dismissed and others of the said town to succeed as aforesaid'. Of the £500 left by Simon, Lord Digby, in 1694 for 'good, pious and charitable uses', the princely sum of £4 per annum was allocated for the teaching of the daughters of the poor in Coleshill, Warwickshire to read, knit, spin and sew, a similar sum being provided to teach boys to read, write and cast accounts so as to qualify them to become bailiffs or gentlemen's servants or undertake 'some honest trade'.[86]

It will be seen that many bequests provided funds which, even if they were regularly forthcoming (which some obviously were not), were so small as to be virtually non-viable. As a result, many produced no subsequent evidence of their survival, whilst others became subsumed under eighteenth-century charity school provision and surfaced later as elementary schools in the nineteenth century. Some wills, however, provided funds which gave a school a much greater chance of survival. In 1611 for example, Marmaduke Longdale of Dowthorpe Hall, Skirlaugh in Yorkshire, left £200 for a school. Richard Aldworth left £4000 to provide an annual income of £215 for a school for 20 boys in Reading which, after much delay, became the Reading Bluecoat School.[87] In 1634 William Smyth left £250 to purchase land, the rents of which were to be used for a schoolmaster to teach 'all youth, rich and poor, female and male' who had been born in West Chiltington, Sussex. Launcelot Bathurst's 1651 bequest of £150 was to make provision for the poor of the parish of Staplehurst to be taught reading and writing, together with 'instruction in their duty to God and man', an initiative which was supplemented in 1656 by a subscription which raised the sum of £40. In 1662 the Reverend John Scargill left £540 for a school at Westhallam in Derbyshire. The schoolmaster was to be paid £10 per annum to teach reading, writing and casting accounts, together with the church catechism. Unusually, a maintenance grant of 9d per week was to be paid to 12 'pensioners' in the school.[88]

Some few will-makers were concerned to direct their bequests to the education of girls only, though examples of this occur only at the end of the period, as in the 1683 will of Bartholomew Hickling. Part of the monies accruing from the rents of land left for the purpose was to be spent in providing Bibles to be distributed to children in the area around Lough-borough. The rest was to be used to found a school for 20 poor girls from Loughborough, with a mistress who would be paid £4 per annum to

> teach and instruct the said 20 poor girls in learning the English alpha-bet of letters and the true spelling and reading of the English tongue, in good manner and behaviour and also in the grounds and principles of Christian religion.

Hickling also took the wise precaution of appointing a trust of eight local men to adminster his bequests after he and his wife had died.[89] Simon Digby's school in Coleshill, Warwickshire, was similarly designated for 'the daughters of the poor' in 1694, as was that founded by Offalia Rawlins, who left £100 for that purpose, in the same year. In 1705 Lady Anne Walter left £600 in her will of 20 July 1705 to provide a school for 24 poor girls of Sarsden and Churchill parishes, to be admitted between the ages of 7 and 9 and to stay for four years, when they would be given a Bible and a Prayer Book.[90]

For the vast majority of these schools we have no evidence of their subsequent history, nor indeed whether the wishes of the benefactor were actually put in train. Some few foundations, however, provide evidence of the provision of elementary education for girls when such provision was not the primary purpose of the institution. Christ's Hospital, founded in 1553 on the site of the old Greyfriars buildings in Newgate Street, London, was such an institution, having at the outset as part of its offerings a school for poor girls. The hospital's 'General Accounts' for the opening year show payments of 6s 8d to the 'governesses' as salary, together with other small occasional payments to 'Goodwife Smoothing' and 'Goodwife Saepsched' for 'the teaching of the women children'. Further supplementary contribu-tions point to a continuing presence as, for example, in 1625 when George Dunn (an 'Old Blue', as former pupils of the attached boys' grammar school were known) bequeathed £4 per annum for 27 years 'for teaching them [the girls] to read English that they may the better attain unto the knowledge of God and an understanding of the Word'. In 1638 Sarah Wale left a messuage (a property) rents of which were to provide for a mistress to teach reading at a salary of £5 per annum, with a further £5 for 'a sufficient able man' to catechise the girls. In 1644 Dame Elizabeth Clere left £100 for the teaching of reading and needlework. The Great Fire of London destroyed the school buildings in 1666, when the schools were evacuated to Islington, and when these were demolished in 1902 both the Boys' and the Girls' schools were removed to Horsham where they both flourish today, though for a rather different clientele.[91]

What is now known as the Red Maids' School in Bristol started in much the same way as Christ's. In 1634 the mayor-elect Andrew Charlton, with other members of the Bristol Common Council, began to plan for a girls' school to be part of John Whiston's hospital foundation known as 'The Queen Elizabeth's Hospital in Bristol', with the sum of £1000 left in 1606 by Dame Mary Ramsey, who with her husband Sir Thomas had been an earlier benefactor of Christ's, and with other benefactions including £200 from Mrs Anne Colston. With these monies a school for 40 'poor women children whose parents, being freemen and burgesses of the said city, shall be deceased or decayed' with a 'grave, painful and modest woman of good life and conversation' as their teacher who would be responsible to see that they were 'kept, maintained and also taught to read English and to sew', from the ages of 8 or 9 until they were 18. As was so often the case, the implementation of these arrangements proved more difficult than their authors might have intended. However, after much coming and going in the Court of Chancery, the school started with a small complement of 12 girls. Like Christ's, it survived and flourishes to this day.[92]

At the end of the seventeenth century the Children's Hospital at Great Yarmouth in Norfolk took in boys and girls from the ages of 5 to 15, either as orphans or when their parents were unable to maintain them. The main aim of the institution was to prepare the children for apprenticeship or work, but the contract of Abraham Bayly, who became master of the hospital in 1696, gives a clue to its limited educational aims:

> To be allowed for teaching of every child, viz. 20s when it can read well the Bible, 20s more when it can write well, 20s when it can cypher well to the rule of three inclusive, and 20s when each girl can sew plain work well.

Moreover, the children were to be given 2s 6d each when they achieved these targets. As each child entered or left the establishment, the master recorded in the hospital's register a comment on his or her level of achievement. It was recorded of Mary Clark, for example, that she 'can't read at all' when she entered in 1700, though after four years in residence 'she reads her testament but indifferently and has gone through her sampler'.[93] It was, of course, only schools such as these, with relatively large endowments and, more importantly, owning property which increased in value over time, which provide documentation of a serial kind over a period of time.

Whilst some founders provided funds for the teaching of 'poor children' or 'youth', others were careful to indicate that they were making provision for both boys and girls in their bequests. William Smyth of West Chiltington in Sussex, for example, left £250 in 1634 to purchase land which would produce a rent of £5 or thereabouts for a master to 'teach all youth, rich and poor, female and male, born in West Chiltington'. Farther north, at Great Marlow in Buckinghamshire, William Borlase made available funds for a more substantial endowment of a school which would provide an elementary education for 24 girls and a similar number of boys.[94] In 1655 Sir Francis Nethersole left an endowment of lands in Warton and Poles-worth in Warwickshire for a school in Polesworth, stipulating that though there was to be one school building to house both boys and girls, they were to be taught in separate classes, with a master and a mistress (for whom he provided houses) who would be responsible for teaching the boys to read and write English and the girls to read and 'work the needle', and all were to be grounded in 'the principles of Christian religion'.[95] In 1663 Robert Towrie, of Aldbrough in East Yorkshire, left 130 acres of land, the rents of which were to go to the general relief of the poor of the area, including the paying of a schoolmaster to teach both boys and girls. The 1674 will of John Bosworth of Yardley in Worcestershire left land from the rents of which a schoolmaster was to be paid £10 per annum to teach the boys and girls of Long Itchington in Warwickshire. In 1678 Joseph King of Ongar in Essex left houses with rents of £35 per annum for a master's salary of £10 per annum and £1 per annum for the purchase of Bibles and devotional books for six boys and four girls. The school was still in operation in 1906.[96] Beside endowing village schools in Skipwith and Nun Monckton in East Yorkshire, Dorothy Wilson, a spinster who died in 1717, founded two schools in that city, one for boys and one for girls.[97] The fact that provision was made explicitly for girls as well as boys, and sometimes for girls only, suggests that it would not be unreasonable to suppose that when the provision was for 'poor children' or 'youth of the parish' this was not intended to exclude girls from the benefits so provided.

The lack of detail in such wills which has been referred to is, of course, highly frustrating to the historian of education. An exception, however, is provided in the will of Sir John Offley, dated 4 October 1645, though not proved until 1658. In it he charged his executors to build

two decent and convenient schoolhouses, both of stone within Great

Madeley in the County of Stafford in a place there called the Parsonage Yard, with a fair, comely, strong and substantial stone wall before both the said schoolhouses to be built in the nature and after the manner of a courtyard before the said schoolhouses towards the king's highway, with a wall or partition in the middle to divide them, viz. one schoolhouse for the teaching of boys English, Latin and to write and cast accounts, and the other for the teaching of girls to read English and to work all kinds of needlework. The schoolhouse for the teaching of boys to be 20 feet in length and 16 feet of breadth within the walls, and the height thereof to be 13 feet, and to have a chimney built of stone therein of 8 feet wide. And the schoolhouse for teaching of girls to be 16 feet of length and 16 feet of breadth within the walls and the height thereof to be 12 or 13 feet and have a chimney likewise built of stone therein of 8 feet wide, and that both the said schoolhouses be floored all over with good strong oaken board. And for the erecting, building and finishing of both the said schoolhouses handsomely, strongly and substantially and sufficiently with all things needful and necessary, decent and fitting, I do give will and bequeath the sum of £100 or £120 or whatsoever more will do, and finish the same in and after the form and manner aforesaid at the decision of my executors. I will and bequeath that my next heir shall assure and settle three score pounds a year . . . £30 per annum for the finding and maintaining of a sufficient schoolmaster for the teaching of the said boys in the said school . . . and £10 for a sufficient usher, and £20 for the finding and maintaining of a sufficient schoolmistress for the teaching of the said girls. And that the Lord or Lady of the manors of Madeley . . . shall have the sole election and choice of the schoolmaster and schoolmistress often as need shall require . . . whom I desire to have a special care in their choice as well of the skill and sufficiency as of the carriage and behaviour of the parties they make choice of, always provided that the now vicar of Madeley John Jackson be none of them, and I will and bequeath that all the boys and girls of Madeley, Onneley and Mucclestone parish be free to come to be taught in the said schools without paying anything at all for their schooling and teaching therein.

In a codicil to his will Sir John also left the sum of £250 for the building of two houses for the master and mistress.

The school is remarkable not only in respect of the detail provided in the will, but also in the fact that it was actually built in accordance with those details, and survived to be included in George Griffiths' 1860 report, *The Free Schools and Endowments of Staffordshire*, by which time 'No Latin has been taught for many years', though the salaries of the master and mistress had been increased by Lord Crewe, the Lord of the Manor, to £60 and £40 respectively and the Madras system of teaching was being used. The School Charity Commissioners reported in 1825 that each school had about 60 pupils in attendance. Moreover, in 1955 the then headmaster was able to report in a local newspaper article that the school continued to flourish, though on the horizon were plans to convert it to a primary school with the building of a new secondary modern school in the village.[98]

Very occasionally alternative forms of provision are to be found, as at Dedham in Essex, where in 1589 the classis (presbytery of elders) determined that every child in the village should be taught to read, a set of 'orders' requiring that

> young children of the town to be taught to read English and that the moity of that which is given at the communion be employed for the teaching of such poor men's children as shall be adjudged able to bear it themselves, and a convenient place to be appointed for the teacher of them.[99]

A quite different kind of support came from the inhabitants of the Fens village of Willingham who, in 1593, joined together to subscribe the impressive sum of £102 7s 8d. The fund was subscribed to by 102 people, with only five donations being more than £2. The articles which were drawn up insisted that only the children of Willingham residents should be taught in the school, with most being required to pay a small fee, the children of the poor alone being taught free of charge. Whether the original subscribers intended that the school should be anything other than an elementary school is not clear, though this quickly did become clear when William Norton, the master, was licensed to teach grammar in 1596. Thereafter the school regularly sent boys to Oxford and Cambridge, though like most very small grammar schools these would be a small minority, with the majority of pupils leaving school when they had acquired the elements of the vernacular. A similar form of financing elementary education is found in the village of Staplehurst in Kent when in 1656 a subscription of £40 was raised to supplement the £150 left by Lancelot Bathurst in his will of 1651 for the education of the poor of the parish in reading, writing and 'instruction in their duty to God and man'.[100] David Underdown has indicated an unusual form of financing a school in uncovering the work of Mrs Hannah Gifford, who in 1651 was appointed by the Town Corporation of Dorchester in Dorset to be mistress of a school at a salary of £10 per annum if fewer than 30 pupils came forward, and £12 if the numbers exceeded that. In fact, at one time she had over 60 pupils in the school. The finance for the school came in part from the receipts at the annual

Gunpowder Plot sermon, which in the later years of the school's history in the 1670s came to only £1 10s. Mrs Gifford was charged to teach her pupils to read and to learn the catechism, though the orientation of the school's curriculum is revealed by her receipt in 1658 of primers, Bibles, testaments and 'other small books' to the value of £3 5s 7d, and in 1666 of eight New Testaments, 11 psalters, 13 primers and 12 horn books.[101]

The evidence for elementary education for girls is scattered and diverse, with the relatively ephemeral nature of such schools as we have been able to note adding to our frustration. But for our purpose there is sufficient evidence to show that at this educational and social level, schooling was provided by both men and women founders for girls to be taught by both masters and mistresses, sometimes alongside boys and sometimes on their own, and that the over-riding aim of such education was a religious one – the fostering of a God-fearing and deferential clientele.

6 Women as agents

GADDERS TO SERMONS

The picture of women as recipients of the various forms of religious education provided by men fits in well with the position in society that patriarchy
ascribed to them. But it is not a complete picture of women in early modern
England by any means, and it becomes necessary to ask whether and in
what ways they acted as agents in their own and others' education.

It was well recognised that women constituted by far the largest part of
the parish church's congregation, a fact attributed by contemporaries to
their apparently 'natural' piety. Thomas Pomfret, at the end of the period,
was merely echoing a commonplace of long standing, when, as memorialist
to Lady Christina Cavendish, Duchess of Devonshire, he referred to

> virtues almost natural to her sex, the devout sex the Fathers called it, as
> if the very inclinations of women were to religion ... The softest
> natures are usually the most pliant, and the softest natures usually are
> women, and devotion takes first and surest roots in their tender
> breasts.[1]

Richard Hooker, on the other hand, *complained* about the 'eagerness' of
women, which made them 'diligent in drawing their husbands, children,
servants, friends and allies in the same way' and noted 'how all near about
them stand affected as concerning the same cause'. That godly women
existed is not difficult to show, though not in any precisely quantifiable way.[2]
Moreover, the evidence of their piety is so diverse, the means available so
varied and the levels of literacy, understanding and motivation so various
that we need not be surprised that no uniform pattern emerges from the
frequent but scattered evidence of their active participation. Some women
were acutely aware of the religious changes that were going on around
them and some, Catholic or Protestant, so firm in their belief that they were

willing to suffer martyrdom as a result. Anne Askew's refusal to bow to her interrogators' insistence on her wrong-headedness was only one of the most famous. Of the 358 Henrican and Marian martyrs recorded in Foxe's *Book of Martyrs*, 48 were women. Of the 305 Cheshire recusants recorded as being presented and punished, 138 were women.[3] Others were willing to risk and actually suffer persecution, torture, whipping or imprisonment for their religious beliefs. During Mary Tudor's reign many women went into exile with their husbands. Under Elizabeth the same was true of some Catholic women. Many of those who remained, whether 'church papists' or not, took great risks to harbour and succour seminary priests. When a parish priest was 'deprived' his wife suffered with him, as did the wives of royalists during the Commonwealth, and of non-conformists after 1660.

As we shall see, women's propensity for religious adherence was not only noticed and commented on, but attested, both by report and by the evidence of the attendance at divine service, by their letters, spiritual diaries, biblical commonplace books, by their family observance and closet prayer and meditation, as well as in some cases by their writing of religious pamphlets and books, and even by their engaging in the act of public preaching. At the same time, of course, we do well to remember the host of 'conformable' women whose piety has gone unrecorded, though their number swelled the ranks of the godly as a matter of dutiful, Christian obedience.

Women's attendance at churches other than their own parish church, and on days other than the Sabbath, was regularly noticed. There were, of course, plenty of men who found it desirable to attend more than one sermon in the week, but it was to women of like mind that the pejorative label 'gadders' was applied, as John Wing, for example, reported in 1620:

> Nay (says many an impious and profane wretch), if she be a churchgoer, a gadder after sermons, let her go, I will have none of her. I cannot endure these precise dames who are all for religion and never well busied but are poring over their Bibles.[4]

Whilst the more conservative of Elizabeth's church, and especially the later Laudians, were inclined to play down the importance of the sermon – even advocating restricting the number of sermons preached, arguing for a praying rather than a preaching ministry and emphasising the efficacy of the sacraments and liturgical prayers, especially those in the authorised Book of Common Prayer and those formulated for special occasions – there were some who approached the matter with a more positive outcome in mind. Henry Smith, for example, was concerned to make each sermon more effective by instructing his flock in what he called 'The Art of Hearing', the heading of two sermons which he devoted to just this issue:

> There is nothing so easy as to hear well . . . the ABC of a Christian is to
> learn the art of hearing . . . You are here like birds and we the dam,
> and the Word the food; therefore you must prepare your mouth to take
> It . . . My exhortation to you is to record when you have gone that
> which you have heard.

In this way, he urged his listeners, 'You will learn more from one sermon
than you reap from ten'.[5]

And many women, concerned to make an active contribution to their
own religious education, earnestly took him at his word. Lady Margaret
Hoby regularly recorded in her diary her attendance at church, either in her
home parish of Hackness in Yorkshire or during her visits to London, where
on several occasions she attended the chapel of St Anne's in Blackfriars at
which Stephen Egerton preached, besides the services at Westminster
Abbey to which she travelled by water from her brother-in-law's house in
the Strand.[6] John Mayer, the memorialist of Lucy Thornton, wife of John
Thornton of Little Wratting in Suffolk, reported in his funeral sermon that

> Neither the length of the way, the cold and wet of winter, neither the
> business of the world, could hinder her feet from coming to the house
> of God upon the Lord's days; upon lecture days and upon every occa-
> sion of preaching she was seen with the forwardest about the Lord's
> service.[7]

Elizabeth Juxon, wife of the London merchant John Juxon, is reported as
having heard 'for the most part nine or ten sermons every week, whereof
four of them constantly on the Sabbath'. She had apparently undergone
some kind of religious conversion during her adult life, since the preacher
of her funeral sermon reported that before that experience she had 'mar-
velled what people meant to run dragling to sermons'.[8] Oliver Heywood
recalled that his mother, Alice,

> hath in her time taken intolerable pains to hear sermons; scarce any
> public exercise, stated or occasional, within many miles, but she went to
> it; she was, as it were, the centre of news for knowing the time and
> place of weekday sermons.[9]

Anne Venn's *A Wise Virgins Lamp Burning*, posthumously published in 1658
as a record of 'God's sweet incomes of love to a gracious soul waiting for
Him, being the experiences of Mrs Anne Venn, daughter of Col. John
Venn, and a member of the church of Christ in Fulham, written in her
own hand and found in her closet after her death', reported her constant

attendance at the sermons of Christopher Love and Isaac Knight, and her practice of taking notes thereof.[10]

Such attendance at sermons (and the examples could have been repeated many times over) would for the most part indicate a high degree of active pious intent – even, in particular cases, of 'spiritual hypochondria'.[11] Not surprisingly, such practice attracted its share of criticism from clerics and laity alike who, supporting those in authority, saw it as a disturbing indication of the trend for women to ignore traditional views about their 'weakness', and thus to claim for themselves a degree of spiritual autonomy hitherto denied them. Lancelot Andrewes was voicing a common view when he complained:

> For what is it to serve God in holiness? Why to go to sermons? All our holiday holiness, yea and our working day too, are come to this, to hear (nay, I dare not say that, I cannot prove it) but to be at a sermon.[12]

For those who were more concerned with uniformity and conformity, what went on outside the church once the service and sermon were over was seen to be as much a danger as an opportunity for reinforcement, though it was certainly reinforcement that Henry Smith had in mind, and indeed did John Donne who, repeating a homely metaphor, likened repetition to chewing the cud: 'The holy rumination, the daily consideration of his Christianity, is a good character of a Christian . . . all good resolutions . . . must pass a rumination, a chewing of the cud, a second examination'. The metaphor had been used in the first sermon of the First Book of Homilies, in 1547, and was used again by Leonard Wright in his *Pilgrimage to Paradise*, 1591, and by William Perkins in his *Art of Prophesying*, 1607.[13] John Preston, on the other hand, likened those who heard a sermon and then did nothing more about it to seasick sailors who, once ashore, quickly forgot what had happened to them at sea: 'Not repeating the Word of God after it is preached quencheth the spirit. Except it be remembered and hid in our hearts we shall get no good by it.'[14] Daniel Featley used a different metaphor again, to the same end: 'Notes of a sermon preached are like the manna that fell on the Sabbath eve, which if it was not presently gathered up was utterly lost.'[15]

Repeating the sermon to oneself would obviously play a part in a woman's self-education in matters religious. Erasmus' report to Budé that Thomas More's daughters could 'recount nearly the whole sermon to you in order' was, however, unusual at that early date, especially as he went on to claim that the majority of women came back from the sermon remembering nothing of what had been said.[16] Doubtless, however, the 'gadders' heeded the advice to repeat to themselves at least the heads of the sermons they had heard in order to 'hide it in their hearts' and 'get some good of it thereby'. At the end of the century Margaret Hoby was noting almost as a matter of course that she 'talked with some of the house of the sermon'; 'after dinner I conferred of the sermon with the gentlewomen that were with me'; 'kept company with my friends talking somewhat of the sermon'.[17] At about the same time in the godly household of Roger and Lucy Thornton (who died in 1619) morning and evening prayers and the reading of the scriptures were supplemented by attendance at preaching on the Sabbath and lecture days, after which at home 'every sermon was carefully rehearsed'.[18] Orphaned at the age of 14, Mary Gunter found herself in the household of Sir Christopher Blount, whose wife, Lettice, Dowager Countess of Leicester, weaned her away from her early Catholic upbringing, causing her to give an account of the sermons that were preached in the house twice a day on Sundays.[19] Oliver Heywood recalled in his autobiography that when he was a boy his mother repeated to him many passages of sermons she had heard preached before she was married.[20] Henry Newcome noted in his diary the several occasions on which the sermon of the day was repeated in his household on Sunday evenings. The preacher of Lady Anne Waller's funeral sermon reported in 1662 that

> Her custom was after the sermon both in the morning and the afternoon to retire to her chamber and to call before her maidservants and such boys as served in the house to give an account of what they had heard, helping their memories, and wherein they failed clearing up the sense of what was delivered ... exhorting and pressing them to be doers of the Word and not only hearers only.[21]

Lucy Apsley, who was born in 1620 and who later married Colonel John Hutchinson, recalled that, by the time she was 4 she was carried to sermons and 'whilst I was very young could remember and repeat sermons exactly, and being caressed, the love of praise tickled me and made me attend more heedfully'.[22] Catherine, the daughter of parliamentarian Sir John Holland and his Catholic wife Alethea, had a different tale to tell. Her father was determined to maintain a strict Protestant upbringing for his daughter and, as she later recounted, having followed her mother's religious persuasion

> Being about ten years of age and my father for my good holding a strict hand over me, severely corrected me; if I learned not my catechism he debarred me from my meat, and if I remembered not the sermons I was made to write them down.[23]

Lady Elizabeth Langham, the second wife of Sir James Langham, had a happier relationship with her step-children, but was equally strict in their religious upbringing. As her memorialist recorded,

> From her [step-]daughter of about eleven years of age she exacted constantly a repetition by heart of the sermons she heard, for which task she had by her instruction so logically methodized the memory of that so young a child that she was able to analyse a discourse of thirty or forty particular heads *memoriter* with the most remarkable enlargements upon them.[24]

In similar fashion Lady Elizabeth Brooke, who died in 1683 aged 81, insisted on a repetition of the Sunday sermon after prayers and scripture readings in her household. In a letter of 11 February 1672 to her husband Sir Edward (Brilliana's 'Ned'), Lady Abigail Harley reported 'We have constant family duties the Sabbath day. Between sermons I repeated the heads of the sermon to the maids.'[25]

In some cases, attendance at sermons and the practice of rehearsing and conferring at home were further reinforced by the habit of taking notes either at the sermon itself or later at home, noting first the text, then the 'doctrine' – the theology arising from the text – and then the various heads into which the preacher had divided his sermon, with finally the examples and the applications which would have further explicated the text and completed the sermon. Note-taking at sermons was not, of course, an entirely new practice in the early modern period. Erasmus had noted in 1521 that in 'ancient days hardly any one preached a sermon without posting secretaries to take down what had been said'.[26] It also became a regular part of the routine of grammar-school boys, who were required by the statutes of their school to attend church with their master (often in a gallery specially built for their accommodation). Some of the older boys were charged to take notes of the sermon – which would then be used on Monday mornings to reconstruct the sermon, as much a part of their rhetorical training as of their religious education. John Brinsley and Charles Hoole both recommended the practice.[27] Comenius reported that he had seen it in action. Another visitor to England, Cosmo III, Duke of Tuscany, reported of English women:

> They are remarkably well-informed in the dogmas of the religion they profess; and when they attend at the discourses of their ministers they write down an abridgement of what they say, having in the letters abbreviations which facilitate to them and to the men also (thanks to their natural quickness and acuteness of their genius) the powers of doing this with rapidity.[28]

Writing to her son Christopher (*c*.1620) when he was at Jesus College, Cambridge, Lady Hatton was firm in her advice:

> Hear sermons, strive to take notes that you may meditate on them, without which you can never practise what is the only end for which you were created, to know God's will and to endeavour to do it.[29]

The memorising of sermons and then making a note of them at home is exemplified in the practice of Margaret Hoby who, not content with merely talking with her friends about the sermon, constantly wrote up her notes once she had returned home. On 13 August 1599 she reported 'and then I wrote out the sermon into my book preached the day before'. Her entry for 30 September of the same year is not unusual: 'went to church, whence after I had heard catechising and sermon, I returned home and wrote notes in my Bible'.[30] Before she married Robert Harley in 1623, Brilliana Conway was in the habit of keeping a commonplace book in which, besides passages from the Bible and extracts from her reading of Calvin's *Institutes*, William Perkins' *Cases of Conscience* and *Exposition of the Lord's Prayer*, and Nathaniel Coles' *Godly Mans Assurance*, she included notes of the sermons preached by Thomas Case, the vicar of Arrow in Warwickshire, the Conways' home parish.[31] That constant note-taker of sermons, Philip Henry, later encouraged his daughter Sarah to write outlines of the sermons she had heard, a practice she continued after her marriage in 1687 to John Savage and into her old age (she died in 1752 aged 78).[32]

Instead of making notes on their return from church some women preferred to take notes in church itself as the sermon progressed. For example, John Barlow, who preached the funeral sermon for Lady Mary Strode in 1619, reported that:

> She was a notary and took sermons which she heard by her own hand . . . She did this when as many much meaner than she come with their fans and feathers, whereas (me seems) a goose quill would be far better befit their fingers . . . Moreover, having taken her notes, she did in her chamber repeat to her maidservants the sermons she had heard and penned.[33]

Mary Bewley, who died in 1659, was another constant noter of the sermons she heard in her parish church. Sometimes, however (as her memorialist reported), 'she refrained from writing in the church that she might exercise her memory and be more attentive to what she heard, which after she came home she committed to writing'.[34] Katherine Overton married the prolific ecclesiastical biographer Samuel Clarke in 1625. Before her marriage, however, her father, who was Rector of Bedworth in Warwickshire, 'caused her to write sermons and repeat the same'. After her marriage, as her husband recalled, 'her usual manner was to write sermons to prevent drowsiness and distractions and to help her memory, whereof she hath left many volumes, and her practice was to make good use of them by frequent reading and meditation upon them'. She later catechised her own nine children, as well as 'enquiring what they remembered of the sermons they heard, reading her notes to them'.[35] Katherine Fowler, later eulogised as 'the matchless Orinda', 'could take down sermons *verbatim* when she was but ten years old', and presumably continued the practice when she was a pupil at Mrs Salmon's academy for the daughters of gentlemen in Hackney.[36]

There is thus a variety of evidence to show that, as now, women constituted the larger part of a preacher's congregation, and that besides those who made a regular practice of repeating sermons at home, some of those who were literate took notes either at or after the sermon, to be used not only for their own spiritual edification but also for that of their 'family' – their children and servants. But in order to make notes once having returned from church, or even to repeat the main heads of the sermon with their family, godly women would have to receive some help in their memorising. The 'art of memory' has a long history and remains important to this day in pre-literate societies relying entirely on oral communication. In the transition from an oral world to a literate world there is no clear chronological dividing line.[37] Paradoxically, early modern England was a highly literate society in which the vast majority were illiterate, in the sense of being unable to read or write in any functional way. The godly illiterates thus had to be helped to a knowledge of God's Word, chiefly by simple repetition. Even so, the historian has to resist the temptation of jumping from Erasmus' hope that the weaver would hum parts of the scripture to the movement of his shuttle, the traveller lighten the weariness of his journey with stories from the Bible, and that 'even the lowliest woman would read the Gospels and Pauline Epistles', to the conclusion that this did indeed come to pass as quickly as Erasmus (and his Protestant successors) expected.[38] Yet this passage from the *Paraclesis* could be interpreted as Erasmus' realistic recognition that a knowledge of the Bible could be achieved by means of constant 'repetition' and 'rehearsal', in the godly family as well as in church, in much the same way as constant hearings over a period of years of, say, the symphonies of Beethoven and Brahms enable one to hum or whistle whole passages without the benefit of a knowledge of musical notation or of being able to read music. The 1538 Injunctions plainly recognised this when it was required of the clergy that

every holy day throughout the year, when they have no sermon, they should immediately after the Gospel, openly and plainly recite to their parishioners in the pulpit the Pater Noster, the Credo and the Ten Commandments in English, to the intent the people may learn the same by heart.[39]

When the psalms are not only translated into the vernacular but are put into metrical form, as they were in mid-sixteenth-century England, the illiterate person is likewise aided in acquiring a knowledge of that part of the Bible. The Lessons in the Book of Common Prayer, constantly repeated in annual cycles, aimed at precisely the same end.

Of course, if it were to stand a chance of being retained, what was spoken had to catch the attention and be memorable in some degree in its vocabulary, its syntax and its structure. Those who wrote on the theory of memory in the sixteenth century made a distinction between what was called natural memory and artificial memory.[40] Presumably it was the former which Henry Smith and others had in mind in their commentaries on the 'art of hearing', in which they gave precise instructions to the godly on what was required of them in order to remember efficiently parts or all of the sermon. Preachers, too, were called upon to play their part in assisting their auditory to remember what had been said. The medieval practice of writing preaching manuals was followed by works such as John Ludham's *The Practis of Preaching* (1577), Richard Bernard's *The Faithfull Shepheard* (1607), William Perkins' *The Art of Prophesying* (1607) and Joseph Glanville's *An Essay Concerning Preaching* (1678), to say nothing of the detailed advice offered in *The Westminster Directory* (1645) and a host of other works which *inter alia* addressed the same problem, such as William Ames' chapter on the construction of a sermon in his *Conscience with the Powere and Cases Thereof* (1639). Luther had recognised the problem early on:

> An upright, godly and true preacher should direct his preaching to the poor, simple sort of people, like a mother that stills her child, dandles and plays with it, presenting it with milk from her own breast, and needing neither malmsey nor muscadin in it. In such sort should preachers carry themselves, teaching and preaching plainly, that the simple and unlearned may conceive and comprehend and retain what they say.[41]

Thomas Wilson likewise reminded preachers that they

> must now and then play the fool in the pulpit, to serve and tickle the ears of their fleeting audience, or else they are like some time to preach to bare walls . . . to delight is needful without the which weighty matters

will not be heeded at all . . . mingle sweet with sour, whether you be a preacher, lawyer, yea or cook.[42]

George Abbot agreed. The ministers, he recommended, should

> use helps of wit, of invention and art (which are God's gifts), to remove away all the disdain and loathing of the Word from the dull hearts of the auditory – similitudes, comparisons, allusions, applications, parables and proverbs, which may tend to edification and illustrating of the Word; for they have to do with weak stomachs as well as strong, with some queasy stomachs, with some dull capacity, with some that must be enticed.[43]

With their wealth of everyday language and homely metaphor the sermons of Latimer and Becon remind us that the call for 'plain language' preaching was not the monopoly of the radical wing of the Elizabethan church and their Stuart successors, though such language became the hallmark of puritan sermonising. Even so, for the preacher seriously concerned to facilitate the remembering and internalising of his sermon, 'plain language' was clearly not enough to achieve the desired end. George Gifford spotted the difficulty:

> But let the preacher speak never so plain, although they sit and look him in the face, yet if ye enquire of them so soon as they be out of the church doors, ye shall easily perceive that (as the common saying goes) it went in one ear and out of the other. They will say peradventure after this manner: it was a good sermon. I would we could follow it. He said very well. He is a perfect ready man in the pulpit. But ask what doctrine did he handle? Then they are at a pause and set at a dead lift.[44]

Equally important, then, was his preparatory structuring of his sermon, and his reminders of that structure as he preached, by way of reinforcement. By the beginning of the seventeenth century the vast majority of clerics would be university graduates, familiar with the tenets of Ramistic rhetoric. It was indeed one of the criticisms of 'mechanick' preachers that they were not so trained, and that therefore their sermons lacked the essential quality of structure. John Collinges provides a not unusual example of attention to structure in his funeral sermon for Mary Sampson in 1649: 'For the better proceeding in the handling of it (his text) and for the helping of your memory, I shall branch the doctrine into these four particulars, which I shall handle distinctly and apply jointly.' He then listed the four 'branches', each to be sub-divided, then going on:

The second thing to be opened . . . I will open it in three or four
particulars . . . I pass on to the third branch. The third branch is . . .
Here for the explanation of this branch I shall do these two things:
firstly . . . secondly . . .[45]

In their different ways, then, many preachers were concerned to help the
men and women of their congregation to leave church with some memory
of what had been said. Note-taking in church, however, was a different and
more difficult matter. Some parishioners would have taken down their notes
in longhand, or used a system of abbreviated writing of their own devising
from which they could have produced a fuller version at a convenient time
later on. Oliver Heywood, for example, reported of his wife's note-taking
that 'She writ long-hand and not characterie, yet she took the heads and
proofs fully and a considerable part of the enlargement.' Margaret Corbet's
memorialist said that 'she left many volumes of sermons in her own hand-
writing, taken with great dexterity'. But most of the reports of women
taking notes of sermons, for whatever purpose, give no indication of how
the notes were taken.[46]

By the end of the sixteenth century, and more frequently in the seventeenth, various systems of shorthand were available for sermon note-takers
and others. Whatever system was used, the authors of shorthand manuals
indicated explicitly that their system was one that could be used to take
notes at sermons. Anthony Tyrell in 'Preface to the Reader', in a version of
a sermon preached by him in 1589 and printed in the same year, wrote:

At the time I made my exhortation publicly in Christ His Church in
London my words were no sooner out of my mouth but a young youth
had penned my sermon verbatim in characterie, an art newly invented,
so that it could be published, but he first sought my permission . . . He
that penned my sermon as I uttered it in the pulpit did it most exactly,
writing word for word.[47]

In 1603 appeared *A Lecture preached by Master Egerton at the Blackfriers and taken
by Characterie by a Young Practitioner in that Facultie and now again Perused, Corrected
and Amended by the author*. Stephen Egerton had obviously thoroughly
involved himself in the publication of his lecture, which he had preached
back in 1589, and was unusually forthcoming about the whole process. In
his preface 'To the Reader' he wrote

And now touching noting at sermons give me leave (gentle reader) in a
word to tell you what I think. For the thing itself I dare not (with some)
condemn it as unlawful, but rather commend it as expedient if there be

judgment, memory and dexterity of the hand in the party. Above all things (in my opinion as in other matters so in this) a good conscience is more requisite . . . To these may be added (which myself I have found by some experience) that the swiftest hand cometh often short of the slowest tongue, as I have perceived by diverse things which I have penned from my own mouth . . . My advice is, to such as have willing hearts and ready hands and convenient places to write at sermons, that they would use it for their own private help and edification, and the comfort and benefit of their families and such Christian friends as they have the occasion to confer withal in private, and not suffer themselves to be seduced by gain or glory to set forth those things which may be not only prejudiced to the preacher but dishonourable to God and unprofitable to the church.

Egerton's preface is followed by another written by the person who had taken down the sermon in the first place, in which he notes 'I have not willingly missed one word whereby either the truth of the doctrine might be permitted or the meaning of the preacher altered.'[48] Henry Smith, on the other hand, had a similar but less satisfactory experience. Two of his sermons were printed in 1590 and 1591 which he felt impelled to reissue in his own version in 1592. Thomas Playfere's sermon of 1596 suffered in similar fashion, with two pirated editions appearing before he published his own version. As he reported to his dedicatee, Lady Elizabeth Cary, 'I had rather have my head broken than to have my sermon so mangled.'[49]

Tyrell's reference to the newly invented art of 'characterie' had its origins in Timothy Bright's *Characterie. An Arte of Shorte Swifte and Secrete Writing by Character* (1588). By the time Heywood came to refer to it, characterie had become a generic term rather than one particular to Bright's system. Bright's manual was, in fact, never reprinted, though in due course it was replaced by a whole stream of texts such as John Willis' *The Art of Stenography or Short Writing* (1602), Henry Dix's *The Art of Brachygraphy or Short Writing* (1641), Jeremiah Rich's *Semography or Short and Swift Writing* (1641), Thomas Shelton's *Tachygraphy. The Most Compendious and Exacte Methode of Short and Swift Writing* (1684), William Addy's *Stenographia or The Art of Short Writing* (1684), Abraham Nicholas' *Theographia or A New Art of Shorthand* (1692), and a host of others, often going into many editions, mostly written by 'teachers of the art' and all claiming that their system was not only new but 'the most easy, exact, lineal and speedy method that hath yet obtained'.[50]

The question remains, however, what evidence is there that women followed men in using shorthand in their sermon note-taking? It is easily established that they took notes, but there is little indication as to how precisely they took them, though Ralph Verney advised William Denton:

Let not your girl learn Latin nor shorthand. The difficulty of the first may keep her from that vice, for so I must esteem it in a woman; but the easiness of the other may be a prejudice to her, for the pride of taking sermon notes hath made multitudes of women most unfortunate.[51]

Elizabeth Dunton used a system of her own devising to write her diary. Elizabeth Bury kept one for 30 years, the first ten years of which, as her husband reported, was 'in shorthand which cannot be recovered by me', and Hannah Allen used shorthand to record 'promises together with temptations and other afflications, and how God delivered me out of them'.[52] But apart from the comments about Elizabeth Heywood and Margaret Corbet, both of whom used longhand, none of the other reports of women's note-taking mention what means were used. Though Egerton's sermon was taken by a shorthand writer his comments about note-taking, though obviously addressed to a wider audience, are couched only in general terms, and refer to the purpose of note-taking rather than to the method of taking notes. The reports seem to indicate that women spent more time in perfecting the art of memorising, a skill in which they were plainly assisted by some preachers, and by texts such as John Willis' *The Art of Memory* (1621), than they did in mastering a system of shorthand. Nor indeed did most church-goers – men and women alike – need a *verbatim* text such as a shorthand writer would have attempted to produce, when their purpose was simply to produce a 'note' for home consumption, as an *aide memoire* in the practice of repetition and rehearsal which was much more common in the godly household as a supplement to family prayer and psalm-singing.

It can readily be established, then, that Protestant women of all persuasions were assiduous attenders at sermon time, and that some took notes either at the sermon or later at home, not simply for their own spiritual enlightenment and as an act of self-education, but also to assist in their participation, as educative agents, in the rehearsing and conferring with their immediate family as with their servants, a practice which was a hallmark of a 'godly' household. Such activities in a conforming family were obviously intended to· reinforce the teachings of the established church. Equally, they could be the means of providing biblical knowledge and argumentation for those who wished to challenge orthodoxy. Whether they resulted in a challenging heterodoxy or a sincerely held orthodoxy it is impossible to tell at anything other than an individual level, confronted as we are by a continuum of beliefs ranging from those of Anna Trapnel to those of a woman such as Margaret Hoby whose diary entries about her sermon-going show no sign of anything other than an active and sincere acceptance of the doctrines she had heard propounded. Sermon-goers included the listening Christian woman and the challenging Christian woman, just as the art of listening and remembering, the skill of note-taking and the practices of rehearsal and conferral were behaviour which disguised a heterogeneity of motivation and response. John Milton was not alone in his belief that 'when there is much desire to learn, there of necessity will be much arguing, much writing, many opinions'.[53]

Notwithstanding the attempts of the vast majority of men in the early modern period to assign to women a passive role in both church and family, the evidence of women attending and paying careful attention to the sermons they heard and of their use of this in their families, suggests that listening, rehearsing, conferring played as important a part in the religious education of women as Bible-reading, psalm-singing, catechising and family prayer. With regard to sermon note-taking, however, a final unresolved question remains, and it concerns the simple logistic of taking notes in church as the sermon was being preached. Most of the godly women who were literate would own or at least have access to an inkpot and a supply of quills and paper, if only to write up their commonplace books, spiritual diaries and sermon notes at home in the privacy of their closet, as Hans Eworth for example showed in his portrait of Mary Neville, Lady Dacre.[54] But nowhere it seems do we have any documentation of the carrying of quill, inkpot and paper into church, nor indeed any references to complaints from ministers of the noise of scratching quills and shuffling papers, though, as we have seen, John Barlow would have preferred that to the 'fans and feathers' which some of his parishioners apparently carried with them into church. There are plenty of woodcuts showing women attending sermons, though I have yet to find one showing them with pen and ink in hand.[55]

PRIVATE PRAYER

Women and girls were thus a target for the receipt of religious education in church and in school, that is, in public with others of their own or the other sex. One kind of provision, collections of prayers and texts providing guidance on the process of prayer, leads to the possibility of their being charged with the responsibility of undertaking in private their own religious practice, with being agents instead of recipients in search of salvation. The two distinctions being used here – public–private and recipient–agent – are not, of course, as mutually exclusive as they appear, any more than is the 'public–private spheres' distinction that patriarchy would have wished in delineating the respective roles of the two sexes. Even so, in the matter of religious education the distinction between recipient–agent is sufficiently clear to be useful in presenting the materials and practice of religious education.

We have seen the importance attached to the role of prayer in the liturgy of public worship, as well as in the family setting, but the prescriptive literature is equally urgent in its recommendation of private prayer, in which the proof-texts Matthew 6.6 and Luke 5.16, where Jesus is reported as withdrawing for prayer into a private room or into 'the wilderness', are used as starting points for exposition. Church-goers would have heard readings of the two-part Homily 'On the place and time of prayer', which urged them to supplement the prayers of public worship with 'secret' prayer at home, when they could use any of the readily available collections of prayers of confession, of petition and of thanksgiving, such as Edward Dering's *Godly Private Prayers for Householders to Meditate Upon and Saye to Their Families* (1575) or John Cosin's *The House of Prayer* (1626), a favourite of those with High Church leanings, amongst many others. Alternatively, as Michael Spark reminded his readers, 'Besides our more special devotions at set times, we may use ejaculations at all times, upon every occasion, which are short desires of the heart lifted up to God with great fervency.'[56] There was, of course, another side to the coin, which Oliver Heywood noted in his *Closet Prayer, A Christian Duty* (1671):

> The power of godliness is much spoken of, but (I am afraid) very rarely to be found amongst (even) famous professors. Most content themselves with external, visible duties, while formalists may carry on with as much seeming zeal and applause as sincere worshippers. A formal spirit is the disease of the present day ... There are thousands in the world will run many miles to hear a sermon ... yet will not set themselves solemnly to the duties of meditation, self-examination or secret prayer.[57]

His remonstration was not, of course, unique to his 'present day'.

Even so, there is evidence that the prescriptions were being heeded, though not, as always, in any quantifiable sense. Justinian Isham, for example, was clear and precise in his advice to his daughters, Elizabeth, Jane, Judith and Susan, the eldest of whom was nine when their mother died in 1642:

> Prayers, meditations and such-like holy treatises I rather commend unto you than knotty disputes, and although your sex is not so learned and knowing as men ought to be, yet be sure to keep your thoughts upright and your affections towards God unfeigned, and there is no doubt but that will be more acceptable unto Him than all the wisdom of the whole world besides. St Augustine's *Meditations*, Kempis on the *Imitation of Christ* and Gerard's *Meditations* I commend unto you, as also Doctor

Fealtie's [sic] *Handmaid to Devotion* and divers treatises of Dr Sibbes, often read over by your mother who was a religious and discreet woman.[58]

Despite his eclectic recommendations he nevertheless went on to insist on a thoroughly conservative set of 'graces and virtues' with which women ought to be endued, including holiness, chastity, obedience, charity, meekness, modesty, sobriety, silence, discretion, frugality, affability. John Foxe provides an early example in the person of 'Mistress Dolly Cottismore' who was presented for insisting to her servant John Bainton

> That if she went to her chamber and prayed there she would have as much merit as though she went to Walsingham on pilgrimage . . . that when women go to offer to image or saints they did it to show their new gay gear, and that folk go on pilgrimage for the green way than for any devotion.[59]

Grace Mildmay, Margaret Hoby and Katherine Brettergh were each assiduous in their practice of private prayer. The memorialist of Elizabeth Gouge reported that she engaged in 'daily exercises of piety in her house and also caused her children and servants to do the like'. These were supplemented by 'private devotions at set hours; with her own hands she penned sundry devout prayers; she hath also left written many divine directions for devotions'.[60] In her *Mothers Blessing* (1616), Dorothy Leigh stressed 'the pre-eminence of private prayer' and in her *Mothers Legacie to her Unborn Child* (1624) Elizabeth Jocelin included a set of prayers for the child to use until it could make up its own.[61] During the absence at sea of her husband Sir Kenelm Digby, his wife Venetia

> secluded herself from the world . . . the greater part of the day she spent at her prayers, and the rest, that was not taken up in ordering domestic business and overlooking her children, she employed in meditating and reading of holy and spiritual books.

It was her normal practice each morning before dressing to spend two hours in prayer, and whilst dressing to have someone to read to her from some godly book.[62]

The preacher of the funeral sermon for Mrs Mary Overman of St Saviour's parish in Southwark (who died in 1646) reminded his listeners that 'her chamber was not a shop of confection (as the fashion is) but an oratory for devotion'.[63] Jeremy Taylor, the preacher of the funeral sermon for Lady Frances Carbery, drew on his personal knowledge of his subject, as chaplain to the family of the Earl of Carbery at Golden Grove in

Carmarthenshire, to praise her as 'a great reader of scripture . . . a constant person at her prayers', one who had 'a very great love to hear the Word of God preached' and was 'a constant reader of sermons'.[64] Elizabeth Livingstone noted in her diary her resolution to 'retire myself to my closet and there to breathe forth all my sorrow betwixt God and my own soul, which is the only true way of finding comfort'.[65] Brilliana Harley made a point of reminding her son 'Ned':

> let nothing hinder you from performing constant private duties of praying and reading. Experimentally I may say that private prayer is one of the best means to keep the heart close to God. O, it is a sweet thing to pour out our heart to God as a friend.[66]

In the absence of her husband, Dorothy Shaw (died 1657) never failed 'to gather her family twice daily for prayer, psalm-singing and scripture reading'.[67] Margaret Baxter, wife of Richard Baxter, was unusual in her refusal to act in his stead if he were at home but not wishing to be interrupted in his task of writing. Susanna Wesley, on the other hand, found herself in conflict with her husband Samuel when she defended her practice of leading prayer and expounding the gospel to her family in her husband's many absences on preaching duties.[68]

Lady Elizabeth Alston, who died in 1677, is reported by her memorialist as being constant in her private devotions whilst maintaining the duties of religious observance within her family. The same was true of Lady Dorothy Drake who 'spent much time day by day in her closet devotions . . . she knew closet prayers were as much a duty as church prayers'.[69] Of Mrs Martha Brooks, the wife of the Rev. Thomas Brooks, the preacher of her funeral sermon reported that

> a near relation [had told him] I never knew any woman spend more time in her closet, nor keep more private days to God than she did. The duties of the closet were her meat and drink, and she was always best when she was with God in a corner.[70]

Edmund Barker had been the chaplain to Lady Elizabeth Capel for 8 years, and thus when she died in 1660 and he preached at her funeral sermon he could reliably report that:

> Her closet was not (as too many ladies' are) an exchange only of curious pictures and of rare and costly jewels, but a private oratory (as it were) chiefly designed for prayer and devotion . . . it was very seldom if ever that I found her alone there without a Bible before her.[71]

Anthony Walker's wife, Elizabeth, 'after she had ceased from child-bearing' rose at 4 a.m. winter and summer and 'spent at least two hours with God', calling her room 'the chamber of her choice mercies and beloved retirements'.[72] Lady Anne Burgoyne, who died in 1694, was

> a great admirer of the public prayers of our church [of England] . . . and not withstanding the prejudices of her education which might easily have created an unconquerable aversion to our stated formes. Yet the follies and indecencies of that bold extempore way soon made her weary and ashamed of that.

Even so, she engaged herself in twice-daily family prayers and 'constant retirements every day for secret prayer, reading of the scriptures and heavenly meditations upon them'.[73]

In cases such as these we have examples of what Peter Lake, referring to the pious Chester housewife, Jane Ratcliffe, has called 'an urgent autodidacticism', with women acting in a positive though private way as agents in their own search for the path to salvation.[74]

CLOSET MEDITATION

We have seen that private prayer featured predominantly in the prescriptive literature of religious education and in the daily practice of godly women, as an essential supplement to participation in public worship. Equally important, it was considered, was the practice of religious meditation, one which a woman could also undertake in private as part of her religious formation. As Richard Braithwait put it, a women's closet should be a place for something more than 'bedecking':

> Make your chamber your private theatre wherein you may act some decent scene to God's honour. Be still from the world, but stirring towards God. Meditation, let it be your companion. It is the perfume of memory, the soul's riser from sin's lethargy, the sweetest solace in straits of adversity. Let it be your key to open the morning, your lock to close the evening.

Richard Rogers called such a practice 'the companion of watchfulness and the sister of prayer'; Leonard Wright, 'the key to conscience'.[75]

'Closet exercises' such as these produced a further kind of evidence which gives an indication not only of female piety, but also of women's contribution to religious education, whether of themselves or of others.

Some meditations were designed to be used for particular occasions, such as that produced by authority in response to the troubles of the plague year of 1553: 'A form of meditation very meet to be daily used of householders in their houses in this dangerous contagious time.'[76] Others were compiled to cover various aspects of Christian life. John Bradford's *Godly Meditations Upon the Lord's Prayer, the Beleefe and Ten Commandments with many comfortable prayers and exercises* (1570), for example, included meditations 'Of Death', 'Of the Coming of Christ', 'Of God's Providence', 'Of the Passion of Christ' and so on. Christopher Sutton's *Godly Meditations upon the Most Holy Sacrament of the Lord's Supper* (1613) was dedicated to Katherine and Francis [sic] Southwell, 'sisters attending upon the Queen's Majesty in her honourable Privy Chamber'. In it each meditation is followed by 'The fruit of meditation' and 'A soliloquy upon meditation', the latter offering guidance on various aspects of the meditation, which should be 'considered in meditative thought'. The Laudian John Cosin compiled his *Collection of Private Devotions Called the House of Prayer* (1627) in reply to the books of devotions for Catholics, which he considered to be superior to those available to Protestants. Sir Richard Baker produced a set of *Meditations and Disquisitions Upon the Lord's Prayer* (1636) and *Meditations and Disquisitions Upon the Seven Psalms of David Commonly Called the Penetential Psalms* (1642).

Bishop Joseph Hall's *Meditations and Vowes Divine and Morall* (1606), which he dedicated to Lady Drury, wife of Sir John Drury, ranged more widely, supplementing his *Art of Divine Meditation* (1606), in which he gave detailed guidance on the state of mind appropriate for meditation, the place and time for such devotion, as well as on the process itself which 'must proceed in due order, not troubledly, not preposterously'. Meditation, he urged, 'begins in the understanding, endeth in the affection; it begins in the brain, descends to the heart'.[77] John Downame gave similar advice in the section on meditation in his *Guide to Godlynesse* (1622). Edmund Calamy devoted several sermons to the practice, which were published posthumously in 1680, as *The Art of Meditation*, and in which he placed prime emphasis on the importance of spending time reflecting on the content of sermons:

> for it is with sermons as with meat, it is not the having of the meat upon your table will feed you, but you must eat it, and not only eat it, but concoct it and digest it, or else your meat will do you no good. So it is with sermons . . . the concocting them, the digesting them by medita-tion . . . One sermon well digested, well meditated upon, is better than twenty sermons without meditation . . . A meditating Christian is one that chews the cud, that chews on the truths of Christ.

Widening his injunction, he stressed the importance of preparing oneself for meditation by choosing a fit subject, from the Bible or a sermon or a godly book, and then finding a quiet or solitary place, if not in the house then out of doors, as Isaac had, 'going into the fields at eventide', or Christ himself had when He 'went up into the mountain'.[78] The Roman Catholic Richard Gibbons produced a similar piece of guidance for his faith in his *The Practical Method of Meditation* which he prefixed to his translation *An Abridgment of Meditations . . . by Vincentius Bruns SJ* (St Omer, 1614), with each meditation followed by a 'Let us learn', for example, 'To be glad of our neighbours', 'To follow divine inspirations', 'To bless and praise God continually'.

Richard Baxter's massive *Saints Everlasting Rest* (1650), which ran into many subsequent editions, provided a most comprehensive consideration of the practice of and justification for the practice, that 'cogitation on things spiritual', as he called it, which nevertheless was 'confessed to be a duty by all, but by the constant neglect denied by most'. As an appendix to his *Method for Meditation or A Manuall of Divine Duties Fit for Every Christians Practice* (1651), James Ussher offered 'six wholesome dishes of spiritual meat . . . six divine duties to be meditated upon and practised by every good Christian', the 'dishes' consisting of particular scriptural passages each of which embodied a Christian duty.[79] In Thomas White's *Method and Instruction for the Art of Divine Meditation* (1655), he claimed 'I have wrote this for the meanest and ignorantest sort of Christians, that they might buy it and understand it; I have made it plain, and spoke to them in their own language'. White made the usual distinction between 'occasional' meditation, when some particular occurrence in daily life gives pause for thought, and 'solemn' meditation, on a sermon, or a prayer, or a passage of scripture or 'a practical truth of religion', and after advice about time and place provided a comprehensive collection of 'Instances of solemn and occasional meditations'. William Spurstowe produced a similar collection in his *The Spiritual Chymist or Six Decades of Divine Meditations on Several Subjects* (1666, posthumously) in which he included meditations 'Upon a crum[b] going the wrong way', 'On the morning dew', 'Upon the galaxy or Milky Way', 'Upon the breast and sucking bottle', 'On the Bible', 'On going to bed'. Thomas Fuller's *Good Thoughts in Bad Times* (1645) was equally down to earth in its approach: 'Lord, I confess this morning I remembered my breakfast, but forgot my prayers'; 'I discover an arrant laziness in my soul, for when I am to read a chapter in thy Bible before I begin it I look where it endeth.' Many sections begin with 'I read that . . .' and then proceed to offer a reflection on it. In his sacred poem 'The Church Porch', a prolonged piece of advice on amongst other things prayer and sermon-listening, George Herbert urged his readers:

Sum up at night what thou hast done by day,
And in the morning what thou hast to do.
Dress and undress thy soul; mark the decay
And growth of it.[80]

Samuel Clarke offered much the same kind of advice: 'When we go to sleep with some holy meditations in our minds it will be an excellent preservative against foolish dreams and fancies, and we shall find our hearts in the better frame when we awake.'[81]

Some meditations written by women appeared in print and were plainly intended for the use of others. An early example was Catherine Parr's *Prayers and Medytacions* (1545), which ran to six editions by 1600. The Roman Catholic Elizabeth Grymestone produced a collection of meditations for the use of her son before she died in 1603. Alice Sutcliffe's *Meditations of Mans Mortalite or A Way to True Blessedness*, published in a second edition in 1634 as a 20-page duodecimo volume, was a thoroughly traditional, though not for that reason unimportant, collection of meditations on death, on repentance, on godly living in all its aspects. Elizabeth Warren modestly cited John 6.12 as the justification for her *Spiritual Thrift or Meditations* (1647) which she liberally provided with marginal proof-texts from the Bible and theological authors, concluding with the injunction 'Follow then the scriptures as an infallible guide, which whoso is led by shall never miscarry, because it is the key which openeth the cabinet of God's sacred counsel'.[82] Another later example was Anne Douglas' *The Countess of Mortons Daily Exercises or A Book of Prayers and Rules how to Spend Our Time in the Service and Pleasure of Almighty God*, first published in 1666 and reaching a 24th edition in 1760. Susanna Hopton's *Daily Devotions* (1673) which appeared in a fifth edition in 1703 and as *A Collection of Meditations and Devotions*, edited by George Hickes in 1717, consisted of meditations on the Six Days of the Creation and on various aspects of the life of Christ, together with a set of devotional prayers for a variety of occasions. Amey Hayward published her *Female Legacy Containing Divine Poems on Several Choice Subjects Recommended to all Godly Women* in 1699, some of them in the form of meditations: 'Upon a bee', 'On deceitfulness and vanity', 'On Adam in Paradise and fallen' (in which no mention is made of Eve breaking the law). The book carried a recommendation by Benjamin Keach and was priced at 1s bound. The British Library copy is inscribed 'Mary Deachy her book'.

Some such meditations by women remained in manuscript until they were posthumously published. Elizabeth Juxon's consisted of a set of 'Markes' which she believed characterised an elect person: 'I find fervency in prayer, in secret'; 'The Word worketh in me as a redress of my ways'; 'I desire to deal faithfully in the charge and calling in which I am, and to discharge it in the conscionable fear of God'; 'I love all God's children, and that for the Truth's sake. I esteem them the only excellent people in the world.' They remained in manuscript until they were abstracted in the funeral sermon preached for her on 21 November 1619 by Stephen Denison, who had lived in her house for five years.[83] Those of Dame Gertrude More, the English nun who died at Cambrai in 1633, were posthumously published under her own name as *The Holy Practices of a Divine Lover* (1657) and *The Spiritual Exercises* (1658). Sarah Davy's were published after her death by an anonymous author who revealed their origins in the sub-title of his work, *Heav'n Realized or The Holy Pleasures of Daily Intimate Communion with God, exemplified in a blessed soul (now in heaven) (Mistris Sarah Davy) dying about the 32 years of her age, being a part of the pretious reliques written by her own hand, stiled by her The Record of My Consolations and the Meditations of my Heart. Published by A. P.* (1670). The devotional writings of Anne Halkett, who died in 1699, were similarly abstracted by an anonymous author, S.C., in his *Life of Lady Halkett* (1701, Edinburgh).

Lady Grace Mildmay reported that the practice of meditating 'hath been the exercise of my mind from my youth to this day and has been the consolation of my soul, the joy of my heart and the stability of my mind'. Some she wrote up in a manuscript book, 'which book hath been to me as Jacob's ladder and as Jacob's pillar, even a book of testimonies between God and my soul'.[84] The survival of a series of devotional pieces written by Elizabeth Egerton, Countess of Bridgewater, we owe solely to a manuscript copy collected together in 1663, the year of her death aged 37. They included a meditation on the death of her daughter 'Keatty', who had died of smallpox before she was two, and another on the death of 'my boy Henry', only 29 days old, who had 'lived as many days as my years', in each case expressing the conventional Christian view that such early deaths were but examples of the 'rod of Christian chastisement'.[85] Though she entitled her manuscript books of observations 'Meditations', Mary Rich's were more in the nature of a spiritual diary, consisting as they did in almost daily, though highly repetitive, comments about her spiritual journey over a period of years (1666–78).[86] Katherine Austen was widowed in 1658 when she was 29, but until her death in 1683 she kept a spiritual diary which, alongside autobiographical notes about her family and relations, included verse meditations on biblical passages, 'On my fall off a tree', and reminders of their religious duties to her daughter Anne and her sons Robert and Thomas.[87] A similar mélange of meditations and autobiographical passages (on which she reflected with some piety) was kept by Elizabeth Delaval in the 1660s, and Lady Elizabeth Mordaunt between 1656 and 1676, both of which have found modern editors.[88] We have evidence of similar collections, no longer extant, only through mention by memorialists of one kind or another, as for example that kept by Elizabeth Bury which, it was reported, she described as 'a witness betwixt God and her own soul'.[89] That of Elizabeth Williams, wife of the Rev. Daniel Williams, we know only by reference to it in Edmund Calamy's funeral sermon for her in 1698. The same was true of those kept by Lady Cutts and by Elizabeth Wilkinson.[90] Elizabeth Annesley kept such a diary, we are told, for nearly 20 years, only for her to leave instructions that it should be burned on her death.[91] Though it was more a set of remembered reflections on past events in her life, Elianor Stockton's spiritual diary has avoided the fate of others, as has that of Sarah Savage who was still keeping a diary of her spiritual life when she was 80 years old.[92]

In all of these cases the writer was plainly taking upon herself the responsibility of contributing to her own religious education, as were those women who kept commonplace books of predominantly religious content, such as Brilliana Conway before her marriage, Venetia Digby, Elizabeth Walker, Katherine Clarke and Dorothy Pakington. Once again we know of such practices in some cases only through reportage, either in a funeral sermon or as Sir Kenelm Digby did in a letter to his three sons soon after the death of their mother Lady Venetia, when he reported her constant reading of godly books 'which she ruminated and digested at leisure, as it appeareth by her books of notes written in her own hand'.[93] We have seen that Grace Mildmay used meditations as 'the exercise of my mind from my youth unto this day'. Margaret Hoby's diary is full of such reportage: 'then I walked till supper time and after catechising, meditated awhile of that which I had heard, with mourning to God for pardon both of my omission and commission wherein I felt myself guilty'. Katherine Brettergh's memorialist reported her meditating 'in closet, garden, orchard and field'. Mary Rich frequently referred to her own practice of retiring to the 'wilderness' in the grounds of the family seat at Leighs Priory.[94] Amelia Lanyer put her recollection of Anne Clifford's practice into verse:

> In these sweet woods how often did you walk
> With Christ and his Apostles there to talk,
> Placing his holy writ in some fair tree
> To meditate what you therein did see.

In his funeral sermon for Susanna Perwich, John Batchiler reminded his congregation of her constant habit of 'prayer, meditation and reading in closet and garden'.[95]

Religious meditation was thus seen to act as 'a riser from lethargy', a 'solace in adversity', 'a companion of watchfulness'. But achieving the status of godliness was more complicated than this, and meditation thus also became a means of struggling to cope not only with the difficulties of understanding God's Word but also with the conflicts of emotion arising from such struggles. In enabling women to feel that they were in some small way contributing to their own passage along the road to salvation, it also introduced them to or increased their awareness of the anxieties which beset such a journey.[96]

WOMEN'S READING

We have seen that there was a plentiful supply of godly books available for women's reading. Extant booksellers' inventories, as well as the advertisements at the end of the books they had for sale, certainly provide evidence that they were kept in stock, and it is unlikely that they would have been printed in such profusion had there not been a ready market for them. There was, of course, nothing new in the fact that women read. The early Renaissance paintings of the Annunciation regularly show the Virgin with a book in her hand, in contrast to the earlier pictures which show her at the well or busy with the distaff and, as the author of *The Book of the Knight of the Tower* insisted, 'a woman that can read may better know the perils of the soul and her salvation than she that knows naught of it',[97] a view that became a commonplace in the early modern period. The printing of books, even their possession by individuals, does not, of course, prove that they were read, especially if the books in question were of the godly kind. Richard Rogers was clearly aware of the difficulty:

> There is so little sound knowledge and conscionable practice of Christianity, seeing it is the custom (in a manner) of most professors rarely or never to read over a good book (of any reasonable bigness) from the beginning to the end thereof; or if they do so, then (as if they have done enough) they lend it, lose it, give it away, or cast it aside for ever to the dust, cobwebs and moths to study and meditate upon, for any more dealing they mean to have with it.

As also was his contemporary, Daniel Rogers: 'it may be once a quarter if they hit upon a new book, read a few pages and cast it away, and so it lies upon the cupboard overgrown with cobwebs'.[98] Even then, there was a good deal of competition for the attention of women readers. If she could read at all, Sir Thomas Overbury's 'chambermaid' would read romances rather than godly books,[99] and some educated readers confessed to succumbing to the same temptation. Lady Elizabeth Delaval, for example, confessed in her spiritual diary that her governess

Had so filled my head with follies that (unless those times which I was forced to perform my tasks in) what I read was altogether romances. I was but a few months past ten years old before I had read several great volumes of them: all Cassandras, the Grand Cyrus, Cleopatra and Astrea. Thus mainly passed the blossom time of my life, which should have been spent in laying a good foundation of what is to be learned in such books as teach of heavenly wisdom.

Mary Rich acknowledged a similar predisposition, in that until she was married in 1641 she spent her 'precious time in nothing else but reading romances, and in reading and seeing plays', whilst Margaret Cavendish, Duchess of Newcastle, complained:

the truth is, the chief study of our sex is romances, wherein reading they fall in love with the feigned heroes and carpet-knights, with whom their thoughts secretly commit adultery, and in their conversation and manner, or forms of phrases of speech, they imitate the romancy-ladies.[100]

Samuel Pepys noted with ill-concealed disapproval his wife's reading of the verbatim love-letters which were a feature of Scudéry's *The Grand Cyrus*, though, on the contrary, Dr Arnold Boate reported of his pious wife Margaret's reading of romances that she was 'wonderfully pleased as with the beauty of their language and conceptions, so with the characters of all kinds of heroical virtues which therein are held forth, most lively in the persons of both sexes'. Hannah Woolley similarly listed approvingly 'such romances which treat of generosity, gallantry and virtue'.[101]

But popular though such literature was, there is plenty, though scattered, evidence of women engaged in the serious matter of reading godly books. Not surprisingly, reading the Bible was considered to be most worthy of mention. In 1554, for example, Lady Jane Grey sent a Bible to her sister Katherine. It is, she wrote, 'the book of the Lord . . . It will teach you to live and learn you to die . . . if you with a good mind read it and with an earnest mind do follow it, it will bring you an immortal and everlasting life'.[102] In the list of books in the possession of Jane's other sister, Mary, made during her confinement in the houses of various notables for marrying without the consent of the Queen, were included copies of both the Bishops' and Geneva Bibles.[103] Imprisoned in the Tower after his part in the Northern Rising of 1569, Thomas Howard, fourth Duke of Norfolk, wrote 'to my loving children, especially Thomas and Nan', urging them to

delight in spending some time in reading of the scripture, for therein is the whole comfort of man's life, and if you be diligent of reading of them they will remain with you continually to your profit and commodity in this world, and to your comfort and salvation in the world to come.[104]

As a young girl, Oliver Heywood's mother Alice experienced a 'conversion' event whereupon she 'took her Bible with her and spent the whole day in reading and praying', a practice she continued for the rest of her life. John Bruen's daughter, Katherine, read eight chapters of the Bible each day. Alice Lucy started the day with a reading of the Bible and other godly books.[105] Mary Gunter, who died in 1622, schooled herself to read the whole Bible through in the course of a year, at the same time making notes of difficult passages to be discussed and clarified in talks with ministers 'and other understanding Christians'. Lady Mary Vere spent 'much precious time in reading holy scriptures and other godly books' and 'getting by heart many select chapters and special psalms, and of every book of the scripture one choice verse'.[106] Lady Elizabeth Langham was another who read the scriptures through once a year. Susanna, Countess of Suffolk, read six chapters each day, enabling her to read it over twice a year.[107] Elizabeth Dunton, too, was a regular reader of her Bible, of which 'her memory was almost as good as a concordance'. Elizabeth Hastings, the unmarrried daughter of Theophilus, seventh Earl of Huntingdon, spent much of her life in the house of her grandfather, Sir John Lewis of Ledstone in Yorkshire, where

> The word of God was a lantern to her feet and a light unto her paths; her delight was in God's Word and every day was her study of it. She held her Bible to her heart as a mirror to the face . . . and she lived in the communion of the Church of England to her dying day.[108]

In much the same way, the memorialist of Lady Elizabeth Capel (who died in 1660) reported that

> her closet was not (as too many ladies' are) an exchange of curious pictures and of rare and costly jewels, but a private oratory (as it were) chiefly designed for prayer and devotion . . . it was seldom if ever that I found her alone there without a Bible in front of her.[109]

Judith Hammond, as might be expected of a clergyman's wife, was similarly assiduous in her reading, though decidedly discerning in her choices:

> she was abundant in reading, especially of the Holy Book; that was her business and delight. She very little cared to concern herself in reading

writings that were merely notional or polemical and disputative. But the most practical ones she was most taken with, such as treated of the other state and of the duties of Christians in the meantime.[110]

For most of the women for whom we have evidence of their godly reading, the references are all too brief and general. For some, however, a little more detail is forthcoming. Catherine Parr was a well-read woman, who also bought books in quantity, presumably for distribution among the members of her household.[111] Margaret Hoby's diary records her reading of the *Book of Martyrs*, the *Book of Discipline* and the works of divines such as Cartwright, Gifford, Gervase Babington, Broughton and Perkins, either alone in her closet, or with her chaplain Richard Rhodes, or with 'the wives', 'some good neighbours', 'the goodwives'.[112] When she married Anthony Mildmay, Grace Sherrington moved from one assiduously puritan family to another. Her mother, Lady Anne, had restricted her reading as a child to the Bible, the *Book of Martyrs*, John Man's translation of Musculus' *Commonplaces of Religion* (1563) and one of the English, Protestantised translations of Thomas à Kempis' *Imitatio Christi*. It was these books that she recommended as improving reading for her only child, Mary.[113] In the Arminian colony founded by Nicholas Farrar at Little Gidding in 1625, a chapter of Foxe was read to the assembled household each Sunday evening. His wife Mary, his daughter Susannah and his granddaughter Mary all proved themselves to be exceptionally well-read women in what was called 'practical divinity', and it was they who virtually controlled the massive scheme of religious education which was undertaken there.[114] Anne Clifford's diary, written between 1616 and 1619, reveals her practice of having books read to her by various male and female servants. Wat Coniston, for example, read St Augustine's *City of God* and the *Supplication of Saints* (1612), the latter having been given to her by her father. Later entries refer to the reading of Montaigne's *Essays* to her by Christopher Marsh, the family steward, and by Edward Rivers, the rector of the Sackville living of Hartfield. St Francis of Sales' *Introduction to a Devout Life* was read to her by her secretary George Sedgwick, by Thomas Strickland, 'one of my chief officers', and by John Taylor. On another occasion Kate Buchin read to her a portion of the Bible, together with 'a book of the preparation of the sacrament'.[115]

Anne Venn, daughter of the regicide Colonel John Venn, also kept a diary, which apparently she began in 1635 when she was about 9 years old, 'written by her own hand and found in her closet after her death', in which she noted her very wide range of godly reading:

I got a book called Mr Rogers' Evidences and another called The

Touchstone of True Grace and another called None But Christ and divers others . . . read Mr Dod upon the commandments . . . a little book called The Marrow of Modern Divinity . . . reading some sermons of Mr Marshall's and others . . . one of Mr Burrowes' books and fifty sermons of Mr Knight's . . . opened Mr Burroughs' book which I did read daily many hours together . . .

Anne also records the influence of the prolific writer of godly books, Christopher Love, chaplain to her father's regiment, and of Isaac Knight, many of whose sermons she summarised in her notebooks, and with whom she corresponded on matters religious.[116] In the 'diary' of Elianor Stockton (which awaits an editor) is found a record of 'short sentences that I have met with in reading', including 'Caryl on Job 30.2 . . . the Christians Daily Wake . . . The Spirits Office Towards Believers . . . Mr Crow on the Lords Supper . . . that small piece of Mr Flavel's entitled A Token for Mourners'.[117] Mary Rich's reading included Foxe's Book of Martyrs, the sermons and other writings of Jeremy Taylor, the poems of George Herbert and Richard Baxter's *Crucifying of the World by the Cross of Christ*, her favourite book.[118] Elizabeth Wilkinson, wife of Dr Henry Wilkinson, principal of Magdalen Hall, Oxford, was not only a great reader of sermons but 'took much pains in writing [down] sermons and collecting notes out of practical divines', as well as keeping 'a diary of God's dealings with her soul'. Her reading included *The Practise of Pietie*, Calvin's *Institutes* and 'Mr Scudder's Works'. Katherine Clark's reading included the works of 'Mr Ambrose and Mr Reyner', from which she transcribed passages into her commonplace book. Elizabeth Bury criticised learned divines for refusing to translate more devotional books for women's use. For her own part,

she devoted most of her secret and leisure hours to the reading of Mr Henry's *Annotations*, which she would often say were the most plain, profitable and pleasant she had ever read, and the last books (next to her Bible) she should ever part with. Next to the Holy Scriptures her chiefest delight was in reading practical divinity

which included the works of Isaac Ambrose, Henry Flavel, William Burkitt and Samuel Craddock. The Bible itself she was able to read in its original languages.[119] The linguistic skills of Lady Elizabeth Langham were also put to good use as part of her religious life. As her memorialist reported:

Her learning rendered her to be a helpmeet for him [her husband] as thereby being made capable of conversing with him in parts both of

Divinity and Humanity, and that very knowingly and judiciously, and that in more languages than one, for she was able to make use of learned authors in other tongues, not needing the help of translations. As for Latin that learnedest piece of Peter Martyr [his *Commonplaces*] she frequently had recourse to and made good use of. For the French she was intimately acquainted with the works of that prodigy of learning Dr du Moulin, out of whose *Buckler of Faith* she was able to defend her own protestant faith.[120]

Susanna Perwich's reading was obviously more extensive than most, including the works of Thomas Watson, Francis Roberts, Thomas Goodwin, William Spurstow, Samuel Craddock, Christopher Love, Thomas Brookes and Richard Baxter. Her contemporary, Mary Wilson, found comfort in those of Brookes, Love and Shepherd.[121] At the very end of our period, Mrs Elizabeth Freke appended to her diary 'an account of what books I put in the deep deal box by the fireside in my own closet', a collection which included

my mother's folio Bible, Andrew's sermons, Feltham's Resolves, Smith's Sermons, Cooper's *Door of Heaven Open'd*, Jeremy Taylor's *Life of Christ*, D. Featley's *Devotions*, *The Practise of Pietie*, *The Whole Duty of Man*, Bishop Andrewes' *Book of the Western Martyrologie*, books of private devotions.[122]

A contemporary of Mrs Freke's, Damaris Cudworth, daughter of the Cambridge Platonist Ralph Cudworth, was brought up under his direct instruction. She later married Sir Francis Masham who received into his household John Locke, with whom Damaris studied philosophy and history. Her well-read piety comes through very clearly in her *Discourse Concerning the Love of God* (1696) and *Occasional Thoughts in Reference to a Virtuous Christian Life* (1705). In the latter she deplored the lack of education for women, not least their consequent inability to provide their children with a rational education. Throughout she insists that as rational creatures women should subject their religious belief to the dictates of reason, as plainly she did her own. Women have souls to be saved equally with men, she claimed, and it was necessary therefore that they should acquire the knowledge to enable them to 'answer opposers of and corrupters of Christianity'. The generality of women, pious attenders at divine service though they were, were nevertheless, in her view shamefully ignorant therein.[123]

It can be seen, then, that references to women's actual reading of religious matter are not uncommon. More often than not, however, the evidence is of a very general nature or alternatively mention is made only of a single work. On her marriage to Thomas Austey, Joan Redman, for example, brought with her a copy of Wyclif's *Wicket*, which had been bequeathed to her by her late husband John Redman. A similar kind of dowry was carried by John Bunyan's first wife (whose Christian name has eluded historians), who brought with her copies of Arthur Dent's *Plaine Mans Pathway* and Lewis Bayley's *Practise of Pietie*.[124] The Roman Catholic Margaret Massey of Waverton in Cheshire was brought before the High Commission in Chester in 1592, with her maids Ellen Wilden and Joan Amos, for refusing to attend church or take the oath. All three were imprisoned in the goal at the Northgate in the city, and when Mrs Massey's house was searched the Commission's officers found 'divers images, beads and popish books among which was an English book entitled *An Epistle of the Persecution of Catholics in England*'.[125] Not surprisingly, a New Testament 'of the Rheims translation' was part of Margaret Clitherow's reading, together with *The Following of Christ*, an English translation of Thomas à Kempis' *Imitatio Christi*, and 'Perins *Exercises*'.[126] Like Elizabeth Langham, Lady Mary Armine was 'not without some competent skill in more languages than her native tongue, particularly in French and Latin'. Armed with these she proved to be

> considerably skilled in Divinity and History, in Divinity not only know-ing in practical things, but was very intelligent in matters notional and polemical or controversial. In History she was well-versed not only in Jewish and Roman histories but especially in the historical part of the sacred scriptures and ecclesiastical affairs.[127]

Though born into a Catholic family (she was the daughter of Henry Talbot, son of George, sixth Earl of Shrewsbury) she converted to the Protestant faith, and thereafter

> she really endeavoured to promote and advance religion in others, not only by counsel, conference, admonition, exhortation etc., but also by many precious letters written with her own hand. She used to give books and some money to others to draw on and encourage them in their progress towards the Kingdom of Heaven.[128]

In a postscript to Elizabeth Poley's letter to her brother Simonds D'Ewes, her husband asked the latter to purchase for Elizabeth 'a Great Bible with the fairest print for her weak eyes', together with copies of 'Withers his *Prophesyings* and Perkins his *Cases of Conscience*'.[129] In 1627, when she was 3 years old, Mary Proude was orphaned. She was taken into the care of her kinsman Sir Edward Partridge, who had married the sister of Mary's mother Anne. Her guardians were (as Mary later recounted in her autobiography)

> a kind of loose protestants, that minded no more about religion than to go to their worship-house of fast days to hear a canonical priest preach in the morning and read common prayers in the afternoon. They said common prayers in the family and observed superstitious customs at days of feasting and fasting, Christmas, Good Friday, Lent etc.

On Sundays, when Mary was about 10 or 11 (she continued), a maid-servant in the household read to her and the other Partridge children 'Smith's and Preston's sermons', and it was about this time that she began to dislike using the formal prayers of the established church. She therefore acquired a book of prayers to read each morning and evening, and ultimately to 'write a prayer of my own composing . . . though then I could scarcely join my letters, I had learned so little a time to write'. In the household was the young William Springett, son of Sir Edward's widowed sister, Catherine, who acted as a kind of schoolmistress to her own and Sir Edward's children, as well as to Mary. William and Mary were married in 1640. William went off to join the Parliamentary army and died of wounds received in 1644, shortly after which their child Gulielma Maria Postuma was born, later to become the first wife of William Penn. In 1654 Mary married Isaac Pennington, their five surviving children all being brought up in the Quaker faith, of which Isaac had finally drawn Mary into membership, though Mary herself reported that it was a reading of 'Preston on prayer' that had been responsible for her conversion.[130]

Nicholas Byfield's *Principles of The Pattern of Wholesome Words* was bought for young Diana Russell at Woburn, together with a copy of 'The Wise Virgin', and it was probably a copy of *Principles* that was bought for the 11-year-old Lucy Barrington, recorded in the family accounts as 'a book by Mr Byfield'.[131] Margaret Ducke was praised by her memorialist William Gouge for her reading of godly books which, he claimed, had 'made her heart . . . a library of Christ'. Mary ('Molly') Verney, daughter of Edmund and Mary Verney, received from her god-mother

> aunt Sherard [Margaret Sherard, wife of Captain Philip Sherard] a noble present of a pair of silver candlesticks, a curious fine Bible, and a *Whole Duty of Man*, as fine, most excellent and best of books, which I have urged her to read and study carefully and seriously.[132]

Lady Elizabeth Brooke was described as an

indefatigable reader of books and scripture, especially, and various commentators upon them. She has turned over multitudes not only of practical treatises but also of learned books, and among many others some of those the ancient philosophers translated into English.[133]

When Richard Whalley sent his daughter Jane to the household of his sister-in-law Lady Joan Barrington, he sent with her in addition to the agreed £20 per half year for her board, 'the third and last volume of Mr Perkins' Works which were her mother's'.[134] Of the Quaker Sister Sheesby's reading we know only, by her own report, that she had 'read many of the books written by a Quaker preacher who had preached in her house'.[135] The memorialist of Anne Terry, who died in 1693 aged 38, reported that

> in prayer and meditation she followed the method she received from the *Directions* of Mr Daniel Burgess, viz. To go over the Creed, the Lord's Prayer and Commandments, all of which she did with many other portions of scripture, as appears from the many papers left under her own hand.[136]

The details to be found in wills and their inventories add a further strand to the web of evidence relating to women's reading. Occasionally the wills show religious books being passed on to a second generation, a very early example being the bequest of Lady Alice West, who died in 1395, 'to my daughter [in-law] . . . a mass book and all the books that I have in Latin, English and French, out-take the aforesaid matins books that I bequeathed to Thomas my son'. Eleanor de Bohun, Duchess of Gloucester (died 1399) left a well-illustrated *Golden Legend*, with other books, to her daughter Anne. The *Golden Legend* was also bequeathed with other books by Cicely, Duchess of York, to her god-daughter Brigitta in 1485. Anne, Duchess of Buckingham, who died in 1480, left a copy of the *Legend* to Margaret Beaufort, together with a primer and various gospels and epistles in French.[137] The *Legend*, of course, went out of favour in the sixteenth century, but the practice of bequeathing religious books continued. In 1552, for example, Giles Levyt of Bury St Edmunds left his daughter Katherine 'two great books, the Bible and the New Testament'.[138] Just before he died in 1593, the martyr John Penry wrote to his wife enclosing a letter to his four infant daughters, Deliverance, Comfort, Safety and Sure Hope. To them he wrote 'I have left you four Bibles, each of you one, being the sole and only partiment or dowry that I have for you', with the enjoinder that their mother teach them to read 'when they come to the years of discretion and understanding'.[139] Though Sir Nathaniel Bacon's will of 1614 gives no more information than to bequeath 'to my wife and three daughters all my English printed and written books', it would be reasonable to suppose that these included some godly books and Bibles.[140]

Lower down the social scale Mary Skeale, a widow of Hornchurch, left her *Book of Martyrs* to her grandson in 1619, and in the same year the widow Alice Berry of Beccles in Suffolk left 'a little Bible' to Agnes Reeve and a 'Great Bible' to Alice Bowen. In the following year Thomas Scott of Ipswich left to his wife Joan a Bible, 'a book called Mr Babbington Upon the Commandments, another book called Mr Moores Sermons, another book called The Christian Righteousness'.[141] John Wright, a yeoman of Tattingstone in the south of the county, left his married daughters Anne Warne and Mary Turner a Prayer Book apiece, whilst Everard Isaac of Beccles left a new Bible together with a silver spoon to his granddaughter, Mary. Hugh Butcher, yeoman of Willby, left all his prayer books to his sisters, Mary and Katherine.[142] Edward Vince of Sternfield left Hannah Forsdike, his goddaughter, 6s 8d to buy a Bible. By his will of 1624, Samuel Tuttell of Ashfield left his Great Bible to his daughter Dinah. Alice Smith of Alderton bequeathed to Ann, daughter of John Man, £5, a Bible and a desk to set it on.[143] In Lancashire, by his will of 1681, the Reverend William Holland of Heaton near Manchester provided that his daughter Elizabeth might have 'what Bible she will choose out of my books, together with *The Practise of Pietie* and all the books written by the author of *The Whole Duty of Man*'.[144] Joseph Midgley, former vicar of Rochdale, in his will of 1637 left to his daughter Rebecca a copy of Richard Rogers' *Practice of Christianity*, the 300-page epitome of his *Seven Treatises Containing Such Direction as is Gathered out of the Holy Scriptures* (1603). In 1647 James Bacon, clerk of Barrgate in Suffolk, bequeathed to his daughter Elizabeth 'my books of Mr Perkins' Works being contained in three volumes', and in 1649 Mary Chapman, a widow of Bury St Edmunds, left her Bible and all her household goods to her daughter Mary.[145] In 1670 Deborah Frohock, a yeoman's Congregationalist widow, left her three Bibles to her son, Samuel. In his will of 1684 John Carter, chandler, left a Bible each to his son and his daughter.[146]

Whether as givers or receivers of godly books, women and girls regularly appear in the wills of the period, though not of course as frequently as do men. It would be reasonable to suppose that such works would also figure in the inventories attached to wills, but though the contents of houses were mostly listed down to the last chamber pot and 'closet stool', Bibles and godly books are listed considerably less frequently, and even then with little precise detail. Sir Henry Unton of Wadley in Berkshire died in 1596. In the inventory of the many rooms and chambers of his residence there is not one mention of books save for the cryptic 'In Sir Henry's study . . . many books of divers sorts to the number of ccxx.' The inventory (1620) and will (1634) of his widow Lady Dorothy have no mention of books at all.[147] In the inventory of Hardwick Hall of 1601, Bess of Hardwick is listed simply as having '6 books in her bedchamber'.[148] The 1634 inventory of the property at Cockesden in Yorkshire of Lettice, Dowager Countess of Leicester, who died in that year aged 92, lists only '2 Testaments embroidered, in a trunk in her bedchamber', though an earlier 1611 inventory shows that 'the study room' had two reading tables, on one of which stood a 'desk whereupon the *Book of Martyrs* now stands', with in addition 24 books which included 'The Serving Man's Comfort . . . Fotherbies Sermons . . . a Bible of very fair print . . . Slaydens Commentaries . . . The Whole Book of Psalms . . . a book of divers godly prayers . . . a book called The Mystery of Redemption'.[149] The 1665 inventory of Deborah Harpur showed that she had a copy of the Bible and of *The Practise of Pietie* in a linen chest. The inventory attached to the will of Lady Mary [Fitz]Howard in 1671 merely reported 'her books and other things in her closet, £50'. Margaret Spufford's scrutiny of the (post-1660) Cambridgeshire inventories showed a similarly poor return for her efforts.[150] However, lower down the social scale, Anne Goodere was obviously fairly affluent. The total value of her inventory came to £675, and included a Eusebius, the Rhenists's Testament, Perkins *Upon the Fifth of Matthew*, and the Song of Solomon. More typical though was the widow Jane Wood who, in 1606, had in her parlour 'a small Bible' which was valued at 2s. A 'Service Book' and 'other small books' to the value of 1s 4d were all that were recorded in the inventory of Anne Barnarde in the same year. In 1631 Frances Jodrell's 'little Bible and two other books' were valued at 5s.[151] Less frequently we find references to the gifting of Bibles and other godly books during a person's lifetime, and we have already noted Lady Jane Grey's gift of a Bible to her sister Katherine. In 1620 Sir John Coke of Melbourne Hall in Derbyshire sent a copy of *The Practise of Pietie* to his wife Marie, and John Haynes, wool merchant of Exeter, before he married Susan Healey in 1635 bought her a copy of Arthur Hildersham's *Lectures Upon the 4th of John* (1632). He continued the practice after their marriage, and together with gifts of rings, gloves, purses and ribbons, he purchased for her 'a Bible worth xxs' and '2 sermon books 4s 6d'.[152]

As some contemporaries duly noted, the possession of books did not necessarily mean that they were read, least of all 'digested' after an appropriate period of reflection, of 'chewing the cud'. Yet the scattered evidence, imperfect as it is, suggests that for some women at least the reading of the Bible and other godly books, within the family but more especially in the closet or some secluded spot, was a very personal experience of 'coming close to God', of widening and deepening their religious understanding. For most, of course, the Bible was a listening book. But for those for whom it was a reading book, providing guidance on every aspect of daily life, it became 'a very present help', and not simply in times of trouble.

7 Mothers as educators

Woman's involvement in education thus ranged much more widely than has hitherto been reported, whether as pupils, as governesses, as schoolteachers, as founders. In a thoroughly patriarchal society it would be reasonable to assume that, in the privacy of the home, the major agent of such education would be the father. But this would be to ignore the large amount of evidence showing the part played by mothers in that situation, where they took on the responsibility of instructing their children and the children of others, and this notwithstanding all kinds of biblical constraints which emphasised their membership of the 'weaker sex', and which insisted that they should not usurp the rights of the husband as the superior being. The relatively new field of family history has, not surprisingly, been dominated by a concern for structure and hierarchy, revolving round the father as 'head' of the family and household. In her consideration of 'The History of the Family as an Interdisciplinary Field', Tamara Hareven hardly mentions the role of the mother. Christopher Hill's long and important chapter on 'The Spiritualization of the Household' is orientated wholly round 'the master of the household', 'the head of the household', 'the father'. Wives are mentioned only in relation to their husbands. The word 'mother' does not occur once.[1] In the same way, William Lazareth's *Luther on the Christian Home* (1960) has no chapter which explicitly considers the educative function of the Christian home, least of all the role of the mother within it. Again, whilst a good deal has been written about the 'learned ladies' of the early modern period (indeed, of all periods) remarkably little consideration has been given to the problem of how far (if at all) and in what ways they transmitted their own learning to their children. Even Shulamith Shamir's specialist monograph *The Fourth Estate: A History of Women in the Middle Ages* (1982) resignedly concludes that 'in few of the contemporary sources do we find mention of woman as mother'. In her more recent *Childhood in the Middle Ages* (1990), mothers suffer a similar fate. Clarissa Atkinson in her *The Oldest Vocation: Motherhood in the Middle Ages* (1991) is concerned more with ideology than reality.

The question of mothers as agents, as having an active role in the early modern household, must of course have as one of its referents their relative status in the hierarchy of social authority. The typical generalisation had it that they were subordinate to their husbands, but the doctrine of total subordination or of total obedience was rarely sustained – either in theory or in practice. William Gouge urged the wife to be obedient to her husband 'providing his command be not against the Lord and his Word'.[2] The qualifying adjectives of 'A Prayer for a Woman with Child' – 'grant me also that I may humbly reverence and faithfully love mine husband and be observant to all his honest, lawful and godly requests' – were typical of many such supplications. The contemporary proverb 'More belongs to a marriage than four bare legs in a bed'[3] put it in a more down-to-earth manner. The question was not 'whether?' but 'in what degree?' and 'in what circumstances?' Reminders that Eve was created from Adam's rib not his foot came not only from seventeenth-century 'feminists' but also from the Tridentine catechism for priests. Most commentaries included some demurral, followed by a conditional clause which accorded a mother a positive role in the education of her children (as also her servants). As William Louth concluded: 'for certain it is that mothers by the Commandment of God ought to have no less care and charge belonging unto them than the fathers and masters, touching the good government of their sons, daughters and servants'. In the words of the Anglican bishop Jeremy Taylor, 'a husband's power over his wife is paternal and friendly, not magisterial and despotic'. Later in the same sermon he spelled out in detail, as many others did, the difficult connection between love and obedience.[4]

As we have seen, glossators on the prime proof-text, Proverbs 22.6, 'Train up a child in the way wherein he should walk and he will not depart from it when he is old', produced a wide range of metaphor and example to emphasise the efficacy of early training in the family. Even so, throughout the period the question remained open as to whether a woman was, by her nature, fitted to undertake such a task, particularly in the light of the much-quoted Pauline insistence 'But suffer not a woman to teach, nor to usurp the authority over man, but to be in silence'. Though glossators were well aware that Paul was referring to women in church (and in particular geographical and historical contexts), this did not prevent some from extending the meaning of the passage in an attempt to justify their insistence on the subordinate position of women. Yet Aquinas had long since made the distinction between teaching and speaking in the public and private domains, exhorting women to fulfil their undoubted duty in the latter. The image of the teaching mother was common in Christian iconography, where there are numerous depictions of Mary holding a book in front of the Child Jesus and of Anne teaching Mary. By the sixteenth century the view had become commonplace, without, however, eradicating the ambivalence of attitude, in women as in men, towards the notion of woman as autonomous being, an ambivalence which expressed itself in that plethora of eulogy and vituperation, *la querelle des femmes*. Thomas Becon obviously had no doubt in his mind as to the answers to his rhetorical questions: 'Is not woman a creature of God as the man? . . . Can mothers bring up their children virtuously when they themselves are void of all virtue?' Roger Carr was more precisely explicit: 'most true it is that women, as men, are reasonable creatures, and have flexible wits both good and evil, the which with use, discretion and good counsel may be altered and turned'.[5] But so too was John Aylmer, Bishop of London, in his reply to John Knox's *First Blast of the Trumpet Against the Monstrous Regiment of Women*:

> Women are of two sorts, some of them wiser, better, learned, discreeter and more constant than a number of men; but another and worse sort of them, and for the most part, are fond, foolish, wanton flibbergibs, tatlers, triflers, wavering, witless, without counsel, feeble, careless, rash, proud, dainty, nice, talebearers, eavesdroppers, and in every way dolti-fied with the dregs of the devil's dunghill . . . No Deborahs, no Judiths, no Hesters, no Elizabeths. For sure, where such there be is as a token of God's wrath.[6]

Underlying all of this lay the fundamental question – 'What makes a good woman?', and its sequential questions 'What makes a good wife? A good mother?' In Aylmer's view, obviously, women 'for the most part' would not make good wives or mothers. At the very end of our period, Mary Wollstonecraft was equally emphatic but over-simple – the character-istic of any polemicist: 'meek wives are, in general, foolish mothers'.[7] It is true that, though those favourite proof-texts Psalms 37.11 and Matthew 5.5 were not gender-specific, when they were cited in the literature their appli-cation was to women much more often than to men. Even so, 'meekness' was for most a sign of pious virtue not of foolishness. Catherine Parr, an intelligent and well-educated woman not given to undue deference, can in no way be classed as either 'meek' or 'foolish' in the Wollstonecraft sense of the words, yet her characterisation of a good woman, wife and mother was typical of many throughout the period:

> If they be women married, they learn of St Paul to be obedient to their husbands and to keep silence in the congregation and learn of their husbands at home. Also they wear such apparel as becometh holiness and comely usage, with soberness; not being accusers or detractors, not given to much eating of delicate meats and

drinking of wine; but they teach honest things to make young women sober-minded, to love their husbands, to love their children, to be discreet, chaste, housewifely, good, obedient to their husbands, and that the Word of God be not evil spoken of. Verily if all sorts of people would look to their own vocation and ordain the same according to Christian doctrine we should not have so many eyes and ears to other men's faults as we have.[8]

Male writers on the matter, whether misogynist or eulogist (or neither), put forward characterisations which are also to be found in the female writers of the period, whether 'feminist-radical' or 'traditional-conservative' in their outlook. Yet even the eulogists couched their justifications for the education of women as much in terms of the benefits for husband and child (she would be more tractable, more efficient) as in terms of her own benefit. As Robert Snawsel put it:

And further know this, that good parents are special instruments to make godly children and good servants, and godly children and good servants make religious men and women, and religious men and women do make a flourishing church and famous commonweal, set forth God's glory and establish the prince's kingdom.[9]

The purpose of the (strictly limited) curriculum proposed for girls 'from twelve till the day of their marriage' by the anonymous author of *The Office of Christian Parents* (1616) was to ensure that 'she may be brought up into her husband's house with . . . great honour and joy'. Francis Cheynell, writing in 1648, was merely echoing earlier humanists when he enjoined husbands: 'do not forget your beloved wife . . . she will never be at your command unless you teach her to be at Christ's command'.[10] The difficulty arose when a wife decided that what appeared to her to be Christ's command did not coincide with that of her husband. Yet, George Keith argued, if there was a disagreement of a fundamental kind the wife should be free to leave, 'for she ought rather obey God than man, and in Christ Jesus there is neither male nor female but all is one in Him, as the apostles said'.[11] There was nothing new in Keith's citing Galatians 3.28; what was becoming, in his day, far more common was a willingness to go beyond the woman's soul to her freedom of action, and this would also apply to her actions as educator of her children.

But there was a nettle to be grasped. Many of those in authority recognised that in a far from perfect world many parents could not be relied on to carry out the task assigned to them. Clergymen and schoolmasters, themselves under critical scrutiny as educators, were nevertheless not slow to point out the inadequacies of parents. As always, some such as the school-master Hezekiah Woodward merely complained 'Now the parent doth just nothing, the master must do all, look to the child's books and manners both.'[12] Others, however, saw that the nettle had to be co-operatively grasped. Materials had to be produced whereby the flock, either by reading for themselves (a very small minority) or by having books and pamphlets read to them, could prepare themselves, or be prepared, for their parental 'vocation' and, since the mother's 'vocation' was deemed to include the education of her children, she had to be prepared for that responsibility with the aid of 'godly books', catechisms, collections of prayers and the like. Whatever was done in church by the clergy (or for some few in school by the schoolmaster or mistress) had, necessarily, to be reinforced by instruction at home. Richard Greenham's prescription may stand exemplar for a long line of writers from the pre-Reformation humanists and their Tridentine successors to the wide range of Protestant writers:

> Aggrieved parents ask 'Do we not as much as is of us required? We send our children to the church to be instructed of the pastor and to the school to be taught of the master: if they learn it will be the better for them, if not they have the more to answer for, what can we do more?' If parents would have their children blessed, at the church and at the school, let them beware they give their children no corrupt example at home by any carelessness, profaneness or ungodliness, and the wise parents will do them more harm at home than both pastor and schoolmaster can do good abroad, for the corrupt example of the one fighteth with the good doctrine of the other . . . and further experience teacheth us that children like or mislike more by countenance, gesture and behaviour than by any rule, doctrine or precept whatsoever.
>
> Speak men of discipline never so much, complain they of want of church government never so loud, preach they, teach they never so much abroad, unless they will begin discipline in reforming their houses, and give religion some room at home, they shall travail much and profit little. It is then, O man, O woman, that mayest do thy child the greatest good and the greatest harm.[13]

Generalised statements about the 'nature' of women and injunctions about a mother's (and father's) duty nevertheless had to be transformed into the practicalities of action in actual family situations. In the early modern period, being a good mother did not start with the birth of her child. Current belief in the efficacy of petitionary prayer, which in Latimer's words 'hath ever remedied all matters', insisted that the future well-being of both mother and child depended first on the sanctifying of the marriage bed by the saying of prayers before husband and wife 'doe lie licentiously together', so that 'our child by carnall generation may be the child of God by regeneration'.[14] Since according to the Church authorities, whether Catholic or Protestant, the chief purpose of coition was the production of a Christian child, the act itself took on an importance beyond mere reproduction, and it was often claimed that monstrous births were the result of indecent sexual relations, the state of mind of the copulating parties helping to give the embryo its distinctive shape.[15]

Nevertheless, prayer was regarded as a supplement rather than an alternative to physical care. During pregnancy the mother-to-be was enjoined to have care for both her physical and spiritual well-being in order to safeguard her child, confirming her limited (Aristotelian) role as nourisher only of what her husband had generated.[16] William Louth, for example, urged that the wife should 'have great care during that time and not give herself to anger'; she should 'forbear all dancing and immoderate stirring, striving, lifting and labour' and avoid any 'intemperance in eating or drinking'.[17] In all of these matters the mother-to-be was well supplied with advice and exhortation which she in turn would be expected to pass on to her daughters, 'whereupon rose the proverb Qualis mater, talis filia: such a mother, such a daughter', echoing the late medieval 'How the good wyf taught her daughter': 'Now I have taught thee my dear daughter the same teaching I had of my mother.'[18]

Throughout the period one further consideration, alongside classical authority and Christian doctrine, was taken into account (by all classes) in matters of conception (and contraception), parturition and infant nurture, and that was astrology. Though reputable astrologers (no contradiction in the early modern period) were careful to insist that their prognostications were not inexorably binding, other, less scrupulous 'conjurors' led their clients to believe otherwise, and there were many who exemplified the willingness of the human race to be persuaded that something or someone other than themselves was, or would be, responsible for their present or future situation. The casting of a 'nativity', declaring the position and movement of the stars at the time of a person's birth, could produce 'prognostications' about the optimum times for conception, birth and marriage, and could indicate the sex of a child, even its future vocation. John Maplet, for example, concluded his *Diall of Destiny* (1581) with a three-page 'Description of such days as are most happy and unhappy throughout the year', claiming that:

> all children which are born on any of these happy days shall never be poor, and being in like sort put to school or to any science or trade or

occupation upon any of these said happy days, if he do persevere and continue in his estate and vocation shall undoubtedly profit greatly and become a rich man.[19]

John Pool's *Country Astrology* (1650) gave astral details to determine 'if a child born shall live long or not', and what would be 'the wit, manners and natural inclination of the child', as well as preferred times of conception, birth and marriage. John Case recommended:

> If thou wantst an heir or man-child to inherit thy land, observe a time when the masculine planets and signs ascend and [are] in full power and force: then take thy female and cast thy seed, and thou shalt have a man-child.[20]

On the other hand, the Salisbury 'professor of physicke', John Securis, whose prognostications, he told his readers, would cost 'only two pence or three pence at the most', made no reference to these matters, though he too provided a list of 'most dangerous and infortunate days . . . and most lucky and prosperous days to do or begin any weighty matter or business'.[21]

It is a moot point as to what proportion of the population preferred to put its trust in astrological prognostication or in prayer and Christian stoicism or, indeed, in the popular medical books such as Jacob Rueff's *The Expert Midwife* . . . (1637), which advised that a male child was the product of sperm from the right testicle and was conceived on the right side of the womb, and a female came from the left.[22] People probably made use of what happened to be available to them, without stopping to consider the incompatibilities therein, notwithstanding constant warnings from their clergy and others – though doubtless some would be inclined to share the sentiment of Sir Thomas More's epigram:

> The starres to thee their prophet do reveal
> The fates of all and nought from thee conceal
> Yet though thy wifes false play the stars all see
> There's none of them so kind to tell it thee.[23]

Since parenting was deemed to be a divinely ordained vocation – 'Go forth and multiply' – the successful production of children ('begotten in the state of matrimony', as Edwin Sandys, for example, was careful to remind his congregation) was a divinely sanctioned reward: 'Children are an heritage of the Lord, and the fruit of the womb is his reward.'[24] Children were, therefore, as a matter of prescription at least, to be regarded as a blessing and voluntary childlessness a denial of holy injunction. For the vast majority, a child successfully reared beyond infancy would be someone who could contribute to the economic production of the household, and though the upper classes had no monopoly of the pleasure of 'continuing the line', very few would have been able to offer an informed expression of either the classical or Christian sense of a child acting as a medium of the immortality of the father's persona.[25] Many, however, would have had an intuitive awareness of such a possibility, either when they noticed a parental likeness in the child, or when they strove to bring up their children 'according to their own lights'.

The arrival of a boy was greeted (for both economic and political reasons) with more enthusiasm than that of a girl, though clerics constantly urged that children of either sex should be equally valued as children of God.[26] The expectant Lady Elizabeth Mordaunt nevertheless entered in her diary for 1657 'if it be thy pleasure let it be a son', and Adam Martindale believed that the death of his infant son, John, named after an earlier child who had died young, was the result of his 'striving with his providence to have a John'.[27] How far most parents continued to regard new additions to the family as 'blessings' is not susceptible of acceptable generalisation. What can no longer be claimed unequivocally, however, is that 'mothers did not care, and that is why their children vanished in the ghastly slaughter that was child-rearing'.[28] All that can be done (in the absence of serial data) is to cite instances, and avoid implying that the much-quoted cases of Elizabeth Paston and Lady Jane Grey were therefore 'typical'.[29] The public whipping of female as well as male offenders was not unusual, and we should not be surprised that this was mirrored in the (relative) privacy of the early modern family. It would, however, be fatal to substitute one unacceptable generalisation by its reverse. For every case of 'harshness', 'indifference' or 'vexation' it is possible to cite 'affection', 'warmth' or 'care', and in between the two to find a prescriptive middle way or the differential treatment of siblings by parents. This means that we have at least to enquire whether Thomas Becon was reporting his wife's, as well as his own, view (or merely personalising a theological stance) when he asked what greater joy could parents have than 'when some little babe shall play in your hall which shall resemble you and your wife? . . . which with a mild lisping or amiable stammering shall call you Dad?'[30]

The prescriptive literature readily recognised the dilemma facing parents, who were in any case facing the same problem in the affective side of their own conjugal relationship – how to be affectionate within a dominant–submissive situation – which itself would play some part, and in most cases a large part, in determining the pattern of their child-rearing behaviour. Here again the historian is faced with a wide variety of practice, both prescribed and actual, though in each case the bulk of it would lead away from the Ariès–Shorter thesis rather than towards it. The proverbial lore of the period, it is true, would more often than not support the thesis than deny it: 'a spaniel, a woman and a walnut tree, the more they are beaten the better still they be': or 'He that fetches his wife from Shrewsbury [play on shrew] must carry her to Staffordshire [play on staff = beating] or else in Cumberland [cumber = care, worry].'[31] But the general prescription was against the beating of wives. Henry Smith's reminder that 'Her cheeks are made for thy lips and not thy fists', and Robert Bolton's emphasis on 'a sweet, loving and tender-hearted pouring out of hearts with much affectionate dearness . . . one toward another',[32] were much more typical expressions of what was to be preferred, and are reflected too in letters between husband and wife. It would be stretching scepticism to cynicism to regard Lady Joan Coke's wording in a letter to her husband Sir John, 'I pray for you and wish you were here, and will ever remain your faithful and loving wife to death', as a mere formality rather than a true expression of her feelings. The same would be true of Henry Oxinden's to his wife Katherine:

> Dear heart, I shall think of the time long till I see you; in the meanwhile I shall most heartily pray to Almighty God to continue your health, which shall ever be more dear to me than mine own. Dear heart, I am your most affectionate, most faithful and most humble servant to command.

Twenty years later he wrote, 'I read thy letters over and over and over, for in them I see thee as well as I can.'[33] Susannah Newdigate's letters to her husband John, away at Parliament, those of Juliana Newdigate to her husband Richard, a judge away on circuit, or the correspondence between Sir John and Lady Anne Oglander whilst he was away in London trying to prevent the sequestration of his estates by a parliamentary committee, tell a similar tale.[34] Alongside these may be cited the well-documented grief of Sir Kenelm Digby on the death of his wife Venetia in 1633, and in a different vein the 'Considerations concerning marriage' of Elizabeth, Countess of Bridgewater, in which she laid the ground rules for a companionate marriage, acknowledging obedience, but 'not to be in such awe of him as a servant . . . showing affection and love to him as a friend, and so to speak their mind and opinion freely to him yet not value him the less'. William Cecil's eulogy of his wife Mildred, Sir Francis Hasting's of Lady Magdalene, and Edward Harley's account of his wife Abigail's last illness and death, 'That for 27 years hath been my crown and the repose and blessing of my life' confirm, with many others, what might be called, in a non-statistical sense, the general picture.[35]

Mary Stanhope married in 1600 aged 26, gave birth to nine children in 16 years and died in 1618 after giving birth to her ninth child; Elizabeth Brownlow, wife of Sir John Brownlow of Belton in Lincolnshire, came to 19 full-time births in the 22 years between 1626 and 1648; Anne Donne, wife of John Donne, produced 12 children in 15 years and died aged 33, seven days after the birth of her still-born thirteenth; Anne Fanshawe had six boys and eight girls 'born and christened, and I miscarried of six more, three at several times and once of three sons when I was about half gone my time'. Whether women such as these (and there were many others like them) continued to think of the products of their fecundity as 'blessings' we cannot precisely document since none of them has left their thoughts on the matter.[36] Frances Clerke, however, writing to her father Sir John Oglander in 1651, reported 'I was brought to bed with a son, which is my tenth child, and I pray God, if it be his blessed will, that it may be my last.' She would obviously have not been inclined, on that occasion at least, to offer up the 'prayer for a woman with child' which sought 'Thy fatherly pity to strengthen me in this my dangerous labour and travail, and grant me speedy deliverance and joyful beholding of my child, that being a merry mother I may render thee wonder, laud, praise and thanks', despite the 'woeful sorrows, laborious pangs and most grievous throws, bitter anguish and unspeakable pains'[37] which the prayer acknowledged to be part and parcel of childbearing.

Obviously, none of these women had made use of the contraceptive devices which were recommended in the medical handbooks and almanacks of the period, perhaps with good reason.[38] Clerics and others (following their medieval predecessors) urged women to resist the temptation to make use of 'physick or any other practice' in order to 'make away their children in their womb'. Yet the theologians would certainly have not felt it necessary to proscribe such practices had the recommendations of such as the perfectly respectable Nicholas Culpepper not been freely available and used. James Sandford (translating Cornelius Agrippa) made specific complaint of the medical books, written especially for women, which were filled with 'recipes to increase carnall desires . . . to restore virginitie at the time of marriage . . . to keep the belly in one state'. Humfre Lloyd, for example, offered remedies 'against great desire to fleshly lust', 'to helpe conception', 'to stop the flows' and 'to provoke the flows'. The Tridentine catechism, on the other hand, recommended that 'to avoid impure lusts' married folk should 'studiously avoid idleness . . . over-eating . . . over-drinking'.[39] The astrologers, too, advertised powders to encourage conception and potions to procure abortions, and in the 1690s Henry Coley, William Lilly's adopted son and successor, was said to be selling sigils (amulets) to servant girls at 4s a piece for use as contraceptives.[40]

Bombarded with a variety of prescriptive advice, and doubtless directly observing as much different practice, the mother nevertheless had to create a milieu in which her child would be brought up. Having been enjoined to prepare herself spiritually and physically for conception and pregnancy, and having survived the hazards of childbirth, she now had to feed her child. For the vast majority this inevitably meant breast-feeding. For some few, however, it was a matter of decision whether to suckle the child or not. Formally and universally,[41] all mothers were reminded that it was God's wish that she should do so, otherwise (it was argued) why would He have provided her with two breasts and a capacity to produce milk after birth? In suckling her child, she would also be reinforcing 'the holy bonds of nature' and demonstrating 'a manifest and undoubted token of absolute kindness and friendship'.[42] Moreover, had not that perfect model, Mary the mother of Jesus, suckled her own son, as had a host of other lauded mothers? Above all, by suckling her own child a mother could ensure that in passing on her own milk she was at the same time passing on her own virtues.[43] Suckling, then, was universally prescribed and justified on a variety of grounds. Never, however, as a prophylactic, though informally a young woman would have been told by her mother (and if not may well have observed for herself), that prolonged suckling would be accompanied by a period of temporary infertility during lactation, as the parish registers recording birth intervals of two, three or four years amongst ordinary women show. The interval was reduced when the infant died (and of course there were many such deaths); nursing therefore ceased and fertility reappeared – unless the mother undertook wet-nursing, which then produced the bonus of additional income.[44]

By contrast, the norm amongst women of the upper class (many of whom sent their infants to a wet-nurse) was for annual births. Such women were included in the strictures of clerics and medical writers alike – 'these dainty half-mothers, who for fear of wrinkling of their faces or to avoid some small labour do refuse this so necessary duty' – as well as by women writers such as Elizabeth Clinton, who castigated those who on grounds of personal convenience preferred not to suckle their own infants.[45] Not that such women were under severe pressure since, again almost universally, exhortations to suckle were immediately followed by advice on how to choose a satisfactory wet-nurse if the mother was prevented from suckling by shortage of milk or illness, or by some vaguely indicated 'weakness'. The difficulty, as Henry Smith noted, was that 'women love to be mothers but not nurses ... committing them forth like a cuckoo to be hatched in a sparrow's nest', and he went on to ask, somewhat uncharitably: 'but whose breasts have this perpetual drought? Forsooth it is like Gout; no beggar may have it, but citizens or gentlewomen'.[46] If a poor woman so suffered her baby would die, either through lack or through illness brought on by artificial feeding methods.

The question here, however, is how far wet-nursing is to be interpreted as a characteristic sign of Christian indifference in the upper middle classes at a crucial period in the rearing of an infant.[47] Even within the upper classes, however, the practice of sending out to a wet-nurse was far from universal, and certainly not common enough to support the Ariès–Shorter–Stone type of generalisation (see note 28 below). For every example of actual children being sent to a wet-nurse, it is possible to cite others who were suckled by their own mothers. As always, members of the younger generation were beset by conflicting advice and practice. Anne Newdigate, for example, daughter of Sir Edward Fytton, who determined in 1598 to nurse her own first child, Mary, found her practice (gently) queried by both her father and the child's godfather, Sir William Knollys:

> I must confess [Sir William wrote] it argueth great love, but yet breedeth much trouble to yourself, and yet would more grieve you if suckling your own milk it should miscarry, children being subject to many casualties. But you may tell me I am over-curious in this point than I need, but I speak it in friendly counsel not meaning either to contrary your own will or dissuade you from your resolution.

Anne went on to breastfeed all five of her children, reporting the fact to Lord Burghley, when she sought his wardship for her son, Jack, then aged 9.[48]

Claims about 'indifference' based on generalisations concerning lack of parental grief at the death of children must also be countered, and on the same grounds. Luther's expression of grief on the death of his daughter Magdalene, aged 14, or Mary Verney's at the death of her 4-month-old son or her husband Ralph's at the loss of 8-year-old Margaret ('Peg'), can in no way be dismissed as untypical.[49] Alice Thornton, indeed, reported that she was reproved by her 4-year-old daughter for her excessive grieving over the loss of a baby son.[50] In similar circumstances, the Countess of Warwick struggled against what she called 'heathenish' impulses. She probably had Thomas Becon's immensely popular *Syck Man's Salve* (1561) in mind, though a reading of Plutarch (in translation) might have saved her from the error.[51] Calvin, Knox and others were careful to remind their readers and listeners that 'that which ye scoffingly call Destiny and Stoical necessity . . . we call God's eternal election and purpose immutable'.[52] 'It hath pleased God', and a citing of Job 1.21 – 'The Lord gave and the Lord hath taken away; as it seemed good to the Lord so hath he done' – were the themes of many a funeral sermon or letter of condolence, and of course the proof-text figured at the opening of the Funeral Service in the Book of Common Prayer. Becon, on the other hand, wished to encourage a more positive response:

> I think that at burials of the faithful there should rather be joy and gladness than mourning and sadness; rather pleasant songs of thanksgiving than lamentable and doleful dirges. Let the infidels mourn for their dead; the Christians ought to rejoice when any of the faithful be called from this vale of misery into the glorious kingdom of God . . . Such as die in the Lord are not to be mourned, but God is rather to be thanked for their Christian departure. For now they are at rest.[53]

For many who felt unable to acquiesce in the practicalities of such advice (though doubtless they would have agreed with its theology), what Shorter and others characterise as 'indifference' was rather a Christian response to 'bear all adversities . . . calmly and patiently, entirely resigning our wills to God's . . . 'Tis this consideration alone that can restrain us from breaking out into immoderate and excessive grief.'[54] When it came to grieving, Hugh Latimer's advice had been to 'do it measurable as beseemeth Christians'.[55] Francis Bacon's essay 'Of Death', having opened with 'Men fear death as children fear to go into the dark', nevertheless concludes: 'But above all, believe it, the sweetest canticle in Nunc Dimittis'. Or as Ben Jonson put it:

> He that fears death or mourns it in the just
> Shows of the resurrection little trust.[56]

Whether expressed in the Christian–humanist theology of pre-Reformation times, or in Protestant manuals, or in the letter-writing manuals which included models of letters of condolence, or in the elegiac poetry of the period,[57] or in actual cases, the relationship between parents and children, and therefore the ambience within which the educative process took place, hardly sustains the extremes of the Ariès–Shorter–Stone thesis. At the very least, prescriptions concerning, and behaviour towards, infant nurture and death were extremely heterogeneous. Moreover, those arguing for 'indifference' virtually ignore another kind of evidence, of which there is no shortage – the perennial complaint that, far from treating their children harshly, many parents treated them too leniently, 'cockering' them, as the contemporary usage put it. When Erasmus and Vives complained[58] that mothers especially were guilty of such behaviour, they were merely repeating what classical writers had complained of much earlier, and their views were echoed throughout the sixteenth and seventeenth centuries. But in so doing, such writers only rarely reverted to an unconditional and absolute reliance on Proverbs.[59] Bullinger reminded his listeners that 'These words [he was citing Proverbs 29.15, 17] ... do utterly condemn the father's cockering and the mother's pampering, which is the marring of many children. For the parents offend God as much in too much cockering their children as they do in over much punishing of them.' Becon's *New Catechisme* (1560) made the same point, criticising parents 'which are so tender over their children that they cannot abide the wind to blow upon them', as much as those 'which furiously rage against their children and without consideration beat them as stock fish'.[60] It was this 'consideration' which, if anything, characterised most of the prescriptive literature.[61] As always, those whose prescriptions advocated 'the golden mean' rarely went on to give parents more detailed advice as to where and in what particular circumstances they should 'draw the line'.

Nor were such prescriptions confined to theologians, clerics, schoolmasters and the like. The few women who wrote in this period and on this topic reiterated the message. Despite her own mother's 'undeserved wrath so virulent' towards her, Elizabeth Grymeston still insisted to her son Berneye that 'there is nothing so strong as the force of love; there is no love so forcible as the love of an affectionate mother to her natural child'. Dorothy Leigh recalled that she was brought up with warmth and affection, and urged her sons 'that you will have your children brought up with much gentleness and patience; what disposition so ever they be, gentleness will soonest bring them to virtue'.[62] The reluctance of the newly widowed Elizabeth Brownlow to accede to the proposal to hand over her 9-year-old son, John, to the care of an entirely benign and benevolent uncle, Sir John Brownlow, is but one example of maternal affection which many other women recalled in their own lives. Alice Thornton, for example, offered 'my faithful thanks and gratitude to my dear and honoured parents, for their love, care, affection and sedulity over me'. Lady Anne Clifford constantly referred with affection to the memory of her mother (who died in 1616), and appeared to have a similarly warm relationship with her own daughter, Isabella, as did both Mary Rich, Countess of Warwick, with her father and her daughter, Joan, and Lady Joan Barrington with her daugher, Elizabeth.[63]

Recollections such as these were not, of course, the monopoly of girls and women. Henry VII himself wrote to his mother, Margaret Beaufort, in her old age, giving thanks 'for the great and singular motherly affection that it hath pleased you at all times to bear me'. Vives paid a similar tribute to his mother in *The Instruction of a Christen Woman*: 'no mother loved her child better than mine did, neither any child did ever less perceive himself loved of his mother than I. She never lightly laughed upon me, she never cockered me.' Gervase Holles acknowledged that 'to be the son of such a mother I ought to rank amongst the chiefest blessings and greatest comforts that

God Almighty in his goodness hath bestowed upon me'. The Quaker William Caton, companion to Judge Fell's son at Swarthmore, remembered 'such fatherly love and motherly affection'. Edward Harley recalled the judiciousness of his parents' attitude to him, and gave thanks to God 'that my parents were noble, wise and godly. They instructed me in the fear of God and never cockered me in my evil but always corrected it . . . [and] that the Lord gave my parents hearts to give me a liberal education and inclined their affection to be very tender to me'. Here again we have evidence of caring, thoughtful parents, which is confirmed in Harley's mother's letters to him whilst he was an undergraduate at Oxford.[64]

There was little debate, then, as to whether a mother should be a prime agent in the education of her children, nor as to her purpose in so doing. The ambience in which it should take place raised more doubts. Maternal influence in a child's education, whether by a precept or by example, was just as likely to take place in a warm and caring setting as in one that was harsh or indifferent. Evidence of actual cases is as varied as that provided by the prescriptive treatises. Yet the former should not, therefore, be dismissed as 'merely anecdotal', any more than the latter should be dismissed as 'merely theoretical'. Whilst it is useful to be reminded of the dangers of assuming a causal link between manual precept and parental practice, it over-simplifies the matter to label the one 'secondary socialisation' and the other 'primary socialisation', with all the value-judgements implied by the two adjectives.[65] Parental practice in the upbringing of children is as much prescriptive as descriptive, implying 'do as I do', even though many parents would recognise, reluctant as they would be to admit to it, the prescriptive stance of 'do as I say and not as I do'. Moreover, the distinction gives little assistance in the difficult task of identifying a child's motive for following or neglecting to follow a parent's practice or precept. It also begs the question of a child's ability to perceptively observe parental behaviour, to consider parental advice before deciding to reject rather than follow its parent's example. The period is littered with evidence of divided religious and political allegiances within families, and the same is true of our own theme. Elizabeth Clinton was more honest than most in openly acknowledging, as she urged her daughters and others to breast-feed their infants, that she had sent her own out to a wet-nurse. Alice Thornton was aware of her mother's practice of sending her children to a wet-nurse, but suckled all nine of her own children. Anne Newdigate was plainly going against her own family's practice when she suckled her own infants. Elizabeth Grymestone was certainly not following her own mother's example in the matter of 'correction' when she advised her son to bring up his children with love and affection.

As was so often the case, the principle having been accepted, debate was more likely to centre on ways and means. The heterogeneity of advice offered in the prescriptive literature – conduct books, 'advices', marriage sermons, letters and the like – is reflected in the heterogeneity of practice to be found in the lives and behaviour of actual women. For those whose means allowed it, or whose social status appeard to demand it, there was no shortage of advice about the qualities required of those who would undertake such education on the parents' behalf – from wet-nurses to domiciliary governesses and tutors (and, in the case of boys, schoolmasters and college tutors). Even within this relatively homogeneous group, however, there were some who insisted on undertaking the task themselves. But for the vast majority of parents such means were not available, nor would their children attend a school. The role of the mother thus became crucial, though any attempt to test whether prescription was actually put into practice will, of necessity, have to rely chiefly on evidence which by definition comes not from the vast majority but from or about those literate classes – ranging from the aristocrat and the university-educated cleric to the merchant and the yeoman farmer, and less frequently, their wives – who have left records of their activities. Evidence of the activities of status groups below these comes perforce from legal or quasi-legal records of complaint and presentation.

Some of the evidence provides only the most general of information, as for example when Vives reported that Queen Isabella of Spain had 'taught her daughers to spin, sew and paint'.[66] Sir Thomas Elyot dedicated his *Education and Bringing up of Children Translated out of Plutarche* (1530) to his sister Margery Puttenham, mother of the future poet George, as a means of helping her in the education of her sons, 'my lyttel nevewes'.[67] Lady Jane Grey spent some of her early years, as a matter of common practice, in the household of Catherine Parr and her husband Sir Thomas Seymour, the Lord Admiral. When the former queen died in 1548, however, Lady Jane was sent for by her father, Sir Henry Grey, on the grounds that 'considering her tender years' (she was then 11 years old) and 'her need of careful education and admonition' she would best be 'committed to the governance of her mother', the Lady Frances.[68] For much the same reason, on the execution in 1547 of Henry Howard, Earl of Surrey, it was considered 'most meetest for my Lady Surrey [i.e. Lady Frances Howard] to have the ordering of her daughters, the Ladies Jane and Margaret Howard'.[69]

Margaret Roper, the well-educated daughter of Sir Thomas More, would surely have followed her father's example of parental participation, yet her father's biographer, Nicholas Harpsfield, records only that 'To her children she was a double mother, one not to bring them forth only into the world, but instructing them herself in virtue and learning.' Again, her husband William Roper, having been sent to the Tower on a heresy charge, and the king's officers being sent to search the house, Harpsfield notes only that they found her 'not puling and lamenting, but full busily teaching her children'.[70] Catherine Willoughby, widow of Charles Brandon, Duke of Suffolk, insisted that her son Peregrine, born in 1555 by her second husband Richard Bertie, should be brought up in the household of Sir William Cecil, urging the latter 'for God's sake, to give the young man her son, good counsel; to bridle his youth, and to help him to despatch him to court'.[71] In his will of 1579, William Whittingham, Dean of Durham, indicated, 'I make Katherine, my wife, tutor to Sarah, Judith, Deborah, Elizabeth and David, my children.' George Newton of Newton in Cheshire, who died in 1580, made the same provision that his wife Elizabeth (who lived on until 1604, when she died aged 84) should 'have the education and bringing up of my four daughters [Jane, Elizabeth, Fortune and Marie] until she see convenient time and place for their better preferment'.[72]

In his will dated 20 March 1598, Sir William Fitzwilliam (1526–99) acknowledged his indebtedness to his 'dear and well-beloved' wife, Anne, who whilst he was 'wholly employed in the king's service' in Ireland 'took the most care of the education' of their surviving sons and three daughters. In much the same way, Sir William Cecil opened his 'Advice' to his son, Robert, with a reminder of 'The virtuous inclination of thy matchless mother [Lady Mildred], by whose tender and godly care thy infancy was governed together with thy education under so zealous and excellent a tutor.' Mildred's sister, Lady Anne Bacon, mother of Anthony and Francis, enjoyed a similar reputation.[73] Dorothy Leigh indicated that one of her reasons for writing *The Mothers Blessing*, addressed to her sons George, John and William, was to 'persuade them to teach their children . . . that all your children, be they males or females, may in their youth learn to read the Bible in their own mother tongue'. William Gouge's funeral sermon in 1646 for Mrs Margaret Ducke, wife of Dr Arthur Ducke, one of the Masters of the Court of Requests, is tantalisingly brief on the matter, recording only her constant private devotions and her care in the education of her two children.[74]

Lady Elizabeth Langham, wife of Sir James Langham, had no children of her own, she was 'not much above a year a wife'. But her own education, her memorialist recounts,

> was in a school or rather academy of learning and nursery of virtue, I mean the constant inspection and converse of her watchful mother the now Countess of Huntingdon [i.e. Lucy, wife of Ferdinando, sixth Earl of Huntingdon] from whose great parts and graces she received in her soul that *vis plastica* which formed her into so eminent both woman and Christian. Under her she received an education (for the most part) and a religious retirement which she hath often blessed God for.[75]

The Dowager Countess's son Theophilus, the seventh Earl (1650–1710), noted in an autobiographical piece that he received his education 'according to the direction of his mother, being wholly domestic' until having attained the age of 21 he married (in 1672) 'by her choice . . . Elizabeth, eldest daughter of Sir John Lewys'. The Catholic Lady Elizabeth Dacre, wife of William, third Lord Dacre, is reported as having educated their daughter Magdalene (later Viscountess Montagu, 1539–1608) until she was 13, before sending her to the household of Anne Russell, Countess of Bedford, for three years to 'perform the office of a gentlewoman'.[76] Sir John Bramston reported of his wife Alice, who died in 1647, that

> she was a virtuous and religious woman, a most careful and indulgent mother to her children, instructed them in the church catechism, teaching them the Lord's Prayer, the Ten Commandments, and the Creed, which she heard them say constantly every morning, and some psalms and chapters, which she selected in both the Old and New Testaments.

A similar situation probably was the case when Christiana, mother of William Cavendish, had oversight of his education after the death of his father William, the second Earl of Devonshire (1591–1628).[77] Adam Littleton was similarly sparing in his reportage when preaching the funeral sermon for Mary Alston, wife of Joseph Alston, who died in 1670, noting only 'the indulgent care and motherly love of her children whose duties she earned by her laborious attendance on their infant years'.[78]

In these various ways, then, whether the reportage be first-, second- or third-hand, mothers are to be found engaged in the early education of their children. Remarkably, we have only isolated examples of mothers (or fathers for that matter) undertaking to teach their children to read. Mothers who did teach their children to read must themselves have been taught the skill by someone else, though it is possible, even likely, that among the literate upper and middle classes learning to read was considered so 'normal', so expected, as to be not worthy of note in reports of the education of their children.

Even so, in one of his last letters before his martyrdom, John Penry urged his wife to teach their daughers to read the Bibles he had left them. William Bedell (1571–1642), later Bishop of Kilmore and Ardagh, related how his mother Alison taught him (and his brother) to read and to learn their catechism, before being introduced to the rudiments of Latin grammar by his father who then dispatched him to Emmanuel College, Cambridge, at the tender age of 12. Sir George Oglander (1609–32) recalled how he was taught to read and write by his mother, Lady Anne, with the assistance of her 'gentlewoman', Bett Leigh, the daughter of a neighbour. Lady Alice

Lucie had one of her children read a passage of the Bible to the others before supper, 'frequently taking occasion of instilling into them some sweet and profitable instructions'.[79] In his autobiography Roger North (1653–1734) reported that it was his mother, Lady Anne, wife of Dudley, fourth Lord North, who made herself responsible for her children 'learning to read, and bringing us to it at set hours, leaving the intervals to remission, which is absolutely necessary to young lungs'. Arnold Boate recalled how his wife, Margaret, had taught their daughter, who was born in 1646, to read,

> which she did with so much success as in a few weeks the child had perfectly learned all her letters and the spelling of all single syllables, with a good progress towards the spelling of more compounded ones, and of some whole words (as well as) begetting and confirming in her the knowledge and love of virtue, piety and civility.

The child was only 4 when her mother died in April 1651.[80]

Lady Elizabeth Delaval (born *c.*1649) indicated in her autobiographical *Meditations* that it was her grandmother, Lady Gorges, who taught her to read during her seasonal visits to London. Mrs Mary Bewley, wife of a London merchant, taught her only son, Thomas, to read, as did Elizabeth Walker, wife of clergyman Anthony Walker, her many children. The third Edmund Calamy (1671–1731) reported in his *Historical Account of My Own Life* that 'my good mother [i.e. Mary, his father's first wife] I well remember took a great deal of pains with me in my infancy and childhood, as it was she chiefly that taught me to read'.[81] Susanna Wesley was unusual in detailing the procedures she used in teaching her children to read:

> None were taught to read until five years old, except Kezzy, in whose case I was overruled and she was more years in learning [to read] than any of the rest had been months. One day was allowed to learn the letters, first of all, except Molly and Nancy, who were a day and a half . . . Samuel the first taught, learned the alphabet in a few hours . . . and as soon as he knew the letters began at the first chapter of Genesis. He was taught to spell the first verse, then to read it over and over till he could read it off-hand and without any hesitation, and so on the second [verse] . . . The same method was used by them all.[82]

Teaching one's children to read is, then, only occasionally noted in the records of family life. However, since the prime purpose of such activity was to enable them to read the Bible and other 'godly books', the lack of direct reportage may simply be a function of the plentiful supply of evidence concerning the participation of mothers in the religious education of their children. Though the 'godly household' has recently caught the attention of historians of religion, they have rarely considered in detail the role of the wife and the mother in such an educative situation. The evidence is very scattered, coming from a wide variety of sources, with some reports merely recording that a particular mother had carried out what was plainly considered to be nothing more than Christian duty. It was certainly not something confined to the households of 'the hotter sort of protestant', though William Whately (1583–1639), son of Thomas Whately, mayor of Banbury, and later a famous puritan preacher in the town of his birth, was obviously brought up in such a household. Even so, all we know of his early upbringing is that his mother Joyce 'carefully bred him up in the knowledge of the scriptures'. On the other hand, Anne Clifford (1590–1676), Countess of Pembroke, Dorset and Montgomery, asserted in her will that she hoped 'to die a true child of the Church of England . . . in which myself was born, bred and educated by my blessed mother', who was Margaret, daughter of Francis Russell, second Earl of Bedford and husband of George, third Earl of Cumberland. Anne herself is reported to have undertaken the same duty for her two daughters, Margaret and Isabella.[83] The diarist Simonds D'Ewes (1602–50), who might have been expected to provide some detail, nevertheless records only that his

> most dear and beloved mother [Cecilia] . . . partaking of her zealous prayers, godly instructions and blessed example, did admirably strengthen and settle me in the love and exercise of the best things, so as now I began to perform holy duties feelingly and with comfort which at first had only taken on trust and performed out of custom.[84]

Towards the end of her life Lady Elizabeth Russell (1528–1609), wife of John Lord Russell, and one of the well-educated daughters of Sir Anthony Cooke of Gidea Hall, Essex, translated from the Latin a work of John Ponet, *A Way of Reconciliation of a Good and Learned Man Touching the Nature of the Sacrament* (1605) and, in dedicating the work to her daughter, Lady Anne Herbert, reveals that

> even as from your first birth and cradle I was most careful, above any worldly things, to have you suck the perfect milk of sincere religion, so willing to end as I began, I have left you, as my last legacy, this book . . . now naturalised by me into English.[85]

Lucy Thornton, wife of Roger Thornton of Little Wratting, Suffolk, is reported to have carefully instructed her children through morning and evening prayers, psalm singing and reading from the scriptures, as did Elizabeth Juxon, wife of the London merchant John Juxon, of whom it is baldly reported that 'she diligently instructed her family and servants in godly ways'.[86]

Dorothy Holmes, who died in 1623, was the wife of William Holmes and sister to prominent Laudian, Richard Neile, Bishop of Durham. The preacher of her funeral sermon, however, merely reported that 'born of honest and religious parentage . . . she was sedulous and very affectionate in the education of her children that they might serve God and the common-wealth'. Elizabeth Stanley, daughter of Ferdinand, fifth Earl of Derby, and wife to Henry Hastings, fifth Earl of Huntingdon, simply 'made the fruit of her body to become the fruit of the spirit', as might be expected since she was part of a 'puritan' but conforming household.[87] Dorothy Constable (1580–1632) was brought up in a Catholic family, her mother Margaret, wife of Sir Henry Constable, having been imprisoned for a time for her faith. Dorothy married the conforming Sir Ralph Lawson, but proceeded to initiate all of her 15 children into her faith, with a son going to school in Douai, and her daughter Mary to the convent at Ghent.[88] In his *Memoirs*, Ambrose Barnes, Merchant Venturer and Alderman of Newcastle-upon-Tyne, reported that his wife Mary, whom he married in 1655, 'took care to instil betimes into her children the ABC of religion, as Bathsheba did her son Solomon', and despite his resorting to a multiplicity of metaphor, Edmund Barker, chaplain to the household of Lord Arthur Capel and his wife Lady Elizabeth, tells us not much more about Lady Elizabeth's contribution to the education of her nine children than that:

> but first and greatest care of all was for their education: to water these tender plants with wholesome precepts and examples, and to infuse early principles of piety and religion into their minds; she well knew of what great importance it is, what liquor the vessel is first seasoned with. Neither could she think it is the only part and office of a mother to bring forth children to her husband.[89]

William Dillingham, in his funeral sermon for Lady Elizabeth Alston, who died in 1678, made the same point:

> towards her children she was a most tender and careful mother, when she did not satisfy herself to have once brought forth, but (as St Paul saith he did of his Galatians 4.19) she travailed again of them that Christ might be formed in them.

Margaret Cavendish (1623–73), wife of William Cavendish, first Duke of

Newcastle, and daughter of Sir Thomas and Lady Elizabeth Lucas, looked back on her mother's influence in almost exactly the same terms.[90]

William Tong was born in 1662. He lost his father whilst still young, and it was left to his widowed mother, 'an excellent zealous Christian of the old puritan stamp, who took great care of their education, and under God it was much owing to her that he was bred a minister and a dissenter'. The parents of William Stout, on the other hand, were 'of the communion of the Episcopal Protestant religion' and (he reports) 'instructed their children in the church catechism so-called, and to repeat it before the parish priest'.[91] Mary Dawes also lost her father when young, and it was her mother who is praised for her 'own good example and wise instructions and careful education of your daughter in the ways of religion and virtue'. Sarah Davy's mother died when Sarah was 11, but her parents 'did not leave me without instruction in the things of God, including the Ten Commandments and the catechism'.[92] Anne, daughter of the famous Presbyterian divine Thomas Manton, recollected, 'I look upon it as no small blessing that I was born of Christian and religious parents such as did truly fear God, and did what in them lay to instruct their posterity in early piety.' She was left motherless at an early age, but when she too died aged 38 the preacher of her funeral sermon reported:

> Great was her prudency and conduct in the management of her household affairs. She had the bowels of a tender mother with the souls as well as the bodies of her dear children, and did endeavour by counsel and instruction to instil in them the principles of true godliness.[93]

Lady Lumley, wife of Sir Martin Lumley, is similarly praised at her death in 1692, though only in the baldest of terms, in that 'like a pious and most affectionate mother she took great care to have her son in his younger years instructed in religion, whom she herself taught the most necessary and fundamental points thereof'. Elizabeth, daughter of Reverend Samuel Annesley, kept a diary for nearly 20 years. Alas, she left instructions that it, with her other papers, should be burned after her death. Timothy Rogers, the preacher of her funeral sermon in 1697, nevertheless reported that 'In her papers she acknowledges the good providence of God in giving her religious parents that with united efforts took almighty care of her education.' Her sister Susannah married Samuel Wesley in 1690, in due course to undertake the rigorously detailed religious education of their many children at the parsonage at Epworth which she later described to her son, John, in a letter of 24 July 1732.[94]

Varied records such as these, their lack of detail notwithstanding, nevertheless give some indication that the contribution of mothers to the religious education of their children was not something to be found only in the prescriptive literature of the period. Fortunately, evidence of a rather more detailed kind is also available. Elizabeth, daughter of Sir Lawrence and Lady Elizabeth Tanfield and wife of Sir Henry Cary, is a case in point. When she was 12 her father gave her a copy of Calvin's *Institutes*. Yet, by the time she was married at 15 she found herself increasingly inclined towards the Catholic religion. She spent the first year of her marriage in the house of her father, and then removed to the home of her mother-in-law, Lady Catherine Cary, who thoroughly disapproved not only of her religious leanings but also of her interest in literature. She saw little of her husband, away in The Netherlands and then in Spain, and her first child was not born until seven years after her marriage. Thereafter she continued to prepare her children for the Catholic faith, though it was not until 1625 that she herself openly acknowledged her adherence. Two of her sons became priests and four daughters became nuns, though Lucius, her eldest son, who succeeded his father as second Viscount Falkland, remained a steadfast Anglican and Royalist. As her memorialist put it:

> her first care (whether by herself or by others) was to have them soon inclined in the knowledge, love and esteem of all moral virtue, and to have them according to their capacities, instructed in the principles of Christianity, not in the manner of a catechist (which would have instructed them in the particular Protestant doctrines of the truth of which she was little satisfied), but in a manner more apt to make an impression on them than things learned by rote and not understood.

Her son Lucius married Lettice (1611–40), youngest daughter of Sir Richard Morison, and it was she who played an active part in the education of her two surviving children in the Anglican faith at Great Tew.[95]

Born in 1581, Mary Tracy was the youngest of the 15 children of Sir John and Lady Tracy. Her mother died three days after she was born, and her father eight years later. When she was 19 she married William Hoby and bore him two children before he died in 1605. She then (1607) married Sir Horace Vere, and the five surviving children of this marriage, all daughters, were largely brought up by their mother, in the absence of their soldier father, one of the 'Fighting Veres'. Lady Mary was active in getting ministers appointed to her livings and supporting them in public worship. But, as her memorialist records, she was equally active in the conduct of her household's worship: 'she brought her religion and devotion home with her, and did not leave it in her pew behind her till she returned to it again the next Sabbath'. With her family chaplain, Obadiah Sedgwick, she supervised family prayers twice a day, including the singing of psalms, and saw to it that the Sunday sermons were repeated at home by her servants as well as her daughters. 'Her closet . . . was excellently furnished with pious books of practical divinity', including presumably Richard Sibbe's *The Bruised Reed and Smoaking Flax: Some Sermons Contracted out of the 12 of Matth. 20* (1630), which the author had dedicated to her and her husband. She was also a frequent correspondent of the puritan divine, John Davenport. Widowed a second time in 1635, she spent the last 30 years of her life at Kirby Hall, Castle Hedingham, where she died in 1671, aged 89.[96]

Like Lady Vere, Lady Alice Lucy of Charlecote, had 'a library of our choicest English authors . . . and . . . an excellent understanding as in secular so in spiritual things', and she too engaged herself in the religious education of her ten surviving children:

> about an hour before supper she appointed one from some of her children to read from a godly sermon in the presence of the rest, frequently instilling into them sweet instructions and instructing them to a religious walking. A little before she betook herself to repose she commanded them all to come into her lodging where they sang a psalm, as the servants did constantly after supper.[97]

In his autobiography, Oliver Heywood reported that his mother, Alice,

> took great care of us all that her children might learn and say the catechism; she highly esteemed and commended that of Mr Ball's. She was continually putting us upon reading the scriptures and good books, and instructed us how to pray, and it was her constant concern when my father was gone to London to make all her children pray. I must say I owe much to her as the instrument of God of that saving good which at first I received, and I hope shall never forget the instructions of a mother.[98]

Arnold Boate provided a fairly detailed account of his wife's contribution to the religious education of their third and only surviving child, a girl born in 1646. As we have seen, Margaret Boate taught her daughter to read. In addition she made herself responsible for

> teaching her to pray, and making her repeat often the Lord's Prayer and several other good prayers, as likewise the Creed and the Commandments; [also] in catechising her in all points of Christian religion making her every day repeat what she had learned before, with some new additions still from time to time.

Lady Catherine Wandesford's memorialist reported that:

This good mother taught her son [Christopher] the English tongue and . . . the rudiments of religion. It was her custom every morning, to call her children together and make such of them as could to read the lessons and psalms for the day, and repeat by memory such select chapters and psalms as were proper to be impressed on their hearts in their earliest years. She also catechised them, explaining things with condescension to their weak capacities.[99]

We know little of the life of Mrs Mary Bewley, who died in 1659, but of her piety there can be little doubt. She was a constant church-goer, and 'sometimes she refrained from writing in the church that she might exercise her memory and be more attentive with what she heard, which after she came home she committed to writing'. In addition she 'instructed her only son to read even the Accidents and like another Eunice to know the scriptures from a child, framing and propounding such questions to him as made him give a good account of the chief histories of the Bible'.[100]

In 1629 Lady Brilliana Harley wrote to her husband Sir Robert, asking him to send 'a little bible' to their eldest son, Edward ('Ned'): 'he begins now to delight in reading, and that is the book I would have him place his delight in'. Given the family's puritan leanings, this would probably have been one of the many quarto or octavo editions of the Genevan Bible then available. Then, years later, in one of her many letters to Ned when he was an undergraduate of Magdalen Hall, Oxford, she sent him a copy of her translation of part of Calvin's *Life of Luther*:

I put it into English and here enclosed have sent it to you; it is not all his life for I put no more into English than was not in the Book of Martyrs . . . thus, my dear Ned, you may see how willingly I impart anything to you in which I find any good.

Her letters to him are full of advice about his religious life.[101]

Barbara, the daughter of Thomas Bellasye, first Viscount Falconberg, married Sir Henry Slingsby in 1631. She never enjoyed good health and died in 1641. Even so she played an active part in the upbringing of her daughter Barbara, as her husband noted in his diary:

She is very tender and careful over her children, having yet [1638] but two and now with child; she has so taught her daughter Barbara, who was born the 14th of May 1633, that she is able already to say all her prayers, answer her catechism, read and write a little.

Her son Thomas had the benefit of a tutor, a Mr Cheney, who taught 'following the pattern of Michel de Montaigne'. Whether Barbara also benefited is not revealed.[102]

Lady Rachel Russell lost her second husband in 1683, when her children were 9, 7 and 3 respectively. Eight years later, in a long letter to them, she put down an account of her own practice in the matter of their religious upbringing, urging them to use it as a guide for the future. Beside recommending particular passages of the Bible for learning by heart and enjoining them to take daily note of their faults, she reminded them of her own thankfulness that she

> was born of Christian parents . . . and that I was baptised and since educated in the Christian religion . . . although I love your bodies but too well, yet if my heart deceive me not, tis nothing in a comparison of your precious souls . . . What is leading a holy life [she continued] you find in the Bible; be constant in the reading of it, and use yourself to make some use of what you read; before you lay away the book, consider what virtue is recommended or what vice is forbid, or what doctrines taught in that chapter, you have there read, and think on it often the rest of the day, and doing this you will in a little while make it habitual to you . . . get by heart the Sermon on the Mount, 5, 6, 7 chapter of Matthew; the 17 of St John is also a fine chapter to get by heart, so is 8 of Romans, the 19 and 37 Psalms, and the penitential ones.

She goes on to give detailed instructions on how to pray, using Jeremy Taylor's *Holy Living* as a guide, together with his *Golden Grove*. Simon Patrick's *Devout Christian* is also recommended, with detailed page references which clearly show her own use of the work. Taylor was, of course, chaplain at Golden Grove in Flintshire, the family seat of the Vaughan family, where she resided with her first husband, Francis Vaughan.[103]

Anne Paget, daughter of William, fourth Lord Paget and his wife Letitia, was a constant writer down of sermons, a habit she continued throughout her two marriages, to Sir Simon Harcourt, a Royalist killed at the battle of Carrickmain Castle in Ireland in 1642, and to Sir William Waller, the Parliamentary general. In their inevitable absences, she was 'careful to keep up the observation of family duty twice a day' and of catechising the children, including her two stepchildren, once a week: 'commending those that were forward, admonishing those who were tardy and averse, and imposing little penalties upon them, payable to the poor'. Anne, daughter of Sir Thomas Murray and his wife Jane, gives rather more detail of her upbringing at the hands of her widowed mother. Her father died in 1622 when she was 'but three months old', Anne related in her autobiographical 'Memoirs' (written late 1677, early 1678). But her mother, who had been 'entrusted twice with the charge and honour of being governess to the Duke of Gloucester and the Princess Elizabeth', nevertheless 'spared no expense in educating all her children'. In addition she

> paid masters for my sister and me to write, to speak French, play the lute and virginals, and dance, and kept a gentlewoman to teach us all kinds of needlework, which shows I was not brought up in an idle life. But my mother's greatest care and for which I will ever owe to her memory the highest gratitude was the great care she took that even from our infancy we were instructed never to neglect the church as often as there was occasion to meet there either for prayers or preaching. So that for many years together I was seldom never absent from divine service at five o'clock in the morning in summer and six o'clock in the winter, till the usurped power put a restraint to that public worship that owned and continued in the Church of England, where I bless God I had my education and the example of a good mother, who kept constant to her own parish church and had always a great respect for the ministers under whose charge she was.[104]

Roger North had similar autobiographical recollections of his early life when 'our childhood passed as usual under the mother's government'. Besides teaching her children to read, Lady Anne,

> to show how virtue may be mixed with delight . . . used to tell us tales, always concluding in morality to which, as children, we were most attentive. On Sundays also she would comply when we solicited for a story, but it must be a Sunday one, as she called it, and then would tell some scriptural history, which were more pleasing to us because more admirable and extraordinary than others. Nothing [Roger concluded] could be more *a propos* than this method for forming the minds of children to a prejudice in favour of what was good.

It is not surprising then that Roger wrote to his sister Anne (Foley) in later years (1689),

> I think there never was such an example in the world as our mother, who was no hector, but never appeared disturbed during all the painful nursing which she had of many of us, and more with my father.

During the three years of her widowhood she was 'never more pleased than when her house was filled with her children, with whom she was merry and free, and encouraged them to be so too'.[105]

Given the stress laid in the Protestant churches on the importance of a married clergy, it would be reasonable to suppose that the wives of clerics would have played a significant part in the religious education of their children. George Herbert, for example, insisted that 'all in his house are either teachers or learners or both, so that his family is a school of religion, and they all account that to teach the ignorant is the greatest of alms'.[106] It might also be expected that their contribution would have been recorded in some detail. In fact, this seems not to have been the case.[107] We know something, but not a great deal, about the wives of Martin Luther, John Calvin and other Protestant reformers, nor surprisingly of the Anglican Bishops' wives, or of those lower down the ecclesiastical scale. Ralph Josselin's relatively detailed diary says almost nothing about his wife Jane's possible participation in the education of their young children. The same is true of Oliver Heywood's diaries, and apart from John Donne's clandestine marriage, his numerous offspring and his wife Anne's early death in child-birth, we know nothing about the education of the children.[108]

This was not always the case, of course. It is likely that Robert Bolton (1572–1631), rector of Broughton in Northamptonshire, was not unusual in having a wife, Anne, 'to whose care he committed the ordering of his outward estate, he himself minding only the studies and weighty affairs of his heavenly calling'. Peter Heylin's wife found herself in the same situation, and by her labours thus freed him 'from that care and trouble which other-wise would have hindered his laborious pen going through so great a work in that short time'.[109] When Thomas Cawton felt obliged to go into exile in The Netherlands, he wrote to his wife back in England, 'Train our children in the catechism and in frequent reading of the scriptures.' This was the sort of training presumably which Elizabeth Montfort, wife of Dr Thomas Montfort, who died in 1632, undertook when, as the preacher of her funeral sermon reported, 'in their tender years she brought them up in nurture and instruction and information of the Lord (Ephesians 6.4) and taught them as Bathsheba did her Lemuel (Proverbs 31.1)'.[110] Margaret Corbet was the wife of Dr Edward Corbet, pastor of Hasely in Oxford-shire. Her memorialist reported in 1657 in his funeral sermon that she

> bestowed great pains in catechising her children and other near rela-
> tions committed to her care . . . God gave her several olive branches
> round her table, well bred, well catechised and governed, and of
> as great hopes as any I know. As Eunice and Lois instructed young
> Timothy, so she instructed her hopeful little ones in holy scripture and
> acquainted them with the knowledge of God in their tender years.[111]

Henry Wilkinson's wife Elizabeth obviously received a sincere religious education from her parents, Anthony and Elizabeth Gifford, since

> she was observed to be from her childhood docile, very willing to learn, industrious in reading and of the swift to hear the word of God preached. She was very careful to remember and took much pains in writing sermons and collecting special notes out of practical divines . . . She kept a diary of God's dealings with her soul . . . and much busied herself in prayer and meditation.

Her marriage with Dr Henry Wilkinson, Principal of Magdalen Hall, Oxford, was marred by continual ill-health, but even so, 'she was tender in her affection to her children, and careful to catechise and instruct them in the fear of God' until her death in 1654.[112] Katherine Overton died in 1671. She was the wife of the ecclesiastical biographer Samuel Clarke, by whom she had five sons and four daughters. Her husband reported that she

> nourished them all with her own breasts, loved them dearly without fondness, careful to give them nurture as well as nourishment, not sparing the rod when there was just occasion . . . As soon as they were capable she was vigilant and diligent to season their tender years with grace and virtue by instilling in them the first grounds and principles of religion . . . by catechising, enquiring what they remembered of the sermons they heard, reading her note to them.[113]

Edmund Calamy (1671–1732), the third of that name, in giving *An Historical Account of My Life* reported that:

> my good mother, I well remember, took a great deal of pains with me in my infancy and childhood, as it was she chiefly that taught me to read, so did she teach me also in my catechism, and when I had learned it she carried me in her hands and delivered me to the care of good old Mr. Thomas Lye, to be publicly catechised by him on Saturday afternoons at Dyers Hall, having herself been catechised by him in her younger years which she seemed to mention with abundance of pleasure.[114]

Whilst many of these accounts of the contribution of clerical wives to the religious education of their children are tantalisingly brief, they nevertheless indicate that such contribution was serious in intent and relatively systematic. We are fortunate, therefore, to have one very full report, that relating to Elizabeth Walker, wife of Anthony Walker, rector of Fyfield in Essex.[115] Though lacking the immediacy of a first-hand account of day-to-day relationships, it was written by her husband very shortly after her death in 1690 whilst the memory was fresh, and was based on documents she herself had written during her life. It is characterised by a wealth of detail which he gathered together under headings such as 'How she did spend her day', and 'Her care of the education of her children'. The detail was drawn not only from his immediate memory but also from a collection of her letters and an autobiographical manuscript 'left under her own hand . . . [in] a large book in octavo of the best paper she could buy, neatly bound, gilded and ruled with red',[116] together with a commonplace book of scriptural passages collected under headings such as 'Prayer', 'Fear of God', 'Promiser of Pardon of Sin', 'An Abbreviation of Faith and Christian Principles', each provided with appropriate proof-texts. The whole was supplemented by her diary entries of the births of their six sons and five daughters, 'besides some abortive or untimely births'. Alas, none of this material appears to have survived. Walker probably destroyed it when he had completed his self-appointed task, possibly at his wife's request.[117]

Elizabeth was the daughter of John Sadler, a druggist of Stratford-upon-Avon, and his wife Elizabeth (Dackum), daughter of a Portsmouth clergyman. She was born in Bucklersbury, London, in 1623. In 1650 she married Anthony Walker, then chaplain to the Earl of Warwick. Her first child was born the following year, and in the next 14 years she had 11 full-term births, of which three including her 11th in 1665 were stillborn. Even so, by her husband's report, she was extremely active in the education of those of her children who survived, as well as of her maids and servants, in needlework, cooking, brewing, baking and dairy management, together with 'the making of all sorts of English wines, gooseberry, currant, cowslip, quince etc',[118] in other words, all those domestic skills which the prescriptive literature had so regularly enjoined.

But, as her husband recalled,

> all this was by-business comparatively . . . she considered her children as the nursery of families, the church and the nation . . . [and] . . . her work and business was to cultivate their minds, improve their intellectuals, to season their tender hearts with a due sense of religion.

This she did in a highly systematic fashion. First of all she

> taught them to read as soon as they could pronounce their letters, yea, before they could speak plain, and sowed the seed of early pious knowledge in their tender minds by a plain, familiar catechism suited to their capacity whilst very young . . . when they arrived at four or five years old she would teach them somewhat a larger prayer and cause them to

go by themselves until they were accustomed to do it of their own accord . . . When they could read tolerably well she caused them to get by heart sentences of scripture, then whole psalms and chapters which she oft called them to repeat, and gave them small pecuniary rewards to encourage them, that they might have somewhat of their own to give to the poor, and when she gave farthings or victuals to travelling people at the door, she would cause a child to give it to them to accustom them to be charitable.[119]

In these ways, the years of their early infancy were attended to. Later she

gave them other books and often heard them read them, and would make prudent choice of books of instruction and devotion, and some-times useful histories as the *Book of Martyrs* and abbreviations of our English Chronicles, and lives of holy exemplary persons so that she might do several things at once, both perfect their reading and inform their judgements and inflame their affections to early piety . . . When they had learned the Church Catechism she would have them answer it publicly that the meaner sort might be ashamed not to send their children . . . and having observed that many would read commendably in the Bible where the sentences are shorter and the distinction of the verses and frequent use much helped them who could scarce do it intelligibly in other books where the periods are longer and not so well distinguished, she would give them other books and would often hear them and would make prudent choice.[120]

In addition she made 'For my dear children Mistress Margaret and Mistress Elizabeth Walker' a collection of spiritual passages under various heads: 'Philanthropy and Charity', 'Meekness of Spirit' and several others, includ-ing a 44-page section on 'The Fear of God', together with an act of 'Direc-tions for my children concerning prayers'. Nor did she confine her efforts to her own family, for she

used also to buy primers, psalters, testaments and Bibles to give away, and other godly books, Crooks *Guide* especially, to give to poor children and families . . . She was Martha and Mary both unto perfection, yet always acted Martha's part with Mary's spirit; she spiritualised her worldly business.[121]

No other husband provides such a detailed record of his wife's activities in the education of their children. The extensive diaries of Ralph Josselin, Oliver Heywood, Samuel Pepys and John Evelyn provide only incidental

references to their respective wives and then rarely to their educative function, and the biographical sections of funeral sermons, as we have seen,
leave something to be desired in both the quality and quantity of their
detail. The question thus arises: was Elizabeth Walker 'typical' and then of
whom? Her assiduity may very well have been matched in the lives of
unsung mothers about whom we have only the slightest of detail. The same
may have been true of the range of her educational programmes. She
appears to be unique in having had a husband who was willing to undertake
the biographical task in the detail that he did. Elizabeth Walker's labours
are not matched, in the records at least, until those of Susannah Wesley
(1670–1742), mother of John and Samuel, who gave her own account in
1732.[122] Elizabeth was, of course, statistically untypical in that she was the
mistress of a fairly prosperous Anglican parsonage. She was a mature
woman when she married at the age of 27, and if the following 14 years are
anything to go by, a remarkably strong and healthy one too, surviving thereafter long enough to take an interest in the well-being of her grandson,
'Johnny' Cox. Remarkable as her husband's report is, we can only regret
that no similarly detailed record survives of how she herself came to acquire
the education which she so systematically used to pass on to her own children. It would be pleasing to report also that her labours had a long-lasting
influence on her descendants. In fact, the only child to survive into adulthood was her daughter, Margaret, who nevertheless died in childbirth in
February 1676, following her marriage to barrister John Cox, leaving a son
John, with whom Elizabeth corresponded whilst he was at Felsted School in
1690, the year of her own death at the age of 67.[123]

But, as we have seen, independent religious activity was foreseen by those
in authority as a means of leading children and adults alike away from
statutory orthodoxy, with some 'godly' households being regarded as a
conventicle to be suppressed for their heterodox practice and teaching. It is
the evidence of complaint and for presentment to the churchwardens of the
parish which enables us to see particular members of the lower classes, the
'labouring poor', appearing in the record. Some of the evidence relates to
their failure to send their children to church to be catechised by the parish
priest. At the same time there is evidence of more positive action by parents
in providing their children with a non-orthodox religious education. John
Pykas, a baker of Colchester, for example, confessed under interrogation
before Bishop Tunstall that in 1523 his mother Agnes introduced him to
Lollard texts and doctrines, providing him also with the Epistles in English,
which together with the Gospels she urged would provide him with a truer
religious understanding. In the same way, Alice and Richard Colyngs
were denounced by a neighbour for teaching their daughter Joan the Ten
Commandments, the Seven Deadly Sins and the Epistle of St James.[124]

Rose Hickman's mother, wife of the London merchant Sir William Locke, secretly read Protestant books to her and her sisters. As Rose recalled in her 'Certain Old Stories Recorded by an Aged Gentlewoman a Time Before Her Death, to be Perused by Her Children and Posterity':

> my mother in the days of Henry the Eighth came to some light of the gospel by means of some English books sent privately to her by my father's factors from beyond the sea; whereupon she used to call me with my two sisters into her chamber to read to us out of the same books very privately for fear of trouble because these good books were then accounted heretical . . . Therefore my mother charged us to say nothing of her reading to us for fear of trouble.[125]

When Elizabeth Young was hauled before the authorities and dared to defend her religious views, one of her interrogators exploded: 'Thou hast read a little in the Bible or Testament, and thou thinkest that thou art able to reason with a doctor that hath gone to school thirty years'. When one of them spoke to her in Latin she replied 'I will not go to church till I may hear it in a tongue that I can understand, for I will be fed no longer in a strange tongue'. Similarly challenged, Anne Askew dissembled with politic skill: 'I told him I was but a woman and knew not the course of the schools.'[126]

The role of the mother, especially in the religious education of her children, was thus far from negligible. Nor did her concern cease with their emergence from infancy. Lady Ellen Mounteagle, for example, wrote a pleading letter to the Duke of Norfolk in 1566 concerning the plight of her daughter 'now left in great and extreme misery by the death of her husband Lord Dacre of the North'. Lady Margaret Howard wrote in 1571 to her nephew the Earl of Sussex, asking that her son William 'might be with her now that she is a widow'. Isabel Stanley also wrote to the earl urging that, her husband having died, he would take their son, his nephew, 'as your man'.[127] Some expressed in letters to their often absent husbands their concern for the progress, or lack of progress, in their children's education. In 1572 Catherine Percy, Countess of Northumberland, wrote to her husband, Henry, the eighth Earl, about the education of their daughter. Lady Mary Coke wrote similarly to Sir John Coke about the inadequacy of a 'Mr Mace' (Peter Mease), who had been engaged as tutor to their sons, Joseph and John. As it turned out, the matter was resolved by Sir John arranging for the boys to go on to university under a tutor recommended by his brother.[128] Despite her undoubted ability to cope with all the vicissitudes resulting from her husband's exile, Lady Mary Verney felt compelled to write to her husband, Sir Ralph, about their son John ('Jack'), he of the malformed legs and speech defect: 'of all things [she wrote] he hates his book; truly it is time you had him with you for he learns nothing here . . . [even though] he is a very ready witted child'. Her two older children, Edmund and Margaret ('Mun' and 'Peg') were already with their father at Blois.[129] In her letters to her oldest son, Edward, whilst he was at Oxford, Lady Brilliana Harley constantly refers to her worries about his younger brothers Robert ('Robin') and Thomas ('Tom'): 'I am greatly troubled to get one to teach them' she wrote on one occasion; on another, 'Your brother Robin seems to be extremely discontented': again, she complains that Thomas spends too much time with the servants, 'and does exceedingly neglect himself, which is a great grief to me'.[130] Lady Trevor Warner, having taken the veil at the convent in Ghent, was nevertheless acutely concerned for the religious upbringing of her children, Susan and Catherine. Writing to her husband Sir John she reported:

> I have seriously considered our obligation of bringing them up for the world of religion, and I find they cannot possibly learn anything that is material as to worldly breeding till they be eleven or twelve years of age, and am therefore apt to think they will be as well here if not better, for four or five years, than in any place else.

She acknowledged the difficulties arising from her own position, but concluded 'I think if they could come hither, 'tis necessary that they should have a good and careful servant . . . I hope the widow Draper, if you can prevail with her to leave her family' – which in the event she did.[131]

More often, of course, the correspondence between mother and son which has survived was concerned less with formal matters and academic progress than with health, diet and above all with religious observance and moral rectitude, at the same time showing all the signs of a caring and affectionate relationship. Signing herself 'Your very loving mother', Lady Alice Hatton, wife of Christopher Hatton, wrote to her son, Christopher, at Jesus College, Cambridge, *c*.1620:

> You must know from me that if I did not strive against the fond affections of a mother, I should send oftener for you than you would be willing to come, if you love your own good, as I hope you do.

She follows up these sentiments with some close though entirely traditional advice about the boy's religious duty.[132] Elizabeth Smyth, wife of Sir Hugh Smyth of Ashton Court near Bristol, was a regular letter-writer to her 13-year-old son, Thomas ('Tom'), whilst he was at St John's College, Oxford, from 1622 to 1626, ending her letters in the most affectionate of ways:

'Thus sweetheart, praying to God to bless you with His best blessing, to His holy protection I committ thee, Ever resting, Thy most careful and loving mother.' Given the age of her son it is not surprising that a typical letter reads: 'I know you will have care to keep yourself as warm as you may when the cold weather comes in. Remember your neck and your feet'. Thomas's father died three days after his son's marriage in 1627, but his mother continued to correspond with him about his wife and their children, as well as about the running of the family estate.[133]

Katherine Paston showed a similar concern in her correspondence with her 14-year-old son, William, whilst he was at Corpus Christi College Cambridge, in the mid-1620s:

> Be careful in your recreations for overheating your blood, and if at any time you sweat or be too hot do not drink till you have made water, for so you know you were wont to do at home ... Your kind Aunt Bell remembers her love to you and sends you a box of juice of liquorice. It will stay the rheum when tobacco will not; I hope to hear you still hate the very smell of tobacco.

Even so, she did not omit to remind her son of his religious obligations:

> I hope thou does ruminate over the psalms and chapters and texts of scripture which long since thou didst learn by heart. I would be sorry thou shouldst forget thy Conduit of Comfort; these things let not slip out of thy mind.[134]

In 1628 Susanna Collett, one of the Ferrar daughters, was similarly concerned about her wayward son Edward, away in London, serving his apprenticeship:

> It would trouble me much if I had but a thought that you would forget those psalms that you have learned. I hope you will not content yourself in duty keeping them in your memory, but learn them more and in particular that book of the Proverbs, which both I desire and you promised to do.

Six years later, when he was about to sail for the West Indies, she wrote: 'I give you in charge not only the reading but the putting into practice those precepts contained in the written book I send you ... also three books of Mr Herbert which are held (and worthily) in great esteem.'[135]

Lady Brilliana Harley obviously had the warmest of relationships with her son Edward, who entered Magdalen Hall, Oxford, just before his 14th birthday. 'My dear Ned [she wrote in 1639], I long to hear from you and I cannot but let you know that your letters are most welcome to me.' Alongside the usual motherly advice about his health, diet and clothing she did not omit to add:

> keep always a watch over your precious soul; tie yourself to a daily examination; think over the company you have been in, and what your discourse was, and how you found yourself affected, how in the discourses of religion ... Let nothing hinder you from performing constant private duties of praying and reading.

Even so she was not above asking a favour of her son; 'if there be any good looking glasses in Oxford choose one about the bigness of that I used to dress me in, if you remember it ... choose one that will make a true answer to one's face'.[136]

Surviving less frequently are letters from a son to his mother when he was at university. William Paston's to his mother Lady Katherine and those of Henry Herbert to his mother Lady Elizabeth, second wife of Sir Henry Herbert, whilst he was at Trinity College, Oxford in the early 1670s, are as brief and uninformative as most dutiful letters from boys to their mothers usually are. Roger Manners's to his mother, the newly widowed Elizabeth, Countess of Rutland, are rather more forthcoming in a boyish kind of way: 'I am longing to see you and desirous to hear of your health', though usually his letters merely report that he is in good health, in need of some particular piece of clothing, and excusing his not writing to her more frequently on the rather spurious grounds of his 'ill-inditing and worse writing'. On one occasion, however, he wrote:

> I give your ladyship humble thanks for your honourable directions in your letters for my good. I do assure your ladyship that the carriage of myself both towards God and my work, my comeliness in diet and gesture, shall be such as your ladyship shall hear and like well of.[137]

Usually when a boy went off to university it was his father who negotiated with a tutor and who received reports about his progress. Occasionally, however, we find the mother undertaking his task. In the late 1580s, Elizabeth Manners engaged in a long correspondence with John Jegon, her son Roger's tutor, first at Queens' College, Cambridge then at Corpus Christi, when Jegon became Master (1590–1603) of that college. In the same way Robert Townshend's mother, Lady Jane Townshend, corresponded with his tutor, Arthur Lake, as did Lady Katherine Oxinden with Robert Hegge, tutor at Corpus Christi College, Oxford, to her son, Henry, in the mid-1620s. At much the same time Lady Katherine Paston corresponded with

Samuel Walsall, Master (1618–26) of Corpus Christi College, Cambridge, when her son William was in residence, Walsall assuring her 'I perceive your ladyship feared his excess in tennis though I am persuaded that there is not any exercise more wholesome and not many more gentlemanlike'. Even so, Lady Katherine persisted in advising William 'to beware of violent tennising or leaping or any other things which shall hinder your health'.[138]

A college tutor's role was concerned, of course, as much with moral overseeing as with academic tuition. In some cases, however, a mother even took up residence in or near the university city the better to oversee her son's progress at first hand. An early example is provided by Catherine, Duchess of Suffolk, the fourth wife and widow of Charles Brandon. She took up residence at Kingston, five or six miles from Cambridge, when her two sons, Henry (aged 14) and Charles (aged 12) were at St John's College. Unfortunately her concern did not prevent both boys from dying of the sweating sickness in July 1551.[139] The newly widowed Lady Magdalen Herbert took up residence in Oxford in 1596 to be near her 14-year-old son, Edward, then at University College, and stayed there until he had completed his studies in 1601. Lady Rachel Russell continued her personal oversight of her children's education by accompanying her newly married son, Wriothesley, to Oxford in 1696 when he was in residence at Magdalen College, his young wife Elizabeth having returned, as was customary, to the home of her parents. Wriothesley was at Oxford for but a year before going on his continental travels with his tutor, John Hicks. Lady Rachel found herself still needing to advise Wriothesley's older sister Katherine in the plainest of terms, even though she was by then married to John Manners, later to succeed his father as second Duke of Rutland. Replying to a complaining letter from Katherine, Lady Russell wrote:

> I hasten to remember you of your former promise to strive to take every providence patiently, and as cheerfully as you can, and not fool-ishly pine and waste your spirits and spoil your health against a better day come, which certainly will if you provoke not the only Giver of all things. Heaviness may endure for a night but joy cometh in the morn-ing and the chiefest blessing on this earth you have, a kind husband and a pretty gentleman . . . Strive to act your part and glory in it . . . take the world as you would find it, and you will I trust find heaviness will endure for a night but joy comes in the morning.[140]

In an age of relatively early death, especially in the case of married women in childbirth, children often found themselves faced with the loss of their biological mother, and with her replacement by a surrogate mother, either by a stepmother or more frequently in the first instance by a grandmother, occasionally by an aunt. In each of these roles women undertook the educative function usually carried out by the biological mother. Stereotypically, stepmothers have not enjoyed the best of reputations, and stepchildren, especially those in their early teens and adolescence, doubtless found it difficult to accept their new situation, seeing their stepmother as a rival for their father's affections. Even so, there is a good deal of evidence of stepmothers establishing a caring relationship with their new charges. For example, in 1625, when she was 51, Anne Crouch, already thrice widowed and childless herself, married, as his third wife, Sir Edward, first Baron Montagu, and set about writing devotions for her stepchildren. Lady Anne Waller took charge of the two sons and two daughters of her second husband's two previous marriages, catechising them (as well as the servants) once a week, 'commending those who were forward, admonishing them and reproving those who were tardy and averse, and imposing little penalties upon them, payable to the poor'.[141] Lady Margaret Hoby, who had no children of her own, undertook the education of her third husband's heir, John Sydenham, as well as that of her young relation Jane Lutton. Lady Elizabeth Langham was particularly concerned for the religious education of her stepdaughter, child of her husband Sir James Langham. The preacher of her funeral sermon in 1655 reported that:

> From her [step]daughter of about eleven years of age she exacted constantly a repetition by heart of the sermons she heard, for which task she had by her instructions so logically methodised the memory of that so young a child that she was able to analyse a discourse of thirty or forty particular heads memoriter with the most remarkable enlargements upon them.[142]

On marrying Sir Francis Masham in 1685, Damaris Cudworth became a caring stepmother to his nine children. Many stepmothers were of course experienced married women with children of their own when they remarried. Sarah Henry, on the other hand, expressed considerable misgivings at the prospect when she agreed, at the age of 23, to marry John Savage, a widower with a young daughter by his previous marriage.[143]

Child brides, as we have seen, usually returned to the home of their parents on their marriage, but occasionally such a girl might find her education continuing at the hands of her mother-in-law, as happened in 1568 when, at the age of 16, Grace Sherrington (1552–1620) married Anthony, the son of Sir Walter and Lady Mary Mildmay. Whilst Grace seems to have found her new situation reasonably satisfactory, the same was certainly not true in the case of the young Elizabeth Tanfield who, in 1602 when she was 15, married Henry Cary, son of Sir Edward and Lady Catherine Cary.

Lady Catherine quickly made plain her disapproval of her new daughter-in-law's leanings towards the Roman Catholic religion, to say nothing of her literary tastes and her ambitions to write herself. Elizabeth's eldest daughter, Catherine (1609–26) on the other hand, who went to live with her mother-in-law when, at the age of 13, she married James, Earl of Home, received nothing but kindness and affection, until she died in childbirth four years later.[144] Catherine and Dorothy Boyle, daughters of Sir Richard and Lady Catherine Boyle, were sent, aged 9 and 8 respectively, to the house of their future in-laws when their marriage treaties were finalised. Their sister Sarah, however, who was married to Sir Thomas Moore in 1621 when she was 12, remained with her parents at Lismore for two years, after which she went to her husband's home in Millifont, only for him to die two months later.[145]

In the gap left between the death of a mother and a father's remarriage children would often be placed in the charge of their grandmother, who for other reasons also might be put in charge of the grandchildren. Very early in our period Lady Margaret Beaufort, mother of Henry VII, found places for her royal grandchildren in her palace school at Eltham. Agnes, the Dowager Duchess of Norfolk, widow of Thomas Howard, the second Duke, was put in charge of her grandchild, Katherine Howard, later to be Henry VIII's fifth queen.[146] In his will of 1572, William Carre of Newcastle-upon-Tyne left instructions that in the event of his death his daughters should be sent to his mother 'to bring up as her own', with his other children to go to various of his relations. Elizabeth Jocelin, who was born in 1595, was brought up in the godly household of her grandmother, Katherine, wife of William Chaderton, her parents, Sir Richard and Lady John Brooke, having separated when she was young.[147] Elizabeth, daughter of Thomas Colpepper and his wife Anne, who was the daughter of Sir Stephen Slaney, was born in 1601. But she lost her mother in infancy and her father a few years later, when her early education was put in the hands of her grandmother, Lady Slaney. At about the same time, her mother suffering from 'deep afflictions of the spirit', Sarah Wight went to live with her grandmother in Braintree, Essex, there to be 'well trained up in the scriptures', before returning home when she was 9 on the recovery of her mother.[148]

Anne Clopton, daughter of Sir William and Lady Anne Clopton and later wife of Simonds D'Ewes, was also brought up by her grandmother, Lady Anne Barnardiston, second wife of Sir Thomas Barnardiston. Elizabeth Livingstone, who was born in 1649 and later married Robert, son of Sir Ralph Delaval, provides her own report of her early years, recalling that 'it was my dear grandmother Gorges that took the greatest care of my mind and laboured to implant early the love of virtue in my heart'. As we have seen, Lady Jane Gorges taught her granddaughter to read during the four or five months each year that Elizabeth spent in London with her, and later 'set her daily tasks of reading, so many chapters in the French Bible and so many in the English'. Alternatively, she would be 'set to learn some parts of the holy scripture by heart before my playfellows might come to me'.[149] Lady Joan Barrington was put in charge of the children of her daughter-in-law, Lady Judith, whilst their parents were in London.

> I hope I shall beg your favour [Lady Judith wrote on 22 May 1632] that if my sons follow not their books well and carry themselves not well in my absence to you or others that you will please use your authority to chide them. I hear they go much abroad to neighbours' houses to fishing. I will be sorry if their eagerness of that sport should make them less mind their books, which must not be neglected.[150]

Mary Moundeford, mother of Bridget Moundeford, who had married Sir John Bramston in 1606, took into her care the six surviving children on her daughter's death at the age of 35. From the age of 3 until he was 12 Isaac Newton, who was born in 1642, was brought up by his maternal grandmother, his father having died before he was born, and his mother, Hannah, marrying Barnabas Smith, rector of North Witham, Lincolnshire. Newton seems never to have recorded any affection for his grandmother. Even her death was not noted by him. On the death of her second husband Hannah returned to join Isaac at the family home at Woolthorpe, together with the son and two daughters by her second marriage.[151] It was to Lady Muriel Knyvett, the grandmother of his pupil Thomas Knyvett, then aged 16, that Elias Travers sent reports about Thomas's studies at Emmanuel College, Cambridge in 1612, whilst Lady Lumley, wife of Sir Martin Lumley, having made herself responsible for the religious education of her own son, 'the like care and pains did she likewise take of her grandchildren having instructed them also in matters of religion as much as their tender years would admit of'.[152] The memorialist of Lady Jane Cheyne, wife of Sir William Cheyne and daughter of William Cavendish, Duke of Newcastle and his first wife Elizabeth, reported that she 'received the first elements of her virtuous education from her pious mother ... and noble grandmother Lady [Catherine] Ogle', wife of Sir Charles Cavendish. In the same way Lady Dorothy Sidney (1617–84, Waller's 'Sacharissa'), widow of Henry, Lord Spencer, Earl of Sunderland, took charge of Henry, Anne, William and George, the children of her daughter Dorothy, wife of George Savile, Marquis of Halifax, when their mother died in 1670. On the death of his wife in 1678, Francis North, Lord Keeper Guildford, sent his two sons Francis and Charles to the house of his mother who (Roger

North reported) 'was wanting nothing of maternal care and nurture of them'.[153]

Occasionally it was an aunt who undertook the charge and care of her young relations. For example, on the execution for treason of his father, Henry, Earl of Surrey, in 1547, Thomas Howard, then aged 8, was removed from the care of his mother, Frances (Vere), and committed to the oversight of his aunt, Lady Mary Fitzroy, Duchess of Richmond, with a view to his being educated in the principles of the Protestant religion under the tutor-ship of John Foxe.[154] Later, Bridget Southwell, mother of the future Jesuit, Robert Southwell, took on the responsibility of educating the younger son of her sister-in-law, Catherine Copley, when the latter fled into exile with her convert husband, Thomas. The childless Catherine Hastings, wife of the 'Puritan Earl', Henry, third Earl of Huntingdon, had in her household and under her close personal supervision many nephews and nieces, as well as the orphaned children of Penelope and Walter Devereux, first Earl of Essex. In 1618 the duchess, perhaps not without justification, claimed, 'I think there will be none make question but I know how to breed and govern young gentlewomen', including the future diarist, Lady Margaret Hoby.[155]

Alongside her only surviving child, Lady Mary Rich took into her care three of her nieces, 'daughters of my soul', and according to her chaplain and memorialist, Anthony Walker, was fully involved in their religious edu-cation. Brilliana Harley's nephew Edward ('Ned') Smith was brought up with her own six children at Brampton Bryan from 1632. Elizabeth Freke's mother Cecily, daughter of Sir Thomas Culpepper, died in 1650 when Elizabeth was only 9, whereupon she, with her younger sisters, Cecillia aged 7, Frances aged 6 and Judith aged 4, was brought up in her mother's house at Hollingbourne, Kent, by her maternal aunt Frances, wife of William Freke.[156] Born c.1649 in The Hague where her father, Sir James Livingstone, was in exile, Elizabeth Livingstone lost her mother the following year, and was sent back to England in the care of her aunt, Lady Dorothy Stanhope, at Nocton, Lincolnshire, with whom, she recalled, she spent an unhappy childhood, relieved only, as noted earlier, by spells in London with her grandmother, Lady Gorges. Whilst she was pregnant with her eighth child, Alice Thornton went to great lengths to ensure the care of her children if she should die and her husband decide to remarry. Fearing the worst, she reported in her autobiography:

> I was indeed the more solicitous for my three children, casting my mind what friends of my own to desire to entrust with their education if he so do. For my son, the hope of my house, I humbly committed him . . . into the care of my dear and honoured uncle, my Lord Frechville [i.e. John, Lord Frechville, half-brother of Alice's mother, Alice

Wandesworth]; my daughter Alice to my dear aunt Norton, and my daughter Catherine to my dear niece Best, with strict charge to bring them up in nurture and fear of the Lord, and the true profession of the Protestant religion, as it was my faithful endeavours so to do while I was with them.

In the event, the outcome was happier than Alice had feared. A daughter, Joyce, was born, and Alice lived on until 1707.[157]

A prolonged case of surrogacy in action is provided by the life of Rachel Wriothesley (1637–1732), daughter of Thomas Wriothesley, fourth Earl of Southampton (1608–67) and his first wife, Rachel Masüe. Born in 1637, Rachel was their third child, but her mother died in 1640 giving birth to her fifth child, Magdalen, who survived her. Rachel was then sent with her brother and two sisters, Henry, Elizabeth and Magdalen, to the care of her grandmother, Elizabeth, the Dowager Countess of Southampton (widow of Henry, the third Earl, patron of Shakespeare). When her father remarried in 1642 to Elizabeth Leigh, daughter of Francis Leigh, Lord Dunsmore, Rachel was returned to the charge of her stepmother, who thus became responsible first for her stepchildren and then for four daughters of her own. On Elizabeth's death, she was replaced in 1652 by Rachel's second stepmother, Frances, daughter of William Seymour, second Duke of Somerset.

In 1654, when she was 17, Rachel married Francis Vaughan (1638–67), son of Richard Vaughan, second Earl of Carbery, and his wife, Alice, daughter of John Egerton (1579–1649), first Duke of Bridgewater, and went to live at Golden Grove in Flintshire, the highly cultured home of her in-laws, where Jeremy Taylor was chaplain. Her first pregnancy ended in a miscarriage and the two children she carried to full term died in 1659 and 1665. In 1667, when Rachel was still only 29, her husband died of the plague. The childless but by now rich Rachel was thus left a widow, until in 1669 she married William Russell, younger son of William Russell, fifth Earl of Bedford and his wife, Lady Anne. A blissfully happy second marriage was however cut short in 1683 when her husband was executed on a charge of treason, which Rachel fought sturdily, but without avail, to have overthrown.

The loss of a mother at 2½ years, successively in the charge of a grandmother and two stepmothers, a teenage marriage followed by miscarriage and the loss of two infant children, and the tragically untimely death of a dear husband, might well have produced fatalistic unhappiness and disaffection in a widow aged 43, with children aged 9, 7 and 3 at the time of their father's death. Yet Rachel's subsequent period of widowhood, lasting 40 years (for she never remarried), is a story of caring affection for her growing children and a later role as a grandmother, as her voluminous correspondence clearly shows. She died in 1723, aged 86.[158]

A similarly complicated story relates to the pious household of Lady Hartopp, widow of Sir Edmund Hartopp who died in 1658. In 1664 she married Charles Fleetwood, former Major-General with the parliamentary army, taking with her the two children, John and Mary, of her first marriage, and joining Fleetwood's own children, Smith and Elizabeth, by his first wife Frances Smith. When Fleetwood married as his second wife Bridget, widow of Henry, Lord Ireton, the household was increased by her three Ireton daughters, Jane, Bridget and Elizabeth and later by two further Fleetwood children, Cromwell and Mary. The Fleetwood house in Stoke Newington, a few miles to the north west of Hackney, was a well-known centre of conventicle worship and study, and it was in this ambience that the nine children, some adolescent, others quite young, passed their formative years.[159]

A wife's educative function was not completed with the upbringing of her own or occasionally others' children. Whilst most prescriptive texts emphasised the duty of the master of the house to maintain an oversight of his servants, it was often the mistress of the household who actually made herself responsible not only for their vocational skills but also for their religious education. This was true as much for those young women and girls who had been sent into the household of another to continue their education as of those in the employ of the house. Lettice Cary, for example, is reported by her chaplain, John Duncon, as having

> spent some hours every day in her private devotions and these were called by those of her family 'her busy hours' . . . Then her maids came into her chamber early every morning and she passed about an hour with them in praying and catechising and instructing them.

In addition, she prepared them for their participation in the sacraments. Lady Elizabeth Langham similarly engaged herself, taking care

> even of the meanest of them . . . calling them that were more immediately under her inspection (her maidens) to account (*in scriptis* if they could write) for the sermons they heard, and helping their deficiencies from her own *exacter* notes. She would call upon them in the morning (as her phrase was) to 'go to God', i.e. to wait upon Him in their morning devotions before they waited on her. And if (for she would examine them concerning it) any one of them confessed or by silence betrayed neglect therein, she would dismiss her immediately to that work from her present attendance not without some reprehension with

all for giving her service the precedency of God's, with final exhortation to women with maidservants to do likewise, and criticising those who would not allow their maidens a moment's privacy to lift up a short prayer in secret, wherewith to sanctify the employment of the day.[160]

Anne Clifford was particularly concerned that her servants were well prepared for the sacraments, and to that end she

> took care that several books of devotions and piety might be provided four times a year, that every one might take her choice of such book as they had not before, by which means those that had lived in her house long (and she seldom turned any away) might be furnished with books of religion and devotion in every kind.[161]

Lady Trevor Hanmer was 'accustomed to read constantly some devout book to her servants'. Mrs Katherine Clarke catechised her maids and 'read her notes [of sermons] to them . . . and for housewifery and household affairs she instructed their ignorance, set them a pattern and gave them example how to order the same'. Margaret Hoby frequently refers in her diary to such responsibilities: 'instructed some of my family' (i.e., members of her household); 'read awhile to my workwomen'; 'conferring of the sermon with the gentlewomen that were with me', as well as having regular Bible readings with them.[162] Lady Mary Strode's memorialist reported that

> she was a notary and took the sermons which she heard by her own pen . . . [and] . . . in her own chamber repeated to her maidservants the sermons she had heard and penned; [in addition] she catechised them in the principles of religion and upon every fit occasion would labour to season them with the true fear of the Lord.

Lady Mary Vere and Lady Anne Waller likewise took on these responsibilities, whilst Lady Lumley not only undertook the religious education of her children and grandchildren but also

> did constantly attend the prayers of the family and did call upon her servants to do so too, thinking it not enough to present herself unless she endeavoured at least to have them there too, so that not only she, but her house might serve the Lord.[163]

One of the fullest accounts we have of a mistress's involvement in the education of her servants is that reported by Samuel Bury of his wife Elizabeth:

> As a mistress [he wrote] she was very careful in the choice of her servants . . . whenever she treated with any she did not only acquaint them with the business of their place but also with the religious orders of the family, to which she had their explicit consent when once they were admitted; it was her first and constant care to inquire into the state of their souls, to instruct and catechise, to reprove and encourage . . . to enjoin to take time for secret prayer, reading the scripture, meditation and self-examination. She always charged it as a duty upon herself to talk over every sermon they heard together, expecially on Sabbaths . . . sometimes together but at other times . . . singly and apart . . . By this means she became a servant to her servants . . . I cannot remember any that were ever brought under her care but had learned something of the method of the sermon before they left her, and very many whose memories were improved.[164]

Anthony Walker reported in similar vein as chaplain to Lady Mary Rich, Countess of Warwick:

> She had a great care of the souls of her servants, and if she had any ambition in her it was in this to be the mistress of a religious family . . . exacting their attendance on God's public worship . . . preparing them for the Lord's Supper . . . scattering good books in all the common rooms and places of attendance . . . making it a footstep to preferment.

Of Mrs Margaret Godolphin, John Evelyn reported that 'she provided her servants not only with wages and bodily food, but gave them books to read to nourish their souls, prayers to use by themselves, and constantly instructed them herself in the principles of religion.[165]

Children received advice and instruction about their religious education in a wide variety of forms. The range of religious texts available for their use, if not always directly addressed to them, rapidly increased in quantity after the early years of the Reformation. The 'Advices' that were offered to them were mostly written by men, though mothers also made a significant contribution to the genre, in a variety of forms but always with a high religious content.

Some such advices appeared in print, obviously seeking a wider readership than the authoress's immediate family, but each in its own way emphasising the need to supplement attendance at public worship with private devotions – prayer, bible reading, meditation. Elizabeth Grymeston

wrote her *Miscelanea. Meditations. Memoratives* (1604), with subsequent additions, adding 'Prayer' to the title, for the use of her only surviving son
Bernye:

> I leave thee this portable *veni mecum* for thy counsellor in which thou
> mayest see the true portraiture of thy mother's mind, and find some-
> thing either to resolve thee in thy doubts or comfort thee in thy distress.
> Remember that prayer is the wing wherein wherewith thy soul flieth to
> heaven; and meditation the eye wherewith we see God.[166]

Dorothy Leigh's *The Mothers Blessing* (1616) was one prolonged piece of
religious advice, addressed to her fatherless sons, George, John and William,
at the same time urging other mothers to care for their children and not to
fear death. The boys were faced with several chapters devoted to the
importance of both public and private prayer, night and morning, in which
the dangers of Satan and the Devil are omnipresent throughout. Unusually,
she went on to urge the importance of their paying strict attention to the
religious upbringing of their own children, even to choosing saints' names
for their children 'as Philip, Elizabeth, James, Susanna, especially Susanna
famed for her chastity'. From about the age of 4 they should be taught 'be
they males or females . . . to read the Bible in their own mother tongue, for I
know it is a great help to true godliness'. In addition they should 'seek a
godly wife that she may help you in godliness . . . Marry with none except
you love her . . . let nothing after you have made your choice remove your
love from her'. Of their servants, 'ask if they can read' and, if not, undertake to teach them. 'Remember, your servants are God's servants as well as
yours . . . they are your brethren. Use them well.' Most unusually, she urged
her boys 'to write a book unto your own children of the right and true way
to happiness which may remain with them and theirs forever'.[167]

Elizabeth Jocelin wrote her *Mothers Legacie to her Unborne Childe* (1624) in
similar vein. Elizabeth Richardson's more substantial *A Ladies Legacie to her
Daughters* (1645) was, she indicated, 'composed of prayers and meditations
fitted for several times and upon several occasions, as also several prayers for
each day of the week'. She addressed it to

> my dearly beloved daughters (of which number I account my two sons'
> wives, my daughters-in-law, the Countess of Marlborough and Mrs
> Francis Ashbournham, to be mine also . . . I know you may have many
> better instructors than myself, yet can you have no true mother but me,
> who not only with great pain brought you into the world, but do now
> travail in care for the new birth of your souls, to bring you to eternal
> life, which is my chiefest desire and the height of my hopes.[168]

The anonymous *Mothers Counsell or Live Within Compass being the Last Will and Testament to her Dearest Daughter* (1630) consisted of a set of aphorisms, grouped under the heads 'Within Compass' and 'Out of Compass', on chastity, temperance, humility and beauty (of the soul as well as the body).

Other women's advices remained in manuscript until they were subsequently published posthumously, as was the case of Mary Rich's 'Rules for a Holy Life', prepared at the request of George, Earl of Berkeley and published in 1686 together with 'Occasional Meditations' and 'Pious Reflections Upon Several Scriptures'. Lucy Hutchinson produced a more organised text in her *Principles of Christian Religion* addressed to her newly married daughter Barbara. She started with a disclaimer:

> You may perhaps, when you have read these common principles and grounds which I have collected for you, think that I might have spared my pains and sent you a twopenny catechism which contains the substance of all this.

But she was convinced this would not suffice: 'You will find it my duty to exhort and admonish you according to the talent entrusted with me, and to watch over your soul, though now under another's authority.' She insisted 'I write not for the press', but went on to provide, with detailed proof-texts adjoined, a comprehensive piece of religious guidance in matters of doctrine as well as Christian practice.[169] Lady Anne Halkett made herself responsible for a similar set of guidelines in her *Instructions for Youth*, 'for the use of those young noblemen and gentlemen whose education was committed to her care'. Alongside comments about the care of the body and secular studies, her religious advice was thoroughly conventional, with emphasis on prayer at the beginning of the day, daily Bible reading so that the whole might be read through once a year, and reading of the psalms once a month. With respect to Bible reading she pointed out that 'whereas other books, with often reading grow weary, this on the contrary, the oftener it is read, is more ravishing and delightful'. Needless to say, constant Sabbath worship and observance was considered essential, and in the section on 'Civility' she concluded, 'Put the best interpretation upon other people's words and actions. Meekness, humility and love are the blessed fruits of the Spirit.'[170]

Some advices from mothers, though written in the form of letters, were more formal in structure and content than the more frequent family letters to which we have already referred. Brilliana Harley, for example, included in her commonplace book a 19-page advice 'For my dear son Edward Harley', in which she reminded him of the difficulties which would face him 'on lancing forth into the seas of this world of many rocks':

You will know it was my constant practice often to put you in mind of those things which tend to your chiefest good, but now distance of place will not give me leave to perform that duty so often as I desire . . . Show the holiness of your heart by a holy life. Let your young eyes, hands and feet be instruments by which you express the good affections of your heart . . . beware of swearing and drunken companions, both are sinful . . . it is the wisdom of young men to follow the counsel of the old.

The advice is undated, but presumably it was written on the occasion of Edward's departure for Magdalen Hall, Oxford, in 1630. At much the same time Lady Anne Montagu of Boughton in Northamptonshire was writing a similar piece for her stepchildren.[171]

Among the many ways in which Elizabeth Walker contributed to the religious education of her children was a collection of scriptural passages which she made 'For my dear children Mistress Margaret and Mistress Elizabeth Walker', arranged under various heads, each supported by appropriate proof-texts: 'Philanthropy and Charity', 'Meekness of Spirit', 'On Secret Prayer', 'Promises of the Pardon of Sin', 'An Abbreviation of Faith and Christian Principles', 'The Marks of a Regenerate State', and several others, the longest of which was a 44-page section on 'Fear of God'. The advice was concluded with a set of questions: 'Is there an abhorring of all sin, though your flesh do tempt you to it?'; 'Can you forgive your enemies?'; 'Are you easily entreated, desirous of grace, and to do good to them?'; 'Do you love and esteem and labour for the powerful preaching of the Word above all earthly treasures?', and concluding 'and if this be truly your case, you are one of God's children and people; as sure as God's promises are true, there is a happy and blessed estate for you'.[172]

Lady Rachel Russell's children were 17, 15 and 11 when in 1691 she wrote a long letter putting down an account of her own practice in the matter of their religious upbringing, and urging them to use it as a guide for the future. Besides recommending particular passages of the Bible for learning by heart and enjoining them to take a daily note of their perceived faults, she reminded them of her own thankfulness that she

was born of Christian parents . . . and that I was baptised and since educated in the Christian religion . . . although I love your bodies but too well, yet if my heart deceive me not, 'tis nothing in comparison of your precious souls . . . What is leading a holy life you find in your Bible; be constant in your reading of it, and use yourself to make some use of what you read; before you lay away the book consider what virtue is recommended or what vice forbid, or what doctrines taught, in the chapter you have read, and think on it often the rest of the day, and doing this you will in a little while make it habitual to you . . . get by heart the Sermon on the Mount, 5,6,7, chapter of Matthew; the 17 of John is also a fine chapter to get by heart, so is 8 of Romans, the 19 and 37 psalms and the penitential ones.

She went on to give detailed instructions on how to pray, using Jeremy Taylor's *Holy Living* as a guide, together with his *Golden Grove*. Simon Patrick's *Devout Christian* was also recommended, with detailed page references which clearly show her own familiarity with the work. Taylor was, of course, chaplain at Golden Grove, the family seat of the Vaughan family where she had resided with her first husband, Francis Vaughan.[173]

Perhaps the most sustained example of a mother's religious advice to her children is to be found at the very end of our period in the letters of Susannah Wesley, who married Samuel Wesley in 1690. After the disastrous fire which destroyed the parsonage at Epworth in 1709 and necessitated the temporary dispersal of the children to the homes of various relatives, she wrote to her daughter 'Sukey' (Susan), who was living with her sister Mehetabel in the home of Matthew Wesley:

since our misfortunes have separated us from each other, and we can no longer enjoy the opportunities we once had of conversing together, I can no other way discharge the duty of a parent or comply with my inclination of doing you all the good that I can but by writing.

In the letter, she provided a section by section exposition of the Creed, together with the reassurance that

I love your body and do earnestly beseech Almighty God to bless it with health . . . But my tenderest regard is for your immortal soul and for its spiritual happiness . . . though perhaps you cannot at present fully comprehend all I say, yet keep this letter by you, and as you grow in years your reason and judgement will improve and you will obtain a more clear understanding of all things . . . you must understand what you say and you must practise what you know.

At the end of the year 1710, she wrote to her eldest son 'Sammy', then away at Westminster School, in response to one of his in which he reported his being 'unstable and inconstant in the ways of virtue'. In her reply she urged him constantly to keep in mind 'the awful and constant presence of God' and the glory for 'those who persevere in the paths of virtue', whilst at the same time meditating 'often and seriously on the shortness, uncertainty and vanity of the present state of things'. In attempting to reassure him she observed, 'Since I love you as my own soul, I will endeavour to do as well as I can, and perhaps as I write I may learn, and by instructing you I may teach myself.' But it was to her second son John, the founder of Methodism, that she wrote most frequently whilst he was at university in the 1720s, attempting on one occasion to resolve his doubts about pleasure and sin, on another about election and predestination. In 1727 she wrote, 'If the foundations of solid piety are not laid betimes . . . and if we neglect while strength and vigour last . . . it is a hundred to one odds that we shall die both poor and wicked' – a form of words that one might not have expected from so formidably pious a matriarch![174]

Alongside the texts written by mothers with specific religious purpose in mind were the family memoirs written, as their dedications make clear, for the express edification of the children of the family whose history is being retold, and incidentally passing on religious and moral advice. Mostly written by fathers, who nevertheless directed their remarks to their daughters as well as their sons, some outstanding examples were written by mothers such as Lady Anne Halkett, Lady Anne Fanshawe and Lady Lucy Hutchinson. These were conscious pieces of historical writing, albeit with the contemporary characteristics of such works, which deliberately set up ancestors as exemplars for the future younger generations. As Lady Fanshawe put it, writing in 1676,

> I have thought it convenient to discourse to you (my most dear and only son) the most remarkable actions and accidents of your family . . . because by the example you may imitate what is applicable to your condition in the world.

This was followed by a passage of Polonius-like advice about daily behaviour, based on Christian principles, and urging him to follow his parents' practice of 'being great lovers and honourers of clergymen'.[175] Less substantial but sharing the same purpose were Susanna Bell's *The Legacy of a Dying Mother to her Mourning Children, Being the Experiences of Mrs Susanna Bell who Died March 13 1672*, and Alice Hayes' *A Legacy or Widows Mite Left by Alice Hayes to Her Children and Others*, which was published three years after her death in 1720. Lady Grace Mildmay's autobiographical notes 'written for my daughter [Mary, wife of Sir Francis Fane] and her children' had to await a modern editor but were plainly explicit:

> unhappy and miserable are those children which are not instructed to lay hold of the Word of Life, whereby they may avoid the snares of death. It were better they had never been born. Instruct your children

from their infancy in the knowledge of Him. Giving a child his will and no correction and he shall never prove good for anything in old age. It is an excellent course to teach a child, as soon as he understands anything, the reason of everything according to his capacity and wherein he may have his will and wherein he must not have it, always laying the foundation upon truth as a principal mark for them to aim at in all things, drawing them gently by reason and familiarity with their parents and delight in their company, and to please their parents better than themselves. But never seek to reclaim them by cruelty and rude, railing speeches, for that is no good example but put an evil custom or nature in them. And in any wise not to speak or do anything before a child but that which is good, whereby we may in teaching them admonish ourselves.[176]

More often, of course, mothers (and fathers) had no further intention than to give advice *en passant* in a letter written in the more normal course of family correspondence. An early example was Catherine of Aragon's affectionate, though a touch fatalistic, letter to her daughter Princess Mary, which, after giving her sound advice about her behaviour and especially towards the king her father, enclosed two books in Latin, *De Vita Christi* and *The Epistles of Jerome that he Did Write to St Paula and St Eustochium*, 'and in them I trust you will see good things'.[177] Lady Anne Bacon's letters to her son Anthony rarely missed an opportunity to remind him of his religious responsibilities. In 1592, for example, she wrote:

> This one chiefest counsel your Christian and natural mother do give you ever above the Lord, that above all worldly respects you carry yourself ever at your first coming as one that doth unfeignedly profess the true religion of Christ, and hath the love of truth now by long continuance fast settled in your heart.[178]

This was to an eldest son, newly returned from France, then aged 34.

Brilliana Harley's son 'Ned' was still at university in 1639 when he received many of her letters full of advice as to his religious well-being:

> keep always a watch over your precious soul; tie yourself to a daily examination; think over the company you have been in, and what your discourse was, and how you found yourself affected, how in the discourses of religion . . . I hope thou do ruminate over the psalms and chapters and texts of scriptures which long since thou did learn by heart. I would be sorry if thou shouldst forget thy Conduit of Comfort; these things let not slip out of thy mind.[179]

Thomas Bouchier, nephew of Lady Joan Barrington, wrote to his aunt in 1631 seeking her help in resolving his 'secret doubts of the truth of grace': 'You cannot be ignorant what need I have of such divine counsel as you may easily enrich me with. I beseech you therefore to give a drop of thy fountain.' Margaret Baxter offered such advice to William, the nephew of her husband Richard, in 1666. After giving advice about the study of Latin, Greek and Hebrew as essential to a study of the Bible, she concluded 'But your soul deserves your chiefest care, for nothing is known to purpose till we attain to the saving knowledge of God in Christ', and to that end she reminded him that 'Experience forces us to say that nothing can be prosperously pursued without solemn applications unto God by prayer.'[180]

All of these offerings were assuming a well-educated or reasonably well-educated reader but, as we have seen, the broadsheet was often used to reach a wider audience. Almost invariably these were written by men, in the expectation that they would be read by or read to both males and females, and it is likely that sheets with titles such as 'The Old Gentlewomans Last Legacy to her Sons and Daughters on her Deathbed', or 'An Hundred Godly Lessons that a Mother on her Deathbed Gave to her Children' and its variant 'An Hundred Devout Admonitions Left by A Dying Mother to her Children' came into this category. Their thoroughly orthodox content, with an emphasis on conformity to traditional female virtues, should not, however, detract from their likely influence, with a typical injunction being couched in the form:

> Fear God and keep his true command
> All things will prosper you take in hand.

'The Complete Gentlewoman' with its

> So constant in her actions still is she
> She may compare with chaste Penelope

echoed the sheet 'The Constancy of Susannah' with its sub-title 'whereby they may know how to guide themselves towards God and man, to the benefit of the commonwealth, the joy of their parents and the good of themselves'.[181]

Despite the instances which have been cited here, the question remains: how did this involvement of women in religious education at home compare in quantity (or indeed quality) with that of their menfolk? Elizabeth Walker and Susannah Wesley were obviously the schoolmistresses of their households, as were by implication the wives of Robert Bolton and Peter Heylin, whose involvement allowed their husbands to devote their time to study and pastoral care. On the other hand, it appears that Philip Henry made himself entirely responsible for the religious upbringing of his children. No amount of statistical manipulation will provide a satisfactory answer to the question, since the nature of early modern society in England as well as the conventions of record-keeping in the period result in women featuring less than men in the historical record. Much of women's involvement in education consisted of individual responses to particular sets of circumstances, but they undoubtedly featured to a much greater extent than many male – and some feminist – historians would allow.

The very randomness of record survival precludes conclusions of any general applicability, whether relating to denomination, class, region or even chronology. Nor do the records show whether most women undertook the prescribed charge or not. What the individual cases here cited do show, however, is the inadequacy of claims, by both contemporaries and some present-day historians, that there was, for a variety of reasons, a general disregard of parental duty, of that sense of responsibility and obligation in the upbringing of children in the household situation, at least in the godly families of those classes which have left records, direct or indirect, of their affairs. The evidence of such activity is scattered and far from systematic, but it does lead to the tentative conclusion that some mothers, unquantifiable in the statistical sense, did follow by a variety of means in the biblical and oft-quoted footsteps of Solomon's mother, Bathsheba, and of Timothy's mother, Eunice, and his grandmother, Lois. To go further would be mere speculation or, even worse, polemical assertion.

Conclusion

That girls and women received a godly education can hardly be doubted. Whether this can be quantified is impossible to tell, not least because the 'silent majority', about whom we have no evidence, would have included not only a number who though not attending church escaped presentment by the churchwarden, but also those who did attend and would have been counted as 'godly' if evidence had survived about their religious life, either in church or at home. Given the prevailing attitudes to the appearance of women in print or in the written record, any count of godly women is bound to be an under-estimate.

Equally, the quality of a person's religious knowledge and understanding of that knowledge are just as remote from measurement, even though there is as much scattered evidence of criticism of that quality as there is of its recognition. It was, of course, part of the perennial misogyny of the whole period to make comments such as that of Thomas Cranmer who, denouncing the western rebels of 1549, criticised the 'fond [i.e. foolish] women who commonly follow superstition rather than true religion'.[1] This was a view which was echoed in the attitudes of many clerics before whom women were brought in the diocesan and higher ecclesiastical courts for challenging the religious orthodoxy of the day. Even when as godly a woman as Lady Cutts is praised for her piety, the praise is couched in terms of a contrast with 'what the language of this loose age is called "a lady's religion"'.[2] The juxtaposition and even opposition of reason and faith, so evident in the Christian church since the time of Tertullian, continued to pose problems for women, whether as agents or recipients of religious education, their preference for 'practical divinity', with its guidance in dealing with the vicissitudes of everyday Christian life, nevertheless posing issues about 'divinity' as well as its practical applications.

It is plain that the schooling of women and girls took place both in the parish church where the priest was their teacher, and round the dining table and in their closet (or some other 'secret' place, indoors or out). In the latter case they were their own teachers, in between times acting in a quite direct way as agents in the religious education of their children and servants, in all of which we see a blurring of the boundaries between priest and lay-woman, and a clash between a claimed primacy of personal experience and a ministerial and magisterial interpretation of 'God's true religion'. But the notion of 'clash' might too easily be over-emphasised, and we would do well to note Patrick Collinson's reminder that the Protestant reformation could as easily and reasonably be interpreted as 'an intensification of certain very old-fashioned preoccupations'.[3] New ideas could certainly be spread by print, but printed material as often served as a conservative reminder and reinforcement of what the reader (or the listener) already knew and believed. Families became divided in their religious allegiances, but even then their preferred form of religious education was based on a remarkably similar set of curricular provisions – the Bible, the sermon, prayer and conference, catechising, and godly books. Yet though the role assigned to the family as an educative agency was generally agreed, the role assumed was as much a function of individual personality as of religious affiliation. Even though an Anglican household was more likely to reinforce what might be called the state provision of the parish church and its priest, and a puritan household more likely to subject to critical scrutiny and attempt to remedy what would be considered its shortcomings, the puritan household had no monopoly of familial and individual piety, even though its members might hold a different view of what constituted a godly life.

In the same way, the religious differences between godly Protestants provide no sure guide to the role assigned to or claimed by women. Individual women Protestants interpreted their Bible to satisfy their own individual needs and views, especially of the man–woman, husband–wife relationships, and female piety was far from being incompatible with current patriarchy. The Protestant message to women was, in any case, rarely unambiguous and, in attempting to understand it, individual women interpreted the message and its exposition by their male clergy in ways that were far from homogeneous, with their search for solace, reassurance and security in their religious life constantly being waylaid by fear and anxiety about its ultimate outcome. Equally, those who taught, whether male or female in whatever situation, were well aware that for most, literate as well as illiterate, belief was primarily a matter of acquired disposition, acquired habit, rather than a rational search for truth. The fact that simple words hid complex meanings was no deterrent, for the reading Christian as well as the listening Christian. Montaigne's piece of introspection accurately reflects the complexity of motivation and behaviour which is to be found in any consideration of our theme:

Sometimes I give my soul one visage and sometimes another, according to the posture or side I lay her in. If I speak diversely of myself, it is because I look diversely upon myself. All contrarities are found in her according to some turn or removing, and in some fashion of another. Shamefast, bashful, insolent, chaste, luxurious, peevish, prattling, silent, fond, doting, laborious, nice, delicate, ingenious, slow, dull, froward, luminous, debonair, wise, ignorant, false in words, true-speaking, both liberal, covetous, and prodigal. All these I perceive in some measure or other to be in me, according as I stir or turn myself . . . We are all framed of flaps and patches, and of so shapeless and diverse a contexture, that every piece and every moment playeth his part.[4]

Or, as Patrick Collinson more concisely put it, of another matter, 'there is no neatly severed end to the strands of this rope, only a mass of loose and straggly threads'.[5] One hopes to have made a start on identifying some of the threads of 'women, religion and education in early modern England'. Much more remains to be done.

Notes

INTRODUCTION

In the footnote reference the place of publication is London, unless otherwise indicated. In quotations in the text, spelling and punctuation have been modernised. The titles of publications have been left unchanged.

1 As Richard Hooker, for example, noted in his *Laws of Ecclesiastical Polity*, 1594, in *The Works of Richard Hooker*, ed. G. Edelen, 5 vols, 1977–90, Cambridge, Mass., vol. I, p. 23.

2 E. Hobsbawm and T. Ranger, *The Invention of Tradition*, 1983, pp. 1–14. See also A. Wood, 'The Place of Custom in Plebeian Political Culture: England 1500–1800', *Social History*, 1997, vol. 33, pp. 46–60.

3 T. S. Eliot, 'Tradition and the Individual Talent', in *Selected Essays*, 1932, pp. 13–22. See also L. Stone, *The Past and the Present*, 1981, p. 208.

4 W. J. Bouwsma, 'Intellectual History in the 1980s', *Journal of Interdisciplinary History*, 1981, vol. 21, pp. 279–91.

5 R. D. Klein, 'The "Man-Problem" in Women's Studies: The Expert, the Ignoramus and the Poor Dear', *Women's Studies International Forum*, 1983, vol. 6, p. 413. (Klein's italics)

6 O. Hufton, 'Women in History: I, The Early Modern Period', *Past and Present*, 1983, no. 101, p. 126.

7 *The Importance of Being Earnest*, Act 1.

8 *The Complete Works of Sir Philip Sidney*, ed. A. Feuillerat, 4 vols, 1912–26, vol. IV, p. 337.

9 *A Room of One's Own*, 1929, pp. 6 and 171.

10 In the 1960 musical, by F. Norman and L. Bart, *Fings Ain't Wot They Used T'Be*.

11 *The Complete Works of Montaigne*, trans. and ed. D. M. Frame, 1957, Stanford: 'Of Experience', p. 834; 'Of the Education of Children', p. 111.

12 Cf. M. Spufford, 'Can We Count the "Godly" and "Conformable" in the Seventeenth Century?', *Journal of Ecclesiastical History*, 1985, vol. 36, pp. 428–38. Cf. R. V. Schnucker, 'Puritan Attitudes towards Childhood Discipline', in V. Fildes, ed., *Women as Mothers in Pre-Industrial England*, 1990, pp. 108–16, where he actually applies the Chi-square Test to his data from prescriptive treatises.

13 Following N. Z. Davis, 'Women's History in Transition: the European Case',

Feminist Studies, 1975, vol. 3, p. 90, and C. N. Degler, *Is There a History of Women?*, 1975, Oxford.

14 L. Fèbvre, 'Sensibility and History: How to Reinstate the Emotional Life of the Past', in P. Burke, trans. and ed., *A New Kind of History and Other Essays of Lucien Fèbvre*, 1973, New York, pp. 12–26.

15 M. Reynolds, *The Learned Lady in England, 1656–1760*, 1920, New York; D. Gardiner, *English Girlhood at School*, 1929; C. Camden, *The Elizabethan Woman*, 1952; R. Kelso, *Doctrine for the Lady of the Renaissance*, 1955, Urbana, Ill.; D. M. Stenton, *English Women in History*, 1957.

16 J. Irwin, *op. cit.*, 1979, New York, p. xix.

17 P. J. Corfield, 'History and the Challenge of Gender History', *Rethinking History*, 1997, vol. 1, pp. 241–58.

1 ATTITUDES TO WOMEN

1 *The Merchant of Venice*, I,iii,93.

2 T. Cogan, *The Haven of Health*, 1589, pp. 191–2; *As You Like It*, II,vii,139–66. The seventeenth-century ballad 'The Ages and Life of Man . . .' illustrates, with woodcuts, 11 stages and occupations. For the variety of classical and medieval calculations inherited by the early modern period, see J. A. Burrow, *The Ages of Man. A Study in Medieval Writing and Thought*, 1986, Oxford; E. Sears, *The Ages of Man. The Medieval Interpretations of the Life Cycle*, 1986, Princeton; M. Dove, *The Perfect Age of Man's Life*, 1986, Cambridge.

3 Harrington, *The Commendacion of Matrimony*, 1528, sig. Eii verso. Cf. Vives (trans. Hyrde), *The Instruction of Christen Women*, 1540, sig. Cii verso; T. Cogan, *The Haven of Health*, 1589, pp. 191–2; S. R. Smith, 'Growing Old in the Seventeenth Century', *Albion*, 1976, vol. 8, pp. 125–41.

4 Elyot, *The Boke Named the Governour*, 1531, ed. E. Lehmberg, 1962, p. 19.

5 Wilson, *The State of England 1600*, ed. J. Fisher, *Camden Miscellany*, 1936, vol. 16, p. 20.

6 An excellent survey of the intricacies of the churches' theology and practice in the matter is provided in R. de Molen, 'Childhood and the Sacraments in the Sixteenth Century', *Archives for Reformation History*, 1975, vol. 66, pp. 49–71; E. W. Bennitt, 'The Diary of Isabella Twysden', *Archaeologia Cantiana*, 1939, vol. 51, p. 126.

7 Calvin, *Institutes of Christian Religion*, 1559, II,12,3, trans. L. Battles, ed. T. McNeil, Library of Christian Classics, 1960, vol. 21, p. 497. The passage does not occur in the original 1536 edition.

8 Augustine of Hippo, *Confessions* I,19, trans, R. S. Pine-Coffin, 1961, Harmondsworth. Cf. the translations of T. Matthew, 1620, p. 50, and W. Watts, 1631, p. 60.

9 Cranmer's *Catechisms*, 1548, sig. Miv verso, G. Nichols, ed., *Two Sermons Preached by the Boy-Bishop, One at St. Paul's Temp. Henry VIII, Other at Gloucester Temp. Mary*, Camden Miscellany, 1875, vol. 7. p. 25. For a history of the boy-bishop rituals see F. Rimbault's introduction to the sermons.

10 Hake, *A Touchstone for This Time Present*, 1574, sig. C3 verso.

11 Woodward, *A Childes Patrimony*, 1640, pp. 2, 7, 9. See also A. Burgess, *A Treatise of Original Sinne*, 1658, p. 415; Bayly, *The Practise of Pietie*, 1613, pp. 79, 81.

12 Downame, *A Guide to Godlynesse or A Treatise of a Christian Life*, 1629, pp. 960–1; though contrast S. Patrick, Bishop of Chichester, 'A Short Prayer for the Use of

a Little Child', in his *The Devout Christian Instructed or A Book of Devotions for Families*, 1673; 4th ed., 1678, pp. 442–3.

13 Wright, *The Passions of the Mind in Generall*, 1604, p. 7.

14 Granger, *Syntagma Grammaticum . . .*, 1616, Epistle to the Reader. Cf. R. Carew, *The Examination of Mens Wits*, 1594, p. 274, for similar reliance on humoral theory to explain women's inferiority.

15 *The Seconde Tome of Homilies*, 1563, fol. 225; Baxter, *A Christian Directory or A Summe of Practical Theology*, 1673, p. 480. Cf. B. Googe, *The Zodiake of Life*, 1576, p. 22; R. Hooker, *The Laws of Ecclesiastical Polity*, Book V, chap. 73, in *Works of Richard Hooker*, ed. G. Edelen, 5 vols, 1977–90, Cambridge, Mass., II, pp. 403–4; J. Brinsley, *A Looking Glasse for Good Women*, 1645, *passim*. Lord Chesterfield made the same kind of observation by way of advice to his son in a letter of 20 September 1748, B. Dobrée, ed., *The Letters of Philip Dormer Stanhope, 4th Earl of Chesterfield*, 6 vols, 1932, IV, p. 1224.

16 J. Marston, *The Wonder of Women or The Tragedy of Sophonisba*, 1606, I,ii,20.

17 Aristotle, *Economics*, I,3 (1343b).

18 Sir William Wentworth's advice to his son Thomas in 1614, *The Wentworth Papers 1597–1628*, ed. J. P. Cooper, Camden Society, 1973, 4th Ser., vol. 12, p. 10; Webster, *The White Devil*, 1612, V,vi,161; Shakespeare, *Julius Caesar*, II,iv,38–9; *Nugae Antiquae*, ed. T. Park, 2 vols, 1804, I, pp. 320–1. Cf. Spenser, *The Faerie Queene*, III,xii,289. Sherley, *Witts New Dyall or The Schollers Prize*, 1604, sig. D2 recto; T. Fuller, *The Holy and Prophane State*, 1645, p. 9.

19 Hooker, *Laws . . .* Book V, Dedication.

20 *A C Mery Talys*, 1526, in W. C. Hazlitt, ed., *Shakespeare Jest Book*, 3 vols, I, pp. 87, 122; Erasmus, 'Courtship' in C. R. Thompson, ed., *The Colloquies of Erasmus*, 1965, Chicago, pp. 88–98; Anon, *Pasquils Jests*, 1604, in Hazlitt, *op. cit.*, III, p. 27; Shakespeare, *Much Ado About Nothing*, II,i,16–17; Dekker, *op. cit.*, IV,iii,9; T. Gataker, *Marriage Duties*, 1620, p. 10.

21 Shakespeare, *Two Gentlemen of Verona*, I,ii,22; Middleton, *Blurt Master Constable*, 1602, I,i,189–90 and Webster, *White Devil*. Cf. Lord Chesterfield in a letter to his son on 5 September 1748: 'Women, then, are only children of larger growth; they have an entertaining tattle and sometimes wit; but for solid, reasoning good sense I never in my life knew one that had it,' Dobrée, *Letters*, IV, 1209.

22 Printed in *Englands Moderate Messenger*, 23 April 1649.

23 Tilney, *The Flower of Friendship*, 1568, sig. E1 verso; Whately, *A Bride Bush or A Directory for Married Persons*, 1619, p. 98; Gouge, *op. cit.*, 1622, p. 658. Cf. John Chamberlain's letter of 12 February 1620, in E. P. Stratham, *A Jacobean Letter Writer. The Life and Times of John Chamberlain*, 1920, pp. 180–3.

24 Shakespeare, *Hamlet*, I,ii,46; Baldassare Castiglione, *The Courtyer of Count Baldessar Castilo . . .*, trans. Sir Thomas Hoby, 1561, sig. Bbiii recto; Milton, *Paradise Lost*, 1667, X, 891–2.

25 Shakespeare, *King Lear*, IV,vi,122–9; Marston, *The Insatiate Countess*, 1613, IV,ii,19; Middleton, *Hengist King of Kent*. See also Webster, *The White Devil*, I,ii,188, and Dekker, *II The Honest Whore*, III,i,176–80; Sherley, *Witts New Dyall . . .*, sig. M2 recto.

26 Johnson, *Volpone*, and *Epicoene or the Silent Woman*; R. Herrick, 'His Wish', in *Poems*, ed., L. C. Martin, p. 294.

27 Heywood, *Gunaikeion*, 1624, p. 236.

28 Shakespeare, *Macbeth*, I,v,38; *King Lear*, IV,ii,17–18. Compare the differing English and French attitudes to Joan of Arc in Shakespeare's *1 Henry VI*.

29 Middleton, *A Mad World My Masters*, III,iii,115–16; D. Underdown, *Revel, Riot and Rebellion. Popular Politics and Culture in England 1603–60*, 1985, Oxford, pp. 36–7. M. Wiesner reports similar attitudes in Germany, *Working Women in Renaissance Germany*, 1986, New Brunswick, pp. 187, 191–2.

30 F. Beaumont and J. Fletcher, *Rule a Wife and Have a Wife*, II,iii,36–7. Cf. Dekker, *II The Honest Whore*, II,ii,108–10.

31 J. G. Nichols, ed., *The Progresses and Processions of Queen Elizabeth*, 4 vols, 1788, I, pp. 20–1. The tableaux were repeated in the Queen's entry to Norwich in 1578, *ibid.*, II, pp. 13–16. Cf. Thomas Deloney's ballad 'The Queens Visiting of the Campe at Tilbury', in F. O. Mann, ed., *The Works of Thomas Deloney*, 1912, Oxford, pp. 174–8. For similar comparisons see J. Peele, *The Arraignement of Paris*, 1584; T. Fuller, *Abel Redivivus or The Dead Yet Speaking*, 1651, p. 566. For discussion see R. M. Healey, 'Waiting for Deborah: John Knox and Four Ruling Queens', *Sixteenth Century Journal*, 1994, vol. 25, pp. 371–86.

32 For the continued celebration of the Queen at Tilbury see, for example, D. Primrose, *A Chaine of Pearle or A Memorial of the Peerless Graces and Heroick Vertues of Queen Elizabeth*, 1630, p. 9; T. Heywood, *Exemplary Lives. . .*, 1640, p. 211; S. Clarke, *The History of the Glorious Reign and Death of the Illustrious Queen Elizabeth*, 1682, pp. 184–7. The fifteenth-century *Book of the Knight of La Tour-Landry*: 'A woman who is not humble and full of pity is mannish and not womanly, and this is a vice in a woman', ed. T. Wright, EETS Orig. Ser., 1868, vol. 33, p. 136. Cf. M. Christy, 'The Queen Elizabeth's Visit to Tilbury in 1588', *English Historical Review*, 1919, vol. 34, pp. 43–61, and W. Schleiner, 'Divina Virago: Queen Elizabeth as Amazon', *Studies in Philology*, 1978, vol. 75, pp. 163–80.

33 Spenser, *Faerie Queene* V,v,25–8.

34 Erasmus, 'The Lower House . . .', in *The Colloquies of Erasmus*, ed. C. R. Thompson, Chicago, 1965, pp. 445–6; Hervet, 1532, 1534 ed., fol. 33 recto–34 verso; Chapman-Marston-Johnson, *Eastwood Ho*, I,i,85–6. See also W. Averell, *A Dyall for Dainty Darlings*, 1584, sig. E4 recto; T. Tuke, *A Treatise Against Painting and Tincturing of Men and Women*, 1616, and Anon., *An Invective Against Pride of Women*, 1657, verse 3. Cf. A. Drew-Bear, 'Cosmetics and Attitudes Towards Women in the Seventeenth Century', *Journal of Popular Culture*, 1975–6, vol. 9, pp. 31–7.

35 T. Becon, *A Newe Catechisme*, in *Works*, ed. J. Ayre, Parker Society, 3 vols, 1844, Cambridge, I, p. 346; *Seconde Tome of Homilies*, 1563, fol. 144, P. L. Hughes and J. F. Larkin, eds, *Tudor Royal Proclamations*, 3 vols, New Haven, 1964–9, *passim*.

36 *The Two Liturgies AD 1549 and AD 1552*, ed. J. Ketley, Parker Society, 1844, Cambridge, pp. 371, 459–60, 465. Cf. K. Charlton, 'The Liberal–Vocational Debate in Early Modern England', in J. Burstyn, ed., *Preparation for Life? The Paradox of Education in the Late Twentieth Century*, 1986, Lewes, pp. 1–18.

37 Augustine, *De Genesi ad Litteram*, 9.18.34 and Aquinas, *Summa Theologiae*, 1a.92.3. The point became a commonplace in the 'defence' literature of the early modern period. See for example, W. Coverdale (translating H. Bullinger), *The Christen State of Matrimony*, 1541, sig. Aiv recto–verso and Hi verso; W. Averell, *Dyall for Dainty Darlings*, 1584, sig. Fiv recto; R. C(leaver), *A Godly Form of Householde Gouvernement*, 1598, p. 201; A. Darcie, *The Honour of Ladies*, 1622, p. 20; T. Heywood, *A Curtaine Lecture*, 1637, p. 170; C. Gerbier, *Elogium Heroinum*, 1650, p. 4. For general discussion, J. G. Turner, *One Flesh: Paradisal Marriage and Sexual Relations in the Age of Milton*, 1987, Oxford, and J. L. Thompson, *John Calvin and the Daughters of Sarah*, 1992, Geneva. For late medieval rewritings of the Fall,

H. Phillips, 'Rewriting the Fall: Julian of Norwich and the *Chevalier des Dames*', in L. Smith and J. H. M. Taylor, eds, *Women, the Book and the Godly*, 1998, Cambridge, pp. 749–56, and R. Bottingheimer, 'Print, Publishing and Change in the Image of Eve and the Apple 1470–1570', *Archives for Reformation History*, 1995, vol. 86, pp. 199–235, using the evidence of mainly German woodcut engravings.

38 G. Chapman, *A Humorous Days Mirth*, 1599, sig. D2 verso.

39 Paynell (translating Vives), *The Office and Dutie of an Husband*, 1550, sig. Pi verso; F. Rogers, ed., *St Thomas More: Selected Letters*, 1961, p. 105. The original Latin is in *Rogers, The Correspondence of Sir Thomas More*, 1947, Princeton, p. 122.

40 Elyot, *The Defence of Good Women*, 1540, 1545 ed., sig. Dvii recto; Montaigne, 'Upon Some Verses of Virgil', in D. M. Frame, ed. and trans., *Complete Works of Montaigne*, 1957, Stanford, p. 128. All such comments were, of course, echoing Plato, *Republic*, V,455; Christine de Pisan had complained in similar terms in 1404 in *The Cyte of Ladyes*, trans. Anslay, 1521, sig. Kk5 recto.

41 R. C(leaver), *A Godly Form of Householde Government*, 1598, p. 157. The passage was repeated *verbatim* (without acknowledgement) in W. Gouge, *Of Domesticall Duties*, 1622, p. 273. Garnett, *Treatise of Christian Renunciation*, 1593, pp. 10–22, 100–11, 144–8; Austin, *Haec Homo Wherein the Excellencie of Woman is Described*, 1637, p. 5.

42 *Jane Angers Protection Against Women*, 1598, sig. Ci recto; Austin, *Haec Homo*, p. 13; Gibson, *A Womans Woorth Defended Against All Men in the World*, 1599, fol. 21 verso, and R. Brathwait, *A Ladies Love Lecture*, 1641, p. 424. See also Elyot, *The Castel of Helthe . . .*, 1539, sig. 3 verso–4 recto; R. Barckley, *The Felicite of Man*, 1598, pp. 576–82; T. Walkington, *The Opticke Glasse of Humors . . .*, 1607, *passim*; B. Rich, *My Ladys Looking Glasse . . .*, 1616, p. 14.

43 See, for example, J. Phillip, *The Play of Patient Grissell,* 1558; T. Dekker, *Patient Grissil, c.*1599; Anon, *The Ancient, True and Admirable History of Patient Grisel*, 1619; T. Deloney, *The Pleasant and Sweet History of Patient Grissel*, 1630. Margaret Spufford reports that a 24-page *Patient Griselda* was still being published and sold at 3d in the 1680s, in *Small Books and Pleasant Histories, Popular Fiction and Readership in Seventeenth-Century England*, 1981, p. 156.

44 See, for example, T. Garter, *The Most Virtuous and Godly Susanna*, 1578; R. Greene, *The Mirrour of Modestie*, 1584; R. Aylett, *Susannah or The Arraignement of the Two Unjust Elders*, 1622; *An Excellent Ballad Intitled The Constancy of Susanna*.

45 N. N., trans., *The Complete Woman*, 1639; (John Paulet), Marquis of Winchester, trans., *The Gallery of Heroick Women*, 1652; A.L., trans., *The Woman as Good as the Man, or the Equality of Both Sexes*, 1677; F. Spence, trans., *Conversations Upon Several Subjects*, 2 vols, 1683; G. Hickes, trans., *Instructions for the Education of a Daughter*, 1707.

46 Savile, *The Ladies New-Year Gift*, 1688; W. Walsh, *Dialogue Concerning Women*, 1691, and *A Further Essay Concerning the Female Sex*, 1696; Defoe, *Essay Upon Projects*, 1697; *Athenian Mercury*, 23 May 1691. 'Madam Philips' was the Welsh poetess, Katherine Fowler Philips, 'the Matchless Orinda'. 'Van Schurman' was Anna Maria van Schurman, author of *The Learned Maid or Whether a Maid should be a Scholler*, trans. C. Barksdale, 1657.

47 G. Gifford, *A Catechisme Conteining the Summe of Christian Religion*, 1582, Title Page. Cf. J. Jewel, *An Exposition Upon the First Epistle of St. Paul to the Thessalonians*, 1583, in *Works*, ed. J. Ayre, Parker Society, 4 vols, 1847, Cambridge, II, p. 837.

48 Milton, *Samson Agonistes*, 1671, lines 904–5.

49 Erasmus, *De Pueris Instituendis*, 1529, Basel, ed. J. K. Sowards, trans. B. C. Ver-

straete, *Collected Works of Erasmus*, 1985, vol. 26, Toronto, pp. 305–6; Ascham, *Scholemaster*, 1578, fol. 10 verso–11 recto; J. Stockwood, *Sermon at Paules Crosse*, 1578, p. 88; R. Carew, *The Examination of Mens Wits*, 1594, p. 62; T. Gataker, *Davids Instructer*, 1620, pp. 20–1; J. Earle, *Microcosmographie*, 1628, sig. Bi recto–Bii verso; H. Woodward, *A Childes Patrimony*, 1640, pp. 8–9; J. Curtois, *An Essay to Persuade Parents to Educate Their Children in Piety and Virtue*, 1697, p. 31. The sources are Plato, *Theaetetus*, 191c and, more frequently cited, Aristotle, *De Anima*, 429b–430c. See K. Charlton, 'The Paradox of Metaphor: A Sixteenth-Century Case Study' in W. Taylor, *Metaphors of Education*, 1984, pp. 54–67.

50 Gouge, *Domesticall Duties*, 1634 ed., p. 545. The opening paragraphs of Erasmus' *De Pueris* are an eloquent reminder of the importance of the early stages of an infant's education.

51 Erasmus, *De Pueris Instituendis*, 1529, Basel, ed. J. K. Sowards, trans. B. C. Verstraete, *Collected Works of Erasmus*, 1985, vol. 26, Toronto, pp. 201 and 312. Plutarch's essay was translated by Sir Thomas Elyot, *The Education and Bringinge Up of Children*, 1533, and also by Thomas Blundeville (1561) and Edward Grant (1571).

52 Primaudaye, *French Academie*, 1586; 1618 ed., p. 72; Brathwait, 1630; 1641 ed., p. 53; Griffith, *Bethel*, 1633, p. 166. George Whitelocke used the story in advising his children, 'Diary', BL Addl. Ms. 53726. fols 6a,b.

53 Bruni, *De Studiis et Literis*, c.1405, in H. Woodward, ed., *Vittorino da Feltre and Other Humanist Educators*, 1963 ed., New York, pp. 119–33.

54 Mulcaster, *Positions*, 1581, pp. 170, 173–4, 175.

55 *Ibid.*, p. 175. Timon of Philius, the Sceptic philosopher.

56 Bacon, *The Essayes or Counsels Civill and Morall*, 1625, p. 229. The essay was not part of the original 1597 edition, though it was included in the 1612 edition. The Aesop story, however, was not added until the 1625 edition.

57 Sandys, *Prima Pars . . .*, 1634, p. 128; W. J. Thoms (ed.), *Anecdotes and Traditions*, Camden Society, 1839, vol. 5, p. 125; Harrington in N. E. McLure, ed., *The Letters and Epigrams of Sir John Harrington*, 1935, Philadelphia, pp. 255–6.

58 Niccoles, *Discourse*, 1615; 1620 ed., p. 9. Cf. Montaigne's essay 'Of Pedantry', in Frame, *op. cit.*, p. 103; Heywood, *Gunaikeion*, 1624, p. 236.

59 Howell, *Provearbs and Old Sayd Saws*, 1660, p. 15; P. Tilley, *A Dictionary of the Proverbs in England in the Sixteenth and Seventeenth Centuries*, 1950, Ann Arbor, p. 742; *An Invective Against the Pride of Women*, 1657, verse 6.

60 Jocelin, *The Mothers Legacie to her Unborne Childe*, 1624, p. 33; Dobrée, ed., *Letters . . .*, III, p. 1108.

61 Vives, trans. Hyrde, *The Instruction of a Christen Woman*, 1540, sig. Dii verso. Cf. K. Charlton, ' "Tak the to thi distaff": the Education of Women and Girls in Early Modern England', *Westminster Studies in Education*, 4, 1981, pp. 3–18. The proof-text for such arguments was Proverbs 31. 19.

62 P. Verney and M. Verney, eds, *Memoirs of the Verney Family During the Seventeenth Century*, 4 vols, 1894, III, pp. 73–4. John Evelyn offered the same advice to his grandson in *Memoirs for My Grandson*, 1704, ed. G. Keynes, 1926, Oxford, pp. 13 and 71. His wife Margaret held a similar view: W. Bray, ed., *The Diary and Correspondence of John Evelyn*, 4 vols, 1850–2, IV, p. 32, revised edition by B. Wheatley, 4 vols, 1906, II, p. 58. Lady Mary Wortley Montagu made the same point in 1710, *Complete Letters*, ed. Halsband, 3 vols, 1965–7, Oxford, I, pp. 44–5.

63 Comenius, *The Great Didactic*, 1657, Amsterdam, ed. and trans. W. Keatinge, 1896, p. 220.

64 *The Roxburghe Ballads*, ed. W. Chappell and W. Ebsworth, 9 vols, 1871–99, Hertford, III, p. 199. Judith Drake, *An Essay in Defence of the Female Sex . . .*, 1696, p. 20, makes the same point, as does Poulain de la Barre, *The Woman as Good as the Man*, 1677, pp. 121, 123.

65 Savile, *The Ladys New-Year Gift*, 1688, p. 32.

66 L. Pollock, ' "Teach Her to Live Under Obedience": The Making of Women in the Upper Ranks of Early Modern England', *Continuity and Change*, 1989, vol. 4, pp. 231–58. Cf. W. Tyndale, *Answer to Sir Thomas More's Dialogue*, ed. H. Walter, Parker Society, 1859, Cambridge, p. 19.

67 From the innumerable commentaries and glosses see, for example, R. Pricke, *The Doctrine of Superioritie and Subjection Contained in the Fifth Commandment of the Holy Law of God*, 1609. For its general applicability, J. S. McGee, *The Godly Man in Stuart England*, 1976, New Haven, chap. 4; R. Tuck, 'Power and Authority in Seventeenth-Century England', *Historical Journal*, 1974, vol. 17, pp. 43–61; R. Rex, 'The Crisis of Obedience: God's Word and Henry's Reformation', *Historical Journal*, 1996, vol. 39, pp. 863–94; M. C. Questier, 'Loyalty, Religion and State Power in Early Modern England', *Historical Journal*, 1997, vol. 40, pp. 311–29.

68 *The Seconde Tome of Homilies*, 1563, 'Against Disobedience and Wilful Rebellion'; C. Goodman, *How Superior Powers Ought to be Obeyed*, 1558; J. Hall, *Of Government and Obedience*, 1654. The proof-text was Romans 13.1.2.

69 See the Catechism's gloss on the Tenth Commandment, in J. Ketley, ed., *The Two Liturgies . . .*, p. 465: 'to do my duty in that state of life unto which it shall please God to call me' – a sentiment stamped on the memories, if not the minds and hearts, of many generations of children (and adults) to come.

70 W. Harrison, *The Description of England*, ed. G. Edelen, 1968, Ithaca, Book II, chap. 4; T. Wilson, *The State of England Anno Domini 1600*, ed. F.J. Fisher, Camden Society Miscellany, 1936, vol. 16, p. 22. Cf. L. Stone, 'Social Mobility in England 1500–1700', *Past and Present*, 1966, no. 33, pp. 16–55; K. Wrightson, 'Estates, Degrees and Sorts: Changing Perceptions of Society in Tudor and Stuart England', in P. J. Corfield, ed., *Language, History and Class*, 1991, Oxford, pp. 30–52; P. Burke, 'The Language of Orders in Early Modern Europe', in M. L. Bush, ed., *Social Orders and Social Classes in Early Modern Europe since 1500: Studies in Social Stratification*, 1992, pp. 1–12.

71 *The Two Liturgies AD 1549 and AD 1552*, ed. J. Ketley, Parker Society, 1844, Cambridge, pp. 298, 371. See also 'Prayers for all Conditions and Sorts of Men', in *Liturgies and Occasional Prayers in the Reign of Queen Elizabeth*, ed. W. K. Clay, Parker Society, 1847, Cambridge, pp. 246ff.

72 'An Exhortation Concerning Good Order and Obedience', in *Certain Sermons and Homilies 1547*, ed. R. B. Bond, 1987, Toronto, p. 161, and 'Against Strife and Contention', *ibid.*, pp. 191–205. See also W. Perkins, 'A Treatise of the Vocations or Callings of Men', in *Works*, 3 vols, 1616, Cambridge, I, pp. 747ff.

73 *Troilus and Cressida*, I,iii,108–10.

74 Ketley, *Two Liturgies*, pp. 371, 459–60, 465, and Clay, *Liturgies*, pp. 246ff.

75 Hogrefe, 'The Legal Rights of Tudor Women and Their Circumvention by Men and Women', *Sixteenth Century Journal*, 1972, vol. 3, pp. 97–105. Cf. A. L. Erickson, *Women and Property in Early Modern England*, 1933; W. R. Prest, 'Law and Women's Rights in Early Modern England', *Seventeenth Century*, 1991, vol. 6, pp. 169–87.

76 E.T., *The Lawes Resolutions of Womens Rights*, 1632, p. 125.

77 E.T., *op. cit*, p. 6.

78 W. J. Jones, *The Elizabethan Court of Chancery*, 1967, Oxford; M. L. Cioni, 'The Elizabethan Court of Chancery and Women's Rights', in D. J. Cuth and J. W. McKenna, eds, *Tudor Rule and Revolution: Essays for G. R. Elton from his American Friends*, 1982, Cambridge, pp.159–82. For general discussion, M. K. Whyte, *The Status of Women in Pre-Industrial Societies*, 1978, Princeton, and K. Thomas, 'The Double Standard', *Journal of the History of Ideas*, 1959, vol. 20, pp. 195–216.

79 Rich, *Faultes, Faultes and More Faultes*, 1606, p. 26. Vaughan, *Golden Grove*, 1600, sig. O2 recto; Donne, 'That Virginity is a Virtue', in J. Hayward, ed., *Complete Poetry and Prose*, 1962, p. 348; *All's Well That Ends Well*, I,i,129–30; *Twelfth Night*, I,v,225–7.

80 M. Sheehan, 'Marriage Theory and Practice in the Conciliar Legislation and Diocesan Statutes of Medieval England', *Medieval Studies*, 1978, vol. 40, pp. 418–60.

81 Babington, *Certaine Plaine Briefe and Comfortable Notes Upon Every Chapter of Genesis*, 1596, p. 190, as also his *Certayne Profitable Questions and Answers Upon the Commandments*, 1596, p. 181.

82 Parker, *Jus Populi*, 1644, pp. 4–5. Cf. T. Rogers *The Character of a Good Woman*, 1697, p. 19.

83 Hieron, *The Bridegroom*, 1613, pp. 12–13, as also his 'The Marriage Blessing', in *Sermons*, 1635, p. 405. A. Niccoles, *A Discourse on Marriage and Wiving*, 1615, p. 7. Erasmus had earlier made the same point, *The Colloquies of Erasmus*, ed. C. R. Thompson, 1965, Chicago, p. 123.

84 Fuller, *The Holy and Prophane State*, 1642, p. 14. Cf. Shakespeare's Anne Page, *Merry Wives of Windsor*, III,iv,31–3 and Fenton, *ibid.*, V,v,216–17. A. Searle, ed., *Barrington Family Letters*, Camden Society, 4th Ser., 1983, pp. 250–1. For Dorothy Osborne's views on the matter, *Dorothy Osborne's Letters to Sir William Temple*, ed. K. Parker, 1987, Harmondsworth, pp. 40, 41, 59, 119, 136, 154, 178. Elizabeth Bury, 'Caution to a Friend About Marrying', in S. Bury, *Account of the Life and Death of Elizabeth Bury*, 1720, Bristol, pp. 193–4.

85 J. Loftis, ed., *Memoirs of Lady Anne Halkett and Lady Anne Fanshawe*, 1981, Oxford, p. 14.

86 Parker, *Osborne Letters*, p. 71.

87 G. C. Williamson, ed., *Lady Anne Clifford*, 1967, p. 76. Cf. Dorothy Deane to Roger Lukin, 'do you not think it a sin of a high nature for me to be rebellious to my father and run away with you ... Can I expect the blessing of God if I should do so?', in D. M. Gardiner, ed., *The Oxinden and Peyton Letters 1642–70*, 1937, p. xxvii, and Elizabeth Livingstone, 'I resolve never more to hear a young man talk of love to me ... unless he is approved by my parents', in H. H. Craster, 'Notes from a Delaval Diary', *Proceedings of the Society of Antiquaries of Newcastle-upon-Tyne*, 3rd Ser., 1905, vol. 1, pp. 149–53. Cf. D. O'Hara, ' "Ruled by my Friends": Aspects of Marriage in the Diocese of Canterbury c.1540–70', *Continuity and Change*, 1991, vol. 6, pp. 9–42.

88 Ballad, 'The Constant Maidens Resolution', BL. Roxburgh Collection.

89 *The Works of Thomas Deloney*, ed. F. O. Mann, 1912, Oxford, p. 484; *The Life and Complete Works of Robert Greene*, ed. A. B. Grosart, 1881–3, 15 vols, VII, pp. 65, 79.

90 Ascham, *The Schoolmaster*, 1570, fol. 13 recto.

91 Allestree, *The Whole Duty of Man*, 1658, p. 291. The work was published anonymously.

92 J. Gairdner, ed., *The Paston Letters*, 6 vols, 1904, vol. 5, pp. 36–40; N. Davis, ed., *The Paston Letters and Papers of the Fifteenth Century*, 2 vols, 1971 and 1976, vol. 1, pp. 341–4, 408–10, 541–3. See also A. S. Haskell, 'Paston Women on Marriage in Fifteenth-Century England', *Viator*, 1973, vol. 4, pp. 459–71.

93 R. C. Bald, *John Donne. A Life*, 1970, Oxford, pp. 128–9; W. G. Hiscock, *John Evelyn and his Family Circle*, 1955, p. 140.

94 M. Carbery, ed., *Mrs Elizabeth Freke, Her Diary 1671–1714*, 1931, Cork, p. 148; G. Goodman, *The Court of King James I*, 2 vols, II, p. 191; *Memoirs of Sir Hugh Cholmley*, 1787, pp. 8–9. The Memoirs were written in the 1650s and relate to the 1620s and thereafter. T. C. Croker, ed., *The Autobiography of Mary Countess of Warwick*, 1848, pp. 3, 5ff, 15.

95 E. Chamberlayne, *Angliae Notitiae*, 1669 ed., pp. 458–9, 461.

96 C. Richmond, *John Hopton Fifteenth-century Suffolk Gentleman*, 1981, Cambridge, p. 127.

97 Verney, *Memoirs*, I, p. 48.

98 E. J. Raine, ed., *Richmondshire Wills and Inventories*, Surtees Society, 1853, vol. 26, pp. 231–2.

99 S. Coppell, 'Will-making on the Death-bed', *Local Population Studies*, 1988, vol. 26, p. 41.

100 R. O'Day, *The Family and Family Relationships 1500–1900. England, France and the United States of America*, 1994, p. 121.

101 Burnet, *op. cit.*, ed. H. C. Foxcroft, 3 vols, 1887–1902, Oxford, III, p. 480.

102 M. Cavendish, *The Life of William Cavendish*, ed. C. H. Firth, 1886, p. 288; Croker, *op. cit.*, p. 4; C. Jackson, ed., *The Autobiography of Mrs Alice Thornton*, Surtees Society, 1875 for 1873, vol. 62, p. 76; Barker, *Osborne Letters*, p. 19.

103 M. H. Lee, ed., *Diaries and Letters of Philip Henry 1631–96*, 1882, p. 331.

104 HMC., *Hastings Mss*, II, pp. 70–1.

105 J. Russell, *The Letters of Lady Rachel Russell*, 1853, 2 vols; M. Berry, *Some Account of the Life of Rachel Wriothesley, Lady Russell*, 1819; L. G. Schwoerer, *Lady Rachel Russell. 'One of the Best of Women'*, 1988, Baltimore.

106 Verney, *Memoirs*, I, p. 116.

107 D. North, *A Forest of Varieties*, 1645, p. 141.

108 L. Stone, *Family, Sex and Marriage*, 1977, New York, p. 182.

109 E. E. Stoll, *Shakespeare Studies*, 1927, New York, p. 61.

110 Hilder, *Conjugall Counsel*, 1652, p. 42. See also C. Gibbon, *A Work Worth Reading by Parents. How to Bestow Their Children in Marriage*, 1591, sig. Bi recto.

111 Stockwood, *A Bartholomew Fairing for Parentes Shewing that Children Are Not to Marie Without Consent of Their Parentes*, 1589, p. 12.

112 Stubbes, *The Anatomie of Abuses*, 1583, sig. V5 recto. Montaigne made the same point in his essay 'Upon Some Verses of Vergill', in Frame, ed., p. 646.

113 Painter, *op. cit.*, 1567, sig. *** i verso.

114 Brooke, *op. cit.*, 1562, Epistle to the Reader; Baxter, *Christian Directory*, 1678, Pt ii, pp.10–12. See also D. Rogers, *Matrimoniall Honour*, 1642, p. 32; S. Denison, *The Monument or Tombstone*, 1620, sig. A4 verso. For examples of romantic love see R. A. Houlbrooke, *The English Family 1450–1700*, 1984, p. 77.

115 Chapman, *Bussy D'Ambois*, III,ii,253–5.

116 Dod and Cleaver, *op. cit.*, 1614, pp. 186, 224–5.

117 Seager, *op. cit.*, sig. B7 recto. *Basilikon Doron*, Roxburghe Club ed., 1887, pp. 97–8. See also J. Brinsley, *A Looking Glass for Good Women*, 1645, p. 39; F. Cheynell, *A Plot for the Good of Posterity*, 1646, p. 28.

118 Sherley, *Wits New Dyall or a Schollers Prize*, 1604, sig. C4 verso. Cf. Dod and Cleaver, *A Godly Fourme of Household Gouvernement*, 1614, sig. L5 recto–verso.

119 Whatley, *Bride Bush*, 1619, 1623 ed., p. 98, and chap. 14, 'Of the Wives Peculiar Duties', pp. 189ff.

120 *The Mothers Counsell or Live Within Compass*, 1630, p. 39.

121 *Two Liturgies AD 1549 and AD 1552*, ed. J. Ketley, Parker Society, 1844, Cambridge, p. 465.

122 *The Colloquies of Erasmus*, ed. C. R. Thompson, 1965, Chicago, p. 126. Cf. J. T. Johnson, 'English Puritan Thought on the Ends of Marriage', *Church History*, 1969, vol. 38, pp. 429–36, and E. Leites, 'The Duty to Desire: Love, Friendship and Sexuality in Some Puritan Theories of Marriage', *Journal of Social History*, 1979, vol. 15, pp. 383–408. For general discussion see D. Ammussen, *An Ordered Society: Gender and Class in Early Modern England*, 1988, Oxford.

123 Gouge, 'Directions for Parents in Providing Marriages', *Domesticall Dueties*, 1600, Ep. Ded., sig. A3 recto and pp. 313, 320–1.

124 Whitgift, *A Most Godly and Learned Sermon Preached at Pauls Crosse the 17th of November . . . 1583*, 1589, sig. A7 verso and B3ff; Donne, *Sermons*, III, p. 242.

125 Taylor, 'The Marriage Ring or The Mysteries and Duties of Marriage', in R. Heber, ed., *Works*, 5 vols, 1828, V, pp. 263ff, and *The Measures and Offices of Friendship*, 3rd ed., 1662, pp. 79–83.

126 Above, p. 18, n. 37.

127 Clapham, *The Commendation of Matrimony*, 1545, sig. Cii recto–verso, Ciii recto; Tilney, *A Briefe and Pleasant Discourse on the Duties of Marriage Called the Flower of Friendship*, 1568, sig. Bii recto. See also Vaughan, *Golden Grove*, 1600, Book II, chap. 13; W. Ames, *Conscience with the Powere and Cases Thereof*, 1639, p. 156; W. Heale, *An Apologie for Women*, 1609, Oxford, p. 10.

128 Smith, *A Preparative for Marriage*, 1591, pp. 56 and 66, and in *The Sermons of Master Henrie Smith Gathered in One Volume*, 1592, p. 42. The 'pair of oars' metaphor was also used in W. Secker, *A Wedding Ring Fit for the Finger*, 1664, p. 20, and W. Penn, *Some Fruits of Solitude*, 1693, pp. 27–8, 32.

129 Gouge, *Domesticall Duties*, 1600, 3rd ed., 1634, pp. 188, 191–2. See also Whately, *Bride Bush*, 1619 ed., p. 85.

130 *The Dramatic Works of Thomas Heywood*, 6 vols, ed. R. H. Shepherd, 1874, II, pp. 95ff; Primaudaye, *op. cit.*, sig. 000 2 recto–verso. Cf. G. L. Finney, 'A World of Instruments', *English Literary History*, 1953, vol. 20, pp. 87–120.

131 Donne, *Sermons*, III, p. 244, V, p. 133, II, p. 335. See also D. Leigh, *The Mothers Blessing*, 7th ed., 1621, pp. 49–52.

132 Dod and Cleaver, *op. cit.*, 1614, sig. A8 verso.

133 D. Gardiner, ed., *The Oxinden Letters 1609–42*, 1933, p. 87. Cotton cited Pollock, *Continuity and Change*, 1989, vol. 4, p. 247. A. Walker, *The Holy Life of Elizabeth Walker*, 1690, p. 90; *Memoirs of the Life of Colonel Hutchinson*, 1854, p. 30. See also Barbara Slingsby's letter to her father in D. Parsons, ed., *The Diary of Sir Henry Slingsby of Scriven*, 1836, pp. 327–8.

134 For comparison see T. M. Saffley, *Let No Man Put Asunder. The Control of Marriage in the German South-West. A Comparative Study 1500–1600*, 1984, Kirksville, Mo., and R. Phillips, *Putting Asunder. A History of Divorce in Western Europe*, 1988, Cambridge.

135 T. Gataker, *Marriage Duties Briefly Couched Together out of Colossians 1.18–19*, 1620, pp. 7–8. See also W. Ames, *Cases of Conscience*, 1639, pp. 208–10.

136 *Op. cit.*, p. 16.

137　Bunney, *op. cit.*, 1610, Oxford, Preface, sig. *3 verso.

138　Smith, *Preparative*, 1591, p. 36; Gouge, *Domesticall Duties*, 1622, in *Works*, 2 vols, 1626–7, I, pp. 127–8; Taylor, *The Rule and Exercise of Holy Living*, 1650, pp. 66–7.

139　Kingsmill, 'A Godly Advise . . . Touching Marriage', annexed to his *A View of Mans Estate*, 1576, sig. Kv verso; as also Vaughan, *Golden Grove*, 1600; 1608 ed., sig. 06 recto–verso.

140　*Select Works of John Bale*, ed. H. Christmas, Parker Society, 1849, Cambridge, p. 199.

141　*A Legacy or Widows Mite Left by Alice Hayes to her Children with an Account of her Dying Sayings*, 1724, p. 39. See also A. Wentworth, *A Vindication of Anne Wentworth . . .*, 1677, explaining why she left her husband.

142　Milton, *The Judgement of Martin Bucer on Divorce*, 1644, and *The Doctrine and Discipline of Divorce*, 1643. Cf. J. G. Halkett, *Milton and the Idea of Matrimony*, 1970, New Haven; S. P. Revard, 'Eve and the Doctrine of Responsibility in *Paradise Lost*', *PMLA*, 1973, vol. 88, pp. 69–78.

143　E. H. Bates, ed., *Quarter Sessions Records for the County of Somerset, I, 1607–25*, Somerset Record Society, 1907, vol. 28, pp. 2, 18, 108. See also J. S. Cockburn, ed., *Calendar of Assize Records: Kent Indictments Elizabeth I*, 1979, nos 2912, 2893, 2950; Cockburn, ed., *Calendar of Assize Records; Sussex Indictments Elizabeth I*, 1975, nos 1622, 1651, 1652; T. G. Barnes, ed., *Somerset Assize Records 1629–40*, Somerset Record Society, 1959, vol. 65, p. 37; E. Cust, *Records of the Cust Family. II, The Brownlows of Belton*, 1909, p. 130.

144　C. Evans, *Friends of the Seventeenth Century*, 1885, Philadelphia, pp. 73–4; Elizabeth Williams cited O. Hufton, *The Prospect Before Her. A History of Women in Western Europe, vol. I 1500–1800*, 1995, p. 414. Cf. W. C. Braithwaite, *The Beginnings of Quakerism*, 2nd ed., 1955, Cambridge, p. 158 and M. Brailsford, *Quaker Women*, 1915, p. 103.

145　Becon, *The Boke of Matrimony*, Preface, in *Worckes*, 2 vols, 1562, I, fol. cccclxv.

146　Whitforde, *A Werke for Householders*, 1530, sig. Niv recto; Anon, *The Anatomy of a Womans Tongue*, 1638, in *Harleian Miscellany*, vol. II, p. 744.

147　Vaughan, *Golden Grove*, 1600; 1608 ed., chap. vii, sig. 05 recto.

148　J. Ray, *A Collection of English Proverbs*, 1670, Cambridge, p. 50.

149　*The Colloquies of Erasmus*, ed. C. R. Thompson, 1965, Chicago, p. 177; Ballad, *The Womans Victory or The Conceited Cuckold Cudgel's into Good Qualities*, BL. C 22 f 6, fol. 207. Cf. D. Kunzle, 'The World Turned Upside Down; The Iconography of a European Broadside Type', in B. A. Babcock, ed., *The Reversible World. Symbolic Inversion in Art and Society*, 1978, Ithaca, pp. 39–94, for German and French examples.

150　*The Second Tome of Homilies*, 1563, in J. Griffiths, ed., *The Two Books of Homilies Appointed to be Read in Churches*, 1859, Oxford, p. 510; Smith, *Preparative*, in *Sermons*, 1592, p. 44; Ames, *Conscience with the Powere and Cases Thereof*, 1639, pp. 207–8; *Glasse of Godly Love*, ed. F. J. Furnival, New Shakespeare Society, 1876, Ser. VI, no. 2, p. 181.

151　Taylor, *The Marriage Ring*, in *Works*, ed. H. Heber, 1831, 5 vols, V, p. 268; Moses à Vaut (pseud.), *op. cit.*, To the Reader, sig. A3 recto and p. 55.

152　Cf. C. Carlton, 'The Widow's Tale; Male Myths and Female Reality in Sixteenth and Seventeenth-century England,' *Albion*, 1978, vol. 10, pp. 118–29.

153　Hannay, *A Happy Husband or Directions for a Maid How to Choose her Mate*, 1618, p. 37; J. P. Cooper, ed., *The Wentworth Papers 1597–1628*, Camden Society, 4th Ser., 1973, vol. 12, p. 20.

154 Cited J. Murray, 'Kinship and Friendship: The Perception of Family by Clergy and Laity in Medieval London', *Albion*, 1988, vol. 20, p. 379.

155 A. Hanham, *The Celys and Their World*, 1985, Cambridge, pp. 310, 414, 423–4; C. Richmond; *John Hopton, a Fifteenth-century Suffolk Gentleman*, 1981, Cambridge, p. 127; A. G. Dickens, ed., *Clifford Letters of the Sixteenth Century*, Surtees Society, 1952, vol. 172, p. 95 and J. W. Clay 'The Clifford Family', *Yorkshire Archaeological Journal*, 1905, vol. 18, pp. 380, 387, 411; L. V. Way, 'The Smyths of Ashton Court', *Bristol and Gloucester Archaeological Society*, 1908, vol. 31, p. 244. For Cambridgeshire evidence see M. Spufford, *Contrasting Communities. English Villagers in the Sixteenth and Seventeenth Centuries*, 1974, Cambridge, pp. 81ff. Cf. R. E. Archer and B. E. Ferme, 'Testamentary Procedure with Special Reference to the Executrix', *Medieval Women in Southern England, Reading Medieval Studies*, 1989, vol. 15, pp. 3–34. For comparative data, B. Diefendorf, 'Widowhood and Remarriage in Sixteenth-Century Paris', *Journal of Family History*, 1982, vol. 7, pp. 379–95, and S. M. Wynter, 'Survivors and Status: Widowhood and Family in the Early Modern Netherlands', *ibid.*, pp. 396–405; J. F. Harrington, *Reordering Marriage and Society*, 1995, Cambridge, offers a timely reminder of similarities in Protestant and Catholic families.

156 R. Almack, 'Keddington alias Ketton and the Barnardiston Family', *Proceedings of the Suffolk Institute of Archaeology and Natural History*, 1874, vol. 4, p. 167; F. P. Wilson, 'Notes on the Early Life of John Donne', *Review of English Studies*, 1927, vol. 3, pp. 272–9; James West cited R. T. Vann, 'Wills and the Family in an English Town. Banbury 1553–1805', *Journal of Family History*, 1979, vol. 4, p. 358; J. A. R. Marriott, *The Life and Times of Lucius Cary*, 1907, p. 327; A. Walker, *Memoir of Lady Warwick*, 1847, p. 47; A. Macfarlane, *The Family Life of Ralph Josselin. An Essay in Historical Sociology*, 1970, Cambridge, p. 213; A. Jessopp, *The Autobiography of the Hon. Roger North*, 1887, p. 288.

157 G. J. Piccope, ed., *Lancashire and Cheshire Wills and Inventories*, Chetham Society, 1861, vol. 54, p. 83; J. M. Bestall and D. V. Fowkes, eds, *Chesterfield Wills and Inventories 1521–1603*, Derbyshire Record Society, 1977, vol. 2, pp. 99 and 103; M. J. Galgano, 'Infancy and Childhood: The Female Experience in the Restoration North-West', in J. Watson and P. Pittman, eds, *The Portrayal of Life Stages in English Literature 1500–1800*, 1989, Lewiston, p. 129.

158 D. MacCulloch, *Suffolk and the Tudors. Politics and Religion in an English County 1500–1600*, 1986, Oxford, p. 297; M. A. E. Wood, ed., *Letters of Royal and Illustrious Ladies*, 3 vols in 1, 1846, I, p. 329; Lady Mary Willoughby in *DNB*; K. O. Asheson, ed., *The Diary of Anne Clifford 1616–19*, 1995, New York, *passim* and pp. 2–6 for a consideration of the basis of the lawsuits.

159 Cf. B. J. Todd, 'The Remarrying Widow: A Stereotype Reconsidered', in M. J. Prior, ed., *Women in English Society 1500–1800*, 1985, pp. 54–92, and V. Brodsky, 'Widows in Late Elizabethan London. Remarriage, Economic Opportunity and Family Orientation', in L. Bonfield *et al.*, eds, *The World we Have Gained*, 1986, Oxford, pp. 122–54.

160 B. Winchester, *Tudor Family Portrait*, 1955; S. Ozment, *Magdalena and Balthasar: An Intimate Portrait of Life in Sixteenth-century Europe Revealed in the Letters of a Nuremberg Husband and Wife*, 1986, New Haven; P. Seaver, *Wallington's World. A Puritan Artisan in Seventeenth-century London*, 1985, Stanford.

161 N. Davis, ed., *The Paston Letters and Papers of the Fifteenth Century*, 2 vols, 1971 and 1976, Oxford, *passim*; C. Richmond, *John Hopton, a Fifteenth-century Suffolk Gentleman*, 1981, Cambridge, pp. 97, 115–16, 119–20. See also R. E. Archer,

'"How Ladies Who Live on Their Manors Ought to Manage Their House-holds and Estates": Women as Landholders and Administrators in the Late Middle Ages', in P. J. P. Goldberg, ed., *Woman is a Worthy Wight. Women in English Society, c.1200–1500*, 1992, Stroud, pp. 149–81.

162 *The Lisle Letters*, ed. M. St Clare Byrne, 6 vols, 1981, Chicago, I, pp. 631–3, III, pp. 468–9, IV, pp. 38–9, V, pp. 311–12. BL Addl. Ms. 19, 191, fols 63,66.

163 J. H. Betty, ed., *Calendar of the Correspondence of the Smyth Family of Ashton Court 1548–1642*, Bristol Record Society, 1982, vol. 38, pp. 40–1, 46, 89, 96.

164 A. Wall, ed., *Two Elizabethan Women: The Correspondence of Joan and Maria Thynne 1575–1611*, Wiltshire Record Society, 1983, vol. 38, pp. 48–9; L. B. Osborne, ed., *The Life, Letters and Writings of Sir John Hoskyns*, 1931, New Haven, pp. 68–9, 75.

165 D. Coke, *The Last Elizabethan, Sir John Coke*, 1937, pp. 37, 82, 99; D. M. Gardiner, ed., *The Oxinden and Peyton Letters 1642–70*, 1937, pp. 111, 112, 154, 209, 276–9; P. Verney, *The Standard Bearer*, 1963, p. 28; Verney, *Memoirs*, II, *passim*.

166 HMC, *De Lisle and Dudley Mss*, II, p. 153; G. C. Williamson, *George Earl of Cumberland*, 1920, pp. 285ff. Lord Braybrooke, ed., *The Private Correspondence of Jane Lady Cornwallis*, 1842, p. 76; M. Cavendish, *A True Relation of My Birth, Breeding and Life*, ed. E. Brydges, 1814, p. 16.

167 HMC *De Lisle and Dudley Mss*, VI, pp. 61, 71, 73, 75, 81, and especially letter of 24 February 1637, pp. 89–90; T. C. Croker, ed. *The Autobiography of Mary, Countess of Warwick*, 1848, *passim*; T. T. Lewis, ed., *The Letters of Brilliana Harley*, Camden Society, vol. 58, 1854, *passim*; A. Searle, ed., *The Barrington Family Letters 1628–32*, Camden Society, 4th Ser., 1983, p. 5; J. Collinges, *Par Nobile. Two Treatises . . . at the Funeralls of Lady Frances Hobart and Lady Catherine Courten*, 1669, p. 10.

168 'Sir Roger Twysden's Journal', *Archaeologia Cantiana*, 1861, vol., IV, pp. 145, 201; B. Schofield, ed., *The Knyvett Letters 1620–44*, Norfolk Record Society, 1949, vol. 20, pp. 110 and 120; M. Blundell, ed., *Cavalier. The Letters of William Blundell to his Friends*, 1933, pp. 10, 54.

169 A. Walker, *The Holy Life of Elizabeth Walker . . .*, 1690, pp. 34–5. E(dward) B(agshawe), 'The Life and Death of Mr Bolton', prefixed to *M. Bolton's Last Learned Worke of the Four Last Thinges*, 1632, sig. B6 verso.

170 Cf. D. Willen, 'Women in the Public Sphere in Early Modern England: the Case of the Urban Working Poor', *Sixteenth Century Journal*, 1988, vol. 19, pp. 559–75.

171 H. Smith, *A Preparative to Marriage*, 1591, p. 66; T. Pritchard, *The Glasse of Godly Love*, 1659, ed., F. J. Furnival, New Shakespeare Society, 6, no. 2, 1876, pp. 187–8.

172 D. M. Meads, ed., *The Diary of Lady Margaret Hoby 1599–1605*, 1930, *passim*.

173 C. Aspinall-Oglander, *Nunwell Symphony*, 1945, p. 39.

174 *The Memoirs of Sir Hugh Chomley*, 1870, p. 30; *A Breviate of the Life of Mrs Margaret Baxter*, 1681, 1826 ed., p. 87; See also E. Scarisbrick, *The Life of Lady Warner*, 1691, p. 22 and A. Jessopp, ed., *The Autobiography of the Hon. Roger North*, 1887, Appendix I.

175 Sir John Maclean, *The Berkeley Manuscripts: Lives of the Berkeleys*, ed. J. Smyth, 3 vols, 1883, II, p. 254.

176 Cf. J. Scheffler, 'The Prison Writings of Early Quaker Women', *Quaker History*, 1984, vol. 73 (2), pp. 25–37; C. Trevett, ed., *Women Speaking Justified and Other Quaker Writings about Women*, 1987.

177 Cited Spufford, *Contrasting Communities. English Villagers in the Sixteenth and Seventeenth Centuries*, 1974, Cambridge, p. 247; Bunyan, *Grace Abounding*, 1666, ed. R. Sharrock, 1966, p. 16.

178 Foxe, IV, p. 238. Cf. R. H. Bainton, 'John Foxe and the Ladies', in L. P. Buck and J. W. Zophy, eds, *The Social History of the Reformation*, 1972, Columbus, Ohio, pp. 205–22. See also C. W. Marsh, *The Family of Love in English Society 1500–1630*, 1993, Cambridge, pp. 21n., 147–8, 260–64, 281.

179 Chidley, DNB; E. B. Underhill, ed., *The Records of a Church of Christ Meeting in Broadmead Bristol 1640–87*, 1848, *passim*; K. Thomas, 'Women and the Civil War Sects', *Past and Present*, no. 13, 1968, p. 45; J. Browne, *The History of Congregationalism and Memorials of the Churches in Norfolk and Suffolk*, 1877, p. 254. See also C. Cross '"He-goats before the Flocks". A Note on the Part Played by Women in the Foundation of Some Civil War Churches', in G. J. Cuming and D. Baker, eds, *Popular Belief and Practice, Studies in Church History*, 1972, Oxford, vol. 8, pp. 195–202. For earlier examples, C. Cross, 'Great Reasoners in Scripture: The Activities of Women Lollards 1386–1520', in D. Baker, ed., *Medieval Women, Studies in Church History*, Subsidia 1, 1978, Oxford, pp. 359–80, and J. Davis, 'Joan of Kent: Lollardy and the English Reformation', *Journal of Ecclesiastical History*, 1982, vol. 33, pp. 225–33.

180 R. A. Marchant, *The Church Under the Law. Justice, Administration and Discipline in the Diocese of York*, 1969, Cambridge; R. Houlbrooke, *Church Courts and the People During the English Reformation 1520–70*, 1979, Oxford for the dioceses of Norwich and Winchester; J. Addy, *Sin and Society in the Seventeenth Century*, 1989, for the diocese of Chester.

181 Foxe, VIII, 388–90.

182 Cited R. Houlbrooke, *Church Courts and the People During the English Reformation 1520–1570*, 1979, Oxford, p. 247.

183 Walsingham to Watson, *Acts of the Privy Council, 1580–81*, New Ser. 12, p. 244.

184 T. F. Thistleton-Dyer, *Church Lore Gleanings*, 1891, p. 192. See also A. C. Heales, *The History and Law of Church Seats or Pews*, 2 vols, 1872, I, p. 137; M. Aston, 'Segregation in Church', *Studies in Church History*, 1990, vol. 27, pp. 237–94; D. Dymond, 'Sitting Apart in Church' in C. Rawcliffe *et al.*, eds, *Countries and Communities: Essays in East Anglian History Presented to Hassell Smith*, 1996, Norwich, pp. 312–24; T. More, *A Treatyse (Unfynyshed) Upon These Words of the Holy Scripture . . . Remember the Last Thynges and Thou Shalt Never Synne*, in *The Workes of Sir Thomas More in the English Tonge*, 1567, p. 88.

185 L. H. Carlson, *Martin Marprelate, Gentleman. Master Job Throckmorton Laid Open in His Colors*, 1981, San Marino, Calif., pp. 77–8. Cf. J. N. McCorkle, 'A Note Concerning "Mistress Crane" and Martin Marprelate Controversy', *The Library*, 4th Ser., 1931–2, vol. 12, pp. 276–83.

186 G. Fullerton, *The Life of Elizabeth, Lady Falkland 1585–1639*, 1883, pp. 153–4 and K. Weber, *Lucius Cary, Second Viscount Falkland*, 1940, New York, pp. 24–5; *The Troubles of Our Catholic Forefathers Related by Themselves*, 3rd Ser., 1887, vol. 3, pp. 381ff, 407, 418; C. S. Durrant, *A Link Between Flemish Mystics and English Martyrs*, 1925, p. 273; Hooker, *Laws of Ecclesiastical Polity*, 1597, Preface, sig. B3 recto; *The Works of Richard Hooker*, ed. E. Edelen, 5 vols, 1977–90, Cambridge, Mass., I, p. 19.

187 C. Read, *Mr Secretary Cecil and Queen Elizabeth*, 1955, p. 336.

188 Hobbes, *Behemoth*, 1679, ed. F. M. Tonnies with new introduction by M. M. Goldsmith, 1969, p. 21; Markham, *op. cit.*, p. 2.

189 Vicars, *The Schismatick Sifted, or A Picture of Independents Freshly and Fairly Washt Over Again*, 1646, p. 34. See also T. Edwards, *Antapologia*, 1644, p. 250.

190 Foxe, VIII, pp. 541, 544.

191 A. F. Scott Pearson, *Thomas Cartwright and Elizabeth Puritanism 1535–1603*, 1925, Cambridge, pp. 306–10. J. E. Neale, *Queen Elizabeth I*, 1973, Harmondsworth, p. 34. Locke, *Essay Concerning Human Understanding*, Book IV, xix, p. 14.

192 K. Thomas, 'Women and the Civil War Sects', *Past and Present*, 1968, no. 13, p. 44.

193 S. R. Gardiner, ed., *Reports of Cases in the Courts of Star Chamber and High Commission*, Camden Society, 1886, vol. 39, p. 309; Foxe, V, pp. 559–61; Hayward, *op. cit.*, sig. A3 recto.

194 Foxe, V, pp. 559–61. In 1545 she chided members of the University of Cambridge for writing to her in Latin rather than 'in our vulgar tongue, aptest for my intelligence'. The full text is in C. H. Cooper, *Annals of Cambridge*, 5 vols, 1842, Cambridge, I, p. 430. Cf. C. F. Hofman Jr, 'Catherine Parr as a Woman of Letters', *Huntingdon Library Quarterly*, 1960, vol. 23, pp. 349–67 at p. 361. Locke, *op. cit.*, Ep. Ded., sig. A4 recto.

195 W. Murdin, *A Collection of State Papers Relating to the Affairs in the Reign of Queen Elizabeth from 1571 to 1596*, 1759, p. 189. See also Elizabeth, Dowager Countess of Rutland's letter to Burghley, 10 November 1588, HMC, *Rutland Mss.*, 1888, p. 265, and *ibid.*, p. 263, letter to John Manners, 8 November, 1588. Tyler, *op. cit.*, sig. A3 recto. Cf. T. Krontiris, 'Breaking the Barriers of Genre and Gender: Margaret Tyler's Translation of the Mirrour of Knighthood', *English Literary Renaissance*, 1988, vol. 18, pp. 19–39; *Poems of Anne Finch, Countess of Winchelsea*, ed. J. M. Murry, 1928, p. 24.

196 L. Pollock, ' "Teach Her to Live Under Obedience": The Making of Women in the Upper Ranks of Early Modern England', *Continuity and Change*, 1989, vol. 4, p. 234, citing Warwickshire Record Office, Throckmorton Mss, CR1998, Box 60, Folder 3; R. B. Gardiner, ed., *The Letters of Dorothy Wadham*, 1904, p. 40.

197 D. Parsons, ed., *The Diary of Sir Henry Slingsby*, 1836, pp. 292, 294; D. Gardiner, ed., *The Oxinden and Peyton Letters 1607–42*, 1933, pp. 120–1; Carey, *op. cit.*, Preface To The Reader.

198 See for example, C. Durston, *The Family in the English Revolution*, 1989, Oxford, chap. 5. For general discussion see P. Zagorin, ed., *Ways of Lying: Dissimulation, Persecution and Conformity in Early Modern Europe*, 1992, Cambridge, Mass.

199 T. T. Lewis, ed., *The Letters of Brilliana Harley*, Camden Society, 1854, vol. 58, pp. xix–xx, 207. HMC, *Bath Mss*, I, pp. 1–33, 'A True Relation of the Siege of Brampton Castle in the County of Hereford'.

200 DNB, George Savile. See also Charlotte, Countess of Derby, in the siege of Lathom House, G. Ormerod, ed., *Tracts Relating to Military Proceedings in Lancashire During the Great Civil War*, Chetham Society, 1844, vol. 2, pp. 159–86, and Mary Charleton in the siege of Apsley Castle, Shropshire, in S. Clarke, *Lives of Sundry Eminent Persons in This Later Age*, 1683, pp. 181, 184–9.

201 J. Sprigge, *Anglia Rediviva*, 1647, p. 139; J. Pruett, *The Parish Clergy Under the Later Stuarts: The Leicestershire Experience*, 1978, Urbana, pp. 16–17; J. Nichols, *The History and Antiquities of Leicestershire*, 4 vols, 1795–1815, II (2), pp. 650–2.

202 *Cal. S. P. Dom. 1547–80*, 1856, pp. 200ff, 301 205, 409, 428, 489; *Memoirs of the Life of Colonel Hutchinson*, ed. J. Sutherland, 1973, p. 261; *The Memoirs of Anne Lady Halkett and Anne Lady Fanshawe*, ed. J. Loftis, 1979, Oxford, p. 135.

203 M. K. Jones and M. G. Underwood, *The King's Mother. Lady Margaret Beaufort,*

Countess of Richmond and Derby, 1992, Cambridge, p. 163; *Cal. S. P. Dom. 1591–4*, pp. 350–51 and *ibid., 1595–7*, pp. 147–8, 310.

204 G. C. Williamson, *The Lady Anne Clifford*, 1922, Kendal, *passim*; G. H. Radford, 'Lady Howard of Fitzford', *Transactions of the Devonshire Association*, 1890, vol. 22, pp. 66–110.

205 *A True Copie of the Petition of the Gentlewomen and Tradesmens Wives in and About the Citie of London*, 1641. See also E. A. McArthur, 'Women Petitioners and the Long Parliament', *English Historical Review*, 1909, vol. 24, pp. 698–709; K. Thomas, 'Women and the Civil War Sects', *Past and Present*, 1958, no. 13, pp. 42–62, and P. Higgins, 'The Reactions of Women with Special Reference to Women Petitioners', in B. Manning, ed., *Politics, Religion and the English Civil War*, 1973, pp. 179–222.

206 J. C. Jeaffreson, ed., *Middlesex County Records*, 1886–92, III, pp. 82, 87–8, 90; P. H. Hardacre, *The Royalists During the Puritan Revolution*, 1956, The Hague, pp. 17–18; A. Fraser, *The Weaker Vessel. Women's Lot in Seventeenth Century England*, 1984, pp. 235–9.

2 THE MEDIA

1 Greenham, 'Of the Good Education of Children', in *Works of Richard Greenham* ed. H. Holland, 1599, p. 160; Milton, *Of Education*, 1644, p. 2. See also J. Dury, *The Reformed School*, 1650, ed. C. Webster, 1970, Cambridge, p. 148.

2 N. Pettit, *The Heart Prepared: Grace and Conversion in Puritan Spiritual Life*, 1996, New Haven.

3 As, for example, in L. Lloyd, *The Choyce of Jewels*, 1607, p. 7.

4 N. H. Nicholas, *Memoirs of the Life and Times of Sir Christopher Hatton*, 1847, p. 309.

5 T. Pomfret, *The Life of the Right Honourable and Religious Lady Christian(a), Late Countess Dowager of Devonshire*, 1685, pp. 36–7.

6 'Doomsday or The Great Day of Judgement', 1637, p. 107. See also R. Sibbes, *Works*, ed. A. B. Grosart, 6 vols, 1862–4, Edinburgh, VI, p. 520.

7 Hooker, *The Laws of Ecclesiastical Polity*, 1597, Preface, sig. B3 recto; *The Works of Richard Hooker*, ed. G. Edelen, 5 vols, 1977–90, Cambridge, Mass., I, p. 17.

8 *The Two Liturgies AD 1549 and AD 1552*, ed. J. Ketley, Parker Society, 1844, Cambridge, p. 527; *Cranmer's Miscellaneous Writings and Letters*, ed. J. E. Cox, Parker Society, 1848, Cambridge, pp. 18–19. See also C. Parr *The Lamentacion of a Sinner*, 1548, sig. Gv recto, and S. Hieron, *The Dignitie of Scripture* in *The Sermons of Master Hieron*, 1624, pp. 72–3, amongst many others.

9 B. Smalley, *The Study of the Bible in the Middle Ages*, 1952, Oxford, pp. 247ff, and G. R. Evans, 'Wyclif on Literal and Metaphorical', in A. Hudson and M. Wilks, eds, *From Ockham to Wyclif, Studies in Church History*, Subsidia 5, 1987, Oxford, pp. 259–66.

10 Cf. C. W. Dugmore, *The Mass and the English Reformers*, 1958; P. N. Brooks, *Thomas Cranmer's Doctrine of the Eucharist*, 1965; J. E. Booty, 'Preparation for the Lord's Supper in Elizabethan England', *Anglican Theological Review*, 1967, vol. 49, pp. 131–48; J. P. Boulton, 'The Limits of Formal Religion; the Administration of Holy Communion in Late Elizabethan England', *London Journal*, 1984, vol. 10, pp. 135–53.

11 E. Hall, *Henry VIII*, ed. C. Whibley, 2 vols, 1904, II, p. 356. See also H. C. Porter, 'The Nose of Wax: Scripture and the Spirit from Erasmus to Milton', *TRHS*, 5th Ser., 1964, vol. 14, pp. 155–74, for a consideration of the metaphor

'nose of wax' – pushing scripture in all directions to suit particular interpretations.

12   L. Wright, *The Pilgrimage to Paradise Compiled for the Direction, Comfort and Resolution of God's Poor Distressed Children*, 1591, sig. A3 recto–verso.

13   See, for example, G. R. Evans, *Problems of Authority in the Reformation Debate*, 1992, Cambridge; R. Pogson, 'God's Law and Man's: Stephen Gardiner and the Problem of Loyalty', in C. Cross *et al.*, eds, *Law and Government Under the Tudors: Essays Presented to Sir Geoffrey Elton*, 1988, Cambridge, pp. 67–89.

14   Hughes and Larkin, II, p. 127. Cf. the similar 'one uniform manner or course of praying throughout all our dominions', Preface to 1545 Primer, in *Miscellaneous Writings and Letters of Thomas Cranmer*, ed. J. E. Cox, Parker Society, 1846, Cambridge, p. 497.

15   Milton, Sonnet XII, in *Works of John Milton*, ed. F. M. Patterson, 1931, New York, vol. 1(1), p. 63; 'Reply of Bishop Ridley to Bishop Hooper on the Vestment Controversy', in *The Writings of John Bradford*, ed. A. Townsend, Parker Society, 1843, Cambridge, vol. 2, p. 377. Cf. E. Sandys, *Sermons*, ed. J. Ayre, Parker Society, 1842, Cambridge, p. 49.

16   J. G. Nichols, *Narratives of the Days of the Reformation*, Camden Society, 1859, vol. 77, p. 349.

17   Frere and Kennedy, p. 35. The edition in question was Coverdale's revision of the 1537 Matthew Bible. The proclamation was repeated in 1541 and 1547, Hughes and Larkin, I, pp. 296–8 and 395.

18   T. Becon, *Works*, ed. J. Ayre, Parker Society, 1843, Cambridge, vol. 1, p. 38; *Miscellaneous Writings and Letters of Thomas Cranmer*, ed. J. E. Cox, Parker Society, 1846, Cambridge, pp. 512–13.

19   The First Book of Homilies was published in 1547, and was reissued with additions in 1563; J. Griffiths, ed., *The Two Books of Homilies Appointed to Be Read in Churches*, 2 vols, 1859, Oxford; R. B. Bond, ed., *Certaine Sermons and Homilies 1547*, 1987, Toronto; Hughes and Larkin, I, 402. Cf. J. N. Wall, 'The "Book of Homilies" of 1547 and the Continuity of English Humanism in the Sixteenth Century', *Anglican Theological Review*, 1976, vol. 58, pp. 75–87, and S. Wabunda, 'Bishops and the Provision of Homilies 1520 to 1547', *Sixteenth Century Journal*, 1994, vol. 25, pp. 551–66.

20   L. B. Smith, *Tudor Prelates and Politics 1536–58*, 1953, Princeton, p. 245.

21   As in J. Standish, *A Discourse Wherein is Debated Wheyther it be Expedient that the Scripture Should be in English for All Men to Reade that Wyll*, 1554, sig. Hiii verso, and *passim*.

22   In a letter to Lord Lisle, 13 July 1539, *Cranmer's Miscellaneous Writings and Letters*, ed. J. B. Cox, Parker Society, 1848, Cambridge, p. 391.

23   As illustrated, for example, on the title page of Foxe's 1570 edition of *Actes and Monumentes*. For later examples see M. Spufford, *Contrasting Communities. English Villagers in the Sixteenth and Seventeenth Centuries*, 1974, Cambridge, p. 263; M. Spufford, *Small Books and Pleasant Histories*, 1981, p. 34. As late as the 1650s the Duke of Newcastle was still complaining that 'The Bible in English under every weaver's and chambermaid's arm hath done much harm', *The Life of the Thrice Noble . . . William Cavendish*, ed. C. H. Firth, 1886, p. 188.

24   Foxe, V, p. 535.

25   D. Cressy, *Literacy and the Social Order*, 1980; E. L. Eisenstein, *The Printing Press as an Agency of Social Change*, 2 vols, 1979, Cambridge; H. J. Graff, ed., *Literacy and Social Development in the West*, 1981, Cambridge. Historians' quantifications of literacy

levels are, of course, based on an ability to write one's name on a particular occasion. Reading literacy, more important to our purpose, is not susceptible to such arithmetic.

26 2 Tim. 4.2, Geneva Bible wording.

27 Latimer, *Sermons*, ed. G. B. Corrie, Parker Society, 1844, Cambridge, p. 200. A similar formulation had been used by John Fisher, *A Sermon Had at St Paul's 1526*, sig. Dii verso, cited M. Dowling, 'John Fisher and the Preaching Ministry', *Archives for Reformation History*, 1991, vol. 82, p. 294, as also by John Hooper, *Early Writings*, ed. S. Carr, Parker Society, 1843, Cambridge, pp. 351, 451; H. Smith, *Thirteene Sermons Upon Several Texts of Scripture*, 1592, sigs A5 recto, B3 verso, and R. Greenham, *Works*, 5th ed., 1612, pp. 708, 834.

28 Donne, *Sermons*, V, p. 55. Cf. R. W. Scribner, 'Oral Culture and the Transmission of Reformation Ideas', *History of European Ideas*, 1984, vol. 5, pp. 237–56, and B. Crockett, '"Holy Cozenage" and the Renaissance Cult of the Ear', *Sixteenth Century Journal*, 1993, vol. 24, pp. 47–65. The proof-text was Rom. 10.17.

29 J. Strype, *Life of . . . Edmund Grindal*, 1821, Oxford, p. 562; Hughes and Larkin, II, p. 127.

30 J. Strype, *Annals of the Reformation*, 2 vols, 1824, Oxford, vol. I (ii), pp. 391–2; Hughes and Larkin, II, p. 103. For licensing and control, cf. W. P. Haugaard, *Elizabeth and the English Reformation*, 1970, Cambridge, pp. 163, 167, 214 and *passim*.

31 E. Cardwell, *Documentary Annals of the Reformed Church of England*, 1884, 2 vols, Oxford, vol. II, pp. 149, 178, 201, 230; 'Royal Directions to Preachers, 1622', in K. Fincham, ed., *Visitation Articles and Injunctions of the Early Stuart Church*, vol. 1, 1994, pp. 211–14; C. Petrie, ed., *Letters, Speeches and Proclamations of King Charles I*, 1935, p. 200.

32 *Op. cit.*, 1605, 10th ed., 1614, p. 220. For examples of parishioners and church wardens reporting the total lack of sermons in the parish, J. S. Purvis, ed., *Tudor Parish Documents in the Diocese of York*, 1948, pp. 20, 22, 134, and J. E. Williams, ed., *Bishop Redman's Visitation 1597*, Norfolk Record Society, 1946, vol. 18, pp. 40, 45, 62, 135.

33 Latimer, *Sermons*, ed. G. E. Corrie, Parker Society, 1844, Cambridge, p. 201. John Angier was making the same complaint in the 1640s when he remarked 'some sleep from the beginning to the end . . . as if the Sabbath were made only to recover that sleep they have lost during the week', O. Heywood, *Life of John Angier*, Chetham Society, NS, 1937, vol. 97, pp. 148–50.

34 N. Tyacke, *Anti-Calvinists. The Rise of English Arminianism c.1590–1640*, 1987, Oxford; P. Lake, 'The Laudian Style: Order and the Pursuit of the Beauty of Holiness in the 1630s', in K. Fincham, ed., *The Early Stuart Church 1603–42*, 1993, pp. 161–85; K. A. Newman, 'Holiness in Beauty? Roman Catholics, Arminians and the Aesthetics of Religion in Early Modern England', *Studies in Church History*, 1992, vol. 28, pp. 303–12; I. M. Calder, *The Activities of the Puritan Faction in the Church of England 1625–1633*, 1957.

35 *Op cit.*, sig. Bi recto. For reading as a cooperative activity, cf. M. Aston, *Lollards and Reformers*, 1984, pp. 106–8, 194–5.

36 *Works of John Whitgift*, ed. J. Ayre, Parker Society, 1853, Cambridge, vol. 3, p. 39.

37 *The Practice of Christianitie*, 1603, p. 598.

38 *Sabbathum Veteris et Novi Testamenti or The True Doctrine of the Sabbath*, 1606, p. 383.

39 Foxe, 1583 ed., pp. 2049–52.

40 W. Hinde, *A Faithfull Remonstrance of the Holy Life and Happy Death of John Bruen of Bruen Stapleford in the County of Cheshire*, 1645, pp. 56–7; Allestree, *Whole Duty of Man*, 1659, 1684 ed., p. 118.

41 T. Watt, 'Piety in the Pedlar's Pack: Continuity and Change 1578–1630' in M. Spufford (ed.), *The World of Rural Dissenters 1520–1725*, 1995, Cambridge, pp. 235–72

42 L. F. Lupton, *A History of the Geneva Bible*, 1966; L. E. Berry, *The Geneva Bible: A Facsimile of the 1560 edition*, 1969, Madison, Wisc.; D. Danner, 'The Contribution of the Geneva Bible of 1560 to the English Protestant Tradition', *Sixteenth Century Journal*, 1981, vol. 12, pp. 5–18; C. Eason, *The Geneva Bible. Notes on its Production and Distribution*, 1937, Dublin.

43 J. C. Cox, *Churchwardens' Accounts for the Fourteenth Century to the Close of the Seventeenth Century*, 1913, pp. 117ff.

44 J. E. Foster, ed., *Churchwardens' Accounts of St Mary the Great, Cambridge 1504–1635*, Cambridge Antiquarian Society, 1905, vol. 35, p. 191; Cox, *Churchwardens' Accounts*, p. 118.

45 R. Davies, *A Memoir of the York Press*, 1868, p. 350; M. Reed, ed., *The Ipswich Probate Inventories 1553–1631*, Suffolk Record Society, 1st Ser., 1854, vol. 58, p. 5, and 18–19, 69–70. See also J. Eales, *Puritans and Roundheads: The Harleys of Brampton Bryan and the Outbreak of the Civil War*, 1990, Cambridge, especially chap. 3, 'The Harleys and the Godly Community'.

46 C. R. Manning, ed., *State Papers Relating to the Custody of Princess Elizabeth at Woodstock 1554*, Norfolk Archaeology, 1855, vol. 4, p. 172.

47 For the book's printing history see W. Haller, *Foxe's Book of Martyrs and the Elect Nation*, 1963, and the checklist in D. M. Loades, ed., *John Foxe and the English Reformation*, 1997, Aldershot.

48 Loades, *op. cit.*, p. 4; W. B. Willcox, *Gloucestershire 1590–1640*, 1940, New Haven, p. 235; *The General Accounts of the Churches of Chipping Campden 1626–1907*, Campden Records Series, 1992, vol. 1, p. 202.

49 J. W. Burgon, *The Life of Thomas Gresham*, 2 vols, 1839, II, p. 415; D. M. Meads, ed., *The Diary of Lady Margaret Hoby*, 1930, pp. 69, 74, 87; T. C. Croker, ed., *The Autobiography of Mary Countess of Warwick*, 1848, p. 22; W. Harrison and W. Leigh, *Deaths Advantage Little Regarded ... and The Souls Solace Against Sorrow ... Two Sermons Preached at the Buriall of Mistris Katherine Brettergh*, 1602, p. 9; P. Seaver, *Wallington's World. A Puritan Artisan in Seventeenth Century London*, 1985, p. 62; T. T. Lewis, ed., *The Letters of Brilliana Harley*, Camden Society, 1st Ser., 1854, vol. 58, p. 5; J. F. Mozley, *John Foxe and His Book*, 1940, p. 180. Foxe had recorded the Marian martydom of Nicholas' ancestor, Dr Robert Ferrar, Bishop of Durham, Foxe, VII, p. 26. A. Walker, *The Holy Life of Elizabeth Walker*, 1690, pp. 71–3.

50 W. Haller, *Foxe's Book of Martyrs and the Elect Nation*, 1963, p. 221; L. B. Wright, *Religion and Empire*, 1943, Chapel Hill, NC, p. 53. A. G. Watson, *The Library of Simonds D'Ewes*, 1966, p. 166; 'A Dyurnall or Catalogue of all my Actions and Expenses from 1st January 1646', ed. H. J. Morehouse, Surtees Society, 1877, vol. 65, pp. 65, 79, 90, 104; W. L. Sachse, ed., *The Diary of Roger Lowe of Ashton-in-Makerfield, Lancashire, 1663–74*, 1938, p. 99; E. Nicholson, 'Eighteenth-Century Foxe. Evidence for the Impact of the Book of Martyrs in the Long Eighteenth Century', in D. M. Loades, ed., *John Foxe and the English Reformation*, 1997, Aldershot, p. 152.

51 J. A. F. Thompson, 'John Foxe and Some Sources for Lollard History: Notes for a Critical Appraisal', *Studies in Church History*, 1965, vol. 2, pp. 251–7;

P. Collinson, 'Truth and Legend: the Veracity of John Foxe's *Book of Martyrs*', in A. C. Duke and A. Tomse, eds, *Clio's Mirror. Historiography in the Netherlands. Britain and the Netherlands*, 1985, vol. 8, pp. 31–54; J. King, 'Fiction and Fact in Foxe's *Book of Martyrs*', in D. M. Loades, ed., *op. cit.*, pp. 12–25. For an early attempt, T. Fuller, *The Holy and Prophane State*, 1644, p. 310.

52 The text was for the first time organised in numbered verses, with chapter and page headings together with maps, illustrations, and marginal glosses on particular passages. Cf. M. Betteridge, ' "The Bitter Notes": the Geneva Bible and its Annotations', *Sixteenth Century Journal*, 1983, vol. 14, pp. 41–62; R. C(leaver), *A Godly Fourme of Household Gouvernement*, 1598, pp. 305,38. The same point is made in R. Greenham, *A Godly Exhortation and Fruitfull Admonition to Vertuous Parents and Modest Matrones*, 1584, sig. Svi recto–verso, and was repeated in R. Baxter, *The Reformed Pastor*, 1655, p. 59. For earlier examples of the point see Erasmus, *De Pueris Instituendis*, 1529, in *Collected Works of Erasmus*, vol. 26, 1985, Toronto, pp. 306–9, 318–19; T. Elyot, *The Boke Named the Governour*, 1531, ed. H. H. S. Croft, 2 vols, 1880, I, pp. 133ff; T. Taverner, *A Catechisme or Institution of Christian Religion*, 1539, sig. Aii verso.

53 W. A. Pantin, *The English Church in the Fourteenth Century*, 1955, Cambridge, pp. 220ff; M. Deanesley, 'Vernacular Books in England in the Fourteenth and Fifteenth Centuries', *Modern Languages Review*, 1920, vol. 15, pp. 349–58; A. Hudson, 'Some Aspects of Lollard Book Production', *Studies in Church History*, 1972, vol. 9, pp. 147–57; H. G. Pfander, 'Dives et Pauper', *The Library*, 4th Ser., 1933–4, vol. 14, pp. 229–312; S. McSheffrey, 'Literacy and the Gender Gap in the Late Middle Ages. Women and Reading in Lollard Communities', in L. Smith and H. M. Taylor, eds, *Women, the Book and the Godly*, 1996, Cambridge, pp. 157–70.

54 See the modern translation by H. Rippenberger and G. Ryan, 2 vols, 1993, Princeton, NJ. For examples of copies in parish churches, J. C. Cox, *Church-wardens' Accounts from the Fourteenth Century to the Close of the Seventeenth Century*, 1913, pp. 106–11.

55 D. Crane, 'English Translations of the *Imitatio Christi* in the Sixteenth and Seventeenth Centuries', *Recusant History*, 1975, vol. 13, pp. 79–100, and E. K. Hudson, 'English Protestants and the *Imitatio Christi* 1580–1620', *Sixteenth Century Journal*, 1988, vol. 19, pp. 541–58. For comparison see F. H. Higman, *Piety and the People. Religious Printing in French 1511–1551*, 1996, Aldershot.

56 The best survey is H. C. White, *The Tudor Books of Private Devotion*, 1951, Madison, Wisc. See also E. L. Eisenstein, *The Printing Press as an Agent of Change*, 2 vols, 1979, Cambridge, I, chap. 4. The importance of the press was noted by Foxe in his digression, 'The Invention and Benefit of Printing', Foxe, III, pp. 718–22.

57 Wastell, *op cit.*, sig. A5 recto–verso.

58 Adams, 'England's Sicknesse', in *The Works of Thomas Adams*, 1636, pp. 317–18. Cf. T. Taylor, *Christs Combate and Conquest . . .*, 1615, Cambridge, p. 124.

59 M. Spufford, *Small Books and Pleasant Histories*, 1981, especially chap. VIII, 'Small Godly Books: Popular Religion'; T. Watt, *Cheap Print and Popular Piety 1550–1640*, 1981, Cambridge. For the European scene, M. U. Chrisman, 'From Polemic to Propaganda: the Development of Mass Persuasion in the Late Sixteenth Century', *Archives for Reformation History*, 1982, vol. 73, pp. 175–95.

60 W. Chappell and J. W. Ebsworth, eds, *The Roxburghe Ballads*, 9 vols, 1871–99, Hertford; J. W. Ebsworth, ed., *The Bagford Ballads*, 3 vols, 1876–80, Hertford; A. Clark, ed., *The Shirburn Ballads 1585–1616*, 1907, Oxford; H. B. Rollins, ed., *The Pepys Ballads*, 8 vols, 1929–32, Cambridge, Mass.

61 For a consideration of contemporary debates about the content and use of the ballad form see K. Charlton, ' "False Fonde Bookes, Ballades and Rimes": An Aspect of Informal Education in Early Modern England', *History of Education Quarterly*, 1987, vol. 27, pp. 449–71.

62 Spufford, *Small Books*, p. 213; E. Duffy, 'The Godly and the Multitude in Stuart England', *The Seventeenth Century*, 1986, vol. 1, pp. 31–5.

63 *Remains of Myles Coverdale*, ed. G. Pearson, Parker Society, 1846, Cambridge, pp. 537, 568.

64 Preface to *David's Harp* . . ., 1542, in *Early Works of Thomas Becon*, ed. J. Ayres, Parker Society, 1843, Cambridge, p. 266.

65 Rogers, *A Garden of Spiritual Flowers*, 5th ed., 1609, sig. G7 verso; Bayly, *The Practise of Pietie*, 3rd ed., 1613, pp. 464–5, 467; Wither, *A Preparation to the Psalter*, 1619, pp. 3, 5.

66 Barton, *A View of Many Errors and Gross Absurdities in the Old Translation of the Psalms in English Metre*, 1656, *passim*. For comprehensive surveys see R. Zim, *English Metrical Psalms: Poetry as Praise and Prayer 1535–1601*, 1987, Cambridge, and R. A. Leaver, *'Goostly Psalmes and Spiritual Songes': English and Dutch Metrical Psalms from Coverdale to Utterhove 1535–66*, 1991, Oxford. See also P. L. Hieray, *Music and the Reformation in English 1549 to 1600*, 1967 and N. Temperley, *The Music of the English Parish Church*, 2 vols, 1979, Cambridge.

67 G. Gifford, *A Briefe Discourse of . . . Countrie Divinitie*, 1582, fol. 72 verso; H. Isaacson, *Institutiones Piae or Directions to Pray*, 2nd ed., 1633, p. 74; R. Allestree, *The Ladies Calling*, 1673, p. 127; F. Norton, *The Applause of Virtue*, 1705, p. 196; T. Cooper, *The Mystery of Witchcraft*, 1617, p. 351. Cf. C. Garrett, 'The Rhetoric of Supplication: Prayer Theory in Seventeenth-Century England', *Renaissance Quarterly*, 1993, vol. 46, pp. 328–57.

68 Parr, *op cit.*, sig. A2 recto–verso and p. 7.

69 In his section on closets, P. Thornton, *Seventeenth Century Interior Decoration in England, France and Holland*, 1978, New Haven, pp. 296ff, says nothing about their religious use.

70 Heywood, *op. cit.*, sigs A2 recto, A3 recto, A4 verso and p. 84.

71 Featley, *op. cit.*, sig. *3 verso. The British Library copy has inscribed on its flyleaf 'Hanna Curtis wishes this whas [sic] her book but the ownere of it is my cus White which I love derely and senserely'. On the back flyleaf 'Hannah Curtisis her book given me by my dear cusin White'. Cf. the similar example given in Collinson, *Godly People: Essays on English Protestantism and Puritanism*, 1983, facing p. 527.

72 For example, in T. Bentley, *The Monument of Matrones*, 1582, a three-volume collection of devotions and prayers exhaustively covering every aspect of a woman's life – a 'domesticall librarie' as he called it – there are 33 prayers devoted to pregnancy and birth.

73 BL Egerton Ms. 607, *passim*. See also the prayers transcribed by Katherine Austen in BL Addl Ms. 4454.

74 Bayly, *op. cit.*, 1685 edition.

75 Dent, *op. cit.*, sig. A2 verso. On Dent see M. Hussey, 'Arthur Dent, Rector of South Shoebury 1553–1603', *Essex Review*, 1948, vol. 57, pp. 196–201, and E. K. Hudson, 'The "Plaine Man's" Pastor: Arthur Dent and the Cultivation of Popular Piety in Early Seventeenth-Century England', *Albion*, 1993, vol. 25, pp. 23–36.

76 Vaughan, *The Golden Grove Moralized in Three Books: A Worke Very Necessary for all*

Such as Would Know How to Governe Themselves, Their Houses and Their Countrey, 1599, 1608 ed., sig. Z7 recto.
77 Rhodes, *The Countrie Mans Comfort or Religious Recreations, Fitte for All Well-disposed Persons*, 1588, 1637 ed., sig. A2 recto–verso.
78 Cf. P. Elmen, 'Richard Allestree and *The Whole Duty of Man*, 1658', *The Library*, 5th Ser., 1951, vol. 6, pp. 19–27.
79 P. Collinson, *The Religion of Protestants. The Church in English Society 1559–1625*, 1982, Oxford, p. 191.
80 J. Downame, *The Guide to Godlynesse*, 1622 p. 626. E. Warren, *Spiritual Thrift or Meditations*, 1647, pp. 10–11.

3 THE METHODS

1 Cf. P. Saenger, 'Silent Reading: Its Impact on Late Medieval Script and Society', *Viator*, 1982, vol. 13, pp. 367–414; A. Manguel, 'The Silent Reader', *A History of Reading*, 1996, pp. 41–53, W. J. Ong, *The Presence of the Word. Some Prologomena for Cultural and Religious History*, 1967, New Haven, pp. 271ff.
2 For general discussion see W. A. Graham, *Beyond the Written Word: Oral Aspects of Scripture in the History of Religion*, 1987, Cambridge, especially pp. 140ff.
3 Queen Elizabeth to Matthew Parker, 22 January 1560, in *The Correspondence of Matthew Parker*, ed. J. Bruce, Parker Society, 1853, Cambridge, p. 133.
4 For example, 1536 and 1538 Royal Injunctions, repeated 1547, Frere and Kennedy, II, pp. 6–7, 36–7, 116, and subsequent diocesan injunctions.
5 Smith, *Thirteene Sermons*, 1592, sigs B3 verso, B5 recto, C8 verso, D2 recto. See also R. Greenham, 'Of Hearing God's Word', in *Workes*, 1612, pp. 707–11, 834–6, and Donne, *Sermons*, VII, p. 327.
6 For example, later editions of L. Bayly, *Practise of Pietie* and T. Doolittle, *A Plain Method of Catechizing*, 1698, sig. A1 verso. Cf. E. Rosen, 'The Invention of Eyeglasses', *Journal of the History of Medicine and Allied Sciences*, 1956, vol. 11, pp. 13–46, 183–218, and compare Dürer's portrait of his mother reading without glasses with Rembrandt's of his mother with glasses.
7 Cf. A. W. Tuer, *The History of the Horn Book*, 2 vols, 1896.
8 H. J. Chaytor, *From Script to Print*, 1945, Cambridge, p. 6. The definitive text is I. Michael, *The Teaching of English from the Sixteenth Century to 1870*, 1987, Cambridge, esp. chaps 2 and 3.
9 Mulcaster, *The First Part of the Elementarie*, 1582, pp. 55, 228, 253.
10 Kempe, *The Education of Children in Learning*, 1558, sigs F2 recto–3 recto.
11 Coote *The English Schoole-Maister*, 1596, sig. B2 verso; Clement, *The Petie Scole*, 1587, sig. B1 verso.
12 Mulcaster, *Positions*, 1581, p. 177.
13 Brinsley, *Ludus Literarius*, 1612, pp. 15–20. Hoole, *New Discovery of the Olde Arte of Teaching School*, 1660, pp. 33–40.
14 The 1702 3rd edition copy in the British Library is inscribed 'Ellen Heap her book'.
15 Ellis, *op. cit.*, To the Reader.
16 Locke, *Some Thoughts Concerning Education*, 1693, pp. 128ff. Such a device had earlier been recommended by Sir Hugh Plat, *Jewel House of Art and Nature*, 1653, p. 42.
17 Cf. C. M. Eire, *War Against Idols. The Reformation of Worship from Erasmus to Calvin*, 1986, New York, pp. 315–16; Manguel, *History of Reading*, pp. 95–107; P. Collinson, *The Birthpangs of Protestant England*, 1988, Basingstoke, pp. 119–20.

18 R. McLean, *Pictorial Alphabets*, 1969, starts with Holbein and then jumps forward to 1820.

19 See also J. Newton, *The School of Pastime for Young Children*, 1669; T. White, *A Little Book for Little Children*, 1674; T. Ellis, *The English School*, 5th ed., 1680.

20 Bourne, *The True Way of a Christian*, 1622, p. 18, a 'newly revised and enlarged' version of the sermon; Gouge, *Domesticall Dueties*, 3rd ed., 1634, p. 548; R. B. Bond, ed., *Certaine Sermons and Homilies 1547 . . .*, 1987, Toronto, p. 65, as also the Homily 'Against Contention and Brawling', *ibid.*, p. 193; Taylor, *A Funeral Sermon Preached at the Obsequies of the Lady Frances Countess Carbery*, 1650, p. 27.

21 Vaughan, *op. cit.*, sig. B1 recto.

22 Bayly, *op. cit.*, p. 312.

23 Patrick, *op. cit.*, p. 312.

24 Whitford, *op. cit.*, sig. Fiv verso.

25 Culverwell, *op. cit.*, sig. A3 recto; Beecher, *op. cit.*, sig. A1 recto.

26 Allen, *op. cit.*, sig. A3 verso.

27 See also R. Robinson, *Certain Selected Histories for Christian Recreations with their Several Moralizations Brought into English Verse*, 1576; H. Clapham, *A Briefe of the Bible Drawne First into English Poesy and then Illustrated by Apte Annotations*, 1596, Edinburgh, and J. Weever, *An Agnus Dei*, 1601, a rhymed version of the life of Christ.

28 Wastell, *op. cit.*, sig. A4 verso.

29 Rhodes, *op. cit.*, sig. A2 recto and A3 recto. See also Francis Quarles' verse paraphrases of various books of the Bible, published during the 1620s and collected in his *Divine Poems*, 1630. The 'divine poems' of George Herbert and George Wither were, of course, on a quite different level. For general discussion see J. N. King, 'Recent Studies in Protestant Poetics', *English Literary Renaissance*, 21, 1991, pp. 283–307, and L. L. Martz, *The Poetry of Meditation*, 1954, New Haven.

30 Bunyan, *op. cit.*, p. 49 and *passim*.

31 Foxe, VIII, p. 541; J. E. Neale, *Queen Elizabeth I*, Pelican ed., 1971, p. 314; Adams, *Works*, 1629, p. 76.

32 From an extensive literature, cf. E. A. Havelock, *The Muse Learns to Write: Reflections on Orality and Literature from Antiquity to the Present*, 1986, New Haven; W. J. Ong, *Orality and Literacy. The Technologising of the Word*, 1982; R. Finnegan, *Oral Literacy in Africa*, 1982, Oxford; M. T. Clanchy, *From Memory to the Written Record: England 1066–1307*, 1979; M. J. Carruthers, *The Book of Memory in Medieval Culture*, 1990, Cambridge; F. A. Yates, *The Art of Memory*, 1966.

33 Sparke, *op. cit.*, p. 4; J. Raine, ed., *The Injunctions and Other Ecclesiastical Proceedings of Richard Barnes Bishop of Durham 1675–87*, Surtees Society, 1850, vol. 22, pp. 15–16; Frere and Kennedy, *passim*, and K. Fincham, ed., *Visitation Articles and Injunctions of the Early Stuart Church*, 2 vols, 1994, 1995, *passim*.

34 The definitive study is I. Green, *The Christian's ABC. Catechisms and Catechising in England c.1530–1640*, 1996, Oxford.

35 Inman, *op. cit.*, sig. A2 recto–verso; Doolittle, *op. cit.*, sig. A1 verso.

36 Ball, *op. cit.*, To the Reader.

37 Greenham, *Workes*, 1599, 5th ed., 1612, p. 664.

38 R. Cawdrey, *A Short and Fruitfull Treatise of the Profit and Necessitie of Catechising . . . Hereunto Added . . . A Brief Method of Catechising . . .*, 1604, sig. Avi recto, Avii recto, Biii verso. See also Cawdrey's letter on the subject to Burghley in Strype, *Aylmer*, p. 89.

39 Egerton, *op. cit.*, p. 3, sig. A3 verso, and *passim*. For discussion see J. Booty,

'Preparation for the Lord's Supper in Elizabethan England', *Anglican Theological Review*, vol. 49, 1967, pp. 31–48.

40 Elyot, *op. cit.*, sig. Fiv recto.

41 Bullinger, trans. Coverdale, *The Christen State of Matrimony*, 1541, fol. lix verso. See also H. Rhodes, *The Booke of Nurture*, 1550, sig. Aii recto; R. C(leaver), *A Godly Form of Household Gouvernement*, 1598, p. 260; Gouge *Domesticall Dueties*, p. 542; Herbert, *Jacula Prudentium*, 1640, in *Remains of George Herbert*, 1836, p. 184.

42 Kempe, *The Education of Children in Learning*, 1588, sig. E3 verso.

43 Bolton, *Some General Directions for a Comfortable Walking with God*, 1625, p. 19. Hilder, *Conjugall Counsell*, 1653, p. 123.

44 Chaderton, *An Excellent and Godly Sermon . . . preached at St Paules*, 1578, fol. 6 recto–verso; Hake, *A Touchstone for This Time Present*, 1574, sig. Ciii verso.

45 Woodward, *A Childes Patrimony*, 1640, pp. 12, 14; *Sermons* IV, p. 100.

46 *A Memorial of Walter Mildmay to his son Anthony*, 1893, Apethorpe; D. Parsons, ed., *The Diary of Sir Henry Slingsby*, 1836, pp. 215, 218; Verney, cited M. Slater, *Family Life in the Seventeenth Century. The Verneys of Claydon House*, 1984, p. 131. See also T. Comber, ed., *A Book of Instructions by Sir Christopher Wandesford to his son and heir*, 1777, Cambridge, p. 78.

47 Salter, *op. cit.*, sig. Biiii recto; Bruto, *The Education of a Young Gentlewoman*, 1598, sig. D8 recto, H2 verso.

48 L. B. Osborne, ed., *The Life, Letters and Writings of John Hoskyns*, 1937, New Haven, pp. 65–6; L. Pollock, *With Faith and Physic. The Life of a Tudor Gentlewoman, Lady Grace Mildmay 1552–1620*, 1993, p. 46; J. Sparrow, ed., *Devotions upon Emergent Occasions*, 1923, Cambridge, p. 8.

49 T. T. Lewis, ed., *Letters of Brilliana Harley*, Camden Society, 1st Ser., 1854, vol. 58, p. 120; A. Walker, *The Holy Life of Elizabeth Walker . . .*, 1690, p. 69; A. Jessopp, ed., *The Autobiography of Roger North*, 1887, p. 4.

50 Earle, *Microcosmographie* 1628, sig. Bi recto.

51 Foxe, 'The Utility of This Story', I, p. xxvi.

52 Puttenham, *The Arte of English Poesie*, 1589, p. 31; Spenser, *op. cit.*, 'A Letter of the Authors Expounding his Whole Intention in the Course of this Work . . .'; Heywood, *op. cit.*, sig. A4 recto. See also Philip Sidney, *An Apologie for Poetry*, 1595, ed. G. Shepherd, 1965, p. 110.

53 Gataker, *Two Funeral Sermons . . .*, 1620, sig. A3 verso.

54 Gouge, *A Funeral Sermon . . . preached August 24 1646*, 1646, sig. A2 verso.

55 W. Pierce, *John Penry, His Life, Times and Writings*, 1923, p. 406; W. Hinde, *The Holy Life and Death of John Bruen*, 1641, p. 54.

56 Jocelin, *op. cit.*, sig. B4 recto; Clarke, *The Lives of Sundry Eminent Persons*, 1683, p. 155.

57 Elyot, *The Education and Bringinge Up of Children Translated oute of Plutarche*, 1583, sig. F3 recto–verso.

58 Becon, *op. cit.*, ed. J. Ayre, Parker Society, 1844, Cambridge, I, p. 354. See also *The Decades of Henry Bullinger*, ed. T. Harding, Parker Society, 1849, Cambridge, I, p. 295, and Montaigne, 'Of the Education of Children', *The Complete Works of Montaigne*, trans. and ed., D. M. Frame, 1957, Stanford, pp. 122–3.

59 Hake, *op. cit.*, sig. F6 verso.

60 Kempe, *The Education of Children in Learning*, 1588, sig. H1 verso–H2 recto.

61 *Op. cit.*, sig. E2 verso, E4 recto. See also Greenham, *Workes*, 5th ed., 1612, p. 278.

62 Leigh, *op. cit.*, pp. 46–7. See also M. Cavendish, 'A True Relation of my Birth,

Breeding and Life', in her *Life of William Cavendish*, 1667, ed. C. H. Firth, 1886, p. 278.

63 Perkins, *Works*, 3 vols, 1626–31, III, p. 694; Codrington, *The Seconde Part of Youths Behaviour*, 1664, p. 8; T. Heywood, ed., *The Diary of the Rev. Henry Newcome 1661–63*, Chetham Society, Orig. Ser., 1849, vol. 18, p. 60; Allestree, *Whole Duty of Man*, 1659, p. 298.

64 Kennett, *The Charity Schools for Children*, 1706, p. 24. For Susannah Wesley see below pp. 206, 209, 236.

65 Erasmus, *De Pueris Instituendis*, 1529, Basel, in *Collected Works of Erasmus*, vol. 26, 1985, Toronto, pp. 305–6, 308–9, 318.

66 Bullinger, trans. Coverdale, *The Christen State of Matrimony*, 1541, fol. lix recto.

67 Greenham, *Workes*, 5th ed., 1612, pp. 664–5; Burroughes, *A Sovereign Remedy for all Kinds of Grief*, 1657, p. 82. See also Becon, *Catechism*, p. 348, and Gouge, *Domesticall Dueties*, 3rd ed., 1634, p. 548.

68 Smith, *Thirteen Sermons*, 1592, fol. 141 recto, 151 recto.

69 Quoted from an unpublished letter in Emmanuel College, Cambridge, by N. I. Matar, 'A Devotion to Jesus as Mother in Restoration Puritanism', *Journal of the United Reformed Church Historical Society*, 1989, vol. 4, p. 307. J. P. Gilson, ed., *Lives of Lady Anne Clifford . . . and of her Parents Summarised by Herself*, 1916, p. 33.

70 Whitford, *op. cit.*, sig. Bii recto; *The Ordynary*, sig. El recto; Perkins, *The Foundation of Christian Religion*, 1591, sig. A2 recto, and *Christian Oeconomie*, in *Works*, 3 vols, 1613, Cambridge, III, p. 694.

71 Gataker, *Davids Instructer*, 1620, p. 32; Hooker, *The Unbelievers Preparing for Christ*, 1638, p. 199.

72 Leigh, *Mothers Blessing*, 7th ed., 1621, p. 46; *The Rev. Oliver Heywood BA 1630–1702: His Autobiography, Diaries etc.*, ed. J. H. Turner, 4 vols, 1882–5, Brighouse, I, p. 58; N. Guy, *Pieties Pillar*, 1636, p. 46; A. Walker, *The Holy Life of Elizabeth Walker*, 1690, p. 70; T. Gwin, *A Memorial of Ann Gwin*, 1715, p. 7. Margaret Spufford has pre-eminently concerned herself with the reading abilities of the poorer sort, on which see her 'First Steps in Literacy: the Reading and Writing Experiences of the Humblest Seventeenth-century Spiritual Autobiographers', *Social History*, 1979, vol. 4, pp. 407–35; 'The Schooling of the Peasantry in Cambridgeshire 1575–1700', *Agricultural History Review*, 1970, vol. 18, pp. 112–47; *Small Books and Pleasant Histories. Popular Fiction and Its Readership*, 1981, chaps I and II.

73 Donne, *Sermons*, IV, pp. 203–4; Charke, *Of the Use of Catechising*, 1580, appended to R. Cawdrey, *A Short and Useful Treatise . . .*, 1604; Herbert, *A Priest to the Temple*, 1671 ed., p. 69.

74 J. Rogers, *Doctrine of Faith*, 1629, p. 32. S. R. Gardiner, ed., *Reports of Cases in the Courts of Star Chamber and High Commission*, Camden Society, NS, 1886, vol. 39, p. 309.

75 C. J. Somerville, 'The Distinction Between Indoctrination and Education in England 1549–1719', *Journal of the History of Ideas*, 1983, vol. 44, pp. 387–406, fails to recognise that the use of the term 'understanding' in early modern texts does not coincide with the usage of twentieth-century educators.

76 S. E. Fish, 'Normal Circumstances, Literal Language, Direct Speech Acts, the Ordinary, the Everyday, the Obvious, What Goes Without Saying and Other Special Cases', *Critical Inquiry*, 1979, vol. 4, pp. 625–44.

77 Erasmus, *Paraclesis*, in J. C. Olin, ed. and trans., *Christian Humanism and the Reformation*, 1965, New York, pp. 96–7.

4 WOMEN AS RECIPIENTS

1 Foxe, IV, p. 557, and J. Fines, 'Heresy Trials in the Diocese of Coventry and Lichfield 1511–12', *Journal of Ecclesiastical History*, 1963, vol. 14, pp. 160–74. For later examples see Foxe, IV, pp. 227, 228, 230, 584; VI, pp. 579, 585, VII, p. 558. See also D. Plumb, 'A Gathered Church? Lollards and Their Society', in M. Spufford, ed., *The World of Rural Dissenters 1500–1725*, 1995, Cambridge, pp. 132–63.

2 Tyndale, *The Obedience of the Christian Man*, 1528, in *Doctrinal Treatises*, ed. H. Walter, Parker Society, 1848, Cambridge, p. 163. Lever, *A Fruitfull Sermon Made at Paules Church 2nd February 1550*, 1550, sig. B3 verso.

3 Whitgift, 'Articles touching Preachers and Other Orders of the Church', in E. Cardwell, ed., *Documentary Annals of the Reformed Church of England*, 2 vols, 1844, Oxford, vol. 1, p. 468; J. E. Neale, *Queen Elizabeth I*, 1973, Harmondsworth, p. 314; Abbot in S. R. Gardiner, ed., *Reports of Cases in the Courts of Star Chamber and High Commission*, Camden Society, 1886, New Ser., vol. 39, p. 309.

4 Milton, Sonnet XII, in F. M. Patterson, ed., *Works of John Milton*, 1931, New York, vol. I(1), p. 63; 'Reply of Bishop Ridley to Bishop Hooper on the Vestment Controversy', in *The Writings of John Bradford*, ed. T. Townsend, 2 vols, 1848, 1853, Parker Society, Cambridge, vol. 2, p. 377. See also *Sermons of Edwin Sandys*, ed. J. Ayre, 1842, Parker Society, Cambridge, p. 49, and F. Bacon, 'Of Unity in Religion', in M. Hawkins, ed., *Essays*, 1972, pp. 8–14.

5 For conventicles see P. Collinson, *The Religion of Protestants*, 1982, Oxford, pp. 242–73. The apparitors were the inevitably unpopular officers of the court whose duty it was to cite offenders and suspects and to see that they duly appeared in court on the appointed day. Cf. F. D. Price, 'The Elizabethan Apparitors in the Diocese of Gloucester', *Church Quarterly Review*, 1942, vol. 133, pp. 37–55.

6 W. H. Hale, *A Series of Precedents in Criminal Causes from the Act Books of the Ecclesiastical Courts of London 1475–1640*, 1847, p. 191, and pp. 184, 188, 192; *The Defence of John Etherington Against Steven Denison*, 1641, pp. 3, 29; J. H. Turner, ed., *The Rev. Oliver Heywood . . . His Autobiography, Diaries Etc.*, 4 vols, Brighouse, vol. 1, p. 77. See also W. J. Pressey, 'The Records of the Archdeaconries of Essex and Colchester', *Transactions of the Essex Archaeological Society*, 1930, vol. 19, pp. 1–21, at p. 14.

7 B. Schofield, ed., *The Knyvett Letters 1620–44*, Norfolk Record Society, 1949, vol. 20, pp. 98–9; Clarke, *The Lives of Sundry Eminent Persons*, 1683, p. 4.

8 *The Decades of Heinrich Bullinger*, ed. T. Harding, 5 vols, 1849, Parker Society, Cambridge, vol. 1, p. 291; Woodward, *op. cit.*, p. 12.

9 Perkins, *Christian Oeconomie*, 1609, Ep. Ded. See also J. Downame, *A Guide to Godlynesse*, 1629, p. 329, and D. Dyke, *Two Treatises*, 1633, sig. A3 recto.

10 R. C(leaver), *A Godly Fourme of Household Gouvernement for the Ordering of Private Families*, 1598, Ep. Ded., sig. A4 recto; Nichols, *The Order of Household Instruction*, 1596, sig. B7 verso, and his *The Plea of the Innocent*, 1602, pp. 212–13.

11 Webbe, in Rogers *et al.*, *A Garden of Spiritual Flowers*, 5th ed., 1609, sig. F8 recto–verso; Baxter, *The Reformed Pastor*, 1655, p. 59. See also D. Cawdrey, *Family Reformation Promoted*, 1656, sig. A7 recto, pp. 3–4.

12 S. Clarke, *The Lives of Ten Eminent Divines*, 1662, pp. 7–8; J. H. Turner, ed., *The Rev. Oliver Heywood . . .*, vol. 1, p. 234; E. Axon, ed., *Oliver Heywood's Life of John Angier of Denton*, Chetham Society, New Ser., 1937, vol. 97, pp. 84–6.

13 W. Bates, ed., *An Account of the Life and Death of Mr. Philip Henry*, 1698, pp. 77–87.

14 Erasmus to Johannes Faber, end of 1532, in P. S. Allen, ed., *Opus Epistolarum Des. Erasmi Roterodami*, ed. H. M. Allen and M. W. Garrod, 1941, Oxford, vol. 10, p. 139.

15 Fairclough, *The Saints Worthiness and the Worlds Worthlessness*, 1653, p. 17; Fuller, *The Church History of Britain*, 1655, pp. 124–5. Cf. B. Donagan, 'The Clerical Patronage of Robert Rich 1619–42', *Proceedings of the American Philosophical Society*, 1976, vol. 120, pp. 388–419.

16 W. Hinde, *A Faithfull Remonstrance of the Holy Life and Death of John Bruen*, 1641, p. 123.

17 N. Parkhurst, *The Faithful and Diligent Christian*, 1684, p. 53; C. S. Durrant, *A Link Between Flemish Mystics and English Martyrs*, 1925, pp. 273–5; Hartopp in DNB.

18 Whitford and Tyndale in DNB; Seton and Parkhurst in Strype, *Annals of the Reformation*, 1824, Oxford, vol. 2(ii), p. 347, and R. Houlbrooke, ed., *The Letter Book of John Parkhurst Bishop of Norwich*, Norfolk Record Society, 1975, vol. 43, pp. 20–1.

19 R. Ascham, *The Scholemaster*, 1570, ed. J. E. Mayor, 1863, p. 34.

20 Foxe in DNB, sub Howard, Thomas, fourth Duke of Norfolk.

21 Fairclough, *The Saints Worthiness*, 1653, p. 111.

22 S. Kanshek, 'Resistance, Loyalty and Recusant Politics: Sir Thomas Tresham and the Elizabethan State', *Midland History*, 1996, vol. 21, p. 66, n. 1; J. Petre, 'The Penal Laws and the Petre Family', *Essex Journal*, 1994, vol. 29, pp. 7–13, and F. G. Emmison, *Tudor Secretary: Sir William Petre at Court and at Home*, 1961, p. 230.

23 G. H. Williams, ' "Called by this name, heare us not": The Case of Mrs Joan Drake. A Formative Episode in the Career of Thomas Hooker in England', *Harvard Library Bulletin*, 1968, vol. 16, pp. 278–300; Hoby, *Diary, passim*.

24 Taylor in DNB; Gataker, in Clarke, *Lives of Ten Eminent Divines*, 1662, pp. 133, 145.

25 G. Fullerton, *The Life of Elizabeth Lady Falkland 1585–1639*, 1883, pp. 153–4, 176–7, 183, 194.

26 K. Weber, *Lucius Cary, Second Viscount Falkland*, 1940, New York, pp. 176–8; J. Sutherland, ed., *Memoirs of the Life of Colonel Hutchinson with a Fragment of Auto-biography by Mrs Hutchinson*, 1973, p. 288; Pierson in BL Harleian Ms. 7517, fols 18 verso–19 recto. He dedicated his edition of Perkins' *Godly and Learned Exposition or Commentarie Upon the First Three Chapters of Revelation*, 1606, to Lady Elizabeth Montagu of Broughton in Northamptonshire. Cf. J. Eales, 'Thomas Pierson and the Transmission of the Moderate Puritan Tradition', *Midland History*, 1995, vol. 20, pp. 75–102.

27 *The Life and Death . . . of Thomas Cawton*, 1662, pp. 14–15.

28 Walker, *The Holy Life of . . . Elizabeth Walker*, 1690, p. 7; Gauden in DNB.

29 Sedgwick in DNB; Abbot, *Milk for Babes*, 1646, Ep. Ded. and p. 230; Barker, *A Sermon Preached at the Funeral of . . . Lady Elizabeth Capel*, 1661. For the chaplaincies of William Chantrell, James Harrison, and Ezekiel Rogers in the Barrington household at Brampton Bryan see A. Searle, ed., *The Barrington Family Letters 1628–32*, Camden Society, 4th Ser., 1983, pp. 258–9.

30 G. S. Thomson, *Life in a Noble Household 1641–1700*, 1937, pp. 74–6. 'Minion print' is a small kind of type, about 10 ½ lines to the inch. Byfield, *Principles or Patterne of Wholesome Words*, 1618, 3rd ed., 1627; Fisher, *The Wise Virgin or A Wonderful Narration of the Hand of God . . . in the Life of Martha Hatfield*, 1653, 5th ed., 1664.

31 C. J. Blaisdell, 'Calvin's Letters to Women: the Courting of Ladies in High Places', *Sixteenth Century Journal*, vol. 13, 1982, pp. 67–84; 'Calvin's and Loyola's Letters to Women', in R. V. Schnucker, ed., *Calviniana. Ideas and Influence of Jean Calvin*, Kirksville, Mo., 1988; H. Rahrer, *Loyola's Letters to Women*, Edinburgh, 1959; H. Robinson, ed. and trans., *Original Letters Relative to the English Reformation*, 3 vols, 1846, Parker Society, Cambridge, vol. 3, pp. 702–3, Calvin to Anne Seymour, 15 July 1549.

32 Robinson, *Original Letters . . .*, vol. 1, pp. 7–8. See also her letter to 'Master Harding', her tutor and her father's chaplain, reviling him for his apostasy and urging him to recant; Foxe, VI, pp. 418–22.

33 Cf. A. D. Frankforter, 'Elizabeth Bowes and John Knox: A Woman and Reformation Theology', *Church History*, 1987, vol. 56, pp. 333–47, and S. M. Feich, 'The Rhetoric of Biblical Authority: John Knox and the Question of Women', *Sixteenth Century Journal*, 1995, vol. 26, pp. 805–22.

34 Dering, *Certain Godly Letters and Comfortable Letters Full of Christian Consolation*, 1597; *The Writings of John Bradford*, II, pp. 91–3, 96–7, 140–7; Careless' letters in Foxe, VI, p. 411, VII, pp. 234, 691–3, 723, 725, VIII, pp. 173–4, 182–3, 192–6, 198–200.

35 Searle, *Barrington Family Letters*, pp. 253–8; I. M. Calder, ed., *The Letters of John Davenport, Puritan Divine*, 1937, New Haven, pp. xix–xx.

36 E. A. B. Bernard, 'The Pakingtons of Westwood', *Transactions of the Worcestershire Archaeological Society*, NS 1936, vol. 13, pp. 28–47; G. G. Perry, *Life of Henry Hammond*, 1862, H. M. Nicholson, ed., *Conway Letters. The Correspondence of Anne Viscountess Conway, Henry More and their Friends, 1642–84*, 1930, chap. 2.

37 Of Norris's many writings, his *Reason and Religion or The Grounds of Devotion*, 1689, and *Practical Discourses*, 1691, would probably have appealed most to these two highly educated ladies.

38 *Memoirs of the Life of Colonel Hutchinson*, ed. J. Sutherland, 1973, p. 288. *Memoirs of Anne Lady Halkett and Anne Lady Fanshawe*, ed. J. Loftis, 1979, Oxford, pp. 10–11.

39 Chaucer, *Canterbury Tales*, trans. N. Coghill, 1951, Harmondsworth, p. 258.

40 N. Orme, *From Childhood to Chivalry. The Education of English Kings and Aristocracy 1066–1530*, 1984, p. 33.

41 For Mary, *Letters and Papers Foreign and Domestic Henry VIII*, II(I), p. 874; *ibid.*, III(I), p. 323; *Cal. S. P. Dom. Henry VIII*, VIII, p. 101, and D. M. Loades, *Mary Tudor. A Life*, 1989, Oxford, p. 42. For Catherine's upbringing see G. Mattingley, *Catherine of Aragon*, 1942, p. 17. For Elizabeth, J. E. Neale, *Queen Elizabeth I*, Harmondsworth, pp. 15–16. J. Strype, *Ecclesiastical Memorials Relating Chiefly to Religion and the Reformation of it*, I(ii), pp. 147, 172; HMC, *Hatfield Mss*, XIX, 1965, p. 412; F. Madden, ed., *Privy Purse Expenses of the Princess Mary*, 1831, pp. xli–ii.

42 F. H. Mares, ed., *Memoirs of Sir Robert Carey*, 1972, Oxford, p. 68; *Cal S. P. Dom., 1603–10*, p. 40.

43 Gardiner, *English Girlhood at School*, pp. 231–2; H. Harrington, ed., *Nugae Antiquae*, 2 vols, II, p. 14; Makin, *Essay*, pp. 4, 10.

44 K. Mertes, *The English Noble Household 1250–1600*, 1987, Oxford, p. 172.

45 HMC, *De Lisle and Dudley Mss*, I, pp. 250, 257, 267–9, 359–60, 417–18, 426. Philip's letter in *ibid.*, p. 272.

46 G. Haddon, *Lucubrationes*, 1567, p. 131. See also M. K. McIntosh, 'Sir Anthony Cooke: Tudor Humanist, Educator and Religious Reformer', *Proceedings of the American Philosophical Society*, 1975, vol. 119, pp. 233–50; M. E. Lamb, 'The

Cooke Sisters: Attitudes Towards Learned Women in the Renaissance', in M. P. Hannay, ed., *Silent But for the Word: Tudor Women as Patrons, Translators and Writers of Religious Works*, pp. 107–25. The More and Cooke daughters were praised for their learning in W. Bercher, *The Nobylyte of Wymen*, 1559, ed. W. Bond, 1904, pp. 154–5 and H. Peacham, *The Compleat Gentleman*, 1622, p. 36.

47 Foxe in DNB.

48 L. Pollock, *With Faith and Physic. The Life of a Tudor Gentlewoman. Lady Grace Mildmay*, 1993, Cambridge, pp. 25–6. See also R. M. Warnicke, 'Lady Mildmay's Journal: A Study in Autobiography and Meditation in Reformation England', *Sixteenth Century Journal*, 1989, vol. 20, pp. 55–68.

49 J. Collinges, *Par Nobile. Two Treatises . . . at the Funerals of Lady Frances Hobart and . . . Lady Katherine Courten*, 1669, pp. 3–5.

50 A. E. Robinson, ed., *The Life of Richard Kidder, Bishop of Bath and Wells Written by Himself*, Somerset Record Society, 1922, vol. 37, pp. 1–2.

51 D. G. Greene, ed., *Meditations of Lady Elizabeth Delaval Written Between 1662 and 1671*, Surtees Society, 1978 for 1975, vol. 190, p. 33.

52 G. C. Williamson, *Lady Anne Clifford, Countess of Dorset, Pembroke and Montgomery 1590–1676*, Kendal, 1922, pp. 15, 58, 61, 66. See also B. Lewalski, 'Recording Patriarchy and Patronage: Margaret Clifford, Anne Clifford and Amelia Layner', *Year Book of English Studies*, 1991, vol. 21, pp. 87–106.

53 W. H. Woodward, ed., *Vittorino da Feltre and Other Humanist Educators*, 1963 ed., New York, p. 127.

54 Peter, *op. cit.*, pp. 14, 73.

55 Hilder, *op. cit.*, sig. ¶2 recto–verso. Hilder reported to his dedicatee, Lady Anne Sackville, that it had been written 'six and twenty years since'.

56 Slingsby, *op. cit.*, p. 54.

57 Robins, *op. cit.*, 4th ed., 1676 sig. A7 recto. See also S. Burrowes, *Good Instructions for All Young Men and Maids*, 1642.

58 Savile, *op. cit.*, p. 9.

59 Wing attributes this to Oliver Heywood, who had only two sons, and a daughter who died in infancy. The author also addresses 'Daughter' with 'Had you died in your childhood as my other children did . . .'. Hickes, *op. cit.*, sections VII and VIII.

60 Spufford, *Small Books and Pleasant Histories*, 1981, *passim*. Cf. P. Morgan, 'Frances Wolfreston and 'Hor Bouks': a Seventeenth-century Woman Book-collector', *The Library*, 1989, vol. 11, pp. 197–219. A small collection of her inscribed chapbooks is located in the British Library at Cup. 408d8, formerly 4404b20. The Dent abbreviation is advertised at the back of A. Jones, *The Black Book of Conscience* (1658).

61 T. W. Bramston, ed., *The Autobiography of Sir John Bramston*, Camden Society, 1845, vol. 32, p. 4.

62 *The Writings of John Bradford*, ed. A. Townsend, Parker Society, 2 vols, 1848, 1853, vol. 2, p. 265. See also the letters of Rowland Taylor and John Careless to their respective wives in Foxe, VI, p. 702 and VIII, pp. 163ff. Penry letter in BL Addl. Ms. 48, 164, fols 23 verso, 24, excerpted in J. Waddington, *John Penry the Pilgrim Martyr*, 1854, 136f. J. Bayley, *The History and Antiquities of the Tower of London*, 2 vols, II, p. 471. See also J. V. H. Pollen and W. MacMahon, eds, *The Venerable Philip Howard 1557–95*, Catholic Record Society, vol. 21, 1919 for 1916–17, pp. 5–6, 13–15.

63 HMC, *Rutland Mss*, 1888, IV, pp. 99, 275.

64 Hill in BL Addl. Ms. 46,500, fol. 48. M. Blundell, *Cavalier. The Letters of William Blundell to his Friends*, 1933, pp. 76–8.
65 BL Addl. Ms. 70,011, fol. 152, and Addl. Ms. 70,130 unbound.
66 Evelyn's letter in H. Sampson, ed., *The Life of Mrs Godolphin*, 1939, Appendix B, pp. 218–23.
67 Harrington, *A Holy Oyl and a Sweet Perfume Taken Out of the Sanctuary of the Most Sacred Scriptures*, 1669, pp. 259ff. Not to be confused with his cousin, James Harrington, the author of *Oceana* (1656).
68 Penn, *op. cit.*, pp. 23, 41.
69 D. Willen, '"Communion of Saints": Spiritual Reciprocity and the Godly Community in Early Modern England', *Albion*, 1995, vol. 27, pp. 19–41; A. Fletcher, *A County Community in War and Peace. Sussex 1600–60*, 1974, pp. 64ff.

5 AWAY TO SCHOOL

1 C. Sneyd, ed., *A Relation or Rather a True Account of the State of England . . . About the Year 1500*, Camden Society, 1847, vol. 37, pp. 24–5.
2 L. Stone, *Family, Sex and Marriage in England 1500–1800*, 1977, p. 108.
3 N. Orme, *From Childhood to Chivalry. The Education of Kings and Aristocrats 1066–1530*, 1984, pp. 58–60.
4 M. St Clare Byrne, ed., *The Lisle Letters*, 6 vols, 1981, Chicago, V, pp. 219–20.
5 *Ibid.*, III, p. 9; V, p. 71.
6 *Ibid.*, IV, pp. 163, 170, 172–4; III, pp. 162–3, 165–9.
7 M. Jones and M. Underwood, *The King's Mother. Lady Margaret Beaufort, Countess of Richmond and Derby*, 1992, Cambridge, pp. 167–70.
8 R. W. Chambers, *Thomas More*, 1938, pp. 98, 181–5.
9 Pole in DNB.
10 D. M. Gardiner, *English Girlhood at School*, 1929, p. 126.
11 C. Goff, *A Woman of the Tudor Age*, 1939, p. 17; A. T. Friedman, *House and Household: Wollaton Hall and the Willoughby Family*, 1989, pp. 17–18.
12 Gardiner, pp. 178–80.
13 A. Hassell-Smith *et al.*, eds, *The Papers of Nathaniel Bacon of Stiffkey, I, 1556–77*, Norfolk Record Society, 1978–9, vol. 46, pp. 24, 39.
14 HMC, *Rutland Mss*, I, pp. 250, 297. BL, Lansdowne Ms., 162, fol. 124.
15 HMC, *De Lisle and Dudley Mss*, II, pp. 261, 268, 279; A. Collins, *Letters and Memorials of State . . . of the Sidney Family*, 2 vols, 1746, pp. 43, 153; BL Lansdowne Ms. 162, fol. 124; Hoby, *Diary*, pp. 5, 8. For her own 'maids' see *Diary*, *passim*, for example entries for 1601. For Lettice Carey's 'maids', J. Duncon, *The Returns of Spiritual Comfort*, 1648, p. 162. H. E. Maiden, ed., *Richard Broughton's Devereux Papers*, Camden Miscellany, 1924, vol. 13, p. 6. See also C. Cross, *The Puritan Earl*, 1966, pp. 24–7, 57.
16 *The Memoirs of Sir Hugh Cholmley*, 1787, pp. 85–6; O. Stockton, *Consolation in Life and Death . . .*, 1681, p. 3; Lord Braybrooke, ed., *The Autobiography of Sir John Bramston*, Camden Society, 1845, vol. 32, pp. 13–15.
17 J. H. Wiffen, *Historical Memoirs of the House of Russell*, 2 vols, 1833, I, p. 399; Hoby, *Diary*, p. 56; Donne, *Sermons*, I, p. 130, n. 36.
18 M. A. E. Wood, *Lives of the Princesses of England*, 6 vols, 1849–63, vol. V, p. 173; C. W. James, *Chief Justice Coke: His Family and Descendants at Holkham*, 1929, p. 85.
19 T. Taylor, *The Pilgrims Profession or A Sermon Preached at the Funeral of Mrs M. Gunter*, 1622, p. 121.

20 Mary Towson in BL Egerton Ms. 2641, fols 205, 234.

21 Molineux and Thorndike in L. Pollock, ' "Teach Her to Live under Obedience":
The Making of Women in the Upper Ranks of Early Modern England', *Continuity and Change*, 1989, vol. 4, p. 236.

22 A. Martienssen, *Queen Katherine Parr*, 1975, p. 31; J. K. McConica, *English Humanists and Reformation Politics Under Henry VIII and Edward VI*, 1965, Oxford, chap. 7, but see also M. Dowling, 'The Gospel and the Court: Reformation Under Henry VIII', in P. Lake, ed., *Protestants and the National Church in Sixteenth-century England*, 1987, pp. 62, 71, n.i. 75 n. 37. For Mary's education, Dowling, *Humanism in the Age of Henry VIII*, 1986, pp. 219–29. For Anne Boleyn's childhood, R. M. Warnicke, 'Anne Boleyn's Childhood and Adolescence', *Historical Journal*, 1985, vol. 28, pp. 939–52, and H. Paget, 'The Youth of Anne Boleyn', *Bulletin of the Institute of Historical Research*, 1981, pp. 162–70. For comparison see C. Niekus, *The Maiden's Mirror*, 1987, Wiesbaden, pp. 42ff, for the education of German upper-class girls, and S. Kettering, 'The Household Service of Early Modern French Noblewomen', *French Historical Studies*, 1997, vol. 20, pp. 162–70.

23 Vernon, Knollys, Carey and Russell in DNB.

24 Mary Sidney in DNB.

25 M. Cavendish, *Natures Pictures*, 1656, p. 370, and 'A True Relation of my Birth and Breeding' in *The Life of William Cavendish Duke of Newcastle*, 1667, ed. C. H. Firth, 1886, p. 286; D. G. Green, ed., *Meditations of Lady Elizabeth Delaval Written Between 1662 and 1671*, Surtees Society, 1978, vol. 190, pp. 123–4.

26 W. G. Hiscock, *John Evelyn and His Family Circle*, 1955, chap. VII; C. Barash, 'The Political Origins of Anne Finch's Poetry', *Huntingdon Library Quarterly*, 1991, vol. 54, p. 330.

27 F. Watson, *The Old Grammar Schools*, 1916, Cambridge, p. 116; N. Carlisle, *A Concise Description of the Endowed Grammar Schools of England and Wales*, 2 vols, 1818, II, p. 137. See also *ibid.*, I, p. 679, Manchester Grammar School; I, p. 432, Felsted School; I, p. 340, Tiverton Grammar School.

28 VCH *Berkshire*, II, p. 251; W. A. L. Vincent, *The Grammar Schools: Their Continuing Tradition 1660–1714*, 1969, p. 46.

29 Becon, *Newe Catechisme*, ed. J. Ayre, Parker Society, 1844, Cambridge, pp. 376–7; Mulcaster, *Positions*, 1581, p. 167.

30 Dury, *The Reformed School*, 1650, ed. H. M. Knox, 1958, Liverpool, pp. 25–6. See also Dury's *Advancement of Learning*, 1653, in C. Webster, ed., *Hartlib and the Advancement of Learning*, 1970, Cambridge, p. 190.

31 E. Chamberlayne, *An Academy or College Wherein Young Ladies and Gentlewomen May at a Very Moderate Expense be Educated in the Protestant Religion*, 1671, pp. 2–8; D. Defoe, *An Essay Upon Projects*, 1697, pp. 282, 285–6, 290, 302.

32 J. Duncon, *The Returns of Spiritual Comfort and Grief in a Devout Soul*, 1648, p. 190; M. Astell, *A Serious Proposal*, 1674, pp. 51–5, 60ff, 73–4, 79, 81, 84, 148–9; Part II, 1695, p. 21; B. Makin, *An Essay to Revive the Antient Education of Women*, 1673, pp. 10, 16, 30, 32. Cf. the revisionary essay of J. R. Brink, 'Bathsua Reginald Makin: Most Learned Matron', *Huntingdon Library Quarterly*, 1991, vol. 54, pp. 313–26.

33 Batchiler, *The Virgins Pattern*, 1661, pp. 2, 6, 19–20.

34 The Cox episode is reported in detail in A. Fraser, *The Weaker Vessel. Woman's Lot in Seventeenth-Century England*, 1984, pp. 22–5.

35 P. Souers, *The Matchless Orinda*, 1931, Cambridge, Mass., p. 20. For her poetry see H. Andreadis, 'The Sapphic-Platonics of Katherine Phillips 1632–64', *Signs*, 1989–90, pp. 34–60.

36 Lord Braybrooke, ed., *The Autobiography of Sir John Bramston*, Camden Society, 1845, vol. 32, pp. 108, 111; Sainthill in F. B. Troup, 'A Cavalier's Notebook Continued by his Son', *Reports and Transactions of the Devonshire Association*, 1889, vol. 21, p. 414.

37 *The Diary of Ralph Josselin 1616–1683*, ed. A. Macfarlane, 1991 ed., Oxford, p. 585.

38 V. Larminie, *Wealth, Kinship and Culture. The Seventeenth-Century Newdigates of Arbury and Their World*, 1995, p. 120; E. Gooder, *The Squire of Arbury. Sir Richard Newdigate Second Baronet (1644–1710) and His Family*, 1990, Coventry, p. 138.

39 *The Diary of Samuel Pepys*, 3 vols, 1953, II, p. 447.

40 B. Makin, *Essay*, 1673, pp. 162ff.

41 *The Diary and Correspondence of Dr John Worthington, I*, ed. J. Crossley, Chetham Society, 1847, vol. 13, p. 196 n. l.

42 Gardiner, p. 210.

43 J. O. Halliwell, ed., *The Autobiography and Correspondence of Sir Simonds D'Ewes Bt*, 3 vols, 1845, vol. 1, pp. 63, 157.

44 J. Nichols, ed., *The Progresses of James I*, 4 vols, 1828, vol. III, p. 283.

45 Gouge, *A Funeral Sermon Preached . . . August 24 1646*, 1646, p. 37; *The Diary of John Evelyn*, ed. E. S. de Beer, 6 vols, 1955, Oxford, II, p. 555.

46 R. North, *Lives of the Norths*, ed. A. Jessopp, 3 vols, 1890, I, p. 110. *The London Gazette*, no. 1839, 25 July 1683. Verney, *Memoirs*, IV, pp. 220–1, 249ff.

47 Verney, *Memoirs*, II, pp. 378, 382.

48 *Ibid.*, II, pp. 382–4.

49 J. Gage, *The History and Antiquities of Hengrave Hall in Suffolk*, 1822, p. 195; T. Dorman, 'The Sandwich Book of Orphans', *Archaeologia Cantiana*, 1886, vol. 16, pp. 180, 189, 198.

50 J. O. Halliwell, ed., *The Private Diary of John Dee*, Camden Society, 1842, vol. 19, p. 34; R. O'Day, *Education and Society 1500–1800*, 1982, p. 186.

51 S. C. Lomas, ed., *The Memoirs of Sir George Courthope*, Camden Miscellany, 1907, vol. ll, p. 104.

52 T. N. Brushfield, 'The Financial Diary of a Citizen of Exeter 1631–42', *Reports and Transactions of the Devonshire Association*, 1901, vol. 33, p. 207; HMC, *The Mss of Lord Kenyon*, 14th Report, App. IV, p. 64.

53 D. Gardiner, ed., *The Oxinden and Peyton Letters 1642–78*, 1937, pp. 128–9, 205–6, 203–4; D. Gardiner, ed., *The Oxinden Letters 1607–42*, 1933, pp. 278–9.

54 A. Macfarlane, ed., *The Diary of Ralph Josselin 1616–1683*, 1976, pp. 367, 574–5, 540.

55 R. Thompson, *Women in Stuart England and America*, 1974, pp. 189–90, 192–3; W. H. D. Longstaffe, ed., *Memoirs of the Life of Ambrose Barnes*, Surtees Society, 1867, vol. 50, p. 58; S. Davy, *Heaven Realiz'd*, 1670, p. 7.

56 L. Pollock, ' "Teach Her to Live Under Obedience": the Making of Women in the Upper Ranks of Early Modern England', *Continuity and Change*, 1989, vol. 4, p. 329.

57 R. W. Blencowe, 'Extracts from the Journal and Account Book of the Rev. Giles Moore, Rector of Horsted Keynes from 1655 to 1679', *Sussex Archaeological Collections*, 1848, vol. 1, pp. 97–8, 101, 105, 109, 112, 116–17.

58 *The Journeys of Celia Fiennes*, ed. C. Morris, 1947, p. 227.

59 Kempe, *op. cit.*, sig. F3 verso. Some grammar schools had, in addition to the master, an usher to teach the 'petties'. See K. Charlton, *Education in Renaissance England*, 1965, chap. 4.

60 Mulcaster, *The First Part of the Elementarie*, 1582, p. 55.

61 Becon, *op. cit.*, ed. J. Ayres, Parker Society, 1844, Cambridge, pp. 376–7.

62 Dell, *The Right Reformation of Learning*, 1646, in *Several Sermons and Discourses of William Dell*, 1709, p. 643.

63 Clement, *The Petie Schole*, 1587, To the Courteous Reader, sig. A2 verso.

64 Hoole, *A New Discovery of the Old Arte of Teaching School*, 1660, p. 28.

65 Walker, *Some Improvements in the Art of Teaching*, 1669, 5th ed., 1693, Preface to the Reader, sig. A4 recto.

66 Frere and Kennedy, II, p. 9.

67 *Ibid.*, II, p. 364.

68 Frere and Kennedy, *passim*; J. V. Bullard, ed., *Constitutions and Canons Ecclesiastical 1604*, 1934. Cf. S. M. Wide, 'The Episcopal Licensing of Schoolmasters in the Diocese of London 1627–85', *Guildhall Miscellany*, 1967, vol. 2, pp. 392–405; W. E. Tate, 'The Episcopal Licensing of Teachers in England', *Church Quarterly Review*, 1965, vol. 157, pp. 426–32; G. Jenkins, 'A Note on "The Episcopal Licensing of Teachers"', *ibid.*, 1958, vol. 159, pp. 78–81; J. Addy, 'A Further Note . . .', *ibid.*, 1959, vol. 160, pp. 251–2.

69 Bullard, *op. cit.*, p. 82.

70 W. Cardwell, *Synodalia*, 2 vols, 1842, Oxford, I, p. 291.

71 Barnwick and Prist in D. Cressy, ed., *Education in Tudor and Stuart England*, 1975, p. 33; Woodwerde in M. Campbell, *The English Yeoman Under Elizabeth and the Early Stuarts*, 1942, p. 273; Palmer in R. O'Day, 'Church Records and the History of Education in Early Modern England 1588–1642', *History of Education*, 1973, vol. 2, p. 121.

72 Bussher in A. Hussey, 'Visitations of the Archdeaconry of Canterbury', *Archaeologia Cantiana*, 1902, vol. 25, p. 32; Hartfield in A. R. Morris, 'The Reformation and Schooling in Sussex in the Early Modern Period', unpublished MA Dissertation, University of London King's College, 1979, pp. 53–4; J. E. Wadey, 'Schools and Schooling in Sussex 1548–1607', *Sussex Notes and Queries*, 1957, vol. 14, p. 221.

73 *Cal. S. P. Dom., Charles II 1682*, p. 609.

74 O'Day, *op. cit.*, and VCH Cambridgeshire, II, p. 338.

75 M. Spufford, *Contrasting Communities*, 1974, Cambridge, Map 11 facing p. 184; P. Clark, *English Provincial Society from the Reformation to the Revolution. Religion, Politics and Society in Kent 1500–1640*, 1977, Hassocks, Maps 4 and 5 facing p. 203; A. Smith, 'Endowed Schools in the Diocese of Lichfield and Coventry 1660–99', *History of Education*, 1975, vol. 4, pp. 5–20, and 'Private Schools and Schoolmasters in the Diocese of Lichfield and Coventry in the Seventeenth Century', *ibid.*, 1976, vol. 5, pp. 117–26; A. J. Fletcher, 'The Expansion of Education in Berkshire and Oxfordshire', *British Journal of Educational Studies*, 1967, vol. 15, pp. 51–9; B. Simon, 'Leicestershire Schools 1625–40', *ibid.*, 1954, vol. 3, pp. 42–58.

76 VCH Suffolk, II, p. 353, for Wentworth and Pepyn.

77 Parrett in J. Morgan, *Godly Learning*, 1986, Cambridge, p. 157.

78 Pym in VCH Buckinghamshire, IV, p. 18; Dewhurst in VCH Hertfordshire, II, p. 99.

79 Calton in VCH Derbyshire, II, p. 273.

80 Collins in VCH Leicestershire, III, p. 243 and V, p. 60.

81 VCH Warwickshire, II, p. 369.

82 VCH Essex, II, p. 560.

83 Wall and Greenwood in W. K. Jordan, *The Charities of Rural England*, 1961, pp. 338, 244–5; Rayment in VCH Huntingdonshire, II, p. 115.

84 Minors in Smith, 'Endowed Schools . . .', pp. 7–8; Willoughby in VCH Warwickshire, II, p. 369

85 Walker in VCH Essex, II, p. 561.

86 Austin in BL Addl. Ms. 5809, fol. 64 (renumbered); Digby in VCH Warwickshire, II, pp. 352, 370.

87 Longdale in J. Lawson, *Primary Education in East Yorkshire 1560–1902*, 1959, Hull, p. 7; Aldworth in VCH Berkshire, II, p. 281.

88 Smyth in VCH Sussex, II, p. 437; Bathurst in W. K. Jordan, *The Social Institutions of Kent 1480–1660, Archaeologia Cantiana*, 1961, vol. 75, p. 85; Scargill in VCH Derbyshire, II, p. 273.

89 B. E. Elliott, *The History of Loughborough College School*, 1971, chap. 11; Elliot, 'The Development of Elementary Education in Loughborough', *History of Education Society Bulletin*, 1980, no. 25, pp. 13–17.

90 Rawlins in VCH Warwickshire, II, p. 370; Walter in VCH Oxfordshire, I, p. 487.

91 W. Lemprière, *A History of the Girls' School of Christ's Hospital, London, Hoddesdon and Hertford*, 1924, Cambridge, pp. 4–6.

92 J. Vanes, *Apparelled in Red. The History of the Red Maids School*, 1984, Gloucester, chaps I and III.

93 D. Cressy, *Literacy and the Social Order*, 1980, Cambridge, pp. 30–4.

94 Smyth in VCH Sussex, II, p. 437; Borlase in VCH Buckinghamshire, II, pp. 214–15.

95 Nethersole in VCH Warwickshire, II, p. 369.

96 Towrie in Lawson, *op. cit.*, p. 8; Bosworth in VCH Warwickshire, II, p. 370; King in VCH Essex, II, p. 560.

97 Wilson in Lawson, *op. cit.*, p. 8.

98 PCC 156 Rivers; Griffith, *op. cit.*, p. 517; Charity Commissioners 13th Report, 1825, p. 269. For the Offley pedigree, *The Genealogist*, 1903, vol. 19, and 1904, vol. 20. *Staffordshire Weekly Sentinel*, 27 May 1955, which also has a photograph of the school buildings.

99 R. G. Usher, *The Presbyterian Movement in the Reign of Queen Elizabeth*, Camden Society, 3rd Ser., 1905, vol. 8, p. 100.

100 VCH Cambridgeshire, II, p. 339, and in detail in Spufford, *Contrasting Communities*, pp. 193–6. Bathurst see above p. 147.

101 D. Underdown, *Fire from Heaven. The Life of an English Town in the Seventeenth Century*, 1992, pp. 225–6, 247.

6 WOMEN AS AGENTS

1 T. Pomfret, *The Life of the Right Honorable and Religious Lady Christian(a) Late Countess Dowager of Devonshire*, 1685, pp. 36–7. For attendance see *The Diary of John Manningham of the Middle Temple 1602–3*, ed. R. P. Sorlien, 1976, New Hanover, NH, pp. 115, 151, and W. J. Shiels, 'Oliver Heywood and his Congregation', *Studies in Church History*, 1986, vol. 23, pp. 268–9. Cf. M. Spufford, 'Can We Count the "Godly" and "Conformable" in the Seventeenth Century?', *Journal of Ecclesiastical History*, 1985, vol. 36, pp. 428–38.

2 Hooker, *Laws of Ecclesiastical Polity*, 1597, Preface, sig. B3 recto; *The Works of Richard Hooker*, ed. G. Edelen, 6 vols, 1977, Cambridge, Mass., vol. 1, p. 17.

3 P. Collinson, *The Birthpangs of Protestant England*, 1988, p. 75; K. R. Wark, *Elizabeth Recusancy in Cheshire*, Chetham Society, 1971, 3rd Ser., vol. 19, pp. 82–4.

4 J. Wing, *The Crown Conjugall or The Spouse Royall*, 1620, p. 88.

5 H. Smith, *Thirteene Sermons*, 1592, sigs B3 recto, B5 recto, C8 verso. See also R. Greenham 'Of Hearing God's Word', in *Workes*, 1612, pp. 707–11, 834–6; Donne, *Sermons*, VII, p. 327; T. Rogers, *The Righteous Mans Evidences for Heaven*, 1624 ed., pp. 18, 44; J. Phillips, *The Way to Heaven*, 1625, p. 7; D. Burgess, *Rules for Hearing the Word of God*, 1693, pp. 10, 14. The proof-text was Romans 10.17.

6 Hoby, *Diary*, pp. 64, 66, 75, 150, 153–4 and *passim*.

7 J. Mayer, *A Pattern for Women*, 1619, p. 9.

8 S. Denison, *The Monument or Tombstone . . . a Sermon Preached 21 November 1619 . . . at the Funeral of Mrs Elizabeth Juxon*, 1620, pp. 85, 86–7, 90–91.

9 *The Rev. Oliver Heywood BA 1630–1702. His Autobiography, Diaries etc.*, ed. J. H. Turner, 4 vols, 1882–5, Brighouse, vol. 1, p. 48.

10 *Op. cit.*, pp. 6–7, 33, 34. See also J. Collinges, *Par Nobile. Two Treatises . . . at the Funerals of Lady Frances Hobart . . . and Lady Katherine Courten*, 1669, pp. 22, 24; W. Harrison, *Deaths Advantage . . .*, 1602, p. 80, for Katherine Brettergh's sermon-going; N. Guy, *Pieties Pillar . . .*, 1626, p. 47, for Elizabeth Gouge's, and Anna Trapnel's report of her own practice, *A Legacy for Saints*, 1654, p. 2.

11 P. Collinson, 'The Role of Women in the English Reformation Illustrated by the Life and Friendships of Anne Locke', *Studies in Church History*, 1965, vol. 2, p. 269. Cf. T. Fuller, *The History of the Worthies of England*, 1662, vol. 2, pp. 85–6, sub Mary Waters.

12 Andrewes, *XCVI Sermons*, 1629, p. 992.

13 Donne, *Sermons*, IV, p. 36, VI, p. 52, and VII, pp. 327–9, 'A Fruitful Exhortation to the Reading and Knowledge of Holy Scripture', in *Certaine Sermons and Homilies*, 1547; L. Wright, *The Pilgrimage to Paradise*, 1591, pp. 29ff and 56; W. Perkins, *The Art of Prophesying or A Treatise on Preaching*, in *Works*, 3 vols, 1612, vol. 1, p. 274. See also E. Calamy, *The Art of Divine Meditation*, posth., 1680, p. 24.

14 J. Preston, *The Riches of Mercy to Men in Misery*, 1658, pp. 286–7.

15 D. Featley, *Ancilla Pietatis or The Handmaid to Private Devotion*, 1626; 6th ed. 1639, p. 63. See also J. Norman, *Family Governors persuaded to Family Godliness or The Masters Charge*, 1657, p. 18; R. Hill, *The Patheway to Prayer and Pietie*, 3rd ed., 1609, p. 103, originally *Christs Prayer Expounded*, 1606; J. Downame, *Guide to Godlynesse*, 1629 ed., pp. 490–92.

16 *Correspondence of Erasmus: Letters 1520 to 1521*, trans. R. A. B. Mynors, in *Collected Works of Erasmus*, vol. 8, 1988, Toronto, p. 298.

17 Hoby, *Diary*, pp. 119, 127, 126, 131 and *passim*. See also the practice of Mary Wilson of Crosfield in Cumberland who died in 1672, S. A., ed., *The Virgin Saint . . .*, 1673, p. 23.

18 J. Mayer, *A Patterne for Women*, 1619, pp. 8–9.

19 T. Taylor, *The Pilgrims Profession or A Sermon Preached at the Funeral of Mrs M. Gunter*, 1622, pp. 121ff.

20 J. H. Turner, *Oliver Heywood*, vol. 1, pp. 53, 36.

21 *The Diary of the Rev. Henry Newcome 1661–63*, ed. T. Heywood, Chetham Society, Orig. Ser., 1849, vol. 18, pp. 14, 36, 41, 83; E. Calamy, *The Happiness of Those Who Sleep in Jesus*, 1662, p. 28. The same procedure was followed in the Catholic household of Sir Edward Montagu of Boughton in Northamptonshire, C. Wise, *The Montagus of Boughton*, 1888, p. 31; at the house of William Dudson, mercer, of Rathwell, Northamptonshire, *Cal. S. P. Dom., 1634–5*, pp. 22–3, as also at that

of Sir Robert and Lady Elizabeth Brooke of Yoxford in Suffolk, N. Parkhurst, *Faithfull and Diligent Christian*, 1684, pp. 51, 53, and of Sir John and Lady Frances Hobart, J. Collinges, *Par Nobile*, 1669, p. 18.

22 L. Hutchinson, *Memoirs of the Life of Colonel Hutchinson*, ed. J. Sutherland, 1973, p. 288.

23 C. S. Durrant, *A Link Between Flemish Mystics and English Martyrs*, 1925, pp. 274–5.

24 S. Ford, *A Christians Acqiescence*, 1665, pp. 132–3.

25 N. Parkhurst, *Faithfull and Diligent Christian*, 1684, p. 53; Abigail Harley, BL, Addl. Ms. 70,012, fol. 10. See also the practice of Ambrose and Mary Barnes of Newcastle-upon-Tyne, W. H. D. Longstaffe, ed., *The Memoirs and Life of Mr Ambrose Barnes*, Surtees Society, 1867, vol. 50, p. 67.

26 Erasmus, *Collected Works*, VIII, p. 289.

27 For example in the statutes of Queen Elizabeth Grammar School, Chipping Barnet, in F. C. Cass, 'Queen Elizabeth School at Chipping Barnet 1573–1665', *Transactions of the London and Middlesex Archaeological Society*, 1876, vol. 5, p. 30; of Steyning Grammar School, in W. B. Breach, 'William Holland, Alderman of Chichester, and Steyning Grammar School', *Sussex Archaeological Society Collections*, 1990, vol. 43, p. 79; of Dedham Grammar School 1579, Essex Record Office Transcript no. 461 (NS); of Durham Grammar School in VCH Durham, ed. W. Page, vol. 1, 1905, pp. 377–8; Brinsley, *Ludus Literarius*, 1612, p. 255; C. Hoole, *A New Discovery of the Olde Art of Teaching School*, 1660, p. 270–1.

28 R. F. Young, ed., *Comenius in England*, 1952, Oxford, p. 65; L. Magalotti, trans., *The Travels of Cosmo the Third Through England During the Reign of Charles the Second*, 1821, p. 399–40.

29 *Correspondence of the Family of Hatton 1601–1704*, ed. E. M. Thompson, Camden Society, New Ser. 1878, vol. 22, p. 3.

30 Hoby, *Diary*, pp. 62–3, 75 and *passim*. For the ability of Lollard women to memorise scripture and sermon see A. Hudson *The Premature Reformation, Wycliffite Texts and Lollard History*, 1988, Oxford, pp. 190–92, and C. Cross, ' "Great Reasoners in Scripture": the Activities of Women Lollards 1380–1530', in D. Baker, ed., *Medieval Women, Studies in Church History*, Subsidia II, 1978, Oxford, pp. 359–80.

31 J. Eales, *Puritans and Roundheads. The Harleys of Brampton Bryan and the Outbreak of the Civil War*, 1990, Cambridge, p. 49.

32 J. B. Williams, *Memoirs of . . . Mrs Savage*, 1818, pp. 2, 33.

33 J. Barlow, *The True Guide to Glory*, 1619, p. 48.

34 E. Reynolds, *Imitation and Caution for Christian Women*, 1659, pp. 6–7.

35 S. Clarke, *Lives of Sundry Eminent Persons*, 1683, pp. 153–4.

36 J. Aubrey, *Brief Lives*, ed. O. L. Dick, 1962, Harmondsworth, p. 307; G. Ballard, *Memoirs of British Ladies*, 1752, pp. 287–8; P. W. Souers, *The Matchless Orinda*, 1931, Cambridge, Mass, p. 19. See also the practice of Elizabeth Heywood, in Turner, *Oliver Heywood*, vol. 1, p. 58; of Elizabeth Jocelin, in T. Goade, 'The Approbation', prefaced to Jocelin's *The Mother's Legacie*, 1624, sigs A3 verso, A4 recto; of Susanna, Countess of Suffolk, in E. Rainbow, *A Sermon Preached . . . at the Interring of Susanna Countess of Suffolk*, 1649, pp. 13–14; of Margaret Corbet, in H. Wilkinson, *The Hope of Glory*, 1657, Oxford, pp. 64–7.

37 From an extensive literature cf. E. A. Havelock, *The Muse Learns to Write. Reflections of Orality and Literature from Antiquity to the Present*, 1986, New Haven; R. Finnegan, *Oral Literacy in Africa*, 1982, Oxford; M. T. Clanchy, *From Memory to the Written Word. England 1066–1307*, 1979; M. J. Carruthers, *The Book of Memory*

in Medieval Culture, 1990, Cambridge; F. A. Yates, *The Art of Memory*, 1966; W. J. Ong, *Orality and Literacy. Technologising of the Word*, 1982.

38 J. C. Olin, ed., *Christian Humanism and the Reformation*, 1965, New York, p. 17.

39 Frere and Kennedy, II, p. 36, repeated in the 1547 Injunctions, *ibid.*, II, p. 116; *Cal. S. P. Dom., 1547–80*, p. 170.

40 C. Camden, 'Memory the Warder of the Brain', *Philological Quarterly*, 1939, vol. 18, pp. 52–72 provides a useful summary of the various theoretical works available in the sixteenth century. See also A. M. Guite, 'The Art of Memory and the Art of Salvation: The Centrality of Memory in the Sermons of John Donne and Lancelot Andrewes', *Seventeenth Century*, 1989, vol. 4, pp. 1–17, and R. B. Knox, ed., *Reformation, Conformity and Dissent: Essays in Honour of Geoffrey Nuttall*, 1977, pp. 92–114.

41 *Luther's Table Talk*, ed. W. Hazlitt, 1848, p. 192. Cf. P. Auski, 'Wyclif's Sermons and his Plain Style' *Archives for Reformation History*, 1975, vol. 60, pp. 5–23.

42 T. Wilson, *The Arte of Rhetorique*, 1553, sig. dii verso and fols 59 verso and 75 verso.

43 G. Abbot, *An Exposition of the Prophet Jonah*, 1600, ed. G. Webster, 1845, vol. 2, p. 331. See also Donne, *Sermons*, VI, p. 55.

44 Gifford, *A Sermon on the Parable of the Sower*, 1582, sigs Aii recto–Bvi recto. See also J. Glanvill, *An Essay Concerning Preaching*, 1678, pp. 11, 30, 40–1.

45 J. Collinges, *The Life of a True Christian*, 1649, p. 24. See also H. Wilkinson, *The Hope of Glory*, 1657, 2nd ed., 1660, p. 7; J. Udall, *Peters Fall: Two Sermons on This History of Peters Denying Christ*, n.d., sig. A7 recto, for the tabular setting out of 'The Method and Order of the Whole Matter of This Book', and the Ramistic table in W. Whately, *The New Birth*, 1619, sig. A3 recto–verso, and J. Vincent, *Christ the Best Husband*, 1672. Even the learned John Donne kept the problem in mind, *Sermons*, VIII, pp. 115, 159.

46 Turner, *Oliver Heywood*, p. 58.

47 A. Tyrell, *A Fruitful Sermon Preached at Christ Church the 13 of Julie Anno 1589 . . . Taken by Characterie*, 1589, sigs Avi verso and Aviii recto.

48 Egerton, *op. cit.*, sigs A4 recto–verso, A7 recto.

49 H. Smith, *A Sermon on the Benefit of Contention . . . Taken by Characterie*, 1590, reprinted as *The Benefit of Contention*, 1592. See also his *The Examination of Usurie in Two Sermons Taken by Characterie*, 1591. T. Playfere, *The Meaning of Mourning. A Sermon Preached at St Maryes Spittle in London in Easter Week 1595*, 1596, Ep. Ded., sig. A2 recto. Cf. the comments of W. Cupper, *Certain Sermons . . . preached at Alphages Church*, 1592, sig. Avii recto.

50 T. Metcalfe, *Short Writing*, 6th ed., 1645, title page. Metcalfe referred to his system as 'this art of Radio-Stenography'.

51 Verney, *Memoirs*, III, pp. 72–3. See also J. Phillips, *A Satyr Against Hypocrites*, 1655, pp. 8–9.

52 T. Rogers, *The Character of a Good Woman*, 1697, preface, sig. e5 recto. S. Bury, *An Account of the Life and Death of Mrs Elizabeth Bury*, 1720, p. 11; H. Allen, *Satan His Methods and Malice Baffled*, 1683, p. 12.

53 Anna Trapnel, *A Legacy of Saints*, 1654; J. Milton, *Areopagitica*, 1644, p. 31.

54 National Portrait Gallery of Canada, Ottowa.

55 See, for example, J. N. King, 'The Godly Woman in Elizabethan Iconography', *Rennaissance Quarterly*, 1985, vol. 38, pp. 41–84, and R. W. Scribner, *For the Sake of Simple Folk. Popular Propaganda for the German Reformation*, 1981, Cambridge, p. 200. For discussion and photographs of the impedimenta of writing see M. Finlay, *Western Writing Implements in the Age of the Quill Pen*, 1990, Wetherall, Carlisle.

56 Sparke, *Crums of Comfort*, TG ed., 1628, sig. A7 recto.

57 Heywood, *op. cit.*, Epistle to the Reader, sig. A2 recto–verso.

58 Isham cited in L. Pollock, *A Lasting Relationship. Parents and Children Over Three Centuries*, 1987, p. 249.

59 Foxe, IV, p. 239.

60 N. Guy, *Pieties Pillar . . . for the Funeral of Elizabeth Gouge*, 1626, pp. 47–8, Dr Williams's Library.

61 Leigh, *op. cit.*, pp. 104–5, 108–12; Jocelin, *op. cit.*, p. 46.

62 V. Gabrieli, 'A New Digby Letter-Book: 'In Praise of Venetia', *National Library of Wales Journal*, 1956, vol. 9, p. 125.

63 B. Spencer, *A Dumb Speech . . .*, 1646, p. 42.

64 J. Taylor, *A Funeral Sermon . . . Preached at the obsequies of . . . Lady Frances, Countess of Carbery*, 1650, p. 28.

65 D. G. Green, ed., *The Meditations of Lady Elizabeth Delaval*, Surtees Society, 1975, vol. 190, p. 118.

66 T. T. Lewis, ed., *The Letters of Brilliana Harley*, Camden Society, 1854, vol. 58, p. 15.

67 P. Crawford, *Women and Religion in England 1550–1720*, 1993, p. 87.

68 A. Clarke, *Memorials of the Wesley Family*, 1823, pp. 328–32.

69 W. Dillingham, *A Sermon at the Funeral of Lady Elizabeth Alston*, 1678, p. 41; *Timely Preparation for Death*, in T. Hervey, ed., *Some Unpublished Papers . . . Relating to the Family of Sir Frances Drake*, 1887, p. 50.

70 J. C., *Strength in Weakness. A Sermon Preached at the Funeral of Mrs Martha Brooks . . .*, 1676, p. 34.

71 E. Barker, *A Sermon Preached at the Funeral of Lady Elizabeth Capel*, 1661, p. 34. See also E. Hall, *A Sermon Preached . . . at the Funeral of Lady Anne Harcourt*, 1664, p. 49.

72 A. Walker, *The Holy Life of Elizabeth Walker . . .*, 1690, p. 33.

73 H. Whyle, *A Sermon Preached at the Funeral of Anne Lady Burgoyne*, 1694, pp. 9, 11, 12, 14.

74 P. Lake, 'Feminine Piety and Personal Potency: the Emancipation of Mrs Jane Ratclifffe', *The Seventeenth Century*, 1987, vol. 2, pp. 143–65.

75 Braithwait, *The English Gentlewoman*, 1631, pp. 45, 48; R. Rogers, *The Practice of Christianity: An Epitome of Seven Treatises*, 1618, p. 261; L. Wright, *The Pilgrimage to Paradise*, 1591, sig. E3 recto.

76 *Liturgies and Occasional Forms of Prayer Set Forth in the Reign of Queen Elizabeth*, ed. W. K. Clay, Parker Society, 1847, Cambridge, p. 503.

77 Hall, *The Art of Divine Meditation*, 1600: 1607, p. 84. He lists topics suitable for meditation on pp. 71–3. See also Rogers' list in his original *Seven Treatises*, 1600, pp. 246–59.

78 Calamy, *op. cit.*, pp. 24, 31, 32, 75, 76.

79 Baxter, *op. cit.*, p. 688; chaps 6–14, pp. 686–856; Ussher, *op. cit.*, To the Reader, sig. *4 verso. His proof-texts were Genesis 24–63 and Mark 1.35. I am grateful to the Keeper of the Archives of Dulwich College for permission to consult this apparently unique copy.

80 White, *op. cit.*, pp. 18, 321. Herbert *The Temple. Sacred Poems and Private Speculations*, 1633, p. 16. For general discussion see R. Tuve, *Protestant Poetics in the Seventeenth-century Religious Lyric*, 1979, Princeton.

81 Clarke, *An Antidote Against Immoderate Mourning*, 1659, p. 41.

82 Warren, *op. cit.*, p. 90.

83 S. Denison, *The Monument or Tombstone . . . a Sermon Preached 21 November . . . at the Funeral of Mrs Elizabeth Juxon*, 1620, p. 83 and *passim*.

84 L. Pollock, *With Faith and Physic. The Life of a Tudor Gentlewoman. Lady Grace Mildmay 1552–1620*, 1993, pp. 24, 25, 70.

85 BL Egerton Ms. 607, fols 119 verso, 114 verso, 22 verso.

86 BL Addl. Mss 27, 351–6 *passim*.

87 BL Addl. Ms. 4454, fols 92, 93, 98 verso, 99 recto and *passim*.

88 D. G. Green, ed., *The Meditations of Lady Elizabeth Delaval Written Between 1662 and 1671*, Surtees Society, vol. 190, 1978 for 1975; *The Private Diary of Elizabeth Viscountess Mordaunt*, 1856, Duncairn.

89 S. Bury, *An Account of the Life and Death of Mrs Elizabeth Bury*, 1720, Bristol, p. 11.

90 E. Calamy, *A Funeral Sermon Preached on the Occasion of the Decease of . . . Mrs Elizabeth Williams Late Wife of Rev. Daniel Williams*, 1698, *passim*; F. Atterbury, *A Discourse Occasion'd by the Death of Lady Cutts*, 1698, pp. 12, 14; E. Staunton, *A Sermon on the Death of Mrs Elizabeth Wilkinson*, 1659, Oxford, p. 24.

91 T. Rogers, *The Character of a Good Woman*, 1697, p. 126.

92 Dr Williams's Library, Mod. Ms. 24.8. Sarah Savage's diaries are excerpted in J. B. Williams, *Memoirs of the Life and Character of Mrs Sarah Savage, Eldest Daughter of Rev. Philip Henry*, 1818, *passim*. See also P. Crawford, 'Katherine and Philip Henry and Their Children: A Case Study in Family Ideology', *Transactions of the Lancashire and Cheshire Historic Society*, 1984, vol. 134, pp. 39–73.

93 *National Library of Wales Journal*, 1956, vol. 9, p. 125.

94 Hoby, *Diary*, p. 63; W. Harrison, *Deaths Advantage*, 1602, p. 8; T. C. Croker, ed., *The Autobiography of Mary Countess of Warwick*, 1848, p. 128.

95 A. Lanyer, *Salve Deus Rex Judaeorum*, 1611, 'The Description of Cooke-ham', sig. H3 recto. See also D. H. J. Clifford, ed., *The Diaries of Lady Anne Clifford*, 1990, Stroud, Glos., p. 32; J. Batchiler, *The Virgins Pattern*, 1661, p. 14.

96 For general discussion see H. Wilcox, 'Exploring the Language of Devotion in the English Revolution', in T. Healey and J. Sawday, eds, *Literature and the English Civil War*, 1990, Cambridge, pp. 75–88.

97 G. de la Tour-Landry, *The Book of the Knight of La Tour-Londres*, ed. T. Wright, EETS, 1868, vol. 33, p. 118.

98 R. Rogers, *The Practice of Christianitie*, 1603, sig. A3 recto; D. Rogers, *Davids Cost*, 1619, p. 304.

99 T. Overbury, *Characters*, 1614, in *The Overburian Characters*, ed. W. J. Paylor, 1936, Oxford, p. 43.

100 M. Cavendish, *Sociable Letters*, 1664, p. 39; R. Burton, *Anatomy of Melancholy*, 1621, Oxford, p. 581, had made the same point about 'silly gentlewomen', though Fynes Moryson, *An Itinerary . . .*, 1617, pp. 14–15, had recommended the reading of *Amadis de Gaule* in the original for precisely the reason Margaret Cavendish deplored: 'for the knights errant and the ladies of courts do therein exchange courtly speeches'.

101 Pepys, *Diary*, 7 December 1660; A. Boate, *The Character of a Trulie Vertuous and Pious Woman. . .*, 1651, Paris, p. 41; H. Woolley, *The Gentlewomans Companion*, 1675, p. 9.

102 Foxe, VI, pp. 422–3.

103 J. W. Burgon, *The Life of Thomas Gresham*, 2 vols, 1839, II, pp. 415–16.

104 T. Wright, ed., *Queen Elizabeth and her Times*, 2 vols, 1838, I, p. 406.

105 J. H. Turner, *The Rev. Oliver Heywood 1630–72: His Autobiography, Diaries etc.*, 4 vols, 1881–5, I, p. 42; *A Brief Discourse of the Christian Life and Death of Mistress*

Katherine Brettergh, p. 8, appended to W. Harrison, *Deaths Advantage Little Regarded*, 1602; S. Clarke, *The Lives of Sundry Eminent Persons*, 1683, p. 137.

106 *A Profitable Memorial to the Conversion, Life and Death of Mrs Mary Gunter Set up as a Monument to Both Protestants and Papists*, appended to T. Taylor, *The Pilgrims Profession*, 1625, pp. 151–2. The British Library copy is inscribed 'Sarah Hayne hur boke'. W. Gurnall, *The Christians Labour and Reward . . . Preached at the Funeral of . . . Lady Vere*, 1672, p. 130.

107 E. Reynolds, *The Churches Triumph Over Death*, 1662, p. 33; T. Rogers, *The Character of a Good Woman*, 1697, pp. 127–8.

108 HMC, *Hastings Mss*, IV, p. 353; E. Rainbowe, *A Sermon Preached at the Interring of the Corps of Susanna Countess of Suffolk*, 1649, p. 21.

109 E. Barker, *A Sermon Preached at the Funeral of . . . Lady Elizabeth Capel*, 1661, p. 34.

110 J. Howe, *A Funeral Sermon on the Death of Mrs Judith Hammond . . .*, 1696, p. 17.

111 F. Rose-Troup, 'Two Book Bills of Catherine Parr', *The Library*, 3rd Ser., vol. 2, pp. 40–8.

112 Hoby, *Diary*, pp. 64, 75 and *passim*.

113 L. Pollock, *With Faith and Physic. The Life of a Tudor Gentlewoman. Lady Grace Mildmay*, 1993, pp. 7, 28 and 23.

114 T. T. Carter, *Nicholas Ferrar. His Household and his Friends*, ed. J. F. M. Carter, 1892, pp. 116, 231, 178.

115 V. Sackville-West, *The Diary of Lady Anne Clifford*, 1923, pp. 41, 56, 64, 68, 70. For a description of the books painted into the Great Picture at Craven Castle see T. D. Whitaker, *The History of the Antiquities of the Deanery of Craven*, 3rd ed., 1878, ed. A. W. Morant, pp. 339–51.

116 A. Venn, *The Wise Virgins Lamp Burning or Gods Sweet Incomes of Love, Written by her Own Hand and Found in her Closet after her Death*, 1658, pp. 2, 4, 31, 36, 50.

117 Dr Williams's Library, Modern Ms. 24.8, fols 20, 22.

118 C. Fell-Smith, *Mary Rich Countess of Warwick 1625–78, Her Family and Friends*, 1901, pp. 170–1.

119 E. Staunton, *A Sermon on the Death of Mrs Elizabeth Wilkinson*, 1659, Oxford, pp. 26–8; S. Clarke, *Lives of Sundry Eminent Persons*, 1683, p. 150; S. Bury, *An Account of the Life and Death of Mrs Elizabeth Bury . . . Together with her Funeral Sermon*, 1720, pp. 7, 20, 155.

120 S. Clarke, *Lives of Sundry Eminent Persons*, 1683, p. 202; S. Ford, *A Christians Acquiescence. A Funeral Sermon for Lady Elizabeth Langham*, 1665, pp. 128–9.

121 J. Batchiler, *The Virgins Pattern in the Exemplary Life and Lamented Death of Mrs Susanna Perwich*, 1661, pp. 14, 19–20.

122 M. Carbery, ed., *Mrs Elizabeth Freke, the Diary*, 1913, Cork, pp. 113–14.

123 D. Masham, *op. cit., passim*. See also P. Morgan, 'Frances Wolfreston and "Hor Bouks": A Seventeenth-century Book Collector', *The Library*, vol. 11, 1989, pp. 197–219. For Susanna Wesley's reading see C. Wallace Jr, ' "Some Stated Employment of Your Mind": Reading, Writing and Religion in the Life of Susanna Wesley', *Church History*, 1989, vol. 58. pp. 354–66.

124 S. Brigden, *London in the Reformation*, 1989 p. 89. Bunyan, *Grace Abounding*, 1666, p. 6.

125 K. R. Wark, *Elizabethan Recusancy in Cheshire*, Chetham Society, 3rd Ser., vol. 19, pp. 89–90.

126 J. Morris, ed., *The Triumphs of Our Catholic Forefathers, III*, 1877, p. 393.

127 Clarke, *Lives of Sundry Eminent Persons*, 1683, pp. 192–6.

128 *Ibid.*, p. 193.

129 BL Harleian Ms., 382, fol. 180 recto.

130 M. Pennington, *A Brief Account of my Exercises from my Childhood, Left with My Dear Daughter G. M. Penn*, 1848, *passim*.

131 G. Thomson, *Life in a Noble Household 1641–1700*, 1937, pp. 74–6, 275; Galpin, 'The Household Expenses of Sir Thomas Barrington, *Transactions of the Essex Archaeological Society*, NS, 1911–12, vol. 12, pp. 205, 210.

132 W. Gouge, *A Funeral Sermon . . . August 24 1646*, 1646, p. 28; Verney, *Memoirs*, IV, p. 177.

133 N. Parkhurst, *Faithful and Diligent Christian*, 1684, p. 49.

134 BL Egerton Ms. 2644, fol. 275, July 1628.

135 M. Spufford, 'The Schooling of the Peasantry in Cambridgeshire 1575–1700', *Agricultural History Review*, 1970, vol. 18, pp. 146.

136 T. Manton, *Advice to Mourners*, 1694, Preface, by Matthew Sylvester, p. xiv. See also H. Allen, *Satan His Methods and Malice Baffled*, 1683, p. 5.

137 F. J. Furnival, ed., *The Fifty Earliest English Wills in the Court of Probate 1387–1439*, EETS, Orig. Ser., 1882, vol. 78, p. 5; Bohun in S. G. Bell, 'Medieval Women Book Owners: Arbiters of Lay Piety and Ambassadors of Culture', *Signs*, 1982, vol. 7, pp. 749–50; C. H. Cooper, *The Lady Margaret*, 1874, Cambridge, p. 17. For Caxton's printing of the *Golden Legend* see N. F. Blake, *Caxton and his World*, 1969, pp. 117–23.

138 S. Tymms, ed., *Wills and Inventories from the Registers of Commissary of Bury St Edmunds*, Camden Society, 1850, vol. 49, p. 142.

139 BL Addl. Ms. 48, 064, fols 23 verso–24 recto; J. Waddington, *John Penry the Pilgrim Martyr 1559–93*, 1854, p. 127.

140 *Cal. S. P. Dom., Addenda, 1580–1625*, p. 544.

141 M. K. McIntosh, *A Community Transformed, The Manor and Liberty of Havering 1500–1620*, 1991, Cambridge, p. 273; M. E. Allen, ed., *Wills of the Archdeaconry of Suffolk 1620–24*, Suffolk Record Society, 1989, vol. 31, pp. 87 and 108.

142 *Ibid.*, pp. 388 and 307; 45–6.

143 *Ibid.*, pp. 234, 339, 193.

144 J. E. Bailey, 'Bishop Lewis Bayly and his *Practise of Pietie*', *The Manchester Quarterly*, 1883, vol. 7, pp. 203–4.

145 R. C. Richardson, *Puritanism in North-west England*, 1972, p. 57; S. Tymms, ed., *Wills and Inventories from the Registers of the Commissary of Bury St Edmunds*, Camden Society, 1850, vol. 49, pp. 199, 220.

146 M. Spufford, *Contrasting Communities*, p. 211; Spufford, 'The Scribes of Villagers Wills in the Sixteenth and Seventeenth Centuries and Their Influence', *Local Population Studies*, 1971, no. 7, p. 39. See also R. C. Richardson, 'Wills and Willmakers in the Sixteenth and Seventeenth Centuries. Some Lancashire Evidence', *ibid.*, 1972, no. 9, pp. 33–42. For comparison, N. Z. Davis, 'Beyond the Market. Books as Gifts in Sixteenth Century France', *TRHS*, 5th Ser., 1983, vol. 33, pp. 69–97.

147 J. G. Nichols, ed., *The Unton Inventories in 1596 and 1620*, 1841, p. 3.

148 L. Boynton, 'The Hardwick Inventory of 1601', *Furniture History*, 1961, vol. 7, p. 32.

149 J. O. Halliwell, ed., *Ancient Inventories*, 1854, pp. 10, 35, 82–3, 103, 105.

150 B. Phillips and J. H. Swift, eds, *Stockport Probate Records 1620–50*, Record Society of Lancashire and Cheshire, 1992, vol. 121, p. 291; G. H. Radford, 'The Lady Howard of Fitzford', *Reports and Transactions of the Devonshire Association*, 1890, vol. 22, p. 106. Spufford, *Contrasting Communities*, p. 210.

151 M. Reed, ed., *The Ipswich Probate Inventories 1583–1631*, Suffolk Record Society, 1981, vol. 22, p. 109; *ibid.*, pp. 66, 64.

152 J. J. Briggs, *The History of Melbourne*, 2nd ed., 1852, p. 86; T. N. Brushfield, 'The Financial Diary of a Citizen of Exeter 1631–43', *Reports and Transactions of the Devonshire Association*, 1901, vol. 33, pp. 201, 202, 231, 232.

7 MOTHERS AS EDUCATORS

1 Hareven, *Journal of Interdisciplinary History*, 1972, vol. 2, pp. 399–414; C. Hill, *Society and Puritanism in Pre-Revolutionary England*, 1964, chap. 13. The same point can be made of J. Morgan, *Godly Learning: Puritan Attitudes Towards Reason, Learning and Education 1560–1640*, 1986, Cambridge, chap. 8, 'The Godly Household'. The claim that the 'spiritualized household' and more 'liberal' attitudes towards marriage were the result of puritan emphases has been effectively countered by K. M. Davies, 'The Social Condition of Equality: How Original were Puritan Doctrines of Marriage?', *Social History*, 1977, vol. 5, pp. 563–80. Cf. M. Todd, 'Humanists, Puritans and the Spiritualized Household', *Church History*, 1980, vol. 49, pp. 18–34, though Todd makes no mention of the earlier article.

2 Gouge, *Of Domesticall Dueties*, 1622, pp. 259, 269.

3 J. Ray, *A Collection of English Proverbs*, 1670, Cambridge, p. 48.

4 Lowth (translating B. Batty), *The Christian Mans Closet*, 1581, fol. 52 recto; Taylor, 'The Marriage Ring or The Mysteries and Duties of Marriage', in R. Heber, ed., *Works*, 15 vols, 1828, vol. 5, p. 263. See also J. Nichols, *The Order of Household Instruction*, 1576, sig. Ci verso; R. Cleaver, *A Plaine and Familiar Exposition of the First and Second Chapters of the Proverbs of Solomon*, 1614, pp. 37–8; J. Dod and W. Hinde, *Bathshebaes Instruction to her Son Lemuel*, 1614, *passim*.

5 R. C(leaver), *A Godly Form of Household Government*, 1598, p. 157. His words echo T. Paynell's (translation of Vives, *De Officio Mariti*, 1529), *The Office and Duetie of an Husband*, 1550, sig. Pi verso.

6 Aylmer, *An Harborrowe for Faithfull and Trewe Subjects Agaynst the Late Blowne Blast Concerning the Government of Women*, 1559, Strasburg, sig. Giii verso (not 'a sermon given before the Queen' as in C. L. Powell, *English Domestic Relations*, 1917, New York, p. 147, and repeated in Morgan, *Godly Learning*, p. 143 n. 9). See also the homily 'On the State of Matrimonie' in the *Second Tome of Homilies*, 1563, fol. 255.

7 M. Wollstonecraft, *A Vindication of the Rights of Women*, 1792, p. 346.

8 C. Parr, The *Lamentacion of a Sinner*, 1544, sig. Gvii verso. For male characterisations, T. Becon, *The Syck Mans Salve*, 1561, p. 217; W. Averell, *A Dyall for Dainty Darlings . . . A Myrrour for Vertuous Maydens*, 1584, sig. Fii verso.

9 Snawsel, *A Looking Glasse for Married Folke*, 1610, sig. A5 verso. For comparison see S. Chojnacki, ' "The Most Serious Duty": Motherhood, Gender and Patrician Culture in Renaissance Venice', in M. Miguel and J. Schiesari, eds, *Refiguring Women: Perspectives on Gender in the Italian Renaissance*, 1991, Ithaca, pp. 133–54.

10 Anon, *The Office of Christian Parents*, 1616, Cambridge, p. 137; Cheynell, *A Plot for the Good of Posterity*, 1648, p. 28. See also Erasmus' letter to John Faber in praise of Catherine of Aragon in P. S. Allen, ed., *Opus Epistolarum Des. Erasmi Roterodami*, 1906, Oxford, vol. 3, p. 602; R. Hyrde's preface to Margaret More's (translation of Erasmus, *Precatio Domenica*, 1523, Basel) *A Devout Treatise upon the Pater Noster*, 1526?, sig. Aiv recto–verso; R. Taverner's (translation of Erasmus, *Encomium Matrimonii*, 1518, Basel), *A Ryght Frutefull Epystle . . . in Laude . . . of*

Matrimonye, 1532, sig. Dii verso; D. Clapam's (translation of Agrippa's *De Nobilitate et Praecellentia Foeminei Sexus*, 1532), *The Commendation of Matrimonie*, 1545, sig. C3 recto, C6 verso.

11 G. Keith, *The Women Preachers of Samaria*, 1674, p. 24. See also S. Torshell, *The Womans Glorie*, 1654, pp. 5, 10–11; G. Fox, *Gospell-Truth*, 1656, pp. 81, 331, 724. John Bale's 1547 relation of the examination of Anne Askew not only praised Anne for her knowledge of scripture, but also condoned her desertion of her husband since he prevented her from following her true faith. Of course, all kinds of legal and economic factors effectively prevented the majority of women from following Anne's example and Keith's prescription.

12 Woodward, *The Childes Patrimony*, 1640, p. 14; Henry Peacham, in V. R. Hetzel, ed., *The Compleat Gentleman*, 1622; 1962, Ithaca, p. 41: 'Nor must all the blame lie upon the schoolmasters. Fond parents have often as deep a share in this precious spoil.' I deliberately leave on one side the 'myth of motherhood' debate, as in E. Badinter, *L'Amour en Plus*, 1980, Paris, trans. R. de Garis, *The Myth of Motherhood*, 1981, and A. Dally, *Inventing Motherhood; The Consequences of an Ideal*, 1982, which needs more cogent historical treatment than either Badinter or Dally affords it. S. Wilson, 'The Myth of Motherhood a Myth; The Historical View of European Child-rearing', *Social History*, 1984, vol. 9, pp. 181–94 provides a salutary reminder of the difficulties. See also F. Mount, *The Subversive Family: An Alternative History of Love and Marriage*, 1982, chap. 7.

13 Greenham, *A Godlie Exhortation and Fruitfull Admonition to Vertuous Parents and Modest Matrones*, 1584, sig. Aviff. R. C(leaver), *Household Government*, p. 305 uses virtually identical wording to make the same point, which is repeated in R. Baxter, *The Reformed Pastor*, 1655, p. 59. Note however that both Mulcaster, *The Firste Parte of the Elementarie*, 1582, sig. Aii verso–iii recto, and Kempe, *The Education of Children in Learning*, 1588, sig. Fi verso, emphasised the need for cooperation between parents and teachers.

14 Greenham, *Godlie Exhortation*, sig. A iii–iv. The apocryphal book of Tobias, chaps 8 and 9, provided the usual proof-texts. For recommended prayers, see T. Bentley, *The Monument of Matrones*, 1582, a three-volume collection of devotions and prayers exhaustively covering every aspect of a woman's life, 'a domesticall librarie' as Bentley called it. See also D. Featley, *Ancilla Pietatis or The Handmaid of Private Devotion*, 1623; 3rd ed., 1628, pp. 713ff.

15 K. Thomas, *Religion and the Decline of Magic*, 1978, Harmondsworth, p. 125.

16 Aristotle's one-semen theory of procreation is discussed from the feminist standpoint in M. C. Horowitz, 'Aristotle and Woman', *Journal of the History of Biology*, 1976, vol. 9, pp. 183–213. Cf. I. Maclean, *The Renaissance Notion of Woman*, 1980, Cambridge, pp. 30ff, and V. L. Bullough, 'Medieval Medical and Scientific Views of Women', *Viator*, 1973, vol. 4, pp. 487–93. The enormous power over the embryo traditionally attributed to the female is discussed in E. Neumann, *The Great Mother: An Analysis of the Archetype*, 1963, Princeton. See also the view of John Donne, *Sermons*, V, p. 162.

17 Lowth (Batty), *Christian Mans Closet*, 1581, fol. 52 verso–53 recto; T. Tryon, *A New Method of Bringing up Children*, 1695, pp. 7–13, gives detailed instructions about diet and exercise during pregnancy, though none of them could be called 'new'; cf. Aristotle, *Politics*, VII, XVI, 1335b.

18 W. Averell, *Dyall for Dainty Darlings . . .*, 1584, sig. Fii verso. See Robert Furse's advice to his son that when seeking a wife he should enquire of her mother's nature too, in H. J. Carpenter, 'Furse of Moreshead: A Family Record of the

Sixteenth Century', *Reports and Transactions of the Devonshire Association*, 1894, vol. 26, p. 172. Richard Allestree emphasised the point in his *The Ladies Calling*, 1673, p. 52. The built-in obsolescence of such a mode of education (in any sphere) remains with us to this day.

19 Maplet, *Diall of Destiny*, 1581, sig. Kiiff.

20 Poole, *Country Astrology*, 1650, pp. 15, 24, 30 and *passim*; Case, *The Angelicall Guide*, 1697, p. 61.

21 Securis, *A Prognostication for the Year . . . 1562*, 1562, and *A Prognostication for . . . 1576*, 1576, 'To the gentle reader', sig. Bii recto.

22 Rueff, *The Expert Midwife*, 1637, p. 65. See also J. Guillimeau, *Child Birth or The Happy Delivery of Women*, 1612, pp. 9ff.

23 L. Bradner and C. A. Lynch, eds, *The Latin Epigrams of Thomas More*, 1953, Chicago, p. 156.

24 E. Sandys, 'A Sermon Preached at a Marriage in Strausborough', in *Sermons and Miscellaneous Pieces by Bishop Edwin Sandys*, ed. J. Ayre, Parker Society, 1842, Cambridge, p. 315. See also H. Smith, *A Preparative to Marriage*, 1591, p. 18.

25 Erasmus, *De Conscribendis*, 1522, Basel, ed. J. K. Sowards, trans. C. Fantazzi, *Collected Works of Erasmus*, 1985, Toronto, vol. 25, pp. 133 and 141. See also H. Bullinger, trans. M. Coverdale, *The Christen State of Matrimony*, 1541, fol. xxiii recto and lix recto–verso; 'for to have children is the greatest treasure; for in the children do partners live in manner each after their death'; Becon, *A Pomander of Prayer*, 1558, p. 77; Donne, *Sermons*, II, p. 335.

26 The matter is referred to in Erasmus' *Colloquies*, trans. C. R. Thompson, 1965, Chicago, p. 269, and in Sir Thomas More's letter to his daughter Margaret Roper, in E. F. Rogers, ed., *Sir Thomas More. Selected Letters*, 1961, New Haven, p. 155.

27 *The Private Diary of Lady Elizabeth Mordaunt*, 1856, Duncairn, p. 235; R. Parkinson, ed., *The Life of Adam Martindale Written by Himself*, Chetham Society, Orig. Ser., 1845, vol. 4, p.154.

28 E. Shorter, *The Making of the Modern Family*, 1976, p. 204 and chap. 5 *passim*. The view is shared by L. Stone, *Family, Sex and Marriage*, 1977, pp. 68–70, 114, 117, 210–11, and originated in P. Ariès, *L'Enfant et le Vie Famille Sous l'Ancien Régime*, 1960, Paris, trans. R. Baldick as *Centuries of Childhood*, 1962. Ariès's views are comprehensively considered and doubted (as they were more briefly by most reviewers) in A. Wilson, 'The Infancy of the History of Childhood: An Appraisal of Philippe Ariès', *History and Theory*, 1980, vol. 19, pp. 132–53, and R. T. Vann, 'The Youth of Centuries of Childhood', *ibid.*, 1982, vol. 21, pp. 279–99. Revisionist versions have been incorporated in K. Wrightson, *English Society 1580–1680*, 1982; Mount, *Subversive Family*; L. Pollock, *Forgotten Children*, 1982; G. Pigman III, *Grief and the English Renaissance Elegy*, 1985, Cambridge – though not in M. Slater, *Family Life in the Seventeenth Century, The Verneys of Claydon House*, 1984.

29 Elizabeth Clere to John Paston I, 29 June (not after 1449), in N. Davis, ed., *The Paston Letters and Papers of the Fifteenth Century*, 2 vols, 1971 and 1976, Oxford, vol. 2, p. 32; Ascham, *The Scholemaster*, 1570, sig. Eiii verso–iv recto.

30 Becon, *The Booke of Matrimonye*, in *Worckes*, 1562, fol. DC1 recto. He was repeating almost verbatim R. Taverner's (translation of Erasmus, *Encomium Matrimonii*, 1518, Basel) *A Ryght Frutefull Epystle . . . in Laude and Prayse of Matrimonye*, 1532, sig. Di recto–verso. See also Sandys, *Sermons*, p. 328, and Taylor 'The Marriage Ring', in Heber, ed., *Works*, vol. 5, p. 269: 'how many delicious accents

make a man's heart dance in the pretty conversations of those dear pledges . . . their childishness, their stammerings, their innocence, their imperfections'. Contrast the view of the Presbyterian minister, Henry Newcome: 'What a deal of patience is requisite to bear any conversation with our little children. How foolish and peevish are they', in T. Heywood, ed., *The Diary of the Rev. Henry Newcome 1661–63*, Chetham Society, Orig. Ser., 1849, vol. 18, p. 16.

31 Ray, *A Collection of English Proverbs*, p. 50; M. P. Tilley, *A Dictionary of Proverbs in England in the Sixteenth and Seventeenth Centuries*, 1950, Ann Arbor, p. 723; B. Capp, *Astrology and the Popular Press 1500–1800*, 1979, pp. 122ff, shows that 'almost without exception' almanack literature was critical of women in general and wives in particular. For a typical collection of male chauvinist stories about women see A. Copley, *Wits Fits and Fancies . . . Newly Corrected*, 1614, pp. 91ff.

32 Smith, 'A Preparative for Marriage', in *The Sermons of Master Smith Gathered in One Volume*, 1592, p. 44 (the passage does not occur in the original edition of 1591). See also R. Bolton, *Some General Directions for a Comfortable Walking with God*, 1625, p. 239, and Vives, trans. Hyrde, *The Instruction of a Christen Woman*, 1529, sig. Xiii recto. Cf. R. Whitforde, *A Worke for Housholders*, 1530, sig. Viv recto: 'a shrew will sooner be corrected by smiling or laughing than by a staff or strokes'; Donne, *Sermons*, II, p. 346; Taylor, 'The Marriage Ring' in Heber, ed., *Works*, vol. 5, p. 268.

33 HMC 12th Report, Appendix Part I, pp. 357–8; D. M. Gardiner, ed., *The Oxinden and Peyton Letters 1642–78*, 1937, pp. 270–1, 274.

34 V. M. Larminie, 'Marriage and the Family: The Example of the Seventeenth-Century Newdigates', *Midland History*, 1984, vol. 9, p. 15; C. Aspinall-Oglander, *Nunwell Symphony*, 1945, pp. 97–101.

35 V. Gabrieli, 'A New Digby Letter-Book: In Praise of Venetia', *National Library of Wales Journal*, 1956, vol. 9, pp. 133–48, 440–62, 1957, vol. 10, pp. 81–106. Bridgewater in BL Egerton Ms. 607, fols 78–83; Cecil in C. Read, *Lord Burghley and Queen Elizabeth*, 1960, New York, p. 447; Hastings in C. Cross, ed., *Letters of Sir Francis Hastings 1579–1609*, Somerset Record Society, 1969, vol. 69, pp. 62–3; Harley in BL Addl. Ms. 70, 130 (unbound), 20 October 1688. See also Harley's earlier letters to Abigail, BL Addl. Ms. 70, 012, fols 5, 16, 45; these, of course, among so many others.

36 H. Owen, *Stanhope, Allanson, Haddon and Shaw: Four North Country Families*, 1985, pp. 12, 109; E. Cust, *Records of the Cust Family II: The Brownlows of Belton*, 1909, pp. 112ff; M. Clive, *Jack and the Doctor*, 1966, p. 65; J. Loftis, ed. *The Memoirs of Anne Lady Halkett and Anne Lady Fanshawe*, 1979, Oxford, pp. 13–14.

37 Aspinall-Oglander, *Nunwell Symphony*, p. 115; Anon, *A Tablet for Gentlewomen*, 1574, sig. Dviii verso and Eiiii recto. Similar prayers are to be found in Bentley, *The Monument of Matrones*, 1582, *passim*, S. Hieron, *A Helpe unto Devotion*, 1616, pp. 144ff, and D. Featley, *Ancilla Pietatis or The Handmaid of Private Devotions*, 1638, pp. 713ff.

38 W. Gouge, *Of Domesticall Dueties*, 1622, p. 502; Donne, *Sermons*, III, p. 245; Ben Jonson's epigrammatic poem 'To Fine Lady Would-be', in B. H. Newdigate, ed., *The Poems of Ben Jonson*, 1936, Oxford, p. 19.

39 N. Culpepper, *A Physicall Directory*, 1649, p. 32; J. Sandford, *Of the Vanitie and Uncertaintie of Artes and Sciences*, 1569, p. 115; H. Lloyd, *The Treasury of Health*, 1550, sigs Ov recto, Piii verso, Qi recto; T. A. Buckley, ed., *The Catechism of the Council of Trent 1566*, 1852.

40 Thomas, *Religion and the Decline of Magic*, pp. 222–3, 759–60.

41 For example, from the pre-Reformation humanists, such as Erasmus, *De Pueris Instituendis*, 1529, p. 315 and *A Playne and Godlye Exposition . . . of the Common Crede and the Ten Commandments*, 1541, fol. 163 verso–164 recto, Vives (Hyrde) *Instruction of a Christen Woman*, sig. Bii verso, and T. Elyot (translating Plutarch) *The Education and Bringing up of Children*, 1533, sig Bii verso; in the Protestant reformers such as Bullinger (Coverdale), *Christen State*, fol. lviii verso, Becon, *New Catechisme* in *Worckes*, fol. cccccxvii verso, R. C(leaver), *Godly Form of Household Government*, pp. 231ff, Smith, *Preparative*, pp. 99–100 and Perkins (Pickering), *Christen Oeconomie*, 135; in the Anglican Jeremy Taylor, in Heber, ed., *Works*, vol. 2, pp. 30–42 and the Catholic Francis de Sales, *A Treatise of the Love of God*, 1616, 18th ed., trans. M. Carr, 1630, Douai, pp. 270, 272.

42 J. Jones, *The Arte and Science of Preserving Bodie and Soule*, 1579, p. 30. See also T. Phaire, *The Boke of Chyldren*, 1544, p. 3, and R. Cleaver, *A Plaine and Familiar Exposition of the Ten Commandments Newly Corrected*, 1614, pp. 199f.

43 R. C(leaver), *Godly Form of Household Government*, p. 231; Bullinger (Coverdale), *Christen State of Matrimony*, 1541, sig. iv verso–vi recto. The point was still being made by Allestree in 1673, *The Ladies Calling*, pp. 50f. Conversely, Sir Hugh Cholmley (born 1600) believed his physical weakness during childhood to be the result of his being wet-nursed by a pregnant woman, *Memoirs of Sir Hugh Cholmley*, 1870, pp. 21–2.

44 D. McLaren 'Marital Fertility and Lactation, 1570–1720', in M. Prior, ed., *Women in English Society 1500–1800*, 1985, pp. 22–53; D. McLaren, 'Fertility, Infant Mortality and Breast-feeding in the Seventeenth Century', *Medical History*, 1978, vol. 22, pp. 378–96, and 'Nature's Contraceptive: Wet-nursing and Prolonged Lactation: the Case of Chesham, Buckinghamshire 1578–1601', *Medical History*, 1979, vol. 23, pp. 426–41. Cf. P. Crawford, '"The Suckling Child": Adult Attitudes to Breast-feeding and Infant Care in Early Modern England and America', *Journal of Social History*, 1994, vol. 28, pp. 247–69; D. Harley, 'The Moral Theology and Godly Practice of Maternal Breastfeeding in Stuart England', *Bulletin of the History of Medicine*, 1995, vol. 69, pp. 198–223; V. Fildes, *Breasts, Babies and Bottles*, 1986, Edinburgh.

45 *The Countess of Lincolnes Nurserie*, 1622, Oxford, p. 15 and *passim*.

46 Smith *Preparative*, pp. 99–100. Smith's words are repeated almost verbatim in R. C(leaver), *Household Government*, pp. 232–4. See also Allestree, *The Ladies Calling*, p. 44: 'It is rather taken up as a piece of state and greatness, and for no other reason.'

47 The opening paragraphs of Erasmus' *De Pueris Instituendis* are an eloquent reminder of the importance of this stage. He was, of course, following Plato, *Republic*, 376aff.

48 A. Newdigate-Newdegate, *Gossip From a Muniment Room Being Passages from the Lives of Anne and Mary Fytton 1574–1618*, 1897, pp. 16, 20; letter to Burghley in C. Bowden, 'Women as Intermediaries: an Example of the Use of Literacy in the Late Sixteenth and Early Seventeenth Centuries', *History of Education*, 1993, vol. 22, p. 221, citing Warwickshire Record Office, CR 136/B307.

49 T. G. Tappert, ed., *Luther: Letters of Spiritual Counsel*, 1955, pp. 50–1.

50 C. Jackson, ed., *The Autobiography of Mrs Alice Thornton*, Surtees Society, 1875, vol. 62, p. 126. Cf. J. D. Marshall, ed., *The Autobiography of William Stout of Lancaster 1665–1752*, Chetham Society, 3rd Ser., 1967, vol. 14, p. 67, on the grief of his mother at the death of his youngest brothers of smallpox in 1681 and 1682.

51 For example in Philemon Holland's translation, *The Philosophie Commonly Called*

the Morals . . ., 1603, 'A Consolatorie Oration, Sent to Appollonius upon the Death of his Son', pp. 509–33, and 'A Consolatorie Letter and Discourse Sent unto his Wife, as Touching the Death of her and his Daughter', pp. 533–8.

52 Knox in D. Laing, ed, *Works*, 6 vols, 1846–64, Edinburgh, vol. 5, pp. 32, 119, echoing Calvin's *Institutes of Christian Religion*, vol. 1, pp. 8, 11. Cf. Bishop James Pilkington in J. Scolefield, ed., *The Works of James Pilkington*, Parker Society, 1842, Cambridge, p. 309; Bishop Thomas Cooper, *Certaine Sermons*, 1580, p. 164, and Gervase Babington's gloss in *Brief Conference Betwixt Mans Frailtie and Faith*, 1590, pp. 123ff. T. Playfere, *The Meane in Mourning*, 1595, pp. 5–9, 21–6. From a comprehensive literature see, for example, R. Houlbrooke, *Death, Ritual and Bereavement*, 1989; C. Gittings, *Death, Burial and the Individual in Early Modern England*, 1984; J. Whaley, *Mirrors of Mortality. Studies in the Social History of Death*, 1981.

53 Becon, *Syck Mans Salve*, pp. 151–2, 184. See also E. Bonner, *A Profitable and Necessary Doctryne*, 1604, sig. Dii verso.

54 T. Pritchard, *A Sermon Preached at the Funeral of Mrs Dawes at Great Barfield in Essex, January 5 1690*, 1690, pp. 1–2. See also E. Staunton, *A Sermon Preached on 9 December 1654* . . . *at the Funeral of Mrs Elizabeth Wilkinson*, 1659, p. 18; T. Whitaker, *A Comfort for Parents Mourning over Their Hopeful Children that Dye Younge*, 1693, Preface, sigs Aii recto–verso, Av verso. The point had been made much earlier by R. Southwell, *The Trumpets Own Death or A Consolatorie Epistle for Afflicted Maids in the Affects of Dying Friends*, 1596, sigs Biff, B4 verso.

55 *Fifth Sermon*, 1553, in *Certayne Godly Sermons Made Upon the Lords Prayer*, 1562, fol. 105 verso. See also L. Cole, *Of Death a True Description and against It a True Preparation*, 1629, p. 167: 'For though the first grief be not condemnable yet is the continuance thereof hurtful'; D. Featley, *The House of Mourning*, 1640: 'let the natural springs of tears swell, but not too much overflow their banks'; J. Flavel, *A Token for Mourners on the Advice of Christ to a Distressed Mother Bewailing the Death of her Dear and Only Son*, 1674, *passim*; Milton, 'On the death of a fair infant dying of a cough', stanza XI, in F. M. Patterson, ed., *The Works of John Milton*, 1931, New York, vol. I(1), p. 18.

56 Bacon, *Essays*, ed. M. J. Hawkins, 1972, pp. 6–7; B. H. Newdigate, ed., *The Poems of Ben Jonson*, 1936, Oxford, p. 11.

57 Cf. Pigman, *Grief, passim*. For the general literature see L. S. Marcus, *Childhood and Cultural Despair: A Theme and Variations in Seventeenth Century Literature*, 1978, Pittsburgh.

58 Erasmus to Roger Wentworth, *Letters* in *Collected Works*, vol. 2, p. 257; Vives (Hyrde), *Instruction of A Christen Woman*, Book II, sig. Miii verso. See also J. M. Osborne, ed., *The Autobiography of Thomas Whytehorne*, 1962, pp. 2–3; R. Legate, *A Brief Catechisme and Dialogue between the Husband and his Wyfe*, 1545, sig. Aii recto; J. Robinson, *New Essayes or Observations Divine and Morall*, 1628, p. 306. Sir John Oglander made the same point in his advice 'For my Grandchildren', in F. Bamford, ed., *A Royalist's Notebook. The Commonplace Book of Sir John Oglander Bt*, 1936, p. 249.

59 Proverbs 19.18; 22.15; 23.14, but most commonly 13.24. Occasionally the apocryphal *Ecclesiasticus* 30.8–9 were used: 'An unbroken horse becometh stubborn and a son left at large becometh headstrong. Cocker the child and he shall make thee afraid.'

60 Bullinger in *Decades*, ed. T. Harding, Parker Society, 1849, Cambridge, pp. 295–6; Becon, *New Catechisme*, p. 34. See also M. Cope, *A Godly and Learned Exposition upon the Proverbes of Solomon*, 1580, fol. 402 verso; Woodward, *Childes Patrimony*, pp. 18ff.

61 Elyot, *Education and Bringing up of Children*, sig. Fi verso; Lowth (Batty), *Christian Mans Closet*, fol. 14 recto; Buckley, *Catechism . . . Trent*, p. 145; J. Newham, *Newhams Nightcrowe*, 1590, p. 2; R. C(leaver), *Household Government*, pp. 323–4; R. Allen, *A Treatise of Catechism on Christian Instruction*, 1600, p. 120; Gouge, *Domesticall Dueties*, pp. 528, 556; C. Hoole, *A New Discovery of the Olde Arte of Teaching Schoole*, 1660, pp. 237, 275, 279–80; Woodward, *Childes Patrimony*, p. 28; W. Penn, *The Fruits of a Fathers Love*, 8th ed., 1790, p. 42.

62 E. Grymeston, *Miscelanea. Meditations. Memoratives*, 1604, sig. Aiii recto; D. Leigh, *The Mothers Blessing*, 7th ed. 1621, pp. 45f. See also H. Woolley, *The Gentlewomans Companion*, 1675, p. 4; M. Astell, *A Serious Proposal*, 1694, pp. 115.

63 Cust, *Records of the Cust Family II: The Brownlows of Belton*, p. 133; C. Jackson, ed., *The Autobiography of Mrs Alice Thornton*, Surtees Society, 1978 for 1975, vol. 190, pp. 37–8, 54, 63–4; V. Sackville-West, ed., *The Diary of Lady Anne Clifford 1616– 1619*, 1923, pp. 29–32 and *passim*; T. C. Croker, ed., *The Autobiography of Mary Countess of Warwick*, 1848, p. 27; A. Searle, ed., *The Barrington Family Letters 1628– 1632*, 1983, Camden Society, 4th Series, vol. 28, pp. 136–41.

64 Mount, *Subversive Family . . .*, p. 115; Vives (Hyrde) *op. cit.*, Book II, sig. Miii verso; A. C. Wood, ed., *Memorials of the Holles Family 1493–1656*, 1937, Camden Society, 3rd Ser., vol. 55, p. 220; W. Caton, *A Journal of the Life of William Caton*, 1689, p. 2; 'Journal of John Banks', in W. and T. Evans, eds, *The Friends Library*, 1838, Philadelphia, vol. 2, p. 8; HMC 14th Report, *Portland Mss*, Appendix Part II, p. 190; T. T. Lewis, ed., *The Letters of Lady Brilliana Harley*, 1854, Camden Society, vol. 58, p. 248, and *passim*.

65 J. Mechling, 'Advice to Historians on Advice to Mothers', *Journal of Social History*, 1975, vol. 9, pp. 44–63. Cf. M. Jeay, 'Sexuality and Family in Sixteenth-century France: Are Literary Sources a Mask or a Mirror?', *Journal of Family History*, 1979, vol. 4, pp. 328–45.

66 Richard Hyrde's (translation of Vives, *De Institutione Foeminae Christianae*, 1523), *Instruction of a Christen Woman*, 1529, sig. Di recto.

67 Elyot, *op. cit.*, sig. Aii recto.

68 S. Haynes, *A Collection of State Papers . . .*, 1740, p. 78. HMC, *Salisbury Mss*, I, p. 55.

69 BL Egerton Ms. 2713, fol. 23.

70 N. Harpsfield, *The Life and Death of Thomas More*, ed. E. V. Hitchcock, EETS, 1932, vol. 186, pp. 78–9.

71 J. Strype, *Annals of the Reformation*, 4 vols, 1824, Oxford, vol. II(ii), p. 400.

72 J. C. Hodgson, 'The Diary of Timothy Whittingham of Holmside', *Archaeologia Aeliana*, 1924, 3rd Ser., vol. 21; *Wills and Inventories of the Registry of Durham II*, Surtees Society, 1860, vol. 38, p.18. Katherine had been criticised for her reformist behaviour, J. T. Fowler, ed., *Rites of Durham*, Surtees Society, 1903, vol. 107, pp. 26, 27. G. J. Piccope, ed., *Lancashire and Cheshire Wills and Inventories*, Chetham Society, 1861, vol. 54, p. 72.

73 'Certain Precepts for the Well Ordering of a Man's Life' (*c.*1584), in L. B. Wright, ed., *Advice to a Son*, 1962, Ithaca, p. 9; J. Walsall, *A Sermon Preached at Paul's Cross 5 October 1578*, 1578, sig. Av verso.

74 Leigh, *op. cit.*, 1616; 7th ed., 1621, p. 24; Gouge, *A Funeral Sermon Preached . . . August 24 1646*, 1646, pp. 28–9.

75 S. Ford, *A Christians Acquiescence . . . Funeral Sermon . . . Lady Elizabeth Langham*, 1665, p. 98.

76 HMC *Hastings Mss.*, IV, 1947, p. 353. Written by Magdalen's confessor Dr

Richard Smith (printed in Rome 1609) and translated from the Latin by Dom John Cuthbert Fursdon 1627), in A. C. Southern, ed., *An Elizabethan Recusant House, Comprising the Life of the Lady Magdalen, Viscountess Montagu 1538–1608*, 1954, pp. 9–11.

77 Lord Braybrooke, ed., *The Autobiography of Sir John Bramston*, Camden Society, 1845, vol. 32, p. 111; T. Pomfret, *The Life of Christian(a), Late Countess Dowager of Devonshire*, 1685, pp. 22, 32ff.

78 A. Littleton, *A Sermon at the Funeral of Mary Alston*, 1671, p. 37.

79 J. Waddington, *John Penry the Pilgrim Martyr 1559–1593*, 1854, p. 141; T. W. Jones, ed., *The Life of William Bedell*, Camden Society, 1872, New Ser., vol. 4, p. 17. Cf. E. S. Shuckburgh, ed., *Two Biographies of William Bedell Bishop of Kilmore*, 1904, Cambridge. Archbishop Ussher was taught to read by two aunts, R. Parr, *The Life of James Ussher*, 1686, p. 2; C. A. Oglander, *Nunwell Symphony*, 1945, p. 70; T. Dugard, *Death and the Grave. A Sermon Preached at the Funeral of Lady Alice Lucie August 17 1648*, 1649, pp. 46–7.

80 A. Jessopp, ed., *The Autobiography of the Hon. Roger North*, 1887, pp. 4–5, vi; A. Boate, *The Character of a Trulie Vertuous and Pious Woman*, 1651, Paris, pp 66–7.

81 D. G. Green, ed., *The Meditations of Lady Elizabeth Delaval Written between 1662 and 1671*, Surtees Society, 1978 for 1975, vol. 190, p. 68; E. Reynolds, *Imitation and Caution for Christian Women*, 1659, p. 4; A. Walker, *The Holy Life of Mrs Elizabeth Walker*, 1690, p. 69; E. Calamy, *op. cit.*, ed. J. T. Rutt, 2 vols, 1829, I, p. 73.

82 A. Clarke, *Memoirs of the Wesley Family*, 1823, p. 256.

83 L. Roper's excellent *The Holy Household; Women and Morals in Reformation Augsburg*, 1989, Oxford, has nothing on mothers as educators. T. Fuller, *Abel Redivivus . . .*, 1650, ed. W. Nichols, 2 vols, 1867, II, p. 348. Cf. H. Scudder, 'The Life and Death of William Whately', prefixed to Whately's posthumously published collection of sermons, *Prototypes or The Primary Presidents out of the Book of Genesis*, 1640. Will printed in J. W. Clay, 'The Clifford Family', *Yorkshire Archaeological Journal*, 1905, vol. 18, p. 401; E. Rainbow, *A Sermon Preached at the Funeral of . . . Anne Countess of Pembroke, Dorset and Montgomerie*, 1677, p. 28.

84 J. O. Halliwell, ed., *The Autobiography of Simonds D'Ewes*, 2 vols, 1845, I, p. 104.

85 Russell, *op. cit.*, 1605, Ep. Ded.

86 J. Mayer, *A Pattern for Women*, 1619, p. 9; S. Denison, *The Monument or Tombstone, or A Sermon at the Funerals of . . . Elizabeth Juxon*, 1620, p. 113.

87 J. Cosin, *Works*, ed. J. H. Parker, 5 vols, 1843–5, Oxford, I, p. 27; I. F., *A Sermon Preached . . . at the Funeral of Lady Elizabeth Stanley*, 1635, p. 36.

88 W. Palmes SJ, *The Life of Mrs Dorothy Lawson*, 1646, ed. G. B. Richardson, 1851, Newcastle-upon-Tyne, pp. 13, 20, 21–2 and 19.

89 W. H. D. Longstaffe, ed., *The Memoirs and Life of Mr Ambrose Barnes*, Surtees Society, 1867, vol. 50, p. 69; E. Barker, *A Sermon Preached at the Funeral of . . . Lady Elizabeth Capel*, 1661, pp. 26, 30.

90 W. Dillingham, *A Sermon at the Funeral of the Lady Elizabeth Alston*, 1678, p. 40; M. Cavendish, *Natures Pictures*, 1655, p. 370.

91 J. Newman, *A Funeral Sermon . . . Mr William Tong*, 1727, p. 33; J. D. Marshall, ed., *The Autobiography of William Stout of Lancaster 1665–1752*, Chetham Society, 3rd Ser., 1967, vol. 15, pp. 68–9.

92 T. Pritchard, *A Sermon . . . at the Funeral of Mrs Mary Dawes*, 1693, Ep. Ded. and p. 15; S. Davy, *Heaven Realiz'd . . .*, 1670, p. 3.

93 T. Manton, *Advice to Mourners . . . Long since Preached . . . and now Occasionally Published on the Much Lamented Death of Mrs Anne Terry who Died 9 November 1693*, 1694, pp. viii and 56.

94 T. Pritchard, *A Sermon Preached at the Funeral of Lady Lumley*, 1693, p. 21; T. Rogers, *The Character of a Good Woman*, 1697, p. 126; A. Clarke, *Memoirs of the Wesley Family*, 1823, pp. 261–7.

95 R. S(impson), ed., *The Lady Falkland her Life*, 1861, p. 12 and *passim*, written by one of her daughters, probably Anne, and revised by her son Patrick; Lady Georgina Fullerton, *The Life of Elizabeth, Lady Falkland 1585–1639*, 1883. Cf. N. C. Pearse, 'Elizabeth Cary, Renaissance Playwright', *Texas Studies in Language and Literature*, 1977, vol. 18, pp. 601–8; E. Cary, *The Tragedie of Mariam*, ed. A. C. Dunstan, Malone Society Reprints, 1914, Oxford; B. Travitsky, 'The "Femme Couvert" in Elizabeth Cary's *Mariam*', in C. Levin and J. Watson, eds, *Ambiguous Realities. Women in the Middle Ages and Renaissance*, 1987, Detroit, pp. 184–96.

96 W. Gurnall, *The Christians Labour and Reward . . . Preached at the Funeral of . . . Lady Vere*, 1672, pp. 126ff, 130, 132, 133–4. *The Bruised Reed* was the book which was later to have such an effect on the religious formation of, among others, Richard Baxter: N. H. Keeble, ed., *The Autobiography of Richard Baxter*, 1974, 'bought by his father of a poor pedlar that had some ballads and some good books', p. 517; I. M. Calder, ed., *The Letters of John Davenport, Puritan Divine*, 1937, New Haven, *passim*.

97 T. Dugard, *Death and the Grave. A Sermon Preached at the Funeral of Lady Alice Lucie August 17 1648*, 1649, pp. 46–7. On Dugard see A. Hughes, 'Thomas Dugard and his Circle in the 1630s: a "Parliamentary Puritan" Connexion?', *Historical Journal*, 1986, vol. 29, pp. 771–93.

98 J. H. Turner, ed., *The Rev. Oliver Heywood BA 1630–72: His Autobiography, Diaries etc.*, 4 vols, 1881–5, I, pp. 51 and 234, referring to John Ball, *A Short Treatise Containing All the Principle Grounds of Christian Religion*, 1629; 34th ed., *A Short Catechism . . .*, 1635; 54th ed., 1688. It was also used in Mrs Salmon's Hackney Academy for the Daughters of Gentlemen, P. W. Souers, *The Matchless Orinda*, 1931, Cambridge, Mass., p. 20.

99 A. Boate, *The Character of a Trulie Vertuous Woman*, 1651, Paris, pp. 65–6; T. Comber, ed., *Memoirs of the Life and Death of . . . the Lady Wandesworth*, 1778, Cambridge, pp. 5–6.

100 E. Reynolds, *Imitation and Caution for Christian Women*, 1659, pp. 3–4, 6–7.

101 T. T. Lewis, ed., *The Letters of Brilliana Harley*, Camden Society, 1854, vol. 58, pp. 5, 18–19, 69–70, 96–7.

102 D. Parsons, ed., *The Diary of Sir Henry Slingsby*, 1836, p. 3.

103 Lord John Russell, ed., *The Letters of Rachel Lady Russell*, 2 vols, 1853, II, pp. 72–85.

104 E. Calamy, *The Happiness of those Who Sleep in Jesus . . . a Sermon . . . at the Funeral . . . of Lady Anne Waller*, 1662, p. 30; J. Loftis, ed., *The Memoirs of Anne, Lady Halkett, and Anne Lady Fanshawe*, 1979, Oxford, pp. 10–11.

105 Jessopp, *Autobiography of Roger North*, 1887, pp. 4–5, vi.

106 Herbert, *A Priest to the Temple*, in *The Works of George Herbert*, ed. F. E. Hutchinson, 2nd ed., 1945, Oxford, p. 240.

107 None of the following offers much help on the role of clerical wives in familial education: A. L. Barstow, 'The First Generation of Anglican Clergy Wives: Heroines or Whores?', *Historical Magazine of the Protestant and Episcopal Church*, 1983, vol. 52, pp. 3–16; J. Berlatsky, 'Marriage and Family in a Tudor Elite:

Patterns of Elizabethan Bishops', *Journal of Family History*, 1978, vol. 3, pp. 6–22; R. O'Day, *The English Clergy. The Emergence and Consolidation of a Profession 1558–1642*, 1979, Leicester; F. Heal, *Of Prelates and Princes. A Study of the Economic and Social Position of the Tudor Episcopate*, 1980, Cambridge; M. Prior, 'Reviled and Crucified Marriages: The Position of Tudor Bishops' Wives', in M. Prior, ed., *Women in English Society 1500–1800*, 1985, pp. 118–48; J. H. Pruett, *The Parish Clergy under the Late Stuarts: The Leicestershire Experience*, 1978, Urbana.

108 R. Bainton, *Women in the Reformation in Germany and Italy*, 1971, Minneapolis; A. MacFarlane, ed., *The Diary of Ralph Josselin . . . 1616–83*, 1976; Halliwell, ed., *The Rev. Oliver Heywood*; R. C. Bald, *John Donne. A Life*, 1970, Oxford; M. Clive, *Jack and the Doctor*, 1966.

109 E. B(agshawe), 'The Life and Death of Mr Bolton', prefixed to *Mr Bolton's Last Learned Worke of the Four Last Things*, 1632, sig. B6 verso; G. Vernon, ed., *The Historical and Miscellaneous Tracts . . . [and] Life of Dr P. Heylin*, 1681, p. ix.

110 Various, *The Life and Death of Thomas Cawton*, 1662, p. 46; Anon, *Two Sermons Preached at the Funerals of Elizabeth Montfort and Dr. Thomas Montfort*, 1632, p. 6.

111 H. Wilkinson, *The Hope and Glory . . .*, 1657, p. 70.

112 E. Staunton, *A Sermon on the Death of Mrs Elizabeth Wilkinson*, 1659, Oxford, 1659, pp. 23–5.

113 S. Clarke, *The Lives of Sundry Eminent Persons*, 1683, pp. 152, 155.

114 E. Calamy, *op. cit.*, ed. J. T. Rutt, 2 vols, I, p. 73.

115 A. Walker, *The Holy Life of Elizabeth Walker . . . with Some Useful Papers and Letters Written by her on Several Occasions*, 1690.

116 *Ibid.*, p. 5.

117 Margaret Verney, wife of Sir Edmund Verney of Claydon Hall, left explicit instructions in her will to this end in 1639. So also did Elizabeth Hastings.

118 *Holy Life*, pp. 9, 67–9.

119 *Ibid.*, pp. 60–9, 70.

120 *Ibid.*, pp 71, 73.

121 *Ibid.*, pp. 90, 86, referring to Samuel Crooke, *The Guide unto True Blessedness*, 1614.

122 A. Clarke, *Memoirs of the Wesley Family*, 1823, pp. 256ff. The Ferrar household at Little Gidding in Oxfordshire, and the activities of Mary (Woolnoth) Ferrar, her daughter Susannah Collett, and her granddaughter Mary Collett, provide similar evidence. J. E. B. Mayor, ed., *Nicholas Ferrar: Two Lives by his Brother John and Dr Jebb*, 1855, Cambridge, and its appendix of Letters; B. Blackstone, ed., *The Ferrar Papers*, 1938, Cambridge; A. M. Williams, *Conversations at Little Gidding*, 1970, Cambridge; T. T. Carter, *Nicholas Ferrar, His Household and His Friends*, J. F. M. Carter, ed., 1892; A. L. Maycock, *Nicholas Ferrar of Little Gidding*, 1938.

123 Walker, *Holy Life*, pp. 270–95.

124 Foxe, IV, pp. 235, 238, 239.

125 J. Shakespeare and M. Dowling, 'Religion and Politics in Mid-Tudor England through the Eyes of a Protestant English Woman: The Recollections of Rose Hickman', *Bulletin of the Institute of Historical Research*, 1982, vol. 55, p. 97.

126 Foxe, VIII, p. 537; V, p. 538.

127 L. Howard, ed., *A Collection of Letters from Original Manuscripts*, 1753, pp. 201, 228–9, 234.

128 W. Murdin, ed., *A Collection of State Papers*, 1759, p. 191; D. Coke, *The Last Elizabethan: Sir John Coke 1563–1644*, 1937, pp. 81–2, 84. See also J. J. Briggs,

The History of Melbourne in the County of Derbyshire, 2nd ed., 1852, pp. 84–9 and HMC, *Mss Of the Earl Cowper*, I, pp. 354–6 for some of their letters.

129 Verney, *Memoirs*, II, pp. 292–3.

130 T. T. Lewis, ed., *The Letters of Brilliana Harley*, Camden Society, 1854, vol. 58, pp. 148, 120.

131 E. Scarisbricke, *Life of Lady Warner*, 1691, pp. 144ff.

132 E. M. Thompson, ed., *Correspondence of the Family of Hatton I*, Camden Society, 1878, New Ser., vol. 22, pp. 3–4.

133 J. H. Bettey, ed., *Calendar of the Correspondence of the Smyth Family of Ashton Court 1548–1642*, Bristol Record Society, 1982, vol. 35, pp. 57, 78–9.

134 R. Hughey, ed., *The Correspondence of Lady Katherine Paston 1603–27*, Norfolk Record Society, 1941, vol. 14, pp. 70, 71, 78, 83, 56.

135 J. E. B. Mayor, ed., *Nicholas Ferrar. Two Lives by his Brother John and Dr Jebb*, 1855, Cambridge, Appendix.

136 T. T. Lewis, ed., *Letters of Brilliana Harley*, pp. 71, 69, 76.

137 HMC, *Rutland Mss at Belvoir Castle*, IV, pp. 244, 239–40, 256, 297. See also her letter to Cecil about Roger, 8 May 1588, *ibid.*, p. 248. For fathers' letters to their sons at university, D. Parsons, ed., *The Slingsby Diaries*, 1836, pp. 302–13, 316–18, and G. W. Thompson, ed., *The Fairfax Correspondence*, 2 vols, 1848, I, p. xxxii.

138 HMC, *Rutland Mss At Belvoir Castle*, IV, pp. 249, 250, 256, 260, 262, 266, 269, 275, 281, 284, 293, 296; New College, Oxford, Archives, Ms. 14, 753; D. Gardiner, ed., *The Oxinden Letters 1607–42*, 1933, pp. 23, 46; Hughey, *op. cit.*, pp. 67, 70.

139 J. Strype, *Ecclesiastical Memorials Relative Chiefly to Religion and the Reformation of It*, 3 vols, 1822–42, Oxford, II(i), pp. 491–2.

140 J. M. Shuttleworth, ed., *The Life of Edward, Lord Herbert of Cherbury Written by Himself*, 1976, pp. xi, 7, 14, 16; M. M. Berry, ed., *Some Account of the Life of Rachel Russell*, 1819, p. xxxvi.

141 E. S. Cope, *The Life of a Public Man: Edward, First Baron Montagu of Boughton 1562–1644*, Memoirs of the American Philosophical Society, 1981, Philadelphia, vol. 142, p. 141; E. Calamy, *The Happiness of Those Who Sleep in Jesus . . . Sermon at the Funeral of . . . Lady Anne Waller*, 1662, p. 30.

142 Hoby, *Diary*, pp. 37, 238, n. 12; S. Ford, *A Christians Acquiescence*, 1665, pp. 131–2.

143 Masham in DNB; P. Crawford, 'Katherine and Philip Henry and their Children: A Case Study in Family Ideology', *Transactions of the Historic Society of Lancashire and Cheshire*, 1985 for 1984, vol. 134, pp. 47, 66, citing diary entries for 29 November 1686.

144 H. A. St J. Mildmay, *A Brief Memoir of the Mildmay Family*, 1913, pp. 59ff; R(ichard) S(impson), *The Lady Falkland, Her Life*, 1861, pp. 7–8; Lady Georgina Fullerton, *The Life of Elizabeth Lady Falkland 1585–1639*, 1883, p. 25.

145 A. B. Grosart, ed., *The Lismore Papers*, 2nd Ser., III, 1888, pp. 80–1; N. Canny, *The Upstart Earl. A Study of the Emotional and Mental World of Richard Boyle, 1st Earl of Cork*, 1982, Cambridge, pp. 60, 91.

146 L. Simon, *Of Virtue Rare: Margaret Beaufort, Matriarch of the House of Tudor*, Boston, pp. 100, 125–6; Agnes Howard in DNB.

147 Jocelin in DNB, and S. Clarke, *Lives of Sundry Eminent Persons*, p. 197; Carre in *Wills and Inventories*, Surtees Society, 1835, vol. 2, p. 384.

148 N. Parkhurst, *The Faithful and Diligent Christian*, 1684, pp. 42–3; H. Jessey, *The Exceeding Riches of Grace Advanced by the Spirit of an Empty Creature*, 1647, p. 133.

149 J. O. Halliwell, ed., *The Autobiography and Correspondence of Sir Simonds D'Ewes Bt*, 2 vols, 1845, I, p. 323; D. G. Greene, ed., *The Meditations of Lady Elizabeth Delaval Written between 1662 and 1671*, Surtees Society, 1978 for 1975, vol. 190, pp. 29, 68.

150 A. Searle, ed., *The Barrington Family Letters 1628–1632*, Camden Society, 4th Ser., 1938, p. 246.

151 Mounteford in DNB sub Bramston; Sir John. R. R. Westfall, *Never at Rest. A Biography of Isaac Newton*, 1980, Cambridge, p. 53.

152 BL Egerton Ms. 2715, fols 127–83; T. Pritchard, *A Sermon Preached at the Funeral of Lady Lumley*, 1693, pp. 21–2.

153 A. Littleton, *A Sermon . . . at the Funeral of . . . Lady Jane, Wife of Charles Cheyne*, 1669, pp. 42, 46; DNB and J. Cartwright, *Sacharissa. Some Account of Dorothy Sidney, Countess of Sunderland*, 1893, p. 89. See also Lady Dorothy's letters to the children's father in M. M. Berry, ed., *Some Account of the Life of Rachel Wriothesley, Lady Russell*, 1819, pp. 111–50. R. North, *Lives of the Norths*, 3 vols.

154 N. Williams, *Thomas Howard 4th Duke of Norfolk*, 1964, pp. 24–7; F. Edwards, *The Marvellous Chance. Thomas Howard, Fourth Duke of Norfolk and the Ridolfi Plot 1570–72*, 1968, p. 32.

155 C. Devlin, *The Life of Robert Southwell, Poet and Martyr*, 1956, p. 11; C. Cross, *The Puritan Earl. The Life of Henry Hastings*, 1967, pp. 52ff, 57.

156 A. Walker, *Memoirs of Lady Warwick . . . Also her Diary 1666–72*, 1847, pp. 83, 88, 92, 93, 131, 136; T. T. Lewis, ed., *Letters of Brilliana Harley*, Camden Society, 1854, vol. 58, pp. 7, 18, 22, 28; J. Eales, *Puritans and Roundheads. The Harleys of Brampton Bryan and the Outbreak of the English Civil War*, 1990, Cambridge, p. 24; M. Carbery, ed., *Mrs Elizabeth Freke, Her Diary . . . 1671 to 1674*, 1913, Cork, p. 2.

157 D. G. Green, ed., *The Meditations of Lady Elizabeth Delaval*, Surtees Society, 1878 for 1875, vol. 190, pp. 37–8, 63–4; C. Jackson, ed., *The Autobiography of Mrs Alice Thornton*, Surtees Society, 1875 for 1873, vol. 62, p. 145.

158 This section is based on Lord John Russell, *The Letters of Lady Rachel Russell*, 2 vols, 1853; M. M. Berry, *Some Account of the Life of Rachel Wriothesley, Lady Russell*, 1819; L. G. Schwoerer, *Lady Rachel Russell: 'One of the Best of Women'*, 1988, Baltimore.

159 G. F. Nuttall, 'Henry Danvers, his Wife and the "Heavenly Home"', *Baptist Quarterly*, New Ser., 1982, vol. 29, pp. 217–19.

160 J. Duncon, *The Holy Life and Death of Lady Lettice . . . Viscountess Falkland*, 3rd ed., 1653, pp. 20, 24–5, 162; S. Ford, *A Christians Acquiescence*, 1665, p. 34.

161 E. Rainbow, *A Sermon Preached at the Funeral of . . . Anne, Countess of Pembroke, Derby and Montgomery . . .*, 1677, pp. 33–4.

162 E. Scarisbricke, *The Life of Lady Warner*, 1691, p. 26; Hoby, *Diary*, pp. 67, 81, 126; S. Clarke, *Lives of Sundry Eminent Persons*, 1683, p. 155.

163 J. Barlow, *The True Guide to Glory*, 1619, p. 48; W. Gurnall, *The Christians Labour and Reward*, 1672, pp. 133–4; E. W. Harcourt, ed., *The Harcourt Papers*, 14 vols, I, p. 30; T. Pritchard, *A Sermon Preached at the Funeral of Lady Lumley*, 1693, p. 22.

164 S. Bury, *An Account of the Life and Death of Mrs Elizabeth Bury*, 1720, p. 27.

165 A. Walker, *Eureka, Eureka*, 1678, p. 44; H. Sampson, ed., *The Life of Mrs Godolphin*, 1938, p. 98.

166 Grymeston, *op. cit.*, sig. A3 recto–verso.

167 Leigh, *op. cit.*, sig. A5 recto–verso, pp. 24–5, 28–9, 58ff, 16.

168 Richardson, *op. cit.*, pp. 4–6.

169 L. Hutchinson, *On the Principles of Christian Religion Addressed to her Daughter*, 1817, Introduction and pp. 5, 7, 90, 91.
170 Halkett, *op. cit.*, appended to S. C., *The Life of Lady Halkett*, 1701, Edinburgh.
171 BL Loan Ms. 29/78; E. S. Cope, *The Life of a Public Man . . . Montagu of Boughton*, 1981, Philadelphia, p. 141.
172 A. Walker, *Holy Life of Elizabeth Walker*, p. 40.
173 Lord John Russell, ed., *The Letters of Rachel, Lady Russell*, 2 vols, 1853, II, pp. 72–85.
174 A. Clarke, *Memoirs of the Wesley Family*, 1823, pp. 283–313, 370–74, 267–81, 273–4.
175 J. Loftis, ed., *The Memoirs of Anne, Lady Halkett and Anne, Lady Fanshawe*, 1979, Oxford, p. 101.
176 L. Pollock, *With Faith and Physic. The Life of a Tudor Gentlewomen. Lady Grace Mildmay, 1552–1620*, 1993, pp. 46, 47.
177 *Letters and Papers Foreign and Domestic: Henry VIII*, VI(ii), no. 1126, April 1534.
178 J. Spedding, ed., *Works of Francis Bacon: VII Letters and Life*, 1862, p. 112.
179 T. T. Lewis, ed., *The Letters of Brilliana Harley*, p. 69.
180 A. Searle, ed., *Barrington Family Letters 1628–32*, Camden Society, 4th Ser., 1983, vol. 28, pp. 176–7.
181 Broadsheet quotations from collections at BL C22f6 and 816m22.

CONCLUSION

1 *Miscellaneous Writings and Letters of Thomas Cranmer*, ed. J. E. Cox., Parker Society, 1846, Cambridge, p. 179.
2 F. Atterbury, *A Discourse Occasioned by the Death of . . . Lady Cutts*, 1698, p. 13.
3 Collinson, *The Birthpangs of Protestantism*, 1988, p. 93.
4 'Of the Inconstancie of Our Actions', in *The Complete Works of Montaigne*, trans. and ed. D. M. Frame, 1957, Stanford, p. 242.
5 Collinson, 'The English Conventicle', *Studies in Church History*, 1986, vol. 23, p. 259.

Bibliography

Place of publication is London unless otherwise stated.

PRIMARY SOURCES: MANUSCRIPTS

British Library Additional Ms. 19, 191.
—— Additional Ms. 70, 012.
—— Additional Ms. 70, 130.
—— Egerton Ms. 607.
—— Egerton Ms. 2641.
—— Egerton Ms. 2713.
—— Lansdowne Ms. 162.
Dr Williams' Library Modern Ms. 24.8.

PRIMARY SOURCES: PRINTED

Abbot, G., *An Exposition of the Prophet Jonah*, 1600, ed. G. Webster, 1845.
Abbot, R., *Milk for Babes*, 1646.
Adams, T., *The Works of Thomas Adams*, 1636.
Allen, R., *An Alphabet of the Holy Proverbs of King Solomon*, 1596.
——, *A Treatise of Catechism on Christian Instruction*, 1600.
Allestree, R., *The Whole Duty of Man*, 1659.
——, *The Ladies Calling*, 1673.
Ames, W., *Conscience with the Powere and Cases Thereof*, 1639.
Andrewes, L., *XCVI Sermons*, 1629.
Anon., *A Tablet for Gentlewomen*, 1574.
——, *Two Sermons Preached at the Funerals of Elizabeth Montfort and Dr Thomas Montfort*, 1632.
——, *The Anatomy of a Womans Tongue*, 1638.
Ascham, R., *The Scolemaster*, 1570.
Astell, M., *A Serious Proposal*, 1674.
Averell, W., *A Dyall For Dainty Darlings. A Myrrour For Vertuous Maydens*, 1584.
Babington, G., *A Briefe Conference betwixt Mans Frailtie and Faith*, 1590.

Babington, G. *Certayne Briefe Plaine and Comfortable Notes upon Every Chapter of Genesis*, 1596.

——, *Certayne Profitable Questions and Answers upon the Commandments*, 1596.

Bacon, F., *Essays*, ed. M. Hawkins, 1972.

Bagshawe, E., *Mr Boltons Last Learned Worke of the Four Last Things*, 1632.

Bale, J., *Select Works of John Bale*, ed. H. Christmas, Parker Society, 1849, Cambridge.

Ball, J., *A Short Catechisme Contayning All the Principle Grounds of Christian Religion*, 1615.

Barker, E., *A Sermon Preached at the Funeral of Lady Elizabeth Capel*, 1661.

Barlow, J., *The True Guide to Glory*, 1619.

Barnes, E. G., ed., *Somerset Assize Records 1629–40*, Somerset Record Society, 1959, vol. 65.

Barton, W., *A View of Many Errores and Gross Absurdities in the Old Translation of the Psalms in English Metre*, 1656.

Batchiler, J., *The Virgins Pattern*, 1661.

Bates, E. H., ed., *Quarter Sessions Records for the County of Somerset: I, 1607–25*, Somerset Record Society, 1907, vol. 28.

Baxter, R., *The Reformed Pastor*, 1655.

——, *The Christian Directory*, 1678.

——, *A Breviate of the Life of Mrs. Margaret Baxter*, 1681.

——, *Reliquiae Baxterianae*, ed. M. Sylvester, 1696.

Bayly, L., *The Practise of Pietie*, 3rd ed., 1613.

Becon, T., *The Pomander of Prayer*, 1558.

——, *The Syck Mans Salve*, 1561.

——, *The Boke of Matrimonie*, 1562.

——, *The Works of Thomas Becon*, ed. J. Ayre, Parker Society, 1843, Cambridge.

Bedell, W., *The Life of William Bedell*, ed. T. W. Jones, Camden Society, 1872, vol. 4.

Beecher, E., *The Christian School or Scriptures Anatomy*, 1676.

Bentley, T., *The Monument of Matrones*, 1582.

Bercher, W., *The Nobylyte of Wymen*, 1559, ed. W. Bond, 1904.

Blackwell, S., *Several Methods of Reading the Holy Scriptures in Private*, 1718.

Boate, A., *The Character of a Trulie Vertuous and Pious Woman*, 1651, Paris.

Bolton, R., *Some General Directions for a Comfortable Walking With God*, 1625.

Bourne, I., *The True Way of a Christian*, 1622.

Bradford, J., *The Writings of John Bradford*, ed. A. Townsend, Parker Society, 1843, Cambridge.

Bramston, J., *The Autobiography of Sir John Bramston*, ed. T. W. Bramston, Camden Society, 1845, vol. 32.

Brinsley, J., *A Looking Glasse for Good Women*, 1645.

Brooke, A., *The Tragicall Historye of Romeus and Juliet Written First in Italian by Bandell and Now in Englishe by Ar. Br.*, 1562.

Buckley, T. A., ed., *The Catechism of the Council of Trent 1566*, 1852.

Bullinger, H., trans. M. Coverdale, *The Christen State of Matrimony*, 1541.

——, *The Decades of Henry Bullinger*, ed. T. Harding, Parker Society, 1849, Cambridge.

Bunney, E., *Of Divorce and Marrying Againe That Thing is No Sufficient Warrant So to Do*, 1610.

Bunyan, J., *Grace Abounding*, 1666, ed. R. Sharrock, 1966.

Burgess, D., *Rules for Hearing the Word of God*, 1693.

Burroughes, T., *A Sovereign Remedy for all Kinds of Grief*, 1657.

Burrowes, S., *Good Instructions for all Young Men and Maids*, 1642.

Bury, S., *An Account of the Life and Death of Elizabeth Bury*, 1720.

Byfield, N., *Principles of the Patterne of Wholesome Words*, 1618.

Calamy, E., *The Happiness of Those Who Sleep in Jesus. A Sermon Preached at the Funeral of Lady Anne Waller*, 1662.

——, *The Art of Divine Meditation*, 1680.

Caton, W., *A Journal of the Life of William Caton*, 1689.

Cavendish, M., *Natures Pictures*, 1656.

——, *The Life of William Cavendish*, ed. C. H. Firth, 1886.

Cawdrey, E., *Family Reformation Promoted*, 1656.

Cawdrey, R., *A Short and Fruitfull Treatise of the Profit and Necessitie of Catechising*, 1604.

Chamberlayne, E., *An Academy or College Wherein Young Ladies and Gentlewomen May at Very Moderate Expense be Educated in the Protestant Religion*, 1671.

Chapman, G., *Bussy D'Ambois*, 1607.

——, *An Humourous Days Mirth*, 1599.

Cheynell, F., *A Plot for the Good of Posterity*, 1648.

Cholmley, H., *The Memoirs of Sir Hugh Cholmley*, 1787.

Clapam, D., *The Commendation of Matrimonie*, 1545.

Clapham, H., *A Brief of the Bible Drawne First into English Poesy and then Illustrated by Apte Annotations*, 1596, Edinburgh.

Clark, A., ed., *The Shirburn Ballads, 1585–1616*, 1907, Oxford.

Clarke, S., *A Collection of the Lives of Sundry Eminent Persons in This Later Age*, 1683.

C(leaver), R., *A Godly Forme of Householde Gouvernement*, 1598.

Clifford, A., *The Lives of Lady Anne Clifford and of her Parents Summarised by Herself*, ed. J. P. Gilson, 1916.

——, *The Diary of Lady Anne Clifford*, ed. V. Sackville-West, 1923.

——, *The Diaries of Lady Anne Clifford*, ed. D. J. H. Clifford, 1990, Stroud, Glos.

Coburn, J. S., ed., *Calendar of Assize Records: Sussex Indictments Elizabeth I*, 1975.

——, *Calendar of Assize Records: Kent Indictments Elizabeth I*, 1979.

Codrington, R., *The Second Part of Youths Behaviour*, 1664.

Cole, L., *Of Death a True Description and against it a True Preparation*, 1629.

Collinges, J., *The Life of a True Christian*, 1649.

——, *Par Nobile. Two Treatises . . . at the Funeralls of Lady Frances Hobart and Lady Catherine Courten*, 1669.

Collins, A., ed., *Letters and State Papers of the Sidney Family*, 1746.

Cooper, T., *Certaine Sermons*, 1580.

——, *The Mystery of Witchcraft*, 1617.

Coote, E., *The English Schole-Maister*, 1596.

Copley, A., *Wits, Fits and Fancies Newly Corrected*, 1614.

Courthope, G., *The Memoirs of Sir George Courthope*, ed. S. C. Lomas, Camden Miscellany, 1907, vol. 11.

Coverdale, M., *The Remains of Myles Coverdale*, ed. G. Pearson, Parker Society, 1846, Cambridge.

Cranmer, T., *Cranmer's Miscellaneous Writings and Letters*, ed. J. E. Cox, Parker Society, 1848, Cambridge.

Culpeper, N., *A Physicall Directory*, 1649.

Culverwell, E., *A Ready Way to Remember the Scriptures*, 1637.

Davenport, J., *The Letters of John Davenport, Puritan Divine*, ed. I. M. Calder, 1937, New Haven.

Davis, N., ed., *The Paston Letters and Papers of the Fifteenth Century*, 1971, 1976.

Davy, S., *Heaven Realiz'd*, 1670.

Dee, J., *The Private Diary of Dr. John Dee*, ed. J. O. Halliwell, Camden Society, 1842, vol. 19.

Defoe, D., *An Essay Upon Projects*, 1697.

Deloney, T., *The Works of Thomas Deloney*, ed. F. O. Mann, 1912, Oxford.

Dent, A., *A Pastime for Parents*, 1606.

Dering, E., *Certain Godly and Comfortable Letters Full of Christian Consolation*, 1597.

D'Ewes, S., *The Autobiography of Sir Simonds D'Ewes Bt.*, ed. J. O. Halliwell, 1845.

Dillingham, W., *A Sermon at the Funeral of Lady Elizabeth Alston*, 1678.

Dod, J. and Hinde, W., *Bathshebaes Instruction to her Son Lemuel*, 1614.

Donne, J., *Devotions upon Emergent Occasions*, ed. J. Sparrow, 1923, Cambridge.

——, *The Sermons of John Donne*, ed. E. M. Simpson, and G. R. Potter, 1953, Berkeley.

——, *The Complete Poetry and Prose*, ed. J. Hayward, 1962.

Doolittle, T., *A Plain Method of Catechising*, 1698.

Downame, J., *The Guide to Godlynesse*, 1622.

Dugard, T., *Death and the Grave. A Sermon Preached at the Funeral of Lady Alice Lucie August 17 1648*, 1649.

Duncon, J., *The Returns of Spiritual Comfort and Grief in a Devout Soul*, 1648.

——, *The Holy Life and Death of Lady Lettice Viscountess Falkland*, 3rd ed., 1653.

Dury, J., *The Reformed School*, ed. C. Webster, 1970, Cambridge.

E. T., *The Lawes Resolutions of Womens Rights*, 1632.

Earle, J., *Microcosmographie*, 1628.

Edwards, T., *Antapologia*, 1644.

Egerton, S., *A Briefe Methode of Catechising*, 1574.

Ellis, T., *The English School*, 5th ed., 1680.

Elyot, T., *The Boke Named the Governour*, 1531, ed. H. H. S. Croft, 1880.

——, *The Education and Bringing Up of Children Translated out of Plutarche*, 1533.

Erasmus, *The Colloquies of Erasmus*, ed. C. R. Thompson, 1965, Chicago.

——, *Paraclesis*, in Olin, J. C., ed. 1965.

——, *The Collected Works of Erasmus*, 1974– , Toronto.

Evelyn, J., *The Diary of John Evelyn*, ed. E. S. de Beer, 1955, Oxford.

F. I., *A Sermon Preached at the Funeral of Lady Elizabeth Stanley*, 1635.

Fairclough, S., *The Saints Worthiness and the Worlds Worthlessness*, 1653.

Featley, D., *Ancilla Pietatis or The Handmaid of Private Devotion*, 1626.

——, *The House of Mourning*, 1640.

Featley, J., *A Fountain of Teares*, 1646, Amsterdam.

Fiennes, C., *The Journeys of Celia Fiennes*, ed. C. Morris, 1947.

Finch, A., *The Poems of Anne Finch Countess of Winchelsea*, ed. J. Murry.

Fincham, K., ed., *Visitation Articles and Injunctions of the Early Stuart Church*, 1994.

Fisher, J., *A Sermon Had at St Paules*, 1526.

Fisher, J., *The Wise Virgin or A Wonderful Narration of the Hand of God in the Life of Martha Hatfield*, 1653.

Flavel, J., *A Token for Mourners of the Advice of Christ to a Distressed Mother*, 1640.

Ford, S., *A Christians Acquiescence. A Funeral Sermon Preached at the Funeral of Lady Elizabeth Langham*, 1665.

Fox, G., *The Gospell-Truth*, 1656.

Freke, E., *Mrs Elizabeth Freke Her Diary, 1671–1714*, ed. M. Carbery, 1931, Cork.

Frere, W. H. and Kennedy, W. McC., eds, *Visitation Articles and Injunctions of the Period of the Reformation*, Alcuin Club Collections, 1910, vol. 15.

Fuller, T., *Abel Redivivus*, 1650.

——, *The Church History of Britain*, 1655.

——, *The History of the Worthies of England*, 1662.

Gairdiner, J., ed., *The Paston Letters*, 1904.

Gardiner, R. B., ed., *The Letters of Dorothy Wadham*, 1904.

Gardiner, S. R., ed., *Reports of Cases in the Courts of Star Chamber and High Commission*, Camden Society, 1886, vol. 39.

Gataker, T., *Marriage Duties Briefly Couched together out of Colossians 1.18–19*, 1620.

Gibson, C., *A Work Worth Reading by Parents How to Bestow Their Children in Marriage*, 1591.

Gifford, G., *A Sermon on the Parable of the Sowere*, 1582.

Glanvill, J., *An Essay Concerning Preaching*, 1678.

Gouge, W., *Domesticall Dueties*, 1600.

——, *A Funeral Sermon Preached August 24 1646*, 1646.

Greene, R., *The Life and Complete Works of Robert Greene*, ed. A. B. Grosart, 1881–3.

Greene, D. G., ed., *Meditations of Lady Elizabeth Delaval Written Between 1662 and 1671*, Surtees Society 1978 for 1975, vol. 190.

Greenham, R., *The Works of Richard Greenham*, ed. H. Holland, 1599.

——, *A Godly Exhortation and Fruitfull Admonition to Vertuous Parents and Modest Matrones*, 1584.

Griffith, J., ed., *The Two Books of Homilies Appointed to be Read in Churches*, 1859, Oxford.

Grosart, A. B., ed., *The Lismore Papers*, 2nd Ser., 1888.

Grymeston, E., *Miscelanea. Meditations. Memoratives*, 1604.

Guillimeau, J., *Child Birth or The Happy Delivery of Women*, 1612.

Gurnall, W., *The Christians Labour and Reward Preached at the Funeral of Lady Vere*, 1672.

Haddon, G., *Lucubrationes*, 1567.

Hake, E., *A Touchstone for This Time Present*, 1574.

Hale, W. H., ed., *A Series of Precedents in Criminal Cases From the Act Books Of the Ecclesiastical Courts of London 1474–1640*, 1847.

Hannay, P., *A Happy Husband or Directions for a Maid How to Choose Her Mate*, 1618.

Harpsfield, N., *The Life and Death of Thomas More*, ed. E. V. Hitchcock, EETS, 1932, vol. 186.

Harrington, J., *A Holy Oyl and a Sweet Perfume Taken out of the Sanctuary of the Most Sacred Scriptures*, 1669.

Harrison, W., and Leigh, W., *Deaths Advantage Little Regarded and The Souls Solace Against Sorrow: Two Sermons Preached at the Buriall of Mistris Katherine Brettergh*, 1602.

Hastings, F., *The Letters of Sir Francis Hastings 1579–1609*, ed. C. Cross, Somerset Record Society, 1969, vol. 69.

Hayes, A., *A Legacy or Widows Mite Left by Alice Hayes to Her Children with an Account of Her Dying Sayings*, 1724.

Heale, W., *An Apologie for Women*, 1609, Oxford.

Herbert, G., *Jacula Prudentium*, 1640.

——, *A Priest at the Temple*, 1671.

——, *The Works of George Herbert*, ed. F. E. Hutchinson, 2nd ed., 1945, Oxford.

Heylin, P., *The Historical and Miscellaneous Tracts and Life of Dr. P. Heylin*, ed. G. Vernon, 1681.

Heywood, O., *Closet Prayer a Christian Duty*, 1671.

——, *The Life of John Angier*, ed. E. Axon, Chetham Society, New Ser., vol. 197, 1937, v.

Heywood, T., ed., *The Diary of the Rev. Henry Newcome 1661–63*, Chetham Society, 1849, vol. 19.

Hieron, S., *The Bridegroom*, 1613.

——, *An Helpe Unto Devotion*, 1616.

——, *Sermons of Master Hieron*, 1624.

Hilder, T., *Conjugall Counsell*, 1652.

Hill, R., *The Patheway to Prayer and Pietie*, 3rd ed., 1609.

Hinde, W., *A Faithfull Remonstrance of the Holy Life and Happy Death of John Bruen of Bruen Stapleford in the County of Cheshire*, 1645.

Historical Manuscripts Commission, *Bath Mss.*

——, *De Lisle and Dudley Mss.*

——, *Hastings Mss.*

——, *The Mss of Lord Kenyon.*

——, *Portland Mss.*

——, *Rutland Mss.*

Hobbes, T., *Behemoth or An Epitome of the Civil Wars of England from 1640 to 1660*, 1679.

Hooker, R., *The Lawes of Ecclesiastical Polity*, 1597.

——, *The Works of Richard Hooker*, ed. G. Edelen, 1977–9, Cambridge, Mass.

Hughes, P. H. and Larkin, J. F., eds, *Tudor Royal Proclamations*, 1964–69, New Haven.

Hutchinson, L., *On the Principles of Christian Religion Addressed to her Daughter*, 1817.

——, *Memoirs of the Life of Colonel Hutchinson*, ed. J. Sutherland, 1973.

Inman, F., *Light unto the Unlearned or The Principles of the Doctrine of Christ Set Down Most Briefly for the Use of Young and Ignorant Persons*, 1622.

Isaacson, H., *Institutiones, Piae or Directions to Pray*, 2nd ed., 1633.

Jocelin, E., *The Mothers Legacie*, 1624.

Jones, J., *The Arte and Science of Preserving Bodie and Soule*, 1579.

Jonson, B., *The Poems of Ben Jonson*, ed. B. H. Newdigate, 1936, Oxford.

Keith, G., *The Women Preachers of Samaria*, 1674.

Kennett, W., *The Charity Schools for Children*, 1706.

Kingsmill, A., *A View of Mans Estate*, 1576.

Latimer, H., *The Sermons of Hugh Latimer*, ed. G. E. Corrie, Parker Society, 1844, Cambridge.

Lee, M. H., ed., *The Diaries of Philip Henry 1631–96*, 1882.

Legate, R., *A Brief Catechism and Dialogue between the Husband and His Wife*, 1545.

Leigh, D., *The Mothers Blessing*, 7th ed., 1621.

Lewis, T. T., ed., *The Letters of Brilliana Harley*, Camden Society, 1854, vol. 58.

Lever, T., *A Fruitfull Sermon Made at Paules Churche 1550*, 1550.

Littleton, A., *A Sermon at the Funeral of Mary Alston*, 1671.

Lloyd, H., *The Treasury of Health*, 1550.

Lloyd, L., *The Choyce of Jewels*, 1607.

Locke, J., *Essay Concerning Human Understanding*, 1690.

——, *Thoughts Concerning Education*, 1693.

Loftis, J., ed., *The Memoirs of Lady Anne Halkett and Lady Anne Fanshawe*, 1981, Oxford.

Longstaffe, W. H. D., ed., *The Memoirs of the Life of Mr Ambrose Barnes*, Surtees Society, 1867, vol. 50.

Makin, B., *An Essay to Revive the Antient Education of Women*, 1673.

Manton, T., *Advice to Mourners long since Preached and now Published on the Death of Mrs Anny Terry*, 1674.

Mares, F. H., ed., *The Memoirs of Sir Robert Carey*, 1972, Oxford.

Markham, G., *Country Contentments or the English Housewife*, 1615.

Martindale, A., *The Life of Adam Martindale Written by Himself*, ed. R. Parkinson, Chetham Society, 1845, vol. 4.

Mayer, J., *A Patterne for Women*, 1619.

Meads, D. M., ed., *The Diary of Lady Margaret Hoby 1599–1605*, 1930.

Milton, J., *The Doctrine and Discipline of Divorce*, 1643.

——, *The Judgement of Martin Bucer on Divorce*, 1644.

——, *The Works of John Milton*, ed. F. M. Patterson, 1931, New York.

Mordaunt, E., *The Private Diary of Lady Elizabeth Mordaunt*, 1856, Duncairn.

More, M., *A Devout Treatise upon the Pater Noster*, n.d.

More, T., *The Workes of Sir Thomas More in the English Tongue*, 1567.

——, *The Latin Epigrams of Thomas More*, ed. L. Bradner and C. A. Lynch, 1953, Chicago.

——, *Sir Thomas More: Selected Letters*, ed. E. F. Rogers, 1961, New Haven.

Mulcaster, R., *Positions*, 1581.

——, *The First Part of the Elementarie*, 1582.

Murdin, W., *A Collection of State Papers Relating to the Affairs of the Reign of Queen Elizabeth From 1571 to 1596*, 1759.

Newman, J., *A Funeral Sermon for Mr William Tong*, 1727.

Newton, J., *The School of Pastime for Young Children*, 1669.

Niccoles, N., *A Discourse on Marriage and Wiving*, 1815.

Nicholas, N. H., *Memoirs of the Life and Times of Sir Christopher Hatton*, 1847.

Nichols, J., *The Order of Household Instruction*, 1596.

Nicholson, H. M., ed., *Conway Letters. The Correspondence of Anne Viscountess Conway, Henry More and Their Friends, 1642–84*, 1930.

Norman, J., *Family Governors Persuaded to Family Godliness or The Masters Charge*, 1657.

Norris, J., *Reason and Religion or The Grounds of Devotion*, 1689.

——, *Practical Discourses*, 1691.

North, R., *The Autobiography of the Hon. Roger North*, ed. A. Jessopp, 1887.

——, *Lives of the Norths*, ed. A. Jessopp, 1890.

Norton, F., *The Applause of Virtue*, 1705.

Osborne, D., *Dorothy Osborne's Letters to Sir William Temple*, ed. K. Parker, 1987, Harmondsworth.

Osborne, L. B., ed., *The Life, Letters and Writings of Sir John Hoskyns*, 1931, New Haven.

Painter, W., *The Seconde Tome of the Palace of Pleasure*, 1567.

Parker, M., *The Correspondence of Matthew Parker*, ed. J. Bruce, Parker Society, 1853, Cambridge.

Parkhurst, N., *The Faithfull and Diligent Christian*, 1684.

Parr, C., *The Lamentacion of a Sinner*, 1544.

Parr, E., *Abba Father. A Plaine Direction Concerning the Framing of Private Prayer* 1615.

Parr, R., *The Life of James Ussher*, 1686.

Paston, K., *The Correspondence of Lady Katherine Paston 1603–27*, Norfolk Record Society, 1941, vol. 14.

Patrick, S., *Search the Scriptures. A Treatise Showing that All Christians Ought to Read the Holy Books*.

Peachman, H., *The Complete Gentleman*, 1622.

Penn, W., *The Fruits of a Fathers Love Being the Advice of William Penn to His Children*, 1726.

Perkins, W., *The Foundation of Christian Religion*, 1591.

——, *The Works of William Perkins*, 1618, Cambridge.

Peter, H., *A Dying Fathers Last Legacy to His Only Child*, 1660.

Petrie, C., ed., *Letters, Speeches and Proclamations of James I*, 1935.

Phaire, T., *The Boke of Chyldren*, 1544.

Pilkington, J., *The Works of James Pilkington*, ed. J. Scholefield, Parker Society, 1842, Cambridge.

Plat, H., *The Jewel House of Art and Nature*, 1653.

Playfere, T., *The Meaning of Mourning. A Sermon Preached at St Marys Spittle in London in Easter Week 1595*, 1596.

Pomfret, T., *The Life of the Right Honourable and Religious Lady Christian(a) Late Dowager of Devonshire*, 1685.

Poole, J., *Country Astrology*, 1650.

Preston, J., *The Riches of Mercy to Men in Misery*, 1658.

Primaudaye, P. de la, *The French Academie*, 1618.

Pritchard, T., *The Glasse of Godly Love*, 1659, ed. E. J. Furnival, New Shakespeare Society, vol. 6, 1876.

——, *A Sermon Preached at the Funeral of Mrs Mary Dawes at Great Barfield in Essex January 5 1690*, 1690.

Pritchard, T., *A Sermon Preached at the Funeral of Lady Lumley*, 1693.

Purvis, J. S., ed., *Tudor Parish Documents in the Diocese of York*, 1948.

Puttenham, G., *The Art of English Poesie*, 1589.

Quarles, F., *Divine Poems*, 1630.

R. M., *The Mothers Counsell*, 1630.

Rainbow, E., *A Sermon Preached at the Interring of Susanna Countess of Suffolk*, 1649.

——, *A Sermon Preached at the Funeral of Anne, Countess of Pembroke Dorset and Montgomerie*, 1677.

Raine, E. J., ed., *Richmondshire Wills and Inventories*, Surtees Society, 1853, vol. 26.

Raine, J., ed., *The Injunctions and Other Ecclesiastical Proceedings of Richard Barnes, Bishop of Durham 1675–87*, Surtees Society, 1850, vol. 22.

Reed, M., ed., *The Ipswich Probate Inventories 1553–1631*, Suffolk Record Society, 1954, vol. 58.

Rhodes, H., *The Booke of Nurture*, 1550.

Rhodes, J., *The Countrie Mans Comfort or Religious Recreations Fitte for All Well Disposed Persons*, 1588.

Rich, B., *Faultes, Faultes and More Faultes*, 1606.

Rich, M., *The Autobiography of Mary Countess of Warwick*, ed. T. C. Croker, 1848.

Robins, T., *The Young Mans Guide in His Way to Heaven*, 1676.

Robinson, A. E., ed., *The Life of Richard Kidder Bishop of Bath and Wells Written by Himself*, Somerset Record Society, 1922, vol. 37.

Robinson, H., ed. and trans., *Original Letters Relative to the English Reformation*, 1846, Parker Society, Cambridge.

Robinson, J., *New Essayes or Observations Divine and Morall*, 1628.

Robinson, R., *Certain Selected Histories for Christian Recreations with Their Several Moralizations Brought into English Verse*, 1576.

Rogers, D., *Matrimoniall Honour*, 1642.

Rogers, R., *The Practice of Christianitie*, 1603.

——, *A Garden of Spiritual Flowers*, 5th ed., 1609.

Rogers, T., *The Righteous Mans Evidences for Heaven*, 1624.

Rogers, T., *The Character of a Good Woman*, 1697.

Rueff, J., *The Expert Midwife*, 1637.

Russell, R., *The Letters of Rachel Lady Russell*, ed. J. Russell, 1853.

Sachse, W. L., ed., *The Diary of Roger Lowe of Ashton-in-Makerfield Lancashire 1663–74*, 1938.

Sales, F. de., *A Treatise of the Love of God*, 1616, 18th ed. and trans. M. Carr, Douai.

Salter, T., *A Mirrhour Mete for All Mothers and Matrones*, 1579.

Sandys, E., *The Sermons of Edwyn Sandys*, ed. J. Ayre, Parker Society, 1842, Cambridge.

Saville, G., *The Lady's New Year Gift or Advice to a Daughter*, 1688.

Seager, F., *The School of Vertue*, 1550.

Secker, W., *A Wedding Ring Fit for the Finger*, 1664.

Sherley, A., *Wits New Dyall or A Scholars Prize*, 1604.

Sibbes, R., *The Works of Richard Sibbes*, ed. A. B. Grosart, 1862–4, Edinburgh.

Sidney, P., *An Apologie for Poetry*, 1595, ed. G. Shepherd, 1965.

Sidney, P., *The Complete Works of Sir Philip Sidney*, 1912–26, ed. A. Feuillerat.

Simpson, H., ed., *The Life of Mrs Godolphin*, 1939.

Slingsby, H., *A Fathers Legacy to his Sonnes*, 1658.

——, *The Diary of Sir Henry Slingsby of Scriven*, ed. D. Parsons, 1836.

Smith, A. H., ed., *The Papers of Nathaniel Bacon of Stiffkey, I, 1556–77*, Norfolk Record Society, 1978–9, vol. 46.

Smith, H., *A Preparative for Marriage*, 1591.

——, *The Sermons of Master Henrie Smith Gathered in One Volume*, 1592.

——, *Thirteen Sermons Upon Several Texts of Scripture*, 1592.

Snawsel, R., *A Looking Glasse for Married Folke*, 1610.

Sneyd, G., ed., *A Relation or Rather a True Account of the State of England About the Year 1500*, Camden Society, 1847, vol. 37.

Southwell, R., *The Trumpets Own Death or A Consolatrie Epistle for Afflicted Maids in the Affects of Dying Friends*, 1596.

Sparke, T., *A Catechisme or Short Kinde of Instruction*, 1558.

Standish, J., *A Discourse Wherein is Debated Wheyther it Be Expedient That the Scripture Should Be in English for All Men to Reade That Wyll*, 1554.

Staunton, E., *A Sermon Preached on 9 December 1654 at the Funeral of Mrs Elizabeth Wilkinson*.

Stockwood, J., *A Bartholomew Faring for Parentes Shewing That Children Are Not to Marie Without Consent of Their Parentes*, 1589.

Stout, W., *The Autobiography of William Stout of Lancaster 1665–1752*, ed. J. D. Marshall, Chetham Society, 3rd Ser., 1967, vol. 14.

Stubbes, P., *The Anatomie of Abuses*, 1583.

Taverner, R., *A Ryght Frutefull Epystle in Laude of Matrimonie*, 1532.

Taylor, J., *A Funeral Sermon Preached at the Obsequies of Lady Frances Countess Carbery*, 1650.

——, *The Rule and Exercise of Holy Living*, 1650.

——, *The Measures and Offices of Friendship*, 1662.

——, *The Works of Jeremy Taylor*, ed. R. Heber, 1828.

Taylor, T., *Christs Combate and Conquest*, 1615, Cambridge.

——, *The Pilgrims Profession or A Sermon Preached at the Funeral of Mrs. M. Gunter*, 1622.

Thornton, A., *The Autobiography of Mrs Alice Thornton*, ed. C. Jackson, Surtees Society, 1875, vol. 62.

Tilney, E., *A Brief and Pleasant Discourse on the Duties of Marriage Called The Flowere of Friendship*, 1568.

Trapnel, A., *A Legacy of Saints*, 1654.

Trevett, C., ed., *Women Speaking Justified and Other Quaker Writings About Women*, 1987.

Tyndale, W., *Doctrinal Treatises*, ed. H. Walter, Parker Society, 1848, Cambridge.

Tyrell, A., *A Fruitfull Sermon Preached at Christ Church the 13 Julie Anno 1589 Taken by Characterie*, 1589.

Tryon, T., *A New Method of Bringing Up Children*, 1695.

Udall, J., *Peters Fall. Two Sermons on This History of Peters Denying Christ*, n.d.

Underhill, E. B., ed., *The Records of a Church of Christ Meeting in Broadmead Bristol 1640–87*, 1848.

Vaughan, E., *A Methode or Brief Instruction Very Profitable for the Reading and Understanding of the Old and New Testaments*, 1590.

Vaughan, W., *The Golden Grove Moralized in Three Books*, 1600.

Vicars, J., *The Schismatick Sifted or A Picture of Independents Freshly and Fairly Washt Over Again*, 1646.

Vincent, J., *Christ the Best Husband*, 1672.

Wall, A., ed., *Two Elizabethan Women. The Correspondence of Joan and Maria Thynne 1575–1611*, Wiltshire Record Society, 1963, vol. 38.

Walsall, J., *A Sermon Preached at Paules Cross 5 October 1578*, 1578.

Warren, E., *Spiritual Thrift or Meditations*, 1647.

Wastell, S., *The True Christians Daily Delight Being the Summe of Every Chapter of the Old and New Testaments*, 1623.

——, *Microbiblion or The Bibles Epitome*, 1629.

Weever, J., *An Agnus Dei*, 1601.

Wentworth, A., *A Vindication of Anne Wentworth*, 1677.

Whateley, W., *A Bride Bush or A Direction for Married Persons*, 1617.

——, *The New Birth*, 1619.

Whitaker, T., *A Comfort for Parents Mourning Over Their Hopeful Children That Dye Young*, 1693.

White, T., *A Little Book for Little Children*, 1674.

Whitforde, R., *A Werke for Householders*, 1530.

Whitgift, J., *A Most Godly and Learned Sermon Preached at Paules Cross the 17 November 1583*, 1589.

——, *The Works of John Whitgift*, ed. J. Ayre, P 1853, Parker Society, Cambridge.

Whytenhorne, T., *The Autobiography of Thomas Whytenhorne*, ed. J. M. Osborne, 1962.

Wilkinson, H., *The Hope of Glory*, 1657, Oxford.

Williams, J. E., ed., *Bishop Redman's Visitation 1597*, Norfolk Record Society, 1946, vol. 18.

Wing, J., *The Crown Conjugall, or The Spouse Royall*, 1620.

Wood, A. C., ed., *Memorials of the Holles Family 1493–1656*, Camden Society, 4th Ser., 1937, vol. 28.

Wood, M. A. E., ed., *Letters of Royal and Illustrious Ladies*, 1846.

Woodward, W. H., ed., *Vittorino da Feltre and Other Humanist Educators*, 1963, New York.

Woolley, H., *The Gentlewomans Companion*, 1675.

Worthington, J., *The Diary and Correspondence of Dr John Worthington*, ed. J. Crossley, Chetham Society, 1847, vol. 13.

Wright, L., *The Pilgrimage to Paradise Compiled for the Comfort and Resolution of Gods Poor Distressed Children*, 1591.

Wright, L. B., ed., *Advice to a Son*, 1962, Ithaca.

SECONDARY SOURCES

Addy, J., *Sin and Society in the Seventeenth Century*, 1989.

Andreadis, H., 'The Sapphic-Platonics of Katherine Phillips 1632–64', *Signs*, 1989–90, vol. 15.

Almnack, R., 'Keddington alias Ketton and the Barnardiston family', *Proceedings of the Suffolk Institute of Archaeology and Natural History*, 1874, vol. 4.

Amussen, D., *An Ordered Society: Gender and Class in Early Modern England*, 1988, Oxford.

Archer, R. E., 'How Ladies Who Live on Their Manors Ought to Manage Their Households and Estates: Women as Landholders and Administrators in the Late Middle Ages', in P. J. P. Goldberg, 1992.

Archer, R. E. and Ferme, B. E., 'Testamentary Procedure with Special Reference to the Executrix', *Medieval Women in Southern England, Reading Medieval Studies*, 1989, vol. 15.

Ariès, P., trans. R. Baldick, *Centuries of Childhood*, 1962.

Aspinall-Oglander, C., *Nunwell Symphony*, 1945.

Aston, M., *Lollards and Reformers*, 1984.

——, 'Segregation in Church', *Studies in Church History*, 1990, vol. 27.

Auski, P., 'Wyclif's Sermons and His Plain Style', *Archives for Reformation History*, 1975, vol. 60.

Babcock, B. A., *The Reversible World: Symbolic Inversion in Art and Society*, 1978, Ithaca.

Bainton, R. H., *Women in the Reformation in Germany and Italy*, 1971, Minneapolis.

——, 'John Foxe and the Ladies', in L. P. Buck and J. W. Zophy, 1972.

Baker, D., ed., *Medieval Women, Studies in Church History*, Subsidia 1, 1978.

Ballard, G., *Memoirs of British Ladies*, 1752.

Bamford, F., ed., *A Royalist's Notebook. The Commonplace Book of Sir John Oglander*, 1936.

Barash, C., 'The Political Origins of Anne Finch's Poetry', *Huntingdon Library Quarterly*, 1991, vol. 54.

Bernard, E. A. B., 'The Pakingtons of Westwood', *Transactions of the Worcestershire Archaeological Society*, 1936, vol. 13.

Berry, L. E., *The Geneva Bible. A Facsimile of the 1560 Edition*, 1969, Madison, Wisc.

Berry, M., *Some Account of the Life of Rachel Wriothesley, Lady Russell*, 1819.

Betteridge, M., '"Bitter Notes": The Geneva Bible and Its Annotations', *Sixteenth Century Journal*, 1983, vol. 14.

Blaisdell, C. J., 'Calvin's Letters to Women: Courting the Ladies in High Places', *Sixteenth Century Journal*, 1982, vol. 13.

Blencowe, R. W., 'Extracts from the Journal and Account Book of the Rev. Giles Moore Rector of Horsted Keynes from 1655 to 1679', *Sussex Archaeological Collections*, 1848, vol. 11.

Bolton, J. P., 'The Limits of Formal Religion: The Administration of Holy Communion in Late Elizabethan England', *London Journal*, 1984, vol. 10.

Bonfield, L., ed., *The World We Have Gained*, 1986, Oxford.

Booty, J. E., 'Preparation for the Lord's Supper in Elizabethan England', *Anglican Theological Review*, 1967, vol. 49.

Bouwsma, W. J., 'Intellectual History in the 1980s', *Journal of Interdisciplinary History*, 1981, vol. 21.

Bowden, C., 'Women as Intermediaries: An Example of the Use of Literacy in the Late Sixteenth and Early Seventeenth Centuries', *History of Education*, 1993, vol. 22.

Braithwait, W. C., *The Beginnings of Quakerism*, 2nd ed., 1955, Cambridge.

Brink, J. R., 'Bathusa Reginald Makin: Most Learned Matron', *Huntingdon Library Quarterly*, 1991, vol. 54.

Brodsky, V., 'Widows in Late Elizabethan London: Remarriage, Economic Opportunity and Family Orientation', in L. Bonfield, 1986.

Brooks, P. N., *Thomas Cranmer's Doctrine of the Eucharist*, 1965.

Browne, J., *The History of Congregationalism and Memorials of the Churches in Norfolk and Suffolk*, 1887.

Brushfield, T. N., 'The Financial Diary of a Citizen of Exeter 1631–42', *Reports and Transactions of the Devonshire Association*, 1901, vol. 33.

Buck, L. P. and Zophy, L. P., eds, *The Social History of the Reformation*, 1972, Columbus.

Burgon, J. W., *The Life of Thomas Gresham*, 1839.

Burke, P., ed., *A New Kind of History and Other Essays of Lucien Febvre*, 1973, New York.

——, 'The Language of Orders in Early Modern Europe', in M. L. Bush, 1992.

Bush, M. L., ed., *Social Orders and Social Classes in Early Modern Europe since 1500. Studies in Social Stratification*, 1992.

Camden, C., ' "Memory the Warder of the Brain" ', *Philological Quarterly*, 1939, vol. 18.

Capp, B., *Astrology and the Popular Press, 1500–1800*, 1979.

Carlisle, N., *A Concise Description of the Endowed Schools of England and Wales*, 1818.

Cardwell, E., *Documentary Annals of the Reformed Church of England*, 1884, Oxford.

Carlson, L. H., *Martin Marprelate, Gentleman. Master Job Throckmorton Laid Open in His Colors*, 1981, San Marino, Calif.

Carlton, C., 'The Widows Tale: Male Myths and Female Reality in Sixteenth- and Seventeenth-century England', *Albion*, 1978, vol. 10.

Carpenter, H. J., 'Furse of Moreshead: A Family Record of the Sixteenth Century', *Reports and Transactions of the Devonshire Association*, 1894, vol. 26.

Cartwright, J., *Sacharissa. Some Account of Dorothy Sidney, Countess of Sunderland*, 1893.

Chambers, R. W., *Thomas More*, 1938.

Charlton, K., *Education in Renaissance England*, 1965.

——, ' "Tak The to Thi Distaff": The Education of Women and Girls in Early Modern England', *Westminster Studies in Education*, 1981, vol. 4.

——, ' "False Fonde Bookes, Ballades and Rimes": An Aspect of Informal Education in Early Modern England', *History of Education Quarterly*, 1987, vol. 27.

——, ' "Not Publike Onely but also Private and Domesticall": Mothers and Familial Education in Pre-industrial England', *History of Education*, 1988, vol. 17.

——, 'Mothers as Educative Agents in Pre-industrial England', *History of Education*, 1994, vol. 23.

Chaytor, H. J., *From Script to Print*, 1945, Cambridge.

Chrisman, M. U., 'From Polemic to Propaganda: The Development of Mass Persuasion in the Late Sixteenth Century', *Archives for Reformation History*, 1982, vol. 73.

Cioni, M. L., 'The Elizabethan Court of Chancery and Women's Rights', in D. J. Cuth and J. W. McKenna, eds.

Clanchy, M. T., *From Memory to the Written Record: England 1066–1307*, 1979.

Clarke, A., *Memoirs of the Wesley Family*, 1823.

Coke, D., *The Last Elizabethan. Sir John Coke*, 1937.

Collinson, P., 'The Role of Women in the English Reformation Illustrated by the Life of and Friendships of Anne Locke', *Studies in Church History*, 1965, vol. 2.

——, *The Elizabethan Puritan Movement*, 1967.

——, *The Religion of Protestants. The Church in English Society 1590–1625*, 1982, Oxford.

——, *Godly People: Essays on English Protestantism and Puritanism*, 1983.

——, 'Truth and Legend: The Veracity of John Foxe's Book of Martyrs', in A. C. Duke and A. Tomse, 1985.

——, *The Birthpangs of Protestant England*, 1988, Basingstoke.

Cooper, C. H., *Annals of Cambridge*, 1842, Cambridge,.

Cope, E. S., *The Life of a Public Man. Edward, First Baron Montagu of Boughton 1562–1644, Memoirs of the Americal Philosophical Society*, 1981, vol. 142, Philadelphia.

Corfield, P. J., ed., *Language, History and Class*, 1991, Oxford.

——, 'History and the Challenge of Gender History', *Rethinking History*, 1997, vol. 1.

Cressy D., *Literacy and the Social Order*, 1980, Cambridge.

Crane, D., 'English Translations of the *Imitatio Christi* in the Sixteenth and Seventeenth Centuries', *Recusant History*, 1975, vol. 13.

Craster, H. H., 'Notes from a Delaval Diary', Proceedings of the Society of Antiquaries of Newcastle-Upon-Tyne, 3rd Ser., 1905.

Crawford, P., 'Katherine and Philip Henry and Their Children: A Case Study in Family Ideology', *Transactions of the Historic Society of Lancashire and Cheshire*, 1985 for 1984, vol. 134.

——, 'The Suckling Child: Attitudes to Breast-feeding and Infant Care in Early Modern England and America', *Journal of Social History*, 1994, vol. 69.

Crockett, B., ' "Holy Cozenage" and the Renaissance Cult of the Ear', *Sixteenth Century Journal*, 1993, vol. 24.

Cross, C., *The Puritan Earl. The Life of Sir Henry Hastings*, 1966.

——, ' "He-Goats Before the Flocks": A Note on the Part Played by Women in the Foundation of Some Civil War Churches', in G. J. Cuming and D. Baker, 1972.

——, ' "Great Reasoners in Scripture": The Activities of Women Lollards 1386–1520', in D. Baker, 1978.

Cross, C. *et al.*, *Law and Government under the Tudors. Essays Presented to Sir Geoffrey Elton*, 1988, Cambridge.

Cuming, G. J., and Baker, D., eds, *Popular Belief and Practice, Studies in Church History*, 1972, vol. 8.

Cust, E., ed., *Records of the Cust Family II: The Brownlows of Belton*, 1909.

Cuth, D. J. and McKenna, J. W., eds, *Tudor Rule and Revolution: Essays for G. R. Elton from his American Friends*, 1982, Cambridge.

Danner, D., 'The Contribution of the Geneva Bible of 1560 to the English Protestant Tradition', *Sixteenth Century Journal*, 1981, vol. 12.

Davies, K., 'The Social Condition of Equality: How Original Were the Puritan Doctrines of Marriage?', *Social History*, 1977, vol. 5.

Davies, R., *A Memoir of the York Press*, 1868.

Davis, J., 'Joan of Kent: Lollardy and the English Reformation', *Journal of Ecclesiastical History*, 1982, vol. 33.

Davis, N. Z., 'Women's History in Transition: The European Case', *Feminist Studies*, 1975, vol. 3.

Deansley, M., 'Vernacular Books in England in the Fourteenth and Fifteenth Centuries', *Modern Languages Review*, 1920, vol. 15.

Degler, C. N., *Is There a History of Women?*, 1975, Oxford.

Devlin, C., *The Life of Robert Southwell Poet and Martyr*, 1956.

Dickens, A. G., ed., *Clifford Letters of the Sixteenth Century*, Surtees Society, 1952, vol. 172.

Diefendorf, B., 'Widowhood and Remarriage in Sixteenth-century Paris', *Journal of Family History*, 1982, vol. 7.

Donagan, B., 'The Clerical Patronage of Robert Rich 1619–42', *Proceedings of the American Philosophical Society*, 1976, vol. 120.

Dorman, T., 'The Sandwich Book of Orphans', *Archaeologia Cantiana*, 1886, vol. 16.

Dowling, M., 'The Gospel and the Court: Reformation Under Henry VIII', in P. Lake, ed., 1987.

Duffy, E., 'The Godly and the Multitude in Stuart England', *The Seventeenth Century*, 1986, vol. 1.

Dugmore, C. W., *The Mass and the English Reformers*, 1958.

Duke, A. C. and Tomse, A., eds, *Clio's Mirror. Historiography in the Netherlands. Britain and the Netherlands*, 1985, vol. 8.

Durrant, C. S., *A Link Between Flemish Mystics and English Martyrs*, 1925.

Durston, C., *The Family in the English Revolution*, 1989.

Dymond, D., 'Sitting Apart in Church', in C. Rawcliffe, 1996.

Eales, J., *Puritans and Roundheads. The Harleys of Brampton Bryan and the Outbreak of the Civil War*, 1990, Cambridge.

——, 'Thomas Pierson and the Transmission of the Moderate Puritan Tradition', *Midland History*, 1995, vol. 20.

Eason, C., *The Geneva Bible. Notes on Its Production and Distribution*, 1937, Dublin.

Eire, C. M., *War Against the Idols. The Reformation of Worship from Erasmus to Calvin*, 1986, New York.

Eliot, T. S., *Selected Essays*, 1932.

Elmen, P., 'Richard Allestree and the *Whole Duty of Man* 1658', *The Library*, 5th Ser., 1951, vol. 6.

Emmison, F. G., *Tudor Secretary. Sir William Petre at Court and at Home*, 1961.

Erikson, A. L., *Women and Property in Early Modern England*, 1993.

Evans, C., *Friends of the Seventeenth Century*, 1885, Philadelphia.

Evans, G. R., 'Wyclif on Literal and Metaphorical', in A. Hudson and M. Wilks, eds, 1987.

——, *Problems of Authority in the Reformation Debate*, 1992, Cambridge.

Fiech, S. M., 'The Rhetoric of Biblical Theology: John Knox and the Question of Women', *Sixteenth Century Journal*, 1995, vol. 26.

Fildes, V., *Breasts, Babies and Bottles*, 1986, Edinburgh.

Fincham, K., ed., *The Early Stuart Church 1603–42*, 1993.

Fines, J., 'Heresy Trials in the Diocese of Coventry and Lichfield 1511–12', *Journal of Ecclesiastical History*, 1963, vol. 14.

Finlay, M., *Western Writing Implements in the Age of the Quill Pen*, 1990, Wetherall, Carlisle.

Finney, G. L., 'A World of Instruments', *English Literary History*, 1953, vol. 20.

Fish, S., 'Normal Circumstances, Literal Language, Direct Speech Acts, the Ordinary, the Everyday, the Obvious, What Goes Without Saying and Other Special Cases', *Critical Inquiry*, 1979, vol. 4.

Fletcher, A. J., *A County Community in War and Peace. Sussex 1600–60*, 1974.

——, 'Man's Dilemma: The Future of Patriarchy', *Transactions of the Royal Historical Society*, 6th Ser., 1996, vol. 4.

Frankforter, A. D., 'Elizabeth Bowes and John Knox: A Woman and Reformation Theology', *Church History*, 1987, vol. 56.

Fraser, A., *The Weaker Vessel. Woman's Lot in Seventeenth-Century England*, 1984.

Friedman, A. T., *House and Household: Wollaton Hall and the Willoughby Family*, 1989.

Fritze, R. H., 'The Role of Family and Religion in the Local Politics of Early Elizabethan England: The Case of Hampshire in the 1560s', *Historical Journal*, 1982, vol. 25.

Gabrieli, V., 'A New Digby Letter Book: In Praise of Venetia', *National Library of Wales Journal*, 1956, vol. 9; 1957, vol. 10.

Gage, J., *The History and Antiquities of Hengrave Hall in Suffolk*, 1822.

Galgano, M. J., 'Infancy and Childhood: The Female Experience in the Restoration North-West', in J. Watson and P. Pittman, eds, 1989.

Gardiner, D., *English Girlhood at School*, 1929.

——, ed., *The Oxinden Letters 1607–42*, 1933.

——, ed., *The Oxinden and Peyton Letters 1642–70*, 1937.

Garrett, C., 'The Rhetoric of Supplication: Prayer Theory in Seventeenth-century England', *Renaissance Quarterly*, 1993, vol. 46.

Goff, C., *A Woman of the Tudor Age*, 1930.

Goldberg, P. J. P., ed., *Woman is a Worthy Wight. Women in English Society c. 1200–1500*, 1992, Stroud, Glos.

Gooder, E., *The Squire of Arbury: Sir Richard Newdigate, Second Baronet, 1644–1710 and His Family*, 1990, Coventry.

Graff, H. J., ed., *Literacy and Social Development in the West*, 1981, Cambridge.

Graham, W. A., *Beyond the Written Word: Oral Aspects of Scripture in the History of Religion*, 1987.

Guite, A. A., 'The Art of Memory and the Art of Salvation: The Centrality of Memory in the Sermons of John Donne and Lancelot Andrewes', *The Seventeenth Century*, 1989, vol. 4.

Harley, D., 'The Moral Theology and Godly Practice of Maternal Breastfeeding in Stuart England', *Bulletin of the History of Medicine*, 1995, vol. 69.

Halkett, J. G., *Milton and the Idea of Matrimony*, 1970, New Haven.

Haller, W., *Foxe's Book of Martyrs and the Elect Nation*, 1963.

Hanham, C., *The Celys and Their World*, 1985, Cambridge.

Hannay, M. P., ed., *Silent but for the Word: Tudor Women as Patrons, Translators and Writers of Religious Works*, 1985, Kent, Ohio.

Hardacre, P. H., *The Royalists during the Puritan Revolution*, 1956, The Hague.

Hareven, T., 'The History of the Family as an Interdisciplinary Field', *Journal of Family History*, 1972, vol. 2.

Harrington, J. F., *Reordering Marriage and Society*, 1995, Cambridge.

Haskell, A. S., 'Paston Women on Marriage in Fifteenth Century England', *Viator*, 1973, vol. 4.

Havelock, E. A., *The Muse Learns to Write: Reflections on Orality and Literature from Antiquity to the Present*, 1986, New Haven.

Heales, A. C., *The History and Law of Church Seats or Pews*, 1872.

Higgins, P., 'The Reactions of Women With Special Reference to Women Petitioners', in B. Manning, 1973.

Higman, F. H., *Piety and the People. Religious Printing in French 1511–1551*, 1996, Aldershot.

Hobsbawn, E. and Ranger, T., *The Invention of Tradition*, 1983.

Hofman, F., 'Catherine Parr as a Woman of Letters' *Huntington Library Quarterly*, 1960, vol. 23.

Hogrefe, P., 'The Legal Rights of Tudor Women and Their Circumvention by Men and Women', *Sixteenth Century Journal*, 1972, vol. 3.

Houbrooke, R. A., ed., *The Letter Book of John Parkhurst Bishop of Norwich*, Norfolk Record Society, 1975, vol. 43.

——, ed., *Church Courts and the People during the English Reformation 1520–70*, 1979, Oxford.

——, *The English Family 1450–1700*, 1984.

——, *Death, Ritual and Bereavement*, 1989.

Hudson, A., 'Some Aspects of Lollard Book Production', *Studies in Church History*, 1972, vol. 9.

——, *The Premature Reformation: Wycliffite Texts and Lollard History*, 1988, Oxford.

Hudson, A. and Wilkes, M., eds, *From Ockham to Wyclif. Studies in Church History*, Subsidia 5, 1987, Oxford.

Hudson, E. K., 'English Protestants and the *Imitatio Christi*, 1580–1620', *Sixteenth Century Journal*, 1988, vol. 19.

——, 'The "Plaine Man's Pastor": Arthur Dent and the Cultivation of Popular Piety in Early Seventeenth Century England', *Albion*, 1993, vol. 25.

Hufton, O., 'Women in History: I, The Early Modern Period', *Past and Present*, 1983, no. 101.

——, *The Prospect before Her. A History of Women in Western Europe, I, 1500–1800*, 1995.

Hughes, A., 'Thomas Dugard and His Circle in the 1630s: A Parliamentary Puritan Connexion?', *Historical Journal*, 1986, vol. 29.

Irwin, J., *Womanhood in Radical Protestantism 1525–1675*, 1979.

Jeay, M., 'Sexuality and Family in Sixteenth Century France: Are Literary Sources a Mask or a Mirror?', *Journal of Family History*, 1979, vol. 4.

Johnson, J. T., 'English Puritan Thought on the Ends of Marriage', *Church History*, 1969, vol. 38.

Jones, M. K. and Underwood, M. G., *The King's Mother. Lady Margaret Beaufort, Countess of Richmond and Derby*, 1992, Cambridge.

Jones, W. J., *The Elizabethan Court of Chancery*, 1967, Oxford.

Kanshek, S., 'Resistance, Loyalty and Recusant Politics: Sir Thomas Tresham and the Elizabethan State', *Midland History*, 1996, vol. 21.

Kelso, R., *Doctrine for the Lady of the Renaissance*, 1955, Urbana, Ill.

Kettering, S., 'The Household Service of Early Modern French Noblewomen', *French Historical Studies*, 1997, vol. 20.

King, J., 'Fiction and Fact in Foxe's *Book of Martyrs*', in D. M. Loades, ed., 1997.

King, J. N., 'The Godly Woman in Elizabethan Iconography', *Renaissance Quarterly*, 1985, vol. 38.

——, 'Recent Studies in Protestant Poetics', *English Literary Renaissance*, 1991, vol. 21.

Klein, R. D., 'The "Man Problem" in Women's Studies: The Expert, the Ignoramus and the Poor Dear', *Women's Studies International Forum*, 1983, vol. 6.

Krontitris, T., 'Breaking the Barriers of Genre and Gender: Margaret Tyler's Translation of the *Mirrour of Knighthood*', *English Literary Renaissance*, 1988, vol. 18.

Kunzle, D., 'The World Turned Upside Down: The Iconography of a European Broadside Type', in B. A. Babcock, 1978.

Lake, P., ed., *Protestants and the National Church in Sixteenth Century England*, 1987.

——, 'The Laudian Style: Order and the Pursuit of the Beauty of Holiness in the 1630s', in K. Fincham, ed., 1993.

Lamb, M. E., 'The Cooke Sisters: Attitudes Towards Learned Women in the Renaissance', in M. P. Hannay, ed., 1985.

Larminie, V., 'Marriage and Family: The Example of the Seventeenth Century Newdigates', *Midland History*, 1984, vol. 9.

——, *Wealth, Kinship and Culture. The Seventeenth Century Newdigates of Arbury and Their World*, 1995.

Leaver, R. A., *'Goostly Psalmes and Spiritual Songes': English and Dutch Metrical Psalms From Coverdale to Utterhave 1535–66*, 1991, Oxford.

Leites, E., 'The Duty to Desire: Love, Friendship and Sexuality in Some Puritan Theories of Marriage', *Journal of Social History*, 1979, vol. 15.

Loades, D. M., *Mary Tudor. A Life*, 1989.

——, ed., *John Foxe and the English Reformation*, 1997.

Lupton, L. F., *A History of the Geneva Bible*, 1996.

Macarthur, E. A., 'Women Petitioners and the Long Parliament', *English Historical Review*, 1909, vol. 24.

McClaren, D., 'Fertility, Infant Mortality and Breastfeeding in the Seventeenth Century,' *Medical History*, 1978, vol. 22.

——, 'Nature's Contraceptive: Wet-nursing and Prolonged Lactation: The Case of Chesham in Buckinghamshire 1578–1601', *Medical History*, 1979, vol. 23.

McClaren, D., 'Marital Fertility and Lactation 1570–1720', in M. Prior, ed., 1985.

McConica, J. K., *English Humanists and Reformation Politics Under Henry VIII and Edward VI*, 1986, Cambridge.

McCorkle, J. J., 'A Note Concerning "Mistress Crane" and the Marprelate Controversy', *The Library*, 4th Ser., 1931–2, vol. 12.

MacCulloch, D., *Suffolk and the Tudors. Politics and Religion in an English County, 1500–1600*, 1986, Oxford.

Macfarlane, A., *The Family Life of Ralph Josselin. An Essay in Historical Sociology*, 1970, Cambridge.

——, ed., *The Diary of Ralph Josselin 1616–1683*, 1991, Oxford.

McIntosh, M. K., 'Sir Anthony Cooke: Tudor Humanist, Educator and Religious Reformer', *Proceedings of the American Philosophical Society*, 1975, vol. 119.

Maclean, I., *The Renaissance Notion of Women*, 1980, Cambridge.

Maclean, J., *The Berkeley Manuscripts. Lives of the Berkeleys*, 1883, ed. J. Smyth.

McLean, R., *Pictorial Alphabets*, 1969.

McSheffery, S., 'Literacy and the Gender Gap in the Late Middle Ages. Women and Reading in Lollard Communities', in L. Smith and H. M. Taylor, 1996.

Maden, F., *The Privy Purse Expenses of the Princess Mary*, 1831.

Manguel, A., *A History of Reading*, 1996.

Manning, B., ed., 'Politics and Religion in the English Civil War', 1973.

Marchant, R. A., *The Church Under the Law. Justice, Administration and Discipline in the Diocese of York*, 1969, Cambridge.

Marcus, L. S., *Childhood and Cultural Despair: A Theme and Variations in Seventeenth Century Literature*, 1978, Pittsburgh.

Mares, F. H., ed., *The Memoirs of Sir Robert Carey*, 1972, Oxford.

Marriott, J. A. R., *The Life and Times of Lucius Cary*, 1907.

Marsh, C. W., *The Family of Love in English Society 1500–1630*, 1993, Cambridge.

Matar, N. I., 'A Devotion to Jesus as Mother in Restoration Puritanism', *Journal of the United Reformed Church Historical Society*, 1989, vol. 4.

Mattingley, G., *Catherine of Aragon*, 1942.

Martz, L. L., *The Poetry of Meditation*, 1954, New Haven.

Mechling, J., 'Advice to Historians on Advice to Mothers' *Journal of Social History*, 1975, vol. 9.

Mertes, K., *The English Noble Household 1250–1600*, 1987, Oxford.

Morgan, P., 'Frances Wolfreston and "Hor Bouks": A Seventeenth Century Woman Book-Collector', *The Library*, 5th Ser., 1989, vol. 11.

Mount, F., *The Subversive Family: An Alternative History of Love and Marriage*, 1982.

Mozley, J. F., *John Foxe and His Book*, 1940.

Murray, J., 'Kinship and Friendship: The Perception of Family by Clergy and Laity in Medieval London', *Albion*, 1988, vol., 20.

Neale, J., *Queen Elizabeth I*, 1973, Harmondsworth.

Neumann, E., *The Great Mother: An Analysis of the Archetype*, 1963, Princeton.

Newdigate-Newdegate, A., *Gossip from a Muniment Room Being Passages from the Lives of Anne and Mary Fitton 1574–1618*, 1897.

Newman, K. A., 'Holiness in Beauty? Roman Catholics, Arminians and the

Aesthetics of Religion in Early Modern England', *Studies in Church History*, 1992, vol. 28.

Nichols, J. G., *Narratives of the Days of the Reformation*, Camden Society, 1859, vol. 77.

——, *The Progresses of James I*, 1828.

Nicholson, H. M., 'Eighteenth Century Foxe. Evidence for the Impact of the Book of Martyrs in the Long Eighteenth Century', in D. Loades, 1997.

Niekus, C., *The Maiden's Mirror*, 1987, Wiesbaden.

O'Day, R., *Education and Society 1500–1800*, 1982.

——, *The Family and Family Relationships 1500–1990: England, France and the United States of America*, 1994.

O'Hara, D., '"Ruled by My Friends": Aspects of Marriage in the Diocese of Canterbury, *c.*1540–70', *Continuity and Change*, 1991, vol. 6.

Ong, W. J., *The Presence of the Word. Some Prolegomena for Cultural History and Religious History*, 1967, New Haven.

——, *Orality and Literacy. The Technologising of the Word*, 1982.

Ozment, S., *Magdalena and Balthasar. An Intimate Portrait of Life in Sixteenth-century Europe Revealed in the Letters of a Nuremberg Husband and Wife*, 1986, New Haven.

Paget, H., 'The Youth of Anne Boleyn', *Bulletin of the Institute of Historical Research*, 1981, vol. 54.

Pantin, W. A., *The English Church in the Fourteenth Century*, 1955, Cambridge.

Pearson, A. F. S., *Thomas Cartwright and Elizabethan Puritanism 1535–1603*, 1925, Cambridge.

Perry, G. G., *The Life of Henry Hammond*, 1862.

Pfander, H. G., 'Dives et Pauper', *The Library*, 4th Ser., 1933–4, vol. 14.

Pierce, W., *John Penry. His Life, Times and Writings*, 1923.

Pigman, G., *Grief and the English Renaissance Elegy*, 1985, Cambridge.

Plumb, D., 'A Gathered Church? Lollards and Their Society', in M. Spufford, ed., 1995.

Pogson, R., 'God's Law and Man's: Stephen Gardiner and the Problem of Loyalty', in C. Cross, ed., 1988.

Pollock, L., '"Teach Her to Live under Obedience": The Making of Woman in the Upper Ranks of Early Modern England', *Continuity and Change*, 1989, vol. 4.

Porter, H. C., 'The Nose of Wax: Scripture and the Spirit from Erasmus to Milton', *Transactions of the Royal Historical Society*, 5th Ser., 1964, vol. 14.

Pressey, W. J., 'The Records of the Archdeaconries of Essex and Colchester', *Transactions of the Essex Archaeological Society*, 1930, vol. 19.

Prest, W. R., 'Law and Women's Rights in Early Modern England', *The Seventeenth Century*, 1991.

Prett, J., *The Parish Clergy under the Later Stuarts: The Leicestershire Experience*, 1978, Urbana.

Price, F. D., 'The Elizabethan Apparitors in the Diocese of Gloucester', *Church Quarterly Review*, 1942, vol. 133.

Prior, M., ed., *Women in English Society 1500–1800*, 1985.

Radford, G. H., 'Lady Howard of Fitzford', *Transactions and Reports of the Devonshire Association*, 1890, vol. 22.

Rahrer, H., *Loyola's Letters to Women*, 1959, Edinburgh.

Rawcliffe, C., *Countries and Communities. Essays in East Anglian History Presented to Hassell Smith*, 1996, Norwich.

Ray, J., *A Collection of English Proverbs*, 1670, Cambridge.

Read, C., *Mr Secretary Cecil and Queen Elizabeth*, 1955.

Revard, S. P., 'Eve and the Doctrine of Responsibility in *Paradise Lost*', *Publications of the Modern Languages Association*, 1973, vol. 88.

Reynolds, M., *The Learned Lady in England 1656–1760*, 1920, New York.

Richmond, C., *John Hopton, Fifteenth Century Suffolk Gentleman*, 1981, Cambridge.

Roper, L., *The Holy Household: Women and Morals in Reformation Augsburg*, 1989, Oxford.

Rosen, E., 'The Invention of Eye-glasses', *Journal of the History of Medicine and Allied Sciences*, 1956, vol. 11.

Saenger, P., 'Silent Reading: Its Impact on Late Medieval Script and Society', *Viator*, 1982, vol. 13.

Saffley, T. M., *Let No Man Put Asunder. The Control of Marriage in the German South-West*, 1984, Kirksville.

Scheffler, J., 'The Prison Writings of Early Quaker Women', *Quaker History*, 1984, vol. 73.

Schnucker, R. V., ed., *Calviniana. Ideas and Influence of Jean Calvin*, 1988, Kirksville.

Schwoerer, L. G., *Lady Rachel Russell. One of the Best of Women*, 1988, Baltimore.

Scribner, R. W., *For the Sake of Simple Folk. Popular Propaganda for the German Reformation*, 1981, Cambridge.

——, 'Oral Culture and the Transmission of Reformation Ideas', *History of European Ideas*, 1984, vol. 5.

Seaver, P., *Wallington's World. A Puritan Artisan in Seventeenth-century London*, 1985, Stanford.

Shakespeare, J. and Dowling R., 'Religion and Politics in Mid-Tudor England through the Eyes of a Protestant English Woman: The Recollections of Rose Hickman', *Bulletin of the Institute of Historical Research*, 1982, vol. 55.

Sheehan, M., 'Marriage Theory and Practice in the Conciliar Legislation and Diocesan Statutes of Medieval England', *Medieval Studies*, 1978, vol. 40.

Shiels, W. J., 'Oliver Heywood and His Congregation', *Studies in Church History*, 1986, vol. 23.

Simon, L., *Of Virtue Rare: Margaret Beaufort, Matriarch of the House of Tudor*, 1982, Boston.

Slater, M., 'The Weightiest Business: Marriage in an Upper-gentry Family in Seventeenth-century England', *Past and Present*, 1976, no. 72.

——, *Family Life in the Seventeenth Century. The Verneys of Claydon House*, 1984.

Smalley, B., *The Study of the Bible in the Middle Ages*, 1952, Oxford.

Smith, L., and Taylor, H. M., *Women, the Book and the Godly*, 1996, Cambridge.

Smith, L. B., *Tudor Prelates and Politics 1536–58*, 1953, Princeton.

Somerville, C. J., 'The Distinction Between Indoctrination and Education in England 1549–1719', *Journal of the History of Ideas*, 1983, vol. 44.

Souers, P., *The Matchless Orinda*, 1931, Cambridge, Mass.

Southern, A. C., *An Elizabethan Recusant House 1538–1608*, 1954.

Spufford, M., 'The Schooling of the Peasantry in Cambridgeshire 1575–1700', *Agricultural History Review*, 1970, vol. 18.

——, *Contrasting Communities. English Villagers in the Sixteenth and Seventeenth Centuries*, 1974, Cambridge.

——, *Small Books and Pleasant Histories. Popular Fiction and its Readership in Seventeenth Century England*, 1981.

——, 'Can We Count the Godly and Conformable in the Seventeenth Century?,' *Journal of Ecclesiastical History*, 1985, vol. 36.

—— (ed.), *The World of Rural Dissenters 1520–1725*, 1995, Cambridge.

Stenton, D. M., *English Women in History*, 1957.

Stoll, E. E., *Shakespeare Studies*, 1927, New York.

Stone, L., 'Social Mobility in England 1500–1700', *Past and Present*, 1966, no. 33.

——, *The Family, Sex and Marriage 1500–1800*, 1977, New York.

——, *The Past and the Present*, 1981.

Strype, J., *Annals of the Reformation*, 1824, Oxford.

Temperley, N., *The Music of the English Parish Church*, 1979, Cambridge.

Thistleton-Dyer, T. F., *Church Lore Gleanings*, 1891.

Thomas, K., 'The Double Standard', *Journal of the History of Ideas*, 1959, vol. 20.

——, 'Women and the Civil War Sects', *Past and Present*, 1968, no. 13.

——, *Religion and the Decline of Magic*, 1978, Harmondsworth.

Thompson, J. A. F., 'John Foxe and Some Sources for Lollard History: Notes for a Critical Appraisal', *Studies in Church History*, 1965, vol. 2.

Thomson, G. S., *Life in a Noble Household 1641–1660*, 1937.

Thornton, P., *Seventeenth Century Interior Decoration in England, Holland and France*, 1987, New Haven.

Tilley, M. P., *A Dictionary of Proverbs in England in the Sixteenth and Seventeenth Centuries*, 1950, Ann Arbor.

Todd, M., 'Humanists, Puritans and the Spiritualized Household', *Church History*, 1980, vol. 49.

Tuer, A. W., *The History of the Horn Book*, 1896.

Tyacke, N., *Anti-Calvinists. The Rise of English Arminianism c.1590–1640*, 1987, Oxford.

Vann, R. T., 'Wills and the Family in an English Town. Banbury 1553–1805', *Journal of Family History*, 1979, vol. 4.

——, 'The Youth of Centuries of Childhood', *History and Theory*, 1982, vol. 21.

Verney, P., *The Standard Bearer*, 1963.

Vincent, W. A. L., *The Grammar Schools: Their Continuing Tradition 1660–1714*, 1969.

Wabuda, S., 'Bishops and the Provision of Homilies 1520 to 1547', *Sixteenth Century Journal*, 1994, vol. 25.

Waddington, J., *John Penry the Pilgrim Martyr*, 1854.

Wall, J. N., 'The Book of Homilies of 1547 and the Continuity of English Humanism in the Sixteenth Century', *Anglican Theological Review*, 1976, vol. 58.

Watson, J. and Pittman, P., eds, *The Portrayal of Lifestyles in English Literature, 1500–1800*, 1989, Lewiston.

Watt, T., *Cheap Print and Popular Piety*, 1981, Cambridge.

Watt, T., 'Piety in the Pedlar's Pack', in M. Spufford, ed., 1995.

Warnicke, R. M., 'Anne Boleyn's Childhood and Adolescence', *Historical Journal*, 1985, vol. 28.

Westfall, R. S., *Never at Rest. A Biography of Isaac Newton*, 1980, Cambridge.

Whaley, J., *Mirrors of Mortality. Studies in the Social History of Death*, 1981.

Whyte, M. K., *The Status of Women in Pre-industrial Societies*, 1978, Princeton.

Wiffen, J. H., *Historical Memoirs of the House of Russell*, 1833.

Willen, D., 'Women in the Public Sphere in Early Modern England: The Case of the Urban Working Poor', *Sixteenth Century Journal*, 1988, vol. 19.

——, ' "Communion of Saints": Spiritual Reciprocity and the Godly Community in Early Modern England', *Albion*, 1995, vol. 27.

Williams, G. H., ' "Called by This Name, Heare Us Not": The Case of Mrs Joan Drake. A Formative Episode in the Career of Thomas Hooker in England', *Harvard Library Bulletin*, 1968, vol. 16.

Williamson, G. C., *Lady Anne Clifford*, 1922, Kendal.

Wilson, A., 'The Infancy of the History of Childhood: An Appraisal of Philippe Ariès', *History and Theory*, 1980, vol. 19.

Wilson, S., 'The Myth of Motherhood a Myth: The Historical View of European Child-bearing', *Social History*, 1984, vol. 9.

Wood, A., 'The Place of Custom in Plebeian Political Satire: England 1500–1800', *Social History*, 1997, vol. 33.

Wright, L. B., *Religion and Empire*, 1943, Chapel Hill, NC.

Wrightson, K., 'Estates, Degrees and Sorts: Changing Perceptions of Society in Tudor and Stuart England,', in P. J. Corfield, ed., 1991.

Wynter, S. M., 'Survivors and Status: Widowhood and Family in the Early Modern Netherlands', *Journal of Family History*, 1982, vol. 7.

Zagorin, P., *Ways of Lying. Dissimulation, Persecution and Conformity in Early Modern Europe*, 1992, Cambridge, Mass.

Index